CREATION, MIGRATION, AND CONQUEST

Creation, Migration, and Conquest

Imaginary Geography and Sense of Space in Old English Literature

FABIENNE L. MICHELET

OXFORD
UNIVERSITY PRESS

Great Clarendon Street, Oxford OX2 6DP

Oxford University Press is a department of the University of Oxford.
It furthers the University's objective of excellence in research, scholarship,
and education by publishing worldwide in

Oxford New York

Auckland Cape Town Dar es Salaam Hong Kong Karachi
Kuala Lumpur Madrid Melbourne Mexico City Nairobi
New Delhi Shanghai Taipei Toronto

With offices in

Argentina Austria Brazil Chile Czech Republic France Greece
Guatemala Hungary Italy Japan Poland Portugal Singapore
South Korea Switzerland Thailand Turkey Ukraine Vietnam

Oxford is a registered trademark of Oxford University Press
in the UK and in certain other countries

Published in the United States
by Oxford University Press Inc., New York

© Fabienne Michelet 2006

The moral rights of the author have been asserted
Database right Oxford University Press (maker)

First published 2006

All rights reserved. No part of this publication may be reproduced,
stored in a retrieval system, or transmitted, in any form or by any means,
without the prior permission in writing of Oxford University Press,
or as expressly permitted by law, or under terms agreed with the appropriate
reprographics rights organization. Enquiries concerning reproduction
outside the scope of the above should be sent to the Rights Department,
Oxford University Press, at the address above

You must not circulate this book in any other binding or cover
and you must impose this same condition on any acquirer

British Library Cataloguing in Publication Data
Data available

Library of Congress Cataloging in Publication Data
Michelet, Fabienne.
Creation, migration, and conquest : imaginary geography and sense of space in Old
English literature / Fabienne Michelet.
p. cm.
Includes bibliographical references.
ISBN-13: 978-0-19-928671-3
1. English literature—Old English, ca. 450-1100—History and criticism. 2.
Geography in literature. 3. Place (Philosophy) in literature. 4. Civilization,
Anglo-Saxon, in literature. I. Title.
PR173.M46 2006 820.9'001—dc22 2006005340

Typeset by Laserwords Private Limited, Chennai, India
Printed in Great Britain
on acid-free paper by
Biddles Ltd., King's Lynn, Norfolk

ISBN 0-19-928671-X 978-0-19-928671-3

1 3 5 7 9 10 8 6 4 2

Contents

Preface	vii
List of Illustrations	xiii
Abbreviations	xv
1. Introduction: An Outline of the Anglo-Saxons' Sense of Space	1

I. CREATION

2. Ordering the World: Creation Narratives and Spatial Control	37
3. The Centres of *Beowulf*: A Complex Spatial Order	74
4. Localization and Remapping: Creating a New Centrality for Anglo-Saxon England	115

II. MIGRATION

5. Integrating New Spaces: Saint's Lives and Missions of Conversion	163
6. Searching for Land: Scriptural Poetry and Migration	198

III. CONQUEST

7. The *descriptiones Britanniae* and the *adventus Saxonum*: Narrative Strategies for the Conquest of Britain	235
Conclusion	270
Select Bibliography	275
Index	293

Preface

> þær wæs hearpan sweg,
> swutol sang scopes. Sægde se þe cuþe
> frumsceaft fira feorran reccan ...[1]
>
> Dæg wæs mære
> ofer middangeard þa seo mengeo for.[2]
>
> Ne wearð wæl mare
> on þis eiglande æfre gieta
> ... siþþan eastan hider
> Engle and Seaxe up becoman,
> ofer brad brimu Brytene sohtan,
> wlance wigsmiþas, Wealas ofercoman,
> eorlas arhwate, eard begeatan.[3]

CREATION, migration, conquest: each of the three quotations selected above evokes in turn one of the major divisions of the present study. The first citation is from *Beowulf*; having been granted success in war, the Danish king Hroðgar decides to build a splendid hall for his people. Once the construction is completed, a *scop* performs in the new edifice a song that memorializes the genesis of the world and of mankind. The scene brings together the coming into being of the royal residence, of the Danish kingdom, and of the cosmos. This passage testifies to the importance of the creation motif which pervades Old English literature.

---

[1] 'there was the sound of the harp, the clear song of the *scop*. He who knew how to recount the origin of men from long ago spoke ...' (*Beowulf* 89[a]–91). *Beowulf and the Fight at Finnsburg*, ed. by F. Klaeber, 3rd edn. (Lexington, MA: Heath, 1922; repr. 1950). Unless otherwise specified, all quotations of *Beowulf* are from this edition and all translations are my own—with the exception of biblical quotations.

[2] 'The day the multitude set forth was famous throughout the world' (*Exodus* 47[b]–48). *The Junius Manuscript*, ed. by George Philip Krapp, Anglo-Saxon Poetic Records, 1 (New York: Columbia University Press, 1931; repr. 1964), 91–107. Unless otherwise specified, Old English poems are quoted from the Anglo-Saxon Poetic Records.

[3] 'Nor had there yet ever been a greater slaughter on this island since from the east the Angles and the Saxons, the proud warriors, the noblemen eager for glory, came hither over the broad sea to seek the land of Britain, to conquer the Welsh, and seize their land' (*Battle of Brunanburh* 65[b]–73). *The Anglo-Saxon Minor Poems*, ed. by Elliott van Kirk Dobbie, Anglo-Saxon Poetic Records, 6 (London: Routledge, 1942; repr. 1968), 16–20.

The *mengeo*, the 'multitude' mentioned in the second extract refers to the Israelites who, as the Old English poem *Exodus* recounts, flee Egypt, wander through the desert, and eventually cross the Red Sea dry-shod. This time, the idea of migration is highlighted, that is, the expedition that led the Chosen People toward the Promised Land. But the poem's military and nautical imagery also gestures toward the Germanic tribes' original journey towards Britain and illustrates the enduring fate of the notion of migration in Anglo-Saxon England.[4]

The third quotation concludes the *Battle of Brunanburh*. Interestingly, the commemoration of this major English victory against hostile invaders ends with an allusion to the Anglo-Saxons' own conquest of Britain. Both their migration and their first, successful appropriation of land are thus remembered in these lines and are juxtaposed with a contemporary military success consolidating their claim to the kingdom of England.

These three passages illustrate the thematic threads directing the study that follows and they emphasize the pre-eminence granted to the shaping, appropriation, and securing of one's own space in the Anglo-Saxons' spatial *imaginaire*. This thematic progression is complemented by a binary development which moves from a static to a dynamic vision of space. After an introductory chapter defining the theoretical questions this book addresses, a first, larger section revolves around the notion of creation, recounting the genesis of various spaces: the entire cosmos, the civilized world of human beings, or a revised view of Britain and northern Europe. The last three chapters, including the two sections devoted to migration and conquest, develop a dynamic vision of space which remodels the world's imagined spatial organization and which foregrounds the movement to and appropriation of new and distant lands.

The three extracts quoted above were also selected because they belong to different poetic and literary traditions. *Beowulf* is of course the most prominent example of heroic verse in Old English; *Exodus* is an instance of scriptural poetry; and the *Battle of Brunanburh* is preserved in the Anglo-Saxon Chronicle, a major historical source for the period, as the entry for the year 937. These three citations thus mirror the varied nature of the corpus discussed in this book, a corpus which includes heroic and religious poems as well as documents of a more historical nature, such as chronicles and maps. Division by literary genre is indeed the

---

[4] For a thorough study of the migration motif, see Nicholas Howe, *Migration and Mythmaking in Anglo-Saxon England* (Notre Dame, IN: University of Notre Dame Press, 2001; first publ. New Haven: Yale University Press, 1989).

most obvious structuring pattern shaping the present study. In addition to acknowledging the possible influence that generic traits may exert on how a particular text chooses to address spatial concerns and on how it elaborates an imagined geography, this grouping by genre suggests stimulating lines of thought within one and the same category. But the links and echoes identified and studied within a given genre go beyond chapter divisions to serve an intellectual and rhetorical progression in the present inquiry into the contours of the Anglo-Saxons' mental map.

Creation, Migration, and Conquest: Imaginary Geography and Sense of Space in Old English Literature examines the role played by the *imaginaire* in spatial representations and in imaginary geography in Old English literature. More specifically, it explores the similarities and points of contact between spatial representations as found both in historical documents and in verse. Tracing the literary, political, and intellectual background to this *imaginaire*, it examines the Anglo-Saxons' perception of geographical space and it contends that its representations should be read as narrative constructs and literary devices shedding light on Old English authors' mental maps. Focusing on what these maps have in common, on their shared characteristics, this book superposes these various and varied spatial representations and attempts to extract from them a collective and imagined mental picture of space. Numerous related issues figure prominently in the pages that follow, namely notions of place, enclosure, boundary, centre, and periphery. The establishment and validity of territorial claims are also recurrent concerns for insular authors who, intent on sanctioning land possession, obsessively write and rewrite their heroes, their saints, and their ancestors as the rightful occupiers of a given tract of ground. Symbolic gestures, such as treading the ground, surveying new lands, naming places, and 'othering' an autochthonous population, ensure a metaphorical appropriation of land and the production of a territory. This book concurrently analyses numerous strategies of remapping and recentring which operate both in poetic and in historiographic writings, strategies through which Anglo-Saxon authors engage in a thorough redefinition of their homeland, and consequently also of themselves. They thereby underscore what is at stake in geographical positioning, highlighting the complex and essential relation between location and identity.

Questions of space and spatial *imaginaire* have found a wide echo in recent scholarship. These issues cut across a number of disciplines, such as archaeology, history, geography, sociology, political and literary studies, and so forth. Derek Gregory's reflections on the history of geography as a branch of knowledge, Martina Löw's study of the sociology of space in the contemporary world, or Edward Casey's project to reinterpret conceptions of space combining maps and landscape painting, all testify to the variety of approaches taken to spatial issues.[5] Several items of the series 'The Transformation of the Roman World' (in particular *Topographies of Power in the Early Middle Ages*) offer significant contributions to the fields of history and archaeology.[6] The recently published *The Transformation of Frontiers from Late Antiquity to the Carolingians* attests to the extensive research devoted to the concept of the 'medieval frontier' in the last few years, an interest corroborated by several other publications.[7]

Imaginary spaces and their representations form an important area of investigation. Christian Hänger looks into their political implications in a book studying Roman military strategies in Germania.[8] Medieval geography and cartography explore the mental images of space elaborated at the time. These disciplines, which are enjoying renewed attention, have been marked out by the work of Patrick Gautier-Dalché, as well as by J. Brian Harley and David Woodward's *History of Cartography*, and they are currently bringing forth numerous contributions, such as those by Naomi Reed Kline, Scott D. Westrem, David Buisseret, and Ute Schneider.[9] Literary studies have responded to this increased interest in issues of space and place, and Jennifer Neville's *Representations of*

---

[5] Edward S. Casey, *Representing Place: Landscape Painting and Maps* (Minneapolis: University of Minnesota Press, 2002); Derek Gregory, *Geographical Imaginations* (Cambridge, MA: Blackwell, 1994); and Martina Löw, *Raumsoziologie*, Suhrkamp Taschenbuch Wissenschaft, 1506 (Frankfurt: Suhrkamp, 2001). See also the recently published collection of essays *Uomo e spazio nell'alto medioevo*, 2 vols. Settimane di studio del Centro italiano di studi sull' allo medioevo, 50 (Spoleto: Centro Italiano di Studi sull'Alto Medioevo, 2003) which offers a wide range of views on issues of space and place in the Middle Ages.

[6] Mayke De Jong and Frans Theuws, with Carine van Rhijn (eds.), *Topographies of Power in the Early Middle Ages*, The Transformation of the Roman World, 6 (Leiden: Brill, 2001).

[7] Walter Pohl, Ian Wood, and Helmut Reimitz (eds.), *The Transformation of Frontiers from Late Antiquity to the Carolingians*, The Transformation of the Roman World, 10 (Leiden: Brill, 2001). See also David Abulafia and Nora Berend (eds.), *Medieval Frontiers: Concepts and Practices* (Aldershot: Ashgate, 2002).

[8] Christian Hänger, *Die Welt im Kopf: Raumbilder und Strategie im Römischen Kaiserreich*, Hypomnemata, 136 (Göttingen: Vandenhoeck and Ruprecht, 2001).

[9] Ute Schneider, *Die Macht der Karten: Eine Geschichte der Kartographie vom Mittelalter bis heute* (Darmstadt: Primus Verlag, 2004); David Buisseret, *The Mapmaker's Quest: Depicting New Worlds in Renaissance Europe* (Oxford: Oxford University Press, 2003); Scott D. Westrem, *The Hereford Map: A Transcription and Translation of the Legends*

the Natural World in Old English Poetry examines the spatial representations found in Old English verse.[10] Following on his now classic *Migration and Mythmaking in Anglo-Saxon England*, Nicholas Howe has recently published major articles inquiring into the Anglo-Saxons' imagined world.[11] My own work, however, develops in a book-length study its analysis of spatial representations and imaginary geography in Anglo-Saxon England. By juxtaposing poetic and historico-geographical sources and by elaborating a theoretical model for its investigation into spatial representations inspired by the work of French philosophers, historians, and literary critics (in particular Paul Zumthor, Jacques Le Goff, Henri Lefebvre, and Patrick Gautier-Dalché), my book offers new interpretative models which allow for the articulation of the political in terms of the discursive or poetical. The critical method developed in the first chapter is then fully integrated into the working practices of this book. *Creation, Migration, and Conquest* thus draws on and complements existing interdisciplinary scholarship of medieval representations of space: it focuses attention on the Anglo-Saxons' spatial *imaginaire* and on the writing strategies underlying its elaboration.

This book is based on a doctoral thesis submitted in 2003 at the University of Geneva. I would like to thank Professor Paul B. Taylor for supervising the thesis despite his official retirement from academic life. I am also indebted to Professor Jean-Yves Tilliette, president of my committee, for his continued support and encouragement.

I would like to express my gratitude to the Berrow Foundation and the late Marquis de Amodio for a generous scholarship that allowed me

---

with Commentary, Terrarum Orbis, 1 (Turnhout: Brepols, 2001); Naomi Reed Kline, *Maps of Medieval Thought: The Hereford Paradigm* (Woodbridge: Boydell and Brewer, 2001); and J. B. Harley and David Woodward (eds.), *The History of Cartography*, 6 vols. (Chicago: University of Chicago Press, 1987–).

[10] Jennifer Neville, *Representations of the Natural World in Old English Poetry*, Cambridge Studies in Anglo-Saxon England, 27 (Cambridge: Cambridge University Press, 1999).

[11] Howe, *Migration and Mythmaking*. See also Nicholas Howe, 'An Angle on this Earth: Sense of Place in Anglo-Saxon England', *Bulletin of the John Rylands University Library of Manchester*, 82 (2000), 3–27; Nicholas Howe, 'The Landscape of Anglo-Saxon England: Inherited, Invented, Imagined', in John Howe and Michael Wolfe (eds.), *Inventing Medieval Landscapes: Senses of Place in Western Europe* (Gainesville: University of Florida Press, 2002), 91–112; and Nicholas Howe, 'Looking for home in Anglo-Saxon England', in Nicholas Howe (ed.), *Home and Homelessness in the Medieval and Renaissance World* (Notre Dame, IN: University of Notre Dame Press, 2004), 143–63.

to complete a two-year course of study at the University of Oxford. During this period, Professor Malcolm Godden supervised my M.Phil. thesis which laid the foundation for the present study. He also invited me to come to Oxford a second time and I would like to thank him for his help on both occasions. A fellowship from the Swiss National Science Foundation enabled me to finance my second stay at Oxford and to devote myself to completing this study.

I am greatly indebted to Professor Margaret Bridges for her characteristic generosity and for her helpful suggestions for revision at several stages of my work. I would also like to thank Dr Heather O'Donoghue for her unfailing support that went beyond any official obligations and for her valuable comments on my work while I was in Oxford. I would like to express special thanks to Lincoln College for welcoming me in its Middle Common Room. Finally, I am grateful to the English Department at the Université de Genève, and more particularly its director Professor Richard Waswo, for granting me leave from my teaching duties.

In addition to the support I have received from these academic institutions and from adepts of Old English, my work owes a great deal to a community of scholars and friends who supported and encouraged me throughout the years. I would like to thank Professor Clare Lees, Karen Junod, and Martin Pickavé, who have all read and commented on parts of my work. I am indebted to Lukas Erne, Frédéric Joye, Corinne Fournier-Kiss, Lise Magnollay, Didier Maillat, Pierre Nicolet, Myriam Perregaux, Pierre Sánchez, Professor David Spurr, and Professor Claude Tricot for their help and encouragement. My deepest gratitude for moral support goes to my friends and family, with special thanks to Saba Bahar and Valeria Wagner.

F. M.

List of Illustrations

1. Lambert of Saint Omer, *Liber Floridus*, depicting Augustus as a cartographer. Paris, Bibliothèque Nationale, MS Lat. 8865, fo. 45. 144
2. The Hereford *mappa mundi* (detail). 146
3. The Albi *mappa mundi*. Albi, Médiathèque Pierre-Amalric, Rés. MS 115 (29), fo. 57^v. 148
4. Sketch of the Albi *mappa mundi*, from Konrad Miller, *Mappae Mundi: die ältesten Weltkarten*, (1895), iii. 58. 149
5. The Ripoll Map. Biblioteca Apostolica Vaticana, Reg. Lat. 123, fos. 143^v–144^v. 150
6. The Ripoll Map (detail), fo. 143^v. 152
7. The Saint-Server *mappa mundi*. Paris, Bibliothèque Nationale, MS Lat. 8878, fos. 45bis^v–45ter. 153
8. The Saint-Server *mappa mundi* (detail), fo. 45bis^v. 154
9. The Cotton *mappa mundi*. British Library, Cotton Tiberius B. v. 1, fo. 56^v. 155

The author would like to thank the following for permission to reproduce material:
Paris, Bibliothèque Nationale (Figs. 1, 7, and 8)
The Dean and Chapter of Hereford Cathedral and the Hereford Mappa Mundi Trust (Fig. 2)
Albi, Médiathèque Pierre-Amalric (Fig. 3)
Biblioteca Apostolica Vaticana (Vatican) (Figs. 5 and 6)
British Library (Fig. 9)

Abbreviations

BT   *An Anglo-Saxon Dictionary*, ed. by J. Bosworth and T. N. Toller (Oxford: Oxford University Press, 1882–98) with a *Supplement* by N. T. Toller (Oxford: Oxford University Press, 1921)

DOE   *Dictionary of Old English*, ed. by A. diP. Healy and others (Toronto: Pontifical Institute of Medieval Studies, 1986–)

OED   *The Oxford English Dictionary*, ed. by J. A. Simpson and E. S. C. Weiner, 2nd edn., 20 vols. (Oxford: Clarendon Press, 1989)

1
Introduction: An Outline of the Anglo-Saxons' Sense of Space

IN the course of the last two hundred years, the relationship of proximity and distance has changed radically. The acceleration of traffic, with the development, spread, and ever-increasing speed of means of transport—the railway, the automobile, the plane—have reduced the intervals separating different locations and have thus facilitated access to new physical spaces. Technological progress, such as the invention of the radio, the television, the telefax, or the Internet, has abolished distance altogether by allowing virtual dimensions to penetrate the familiar sphere of the home. All these innovations have proved instrumental in modifying our spatial perceptions, for electronic proximity no longer requires physical contact. They force us to question the common and unsophisticated notion that conceives of space as an empty container and a unified whole. Scientific developments, for instance Einstein's relativity theory, challenge the way we think about space. The arts have also given voice to such alterations; one need only recall the demise of the perspective in the plastic arts and the appearance of currents such as cubism, expressionism, and abstraction.[1] Moreover, as Henri Lefebvre points out, our consumer society generates new rarities that are often related to the earth, such as the natural resources of the soil and of the substratum. Space too can become scant, especially in the case of natural spaces around urban centres: our era has discovered that nature is finite.[2] Although the above enumeration refers to different concepts of space, they all combine to modify the relationship we have with our surroundings.

A second aspect of our cultural history influences the way we conceive of and relate to our milieu. The development of modern nationalism,

---

[1] On these new spatial perceptions, see Martina Löw, *Raumsoziologie*, Suhrkamp Taschenbuch Wissenschaft, 1506 (Frankfurt: Suhrkamp, 2001), esp. 69–73.
[2] Henri Lefebvre, *La Production de l'espace* (Paris: Anthropos, 1974), 380–1.

whose origins Benedict Anderson traces to the end of the eighteenth century, together with the efforts of recent history to redraw the map of Europe in an attempt to define clear national boundaries, have altered the way we perceive our spatial environment.[3] Two concepts inherent in the idea of nation deserve particular attention; first, in the mental framework of nationalist thinking, history becomes a record of oppression and resistance of a given people progressing toward freedom.[4] Second, to constitute itself, an ethnic group needs, among various other elements, a territory that it can call its own—as Anthony Smith postulates in his reflections on the ethnic origins of nations.[5] This locus need not be a physical location; it can be an imaginary space, a remembered homeland, or a desired, promised land. These two elements often mingle and link a group's sense of self and its destiny with the possession and control of a given territory.

While the ways in which we conceive of and situate ourselves in space are evolving, the land and the boundaries that delimit one's territory remain crucial for communities in search of their identity. The tension that exists between, on the one hand, a globalization of space and what seems to be an ever-increasing need to anchor one's own group to a particular place in an imagined geography, on the other, calls for an investigation both of the history of space and of our culturally changing attitudes to it. As part of this pressing reassessment of issues of space, this study intends to examine the Anglo-Saxons' spatial *imaginaire* and to discuss their sense of space as it emerges from a close reading of Old English literature. A number of questions linked to the notion of frontiers, to the nature of geographical distance, or to the definition of centrality and marginality, as well as various strategies of territorial control will also be considered. Although this study is limited to the Anglo-Saxon period, it is the ambitious hope of the chapters that follow to offer some incentives to reflect on our own attitudes toward space.

This first, introductory chapter elaborates a theoretical model for its analysis of spatial representations. It discusses various notions of

---

[3] Benedict Anderson, *Imagined Communities: Reflections on the Origin and Spread of Nationalism* (London: Verso, 1983; repr. 1989), 14, and Walter Pohl, 'Conclusion: The Transformation of Frontiers', in Walter Pohl, Ian Wood, and Helmut Reimitz (eds.), *The Transformation of Frontiers from Late Antiquity to the Carolingians*, The Transformation of the Roman World, 10 (Leiden: Brill, 2001), 247–60 (248).
[4] Henry Baudet, *Paradise on Earth: Some Thoughts on European Images of Non-European Man*, trans. Elisabeth Wentholt (New Haven: Yale University Press, 1965), 60.
[5] Anthony D. Smith, *The Ethnic Origins of Nations* (Oxford: Blackwell, 1986), 28–9.

space and engages with conceptual and methodological problems. It also addresses a number of issues related to the elaboration of a spatial *imaginaire*, such as the relevance of the concept of the mental map or the close links uniting representations of space and the constitution of identity. Focus is then placed on a medieval or, more precisely, an Anglo-Saxon sense of space, and the wider cultural context against which Old English authors wrote is sketched. To do so, I consider the intellectual tools the Anglo-Saxons had at their disposal when thinking about space: the vernacular terminology they used, the geographical and cosmological learning they inherited from classical antiquity and the Bible, and the contrasting pulls towards unity and fragmentation that, following the collapse of the Western Roman Empire, characterize these traditions. This section concludes by tracing the contours of the Old English authors' mental map, a crucial notion that affects both the spatial imagery of a given text and the various models according to which the world is represented. A quick overview of the corpus under consideration and of the subsequent chapters closes this general presentation.

NOTIONS OF SPACE

Definitions and Concepts

In light of the works of Henri Lefebvre and Jacques Le Goff, an inquiry into how a particular society thinks about space, produces a certain spatial organization, positions itself into and represents space, leads to the identification of three levels of analysis.[6] First of all, there is topographical space. It calls for a study of the physical ground on which a group lives, of the salient features of its landscape, of the spatial distribution of its population in villages or in the countryside. It examines how a society appropriates, dominates, and transforms a physical space.[7] The second level of analysis deals with the culture of space, that is, with spatial concepts as they are inscribed in tradition.

---

[6] Jacques Le Goff, 'Discorso di chiusura', in *Popoli e paesi nella cultura altomedievale*, 2 vols., Settimane di studio del Centro italiano di studi sull'alto medioevo, 29 (Spoleto: Centro Italiano di Studi sull'Alto Medioevo, 1983), 805–38 and Lefebvre, *Production de l'espace*. Although Lefebvre clearly adopts a Marxist approach, there are numerous points of comparison between his and Le Goff's classifications.

[7] On this particular field of study, see the works of Maurice Beresford, W. R. Hoskins, and Oliver Rackham.

It refers to a 'conceived' space, that of the scholar, and it includes views inherited from the past, namely information about geography and cosmology transmitted to the learned man or woman, which he or she endorses and possibly modifies. This investigation adopts a historical perspective which traces the evolution of spatial knowledge. Finally, space as a mental structure constitutes the last aspect of this threefold division. It differs from the preceding notion in that it examines the worth and affective properties that are conferred to space and orientation, that is, it reflects on the spatial imagination of an individual or of a society. Such perceptions are shaped by basic images such as inside/outside, open/closed, high/low, and so forth, to which symbolic meaning is always attached. These values survive through the ages and are transmitted down the generations. A culture of space—a given body of knowledge—may disappear as progress modifies existing models of the representation of the world and changes the insights and understanding of the nature of the environment. But the values granted to space as a mental structure endure and infuse spatial imagination with worth and meaning.[8]

My investigation of spatial questions in Anglo-Saxon England, especially of the sense of space Old English authors developed and of the spatial representations that followed from it, focuses on the juncture between the second and the third levels of analysis defined above. It determines how they combine and possibly influence each other. It is difficult to trace a clear-cut boundary between these two aspects, for the overlaps are numerous. Space as a mental structure, the third level of analysis, is experienced through symbols and imagery, but of course the second level, which concentrates on the culture of space, also deals with concepts and mental constructs. These two levels of analysis address different aspects of space and spatial representations, but their objects are always creations of the mind. Likewise, symbolic values and meanings are not only associated with space as a mental structure, but also with a culture of space, since tradition hands down ideas and concepts of space that belong to the realm of the *imaginaire*. For instance, Lefebvre rightly notes that the antique culture of space which described the cosmos as a series of concentric spheres collapsed long ago, whereas space as mental structure has retained some of these ancient values, such as the different

---

[8] Le Goff, 'Discorso di chiusura', 805. See also Lefebvre, *Production de l'espace*, 42–3 and 48–9 for another threefold division underlying spatial analysis: 'la pratique spatiale', 'les représentations de l'espace', and 'les espaces de représentation'.

meanings inherent in the opposition between high and low or between light and darkness.[9]

The mental schema according to which an empty space pre-exists and is subsequently populated and modified by what happens in it is still current.[10] It underlies, for instance, the common notion that human beings live 'in space'.[11] This idea overlooks the crucial fact that space is produced, the central premise of Lefebvre's study which is valid for all three levels of analysis sketched above.[12] The production process goes both ways. A given society inherits from tradition a mental image of space that will be operative in shaping this group's perception of its surroundings and of the interactions between individuals. This perception influences the way a community represents and thinks about itself. It bears on the group's approach to self-definition and on the emergence of a particular sense of identity, which in turn eventually modify the spatial image that was received from tradition. As a result, a different spatial image is transmitted to posterity. Thus, if space is not an absolute, pre-existing void but is indeed a cultural construct, it necessarily has, as Michel Foucault reminds us, a history in Western experience.[13] This book examines both Anglo-Saxon England's culture of space and space as a mental structure from a historical perspective, bearing in mind that spatial perceptions do not simply derive from the surrounding physical world but are indeed cultural conceptualizations.[14]

Space is therefore never neutral; it is not a given of experience to be grasped and known immediately.[15] A certain sense of space is shaped by pre-existing representations of the surrounding world and mediated by conceptions about the significance and value of the space one experiences. In his seminal study of medieval notions of space,

---

[9] Lefebvre, *Production de l'espace*, 267. [10] Ibid., 220.
[11] Löw, *Raumsoziologie*, 19. [12] Lefebvre, *Production de l'espace*, 23.
[13] Michel Foucault, 'Of Other Spaces', *Diacritics*, 16 (1986), 22–7 (22). See also Löw, *Raumsoziologie*, 17–24.
[14] Mary W. Helms, *Ulysses' Sail: An Ethnographic Odyssey of Power, Knowledge, and Geographical Distance* (Princeton: Princeton University Press, 1988), 8–9.
[15] Joachim Frenk's 'Introduction' calls for an analysis of the ways in which space was and is fashioned by culture. Frenk does not, however, consider how a culture of space in turn influences space as a mental construct. Joachim Frenk, 'Introduction', in Joachim Frenk (ed.), *Spatial Change in English Literature* (Trier: Wissenschaftlicher Verlag, 2000), 9–23 (12). See also Dick Harrison, 'Invisible Boundaries and Places of Power: Notions of Liminality and Centrality in the Early Middle Ages', in *The Transformation of Frontiers From Late Antiquity to the Carolingians*, The Transformation of the Roman World, 10 (Leiden: Brill, 2001), 83–93; Paul Zumthor, *La Mesure du Monde* (Paris: Seuil, 1993), 45; and Helms, *Ulysses' Sail*, 8–9.

Paul Zumthor acknowledges that it is impossible to apprehend space as an objective and unbiased category. It can only be a modality of the self and of its surrounding objects.[16] The historian concludes his reflections on the preconditions necessary to an analysis of space as follows: 'l'historien des cultures ne peut donc le [l'espace] saisir que comme une catégorie irrationnelle, relative à la condition de l'homme sur son fragment d'univers: grâce à elle, l'homme déchiffre celui-ci tandis que, dans cet acte même, il se crée un environnement symbolique, en rapport instable de complémentarité ou de contradiction avec la nature ainsi pensée.'[17] I would like to highlight three elements in this quotation. The first is that space can be approached *only* as a mental category: the human factor is unavoidable and always has to be taken into consideration. The second is that space as a mental category has a purpose: it makes sense of the surrounding world, of the portion of space to which human beings are tied. Zumthor postulates that it is one of the fundamental categories according to which an individual organizes the other domains of his or her reality.[18] Any reflection on space and spatial organization is inscribed in a particular time and place. Finally, the very process through which human beings understand their milieu generates a symbolic environment. As a consequence, no location is ever neutral or devoid of meaning, and the place individuals assume they occupy becomes significant.

The notion of place is of major importance for this study. The meanings of 'place' relevant here are, and I follow the definitions given by the *OED*, 'a particular part of space, of defined or undefined extent, but of definite situation', 'a portion of space actually occupied by a person or a thing'. Any sense of place is necessarily bound to an individual's spatial experience, for reflections about space always result from a particular point of view. Notions of the cosmos, of the surrounding world are always situated, located, 'embodied' in a subject; for any practice of spatial representation—whether a geographical description, a map, or even a poetic space created by literary texts—entails a process of enframing that is partial and conditioned by a particular viewpoint. It establishes a centre and a margin, it views the world as a unified and ordered whole arranged around a definite point.[19] Conversely, place and spatial location, precisely because they are never neutral, also play a part in a subject's or a society's self-definition. In an article entitled

---

[16] Zumthor, *Mesure du Monde*, 15.   [17] Ibid., 30.   [18] Ibid., 27.
[19] Derek Gregory, *Geographical Imaginations* (Cambridge, MA: Blackwell, 1994), 36.

'Niemand will im Osten sein', the historian Philipp Ther discusses the metamorphoses of the concept of *Osteuropa* from its appearance at the beginning of the nineteenth century to the present day.[20] He mentions the haziness of its frontiers and its changing location on the map, while detailing its function as the 'constituting other' of Western Europe, a place of poverty and backwardness. At the same time, he recalls the reluctance of numerous nations such as Poland, the Czech Republic, Slovakia, the Baltic states and, more recently, of the Ukraine, to be part of this eastern area. By refusing a particular geographical location, these countries in fact contest a negative vision of themselves, thereby demonstrating that there is indeed a link between situation and identity.

When I talk of space, therefore, I do not mean a philosophical, abstract category, or a void filled by various bodies and objects. Even though the physical environment experienced by the Anglo-Saxon man and woman certainly played its part in shaping their mental map, I do not wish to adopt a cognitive model of investigation; for, the mental map to which this study is devoted depends on cultural and social circumstances, and not on personal and inner factors, a fact which complicates the articulation of individual and of collective or cultural spatial perceptions.[21] The Anglo-Saxons' immediate reactions to their surroundings are forever lost to us, and the surviving evidence is culturally and socially embedded. Maps, geographical descriptions, and poetic spaces: none of these offers unmediated access to the Anglo-Saxons' experience of their environment. Neither do I attempt here a faithful description of the topography of England in Anglo-Saxon times or an analysis of its landscape. Although descriptions of the natural world are found in the Old English corpus,[22] the very notion of landscape, that is, the representation of natural beauty to which the human being is exterior and with which he or she does not interact was not current

---

[20] Philipp Ther, 'Niemand will im Osten sein: Barbarisch, rückständig und despotisch: Die Erfindung Osteuropas von der Aufklärung bis heute', *Süddeutsche Zeitung am Wochenende*, 2–3 December 2000, p. I.

[21] For a presentation of the cognitive model, and objections against it, see Christian Hänger, *Die Welt im Kopf: Raumbilder und Strategie in Römischen Kaiserreich*, Hypomnemata, 136 (Göttingen: Vandenhoeck and Ruprecht, 2001), 14.

[22] On this point, see Jennifer Neville, *Representations of the Natural World in Old English Poetry*, Cambridge Studies in Anglo-Saxon England, 27 (Cambridge: Cambridge University Press, 1999). See also John Howe and Michael Wolfe (eds.), *Inventing Medieval Landscapes: Senses of Place in Western Europe* (Gainesville: University of Florida Press, 2002).

during the Middle Ages.[23] Without wishing to deny the Anglo-Saxons any aesthetic emotions and to grant them only symbolic perceptions of space, one nevertheless has to recognize that vernacular authors do not speak of the landscape as a vista to be enjoyed. Rather, they mention salient topographic features when these relate to the unfolding of the events or adventures recounted.[24] Consequently, my analysis of the Anglo-Saxons' spatial *imaginaire* and of their mental map is organized around two axes: I shall examine on the one hand expressions of a given culture of space as they transpire in geographical descriptions or in maps, and on the other the spatial imagery and settings created by space as a mental structure.

Spatial *Imaginaire* and Mental Map

Two notions will prove crucial to outline the Anglo-Saxons' sense of space: the *imaginaire* and the mental map. Le Goff defines the *imaginaire* as part of the field of representation, and yet as extending beyond it, for it is the creative, as opposed to the reproductive part of the mental depiction of reality that is fundamental to any process of representation.[25] It is always a cultural production and, as Le Goff clearly states, 'l'imaginaire est une réalité historique'.[26] My interest resides in representations and conceptualizations of the surrounding world and of the cosmos which are not stable and enduring objects of scrutiny offered to a neutral and impersonal gaze, but which are reconstructed

---

[23] Zumthor, *Mesure du Monde*, 86–90. BT mentions only one occurrence of the word *landscipe* in Old English, in *Genesis B* 376. But *Genesis B* is a translation from Old Saxon and it contains several compounds which are not found anywhere else in Old English. *Landscipe* is borrowed from Old Saxon; the modern English 'landscape' was taken from Dutch in the seventeenth century. Charles T. Carr, *Nominal Compounds in Germanic*, St Andrews University Publications, 41 (London: Oxford University Press, 1939), 7–8. The *OED* also indicates that the word was introduced as a technical term of painters and the earliest occurrences it lists date from around the year 1600.

[24] Nicholas Howe, 'The Landscape of Anglo-Saxon England: Inherited, Invented, Imagined', in John Howe and Michael Wolfe (eds.), *Inventing Medieval Landscapes: Senses of Place in Western Europe* (Gainesville: University of Florida Press, 2002), 91–112 (102). See also Patrick Gautier Dalché, *Conférence d'Ouverture de M. Patrick Gautier Dalché: 8 janvier 2001*, École Pratique des Hautes Études: Sections des Sciences Historiques et Philologiques (Paris: La Sorbonne, 2002), 35–60 (43–4).

[25] Jacques Le Goff, *L'Imaginaire médiéval* (Paris: Gallimard, 1985), p. ii.

[26] Jacques Le Goff, 'Qu'est-ce que l'histoire de l'imaginaire?', in *Sens et place des connaissances dans la société*, 3 vols. (Paris: Centre National de la Recherche Scientifique, 1986–7), i (1986), 217–50 (239). See also Michèle Le Doeuff, *Recherches sur l'imaginaire philosophique* (Paris: Payot, 1980), 13.

from the geographical descriptions, the cosmological models, and the wider spatial imagery found in Old English literature. They are therefore functions of a particular time and place: they are socially and culturally conditioned.

By 'mental map', I understand an imaginary picture of the world, made up of representations of the immediate environment, of the entire earth, and/or of the whole cosmos, influenced by tradition and invested with meaning. It entails an awareness of the place one occupies in this world picture. At the same time, it generates a particular spatial imagery which reflects values and assumptions that shaped and still continue to bear on the contours of this mental map. The concept itself is important because it affects not only textual spatial imagery—I am thinking here for instance of the nearly universal desirable character of centrality—but also the articulation of discourses about space and the elaboration of models with which to represent the world. Maps for instance mediate between the world and the viewer; they are graphic representations and yet they seem to disappear from sight. The apparent transparency of the artefact, which is in fact a condition of its effectiveness, is misleading, for a map always conveys more than purely geographical information. 'La carte donne à penser autant qu'à voir,' says Christian Jacob, 'Elle matérialise une vue de l'esprit plus qu'une image du réel.'[27] This is most clearly the case with medieval *mappae mundi* which exhibit a reality that will always escape perception. These maps are a means to articulate and structure the world according to various social and political relationships.[28] They also mobilize a body of knowledge without which they would forever remain incomprehensible and unreadable.[29] A mental map therefore always pre-exists to and influences mapping practices. It complicates the relationship between 'objective' geographical and spatial realities on the one hand, and their various representations on the other.

To analyse a mental map raises a number of issues which I will briefly mention here and to which I will come back in more detail below when delineating the Anglo-Saxons' sense of space. I will concentrate on six main points. First, the mental map conjures up issues linked to the complex evaluation of geographical distances and to the institution

---

[27] Christian Jacob, *L'Empire des cartes: approche théorique de la cartographie à travers l'histoire* (Paris: Albin Michel, 1992), 16. On this point, see also Gautier Dalché, *Conférence . . . 8 janvier 2001*, 54–5.
[28] Jacob, *Empire des cartes*, 45.   [29] Ibid., 53 and 349.

of stable boundaries. Distance can be ideologically and politically significant. Edward Said reminds his readers that imaginary geography often dramatizes the gap and difference between what is near and what is remote, and that it always complexifies what appears to be purely positive geographical knowledge.[30] What is conceived of as far-away need not always lie in the distance; it may simply be on the other side of an imaginary boundary. Frontiers are necessary to think space, for they allow us to objectify, to cut out a given expanse in an otherwise unbroken continuum. They distinguish between two spaces which, more often than not, reflect a difference between two peoples and their territories.[31] Frontiers are indeed ancient demarcations establishing the distinction between 'us' and 'not us'. They need not always be clear lines drawn on a map, for even when their situation remains vague or when it contradicts actual geographical facts, imaginary boundaries fulfil their role, that is, they delimit a community's territory and, beyond it, the realm of its constituting others.

The establishment of frontiers inevitably brings to mind the contrasting pair centre/periphery. Centrality and marginality cannot be thought of separately, for they are of course the two sides of the same coin.[32] The localization and preservation of the centre, together with its complex relationships with the periphery, is the second point which my discussion of the notion of the Anglo-Saxons' mental map will raise.

To control space is vital and various strategies are elaborated to secure it. Knowledge, processes of 'othering', and narratives are three of these procedures, and they are respectively the third, fourth, and fifth issues I will address in relation to the notion of the mental map. An analysis of the familiarity with distant lands powerful leaders display constitutes the third step in my inquiry. Mary Helms reminds us that 'the importance of knowledge as an attribute of leadership... can hardly be overemphasized'.[33] Maps for instance are not only objects of knowledge, but also of power.[34] To represent distant reaches of the world is to know and to appropriate them.[35] One thinks here of the

---

[30] Edward W. Said, *Orientalism: Western Conceptions of the Orient* (London: Penguin, 1978; repr. 1995), 55.
[31] Hänger, *Welt im Kopf*, 16.   [32] Harrison, 'Invisible Boundaries', 91.
[33] Helms, *Ulysses' Sail*, 11.
[34] Le Goff, 'Discorso di chiusura', 836, and Patrick Gautier Dalché, 'Tradition et renouvellement dans la représentation de l'espace géographique au XIe siècle', in *Géographie et culture: La représentation de l'espace du VIe au XIIe siècle* (Aldershot: Ashgate, 1997; first publ. in *Studi Medievali*, 24 (1983)), iv. 121–65 (125).
[35] Jacob, *Empire des cartes*, 44.

famous scene of Chaplin's *The Great Dictator* where Hynkel/Hitler, under frenzied delusions of grandeur, plays with a terrestrial globe. The fourth stage in my discussion analyses strategies of 'othering' as means to disqualify rival claimants to a tract of land: they justify territorial dispossession. Anderson identifies one such design in the use of the words 'inlanders' or 'natives' to designate people who are 'inferior' and who therefore belong *there*, that is, to a given colony.[36] Such words establish a difference between 'us' and 'the others', and at the same time they deprive the latter from their right to the territory and they confine them to the periphery.

Narrative also constitutes a powerful weapon in the struggle for control and appropriation of space: it is the fifth aspect of my inquiry into the issues related to the mental map. As Zumthor declares: 'toute prise de possession territoriale s'opère par le biais d'un récit, serait-ce celui qui produit ou falsifie la preuve d'un droit.'[37] A narrative always grounds claims to a given land, justifies its possession, and defines the limits of the space thus occupied. The chapters that follow focus on three instances in which narrative fashions space: when it recounts the events of creation, when it commemorates an original migration, and when it tells of the first conquest of land. All the texts under consideration can therefore be read as myths of origin because they conjure up the genesis of the current spatial organization. And they prove that the making of poetry is always linked to the making of worlds.

Special attention will finally be paid to the intersection between narratives—more precisely myths of origin—and claims to a real or imaginary territory; for this juncture allows the 'articulation of culture in terms of geographical space', to quote Kathleen Davis, and it favours the emergence of a national sense of identity.[38] Such national feelings are always inscribed in space and articulated in narrative. The spatial components operative in the development of such feelings form the sixth and last aspect I will address.

I am aware that to use words such as 'nation' or 'national' in relation to Anglo-Saxon England may sound anachronistic. For the term 'nation'

---

[36] Anderson, *Imagined Communities*, 112.

[37] Zumthor, *Mesure du Monde*, 302. See also Edward Said, *Culture and Imperialism* (London: Vintage, 1994), p. xiii.

[38] Kathleen Davis, 'National Writing in the Ninth Century: A Reminder for Postcolonial Thinking about the Nation', *Journal of Medieval and Early Modern Studies*, 28 (1998), 611–37 (614).

does not appear in English before the fourteenth century, according to the *OED*, and the concept of the modern nation cannot be transposed as such to the Middle Ages. And yet, as Davis rightly points out, 'imagining national identity is not restricted to one set of historically specific conditions such as print culture, democracy, capitalism and secularization', the conditions Anderson deems necessary to the emergence of the nation.[39] Quite obviously, a group constantly needs to reassert its sense of identity, and the articulation of nationalist or proto-nationalist feelings is an ongoing process. Davis detects antecedents to these phenomena in ninth-century Alfredian writings while Patrick Wormald situates them towards the end of the tenth or the beginning of the eleventh century.[40] Thorlac Turville-Petre studies how thirteenth-century writers express their sense of England as a nation,[41] while Bernhard Klein examines the new modes of representing the nation emerging in the Early Modern period.[42] Finally, as already mentioned, Anderson locates the origins of the nation in the eighteenth century.[43] In view of these contrasting positions, I believe that hegemonic processes and attempts at delineating a national community are of all times. The focus of this book is on the Anglo-Saxon period, and more precisely on how insular authors expressed their own sense of self and their national consciousness.

SENSE OF SPACE: THE MIDDLE AGES AND ANGLO-SAXON ENGLAND

Geographical and Cosmographical Traditions

Before turning to the Anglo-Saxons and their spatial *imaginaire*, a brief survey of the culture of space which they inherited from tradition and which informed their view of the world is required. This aspect,

---

[39] Davis, 'National Writing', 613.
[40] Patrick Wormald, 'Bede, the *Bretwaldas* and the Origins of the *Gens Anglorum*', in P. Wormald, D. Bullough, and R. Collins (eds.), *Ideal and Reality in Frankish and Anglo-Saxon Society* (Oxford: Blackwell, 1983), 99–129 (103).
[41] Thorlac Turville-Petre, *England the Nation: Language, Literature and National Identity, 1290–1340* (Oxford: Clarendon Press, 1996), pp. v–vi.
[42] Bernhard Klein, 'Constructing the Space of the Nation: Geography, Maps, and the Discovery of Britain in the Early Modern Period', *Journal for the Study of British Cultures*, 4 (1997), 11–29 (11).
[43] Anderson, *Imagined Communities*, 14.

which pertains to the second of the three levels of analysis identified above, plays an important part in the elaboration of any world-view during the Middle Ages, and it forms the background against which the Anglo-Saxons developed their own picture of the world. For medieval cosmography and geography result from a complex interaction between tradition and experience.[44] The use of the expression 'medieval geography' may, however, be disputed, since there was at that time no geography in the literal sense of the term. And yet, the period fostered complex reflections on space and on how best to represent it,[45] as illustrated in this outline of the mental frameworks that shaped medieval thinking on geography and cosmology.[46]

During the Middle Ages the corpus of cosmographical doctrines consists mainly of a body of knowledge inherited from late antiquity, and any reflection on the world entails a careful examination of classical authors. As Zumthor argues: 'On recueille tout, et l'on juxtapose sans risquer de synthèse. On ignore la notion moderne d' "univers", objet autonome régi par ses lois propres: il y a le monde, œuvre de Dieu, observable, concevable en tant que création mais dont l'intelligence globale reste un privilège divin.'[47] To speak about the world was not a 'neutral', scientific exercise; for to comment on the organization of the cosmos or on the nature and distribution of various locations always implied, in one way or another, speaking about God and his divine plans for the world. However, a small number of principles remained unchallenged for over a millennium; Zumthor enumerates three of them: the idea that the earth constitutes the centre of the universe, the notion that the celestial spheres organize the universe, and finally the idea that 'le monde est fini et clos... l'infini spatial est, jusque tard dans le xve siècle, aussi inconcevable que l'éternité de la matière'.[48]

---

[44] On this point, see Patrick Gautier Dalché's warning against anachronism and against a light dismissal of the role played by contemporary geographical 'realities' in Gautier Dalché, *Conférence... 8 janvier 2001*, 46–7 and 49–50. See also Patrick Gautier Dalché, 'Principes et modes de la représentation de l'espace géographique durant le haut moyen âge', in *Uomo e spazio nell'alto medioevo*, 2 vols., Settimane di studio del Centro italiano di studi sull'alto medioevo, 50 (Spoleto: Centro Italiano di Studi sull'Alto Medioevo, 2003), 117–50 (117–19).

[45] Gautier Dalché, *Conférence... 8 janvier 2001*, 40 and 44–9.

[46] Please note that I am mainly considering the world of clerical learning. I do not wish, however, to deny that other influences shaped the Anglo-Saxons' view of the world—I am thinking in particular of an orally preserved Germanic poetic tradition and of a Celtic form of learning.

[47] Zumthor, *Mesure du Monde*, 220.   [48] Ibid., 223.

Medieval people therefore did not conceive of space as an absolute, infinite, homogeneous, and empty extension.

Medieval cosmography and geography belong to the field of authority. During the early Middle Ages, their two main sources of information about the shape of the world and of the cosmos were the Bible and what was known of classical learning. Although the Bible offers no systematic cosmographical description, the opening of the Book of Genesis is fundamental when dealing with these questions.[49] The following picture can be reconstructed from it: God gathers the waters in one place and the earth appears.[50] It is surmounted by the vault of the firmament and, on this cupola, the stars, the sun, and the moon are fixed.[51] Above the firmament are the heavenly waters that give rain to the earth.[52] Still further above it is the throne of God. At the other end of this vertical axis lies the realm of the dead, situated under the earth. The universe is a hierarchical structure organized vertically. But it is also ordered along a horizontal plane: at the centre of the Garden of Eden is the Tree of Life, and the four rivers that irrigate the whole earth have their source in paradise.[53] The creation of mankind and the beginning of human history took place in Eden. Christ's incarnation, resurrection, and ascension subsequently remap the world and situate the Holy Land at its centre.[54] This picture of the earth was considered part of the divine revelation.

Classical learning is the second cosmographical authority to which medieval thinkers resort. Investigation and discovery in this field of study originated with the Greeks, and it culminated with Ptolemy's *Almagest*. But when the Roman Empire split into a western and an eastern part, the West was left with only a small number of works that had been translated into Latin. Much was lost, and classical knowledge was transmitted mostly through encyclopaedias. This situation prevailed until the intellectual revolution of the twelfth century, when Greek and Arabic scholars began to be widely translated into Latin. The Anglo-Saxons therefore derived most of their cosmographical knowledge

---

[49] On the biblical description of the cosmos, see Christian Cannuyer, 'Cosmologie', in *Dictionnaire Encyclopédique de la Bible*, ed. by Centre: Informatique et Bible, Abbaye de Maredsous, resp. scient. Pierre-Maurice Bogaert and others ([Turnhout]: Brepols, 1987), 307–8 (307).

[50] Genesis 1: 9.   [51] Genesis 1: 14–19.   [52] Genesis 1: 6–8.

[53] Genesis 2: 9, 3: 3, and 2: 10–14.

[54] R. Simek, 'Weltbild: II. Geographisch', in *Lexikon des Mittelalters*, ed. by Robert Auty and others (Munich: Lexma, 1980–99), viii (1997), 2159–66 (2163).

from only a handful of texts: Pliny's *Natural History* and Isidore of Seville's *Etymologies* were standard works of reference among the Anglo-Saxons. Macrobius's *Commentary on the Dream of Scipio* and Martianus Capella's *The Marriage of Philology and Mercury* were both known early in Ireland but were slow to reach England.[55] Finally, Boethius's *Consolation of Philosophy* occupied a unique position in Anglo-Saxon England.[56]

The basic model which organizes the universe in celestial spheres goes back to Pythagorean thinking and was very influential on philosophical developments in antiquity and during the Middle Ages. It can roughly be described as follows: the planets are fixed upon a series of concentric and mobile spheres, at the centre of which is the earth. After the orbit of the moon follow those of the planets known at the time: Mercury, Venus, the sun, Mars, Jupiter, and Saturn. The moon marks the limit between the decaying and the eternal worlds; change is possible only in the sublunary realm. Beyond the orbits of the planets, there is one last, immobile sphere that marks the outer edge of the cosmos. This model clearly departs from the biblical one, although some of its aspects are easily reconcilable with a scriptural picture of the cosmos. The *firmamentum* of the Bible, for instance, was often equated with the sphere of the fixed stars. But such an agreement was not always possible and tensions between the two cosmographical systems endured.

Similar discrepancies also existed between the Bible and classical learning on geography. One controversial point was, for example, the shape of the earth: Genesis 1: 9–10 presents the earth as emerging dry from the waters that God gathers in one place, and Isaiah 40: 22 depicts it as a circle. But the sphericity of the earth had been firmly

---

[55] J. D. A. Ogilvy, *Books Known to the English, 587–1066* (Cambridge, MA: Medieval Academy of America, 1967), 166–70 (Isidore), 196–7 (Macrobius), 199–200 (Martianus Capella), and 222–3 (Pliny). See also J. D. A. Ogilvy, 'Books Known to the English, AD 597–1066: *Addenda et Corrigenda*', *Mediaevalia*, 7 (1981), 281–325 and Gopa Roy, 'The Anglo-Saxons and the Shape of the World', in Jane Roberts and Janet Nelson (eds.), *Essays on Anglo-Saxon and Related Themes in Memory of Lynne Grundy* (London: King's College London, 2000), 455–81 (459 and 463).

[56] D. K. Bolton, 'The Study of the Consolation of Philosophy in Anglo-Saxon England', *Archives d'Histoire Doctrinale et Littéraire du Moyen Age*, 44 (1977), 33–78 (33) and Ogilvy, *Books Known to the English, 587–1066*, 199–200. See also Helmut Gneuss, 'Bücher und Leser in England im zehnten Jahrhundert', in *Books and Libraries in Early England* (Aldershot: Variorum, 1996; first publ. in H. L. C. Tristram (ed.), *Medialität und mittelalterliche insulare Literatur*, Scriptoralia, 43 (Tübingen: Günter Narr, 1992)), iv, 104–31 (128).

established and was conventional wisdom among medieval thinkers.[57] The two authorities therefore disagree on this particular question. Another tension between them is due to the appearance, in the Middle Ages, of previously unknown peoples,[58] for the lists of continents, peoples, and lands drawn up from the Bible and classical learning are deemed complete and exhaustive. When the Mongols are first heard of in the West in the thirteenth century, they are understood to be descendants of Prester John and their ruler is thought to be a new King David. They are incorporated into familiar intellectual categories and are not recognized for what they are: an entirely new people.

For their knowledge of classical geography, the Anglo-Saxons rely mostly on encyclopaedias such as Pliny's *Natural History* or Solinus's *Collectanea Rerum Memorabilium*. They also know Pomponius Mela's *Chorography*, Orosius's *History against the Pagans*, and geographers such as Aethicus Ister or the Ravenna Geographer. Even though Europe is the best known continent at the time, its description will nevertheless remain for long under the influence of classical and biblical knowledge. In the early Middle Ages, therefore, cosmography and geography are conditioned by biblical teaching and by the fragmentary survival of classical sources.[59]

In addition to the textual evidence considered above, *mappae mundi* constitute another important source of information on medieval views of the world. Several types of map coexisted, the principal models being the TO schema and the zonal representation. TO maps depict the inhabited world. The O pictures the Outer Ocean that was believed to encircle the land masses, and the T stands for the inland waterways—rivers and seas—that divide the continents. The world is organized in three parts: Asia, Europe, and Africa. Zonal maps do not limit themselves to the depiction of the northern hemisphere but they include what is located south of the equator. There are five climatic zones, two cold ones at the poles, a hot one at the equator, and two temperate ones in between.

From antiquity to the Middle Ages, and under the influence of Christian doctrine on geographical knowledge, *mappae mundi* lend themselves to an allegorization of spatial organization.[60] East is the

---

[57] On this question, see Jeffrey Burton Russell, *Inventing the Flat Earth* (New York: Praeger, 1991).
[58] See Gautier Dalché, *Conférence...8 janvier 2001*, 46–7 and Gautier Dalché, 'Principes et modes' 142–4.
[59] H. Hunger, 'Geographie', in *Lexikon des Mittelalters*, iv (1989), 1265–9.
[60] Le Goff, 'Discorso di chiusura', 829–30.

source of light and life; it indicates the direction of Eden—forever lost—and, from a European point of view, of Jerusalem, cradle of the Incarnation. The north is often associated with negative values. It is, for instance, the place where Gog and Magog are confined.[61] The end of time will take place in the west, according to the theory of the *translatio imperii*, the model that understands history as a succession of four world empires, from the first in Babylon to the last in Rome. These values, attributed to the various directions, exemplify the intermingling of the second and third levels of analysis outlined at the beginning of this chapter, that is, of the culture of space and of space as a mental structure; for an affective interpretation is here made of 'scientific' data.

This imaginary dimension informs not only religious geography and cosmography; it also shapes classical world-views, as a reflection on the dialectic of unity and diversity inherent in both Roman imperial ideology and in Christian thinking illustrates. The former promotes the idea that the empire is without limit, that it is destined always to expand and to incorporate new territories. Poetry offers abundant evidence of this tenet; let me here just mention the first book of the *Aeneid*, where Jupiter promises Venus that he will give the Romans a new city whose time and space are infinite: 'His ego nec metas rerum nec tempora pono: | imperium sine fine dedi'.[62] Yet at the same time an awareness of the particularities of provinces and regions coexists with this imperial ideology and develops in the course of the first centuries AD.[63]

When the Empire dissolves in the fifth and sixth centuries, Christianity recuperates and endorses the imperial ambition. The lost unity of the Roman Empire is transformed into a desired Christian totality. Christian theology develops the idea of a universal mission, according to which no corner of the world should be denied knowledge of the Christian faith. Its horizon is as limitless as that of imperial ideology. But Christianity proved to be no more immune to fragmentation than the Empire had been. The emergence of local saints promotes the apparition and development of

---

[61] See e.g. Ezekiel 39: 2.

[62] 'To these I give no bounds of power and no time: I gave them an empire without end'. Virgil, *Aeneid* 1. 278–9. See also Hänger, *Welt im Kopf*, 235.

[63] See Jacques Fontaine, 'De l'universalisme antique aux particularismes médiévaux: la conscience du temps et de l'espace dans l'antiquité tardive', in *Popoli e paesi nella cultura altomedievale*, 2 vols., Settimane di studio del Centro italiano di studi sull'alto medioevo, 29 (Spoleto: Centro Italiano di Studi sull'Alto Medioevo, 1983), 15–45.

local Churches, and the particular history of these communities further strengthens the specific character of cities and provinces.⁶⁴

Despite the contrasting pulls of unifying ideologies, division eventually prevails, both politically and religiously. It does so politically with the coming and the settlement of the barbarian peoples in the Empire. These newcomers, with all their particularities, help to disintegrate the traditional concept of the 'Barbarian', which had for centuries been used to define negatively a united and clearly delimited spatial entity on the face of the earth, the place where 'we' are, as opposed to where 'they' are.⁶⁵ Experience, that is, the confrontation with real and diverse peoples, complicates the Christian world picture. Religiously, division spreads because of the increasing tensions between the Eastern and the Western Christian Churches, because of the threat represented by Islam, and because of the development of various heresies. From these political and religious changes arises the idea that Christianity is a closed and limited space, possibly under threat, and that its areas of extension are not infinite. Le Goff calls it 'la Chrétienté close', characteristic of a period which, for the historian, ends in the eleventh century.⁶⁶ He defines the geography of the early Middle Ages as a 'géographie de la nostalgie', of a double nostalgia in fact: 'nostalgie du savoir géographique antique maintenue tant bien que mal contre l'assaut de la fragmentation et de l'ignorance, nostalgie d'une géographie chrétienne qui serait une nouvelle forme idéale de l'unité spatiale antique et inclurait le berceau palestinien du christianisme'.⁶⁷ The first half of the Middle Ages is conditioned by a dialectic of unity and diversity. This tension is reflected in the Old English corpus by some of the specific issues that emerge from a close analysis of its spatial imagery, of space as a mental structure. Anxieties linked to the establishment of a fixed centre and of secure boundaries are recurrent concerns. So are the nature of outsiders and the potential threat they pose to a given community. At the same time, this mental geography is broadened by the need for Anglo-Saxon rulers to anchor their genealogies in a wider Christian and/or Germanic world or by the numerous narratives recounting missions of conversion that holy men and holy women undertake in distant lands.

---

⁶⁴ Fontaine, 'De l'univeralisme', 28. See also Peter Brown, *The Cult of the Saints: Its Rise and Function in Latin Christianity* (Chicago: University of Chicago Press, 1981).
⁶⁵ Zumthor, *Mesure du Monde*, 147–8.
⁶⁶ Le Goff, 'Discorso di chiusura', 837.   ⁶⁷ Ibid., 837.

The Anglo-Saxons' Sense of Space

Terminology

So far, I have been talking of space and place, of geography and cosmology, using terms such as territory, situation, or position. Interestingly, none of these words was current in Old English; 'geography', for instance, appears in English only during the sixteenth century.[68]

Spatium, the Latin form that will give the modern English 'space', was also absent from the Old English language. Adopted by popular usage only quite recently, it remained a *mot de lettrés* as late as the sixteenth and the seventeenth centuries.[69] Space first denoted a period of time, and only later was it used to speak about a physical extension. The oldest occurrence of the word with this meaning listed in the *OED* dates from the fourteenth century and refers to an interval between two points. Only in the seventeenth century does an occurrence of the word mean an unlimited area or extension.

'Place' briefly appears in Old English, in Northumbrian, under the forms *plæce* or *plæts*, to translate the biblical *platea*, 'a broad way, street, avenue'.[70] But it is properly integrated into English only in the eleventh century when it supersedes *stow* and *stede*. In the early Middle Ages therefore, people did not have at their disposal a terminology similar to ours, and Old English does not possess a word that correlates with our notion of 'space'.

What terminology therefore did Anglo-Saxon authors use to speak about space? *Rum* is the Old English term referring to space, and it has numerous cognates in other Germanic languages. Here too, notions of space and time are combined, for the word can be translated either as 'space, dimensional extent' or as 'space of time'. In its spatial sense, the word designates either an enclosed area or the distance between two points. This latter meaning is exemplified in a seventh-century land charter where *rum* refers to the distance that should be kept when building between the public way and the limits of one's possession.[71] The instances BT lists for the spatial sense of *rum* designate either an enclosed extension, a building, or a distance between two points. For instance, in the Old English version of the Gospel of Luke (in all

---

[68] Zumthor, *Mesure du Monde*, 227.   [69] Ibid., 51.
[70] For the following discussion on terminology, see BT and the *OED*.
[71] *A Hand-Book to the Land Charters and other Saxonic Documents*, ed. by John Earle (Oxford: Clarendon Press, 1888), 141 n.

versions except the Lindisfarne and the Rushworth manuscripts), the word appears in the context of the birth of Jesus. Arriving at Bethlehem, his parents cannot stay at the inn, for there is no space, *rum*, in the guesthouse.[72] The word clearly refers to an enclosed extension.

Stede and *stow* are two other Germanic contributions to spatial terminology. BT translates the first of these as 'a place, spot, locality' or 'the place a person or a thing occupies'. In *The Battle of Maldon*, Byrhtnoð harangues his troops and the poet tells us that he shows them 'hu hi sceoldon standan and þone stede healdan'.[73] The meaning of *stede* in this case is quite specific and it refers to a precise location on the ground. Similarly with *stow*: BT translates it as 'a place, spot, locality, site', 'a place on the body', 'a place which is built, a house or collection of houses, a habitation', 'a place, position, station' etc. The most famous occurrence of *stow* is undoubtedly found in *Beowulf*, when Hroðgar concludes his ghastly description of Grendel's mere with his remarkable understatement: 'nis þæt heoru stow!'[74] *Stow* often glosses *locus* in the *Vespasian Psalter* and so does *stede* in Ælfric's vocabulary printed by Thomas Wright.[75] The root sense of these two words is therefore very close to that of 'place', and both derive from an ancient Indo-European root **sta-*, the place where one stands.[76]

The various meanings and occurrences of *rum*, *stede*, and *stow* reveal that these words never meant anything like our infinite space. Other terms, such as *tun*—an enclosed piece of ground, the enclosed land surrounding a single dwelling[77]—or *wic*—a dairy farm[78]—also indicate that spatial terms in Old English designate a concrete and

---

[72] *The Gospel according to Saint Luke and according to Saint John*, ed. by Walter W. Skeat (Cambridge: Cambridge University Press, 1874; repr. Darmstadt: Wissenschaftliche Buchgesellschaft, 1970), 28–9.

[73] 'how they should stand and hold this place' (*The Battle of Maldon* 19). *The Anglo-Saxon Minor Poems*, ed. by Elliott van Kirk Dobbie, Anglo-Saxon Poetic Records, 6 (London: Routledge, 1942; repr. 1968), 7–16.

[74] 'this is not a pleasant place!' (*Beowulf* 1372^b). *Beowulf and the Fight at Finnsburg*, ed. by F. Klaeber, 3rd edn. (Lexington, MA: Heath, 1922, repr. 1950).

[75] *The Oldest English Texts*, ed. by Henry Sweet, EETS os. 83 (London: Oxford University Press, 1885; repr. 1966), 215, 219, 235, 284, and 293; *Anglo-Saxon and Old English Vocabularies*, ed. by Thomas Wright, 2nd edn., ed. by Richard Paul Wülcker, 2 vols. (London: Trübner, 1884), ii. 139 and 187.

[76] Stephen A. Barney, *Word-Hoard: An Introduction to Old English Vocabulary* (New Haven: Yale University Press, 1977), 8–9.

[77] See the etymology given in the *OED*. *Tun* glosses *cohors* in the Erfurt and the Corpus glossaries; *The Oldest English Texts*, 52–3.

[78] G. B. Grundy, 'The Development of the Meanings of Certain Anglo-Saxon Terms', *Archaeological Journal*, 99 (1943), 67–98 (87).

The Anglo-Saxons' Sense of Space 21

definite space. Similarly, in his study of the landscape of Anglo-Saxon England, Nicholas Howe points out that land charters record the boundary landmarks of a given estate, that the periphery is more important than what fills the centre. These documents, the scholar observes, 'speak of landscape as bounded, as contained by human-defined purposes'.[79] In such an intellectual environment, it is not surprising that the Anglo-Saxons conceived of space not as a boundless, but as an enclosed extension.

Mental Map and Related Issues

My inquiry into the Anglo-Saxons' sense of space now returns to the six aspects associated with the concept of the mental map enumerated and briefly discussed above. They were: the affective evaluation of distance, the complex notion of boundary, the question of identity, together with knowledge of space, processes of 'othering', and narratives as modes of spatial control. These questions will be addressed now specifically in relation to Old English literature and to its manifestations of space as a mental structure. Alongside the above examination of a culture of space, a detailed exposition of issues raised by my analysis of spatial representations, issues which pervade the chapters that follow, will complete the present outline of the Anglo-Saxons' spatial *imaginaire*.

Always meaningful, geographical distance is not on all occasions measured according to objective criteria. For instance, a number of places described in Old English literature, such as Grendel's mere and the dragon's barrow in *Beowulf*, or the *beorg* that the saint occupies in *Guthlac A*, are both mysterious and yet near at hand, appearing only when a suitable visitor approaches. In these examples, the evaluation of the distance varies according to the context. Similarly, a comparison between, on the one hand, the anecdote of the Anglo-Saxon slave boys who catch Pope Gregory's eye in a Roman market and spur the holy man to launch a mission of religious conversion to England in Bede's *Ecclesiastical History of the English People*, and, on the other hand, a passage from one of Gregory's letters, provides another example illuminating different attitudes to distance. In the first case, the pun attributed to the Pope translates the *Angli* into angels and transforms strangeness into election.[80] The Anglo-Saxons' difference, the alterity caused by

---
[79] Howe, 'Landscape', 102.
[80] *Bede's Ecclesiastical History of the English People*, ed. and trans. by Bertram Colgrave and R. A. B. Mynors (Oxford: Clarendon Press, 1969; repr. 1991), ii. 1, pp. 132–4.

their remoteness, becomes something positive. In the second instance, Gregory talks about the missionaries he has sent to Britain and he describes the English as 'gens Anglorum in mundi angulo posita'.[81] The Pope offers another pun here—on *Angli* and *angulus*—that associates the English with a distant location. The link between the Anglo-Saxons, their distant situation, and the need for a mission of conversion may or may not be linguistically stressed, depending on the context. As a consequence, the distance separating England from the continent is connoted once as something positive and once as something negative.

A political power—its limits and unacknowledged assumptions about its extent—is always, implicitly or explicitly, inscribed on a mental map. Because it necessarily entails the establishment of imaginary boundaries—and I now move to my second point—a mental map defines a dominion's territorial borders and mirrors the actual or desired range of a jurisdiction. When at the beginning of *Beowulf*, Hroðgar builds Heorot, he imposes his power on the surrounding lands over which the hall towers. The building of Heorot is a founding act, the establishment of a new territory. Foregrounded in this episode, the boundaries of Hroðgar's dominion, metonymically represented by the walls of the hall, will again play an important role during Beowulf's fights against Grendel and against his mother.

Historically speaking, frontiers grow in importance in the course of the early Middle Ages. Hans-Werner Goetz shows how the disintegration of the Roman Empire, contradicting ideological convictions of a

---

[81] 'the people of the English situated in a corner of the world' (*S. Gregorii Magni: Registrum Epistularum Libri VIII–XIV, Appendix*, ed. by Dag Norberg, Corpus Christianorum Series Latina, 140A (Turnhout: Brepols, 1982), viii. 29, p. 551). Other instances of this pun are found in Widukind i. 8. 28 and Thietmar von Merseburg, vii. 36. 392. Widukind names England's inhabitants *Anglisaxones* and Thietmar brings together the two puns associated with *Angli*, namely *angeli* and *angulus*. Thietmar von Merseburg, *Chronik*, ed. by Werner Trillmich, Ausgewählte Quellen zur Deutschen Geschichte des Mittelalters, 9 (Darmstadt: Wissenschaftliche Buchgesellschaft, 1957; repr. 1970); [Widukind], *Quellen zur Geschichte der Sächsischen Kaiserzeit: Widukinds Sachsengeschichte, Adalberts Fortsetzung der Chronik Reginos, Liudprands Werke*, ed. by Albert Bauer and Reinhold Rau with the transl. of Paul Hirsch, Max Büdinger, and Wilhelm Wattenbach, Ausgewählte Quellen zur Deutschen Geschichte des Mittelalters, 8 (Darmstadt: Wissenschaftliche Buchgesellschaft, 1971). On this point, see Nicholas Howe, 'An Angle on this Earth: Sense of Place in Anglo-Saxon England', *Bulletin of the John Rylands University Library of Manchester*, 82 (2000), 3–27 (3–6); Kathy Lavezzo, 'Another Country: Ælfric and the Production of English Identity', *New Medieval Literatures*, 3 (1999), 67–93 (83); and Sarah Foot, 'The Making of *Angelcynn*: English Identity before the Norman Conquest', *Transactions of the Royal Historical Society*, 6th ser., 6 (1996), 25–49 (43).

world-wide empire, brings with it a change in the notion of frontier. In Merovingian times chroniclers develop new perceptions of boundaries between provinces and kingdoms, an evolution that culminates with Carolingian authors who clearly conceive of various kingdoms delimited by precise, though possibly contested, borderlines.[82] A similar development occurs in Anglo-Saxon England. W. G. Hoskins, studying the history of the landscape, suggests that as the countryside fills up it becomes increasingly necessary to define territorial bounds, for it is no longer sufficient to associate them with natural features in an untamed landscape, such as rivers or the edges of forests.[83] Maybe the most famous example of boundary drawing in Anglo-Saxon England is the treaty between Alfred and Guthrum, originating in or soon after 886, when the West Saxon king seized London. It establishes the limit between Alfred's dominion and the Danelaw, and it defines both the Norsemen as outsiders and the English people not under Danish law as subjects to King Alfred.[84] The treaty's prologue distinguishes between the two groups, for it says that 'ðis is ðæt frið, ðæt Ælfred cyninc 7 Gyðrum cyning 7 ealles Angelcynnes witan 7 eal seo ðeod ðe on Eastænglum beoð ealle gecweden habbað 7 mid aðum gefeostnod for hy sylfe 7 for heora gingran'.[85] The first article of the treaty actually draws the boundaries: 'Ærest ymb ure landgemæra' which are to go up the Thames, and then up the Lea, and along the Lea to its source, then in a straight line to Bedford, then up the Ouse to Watling Street.[86]

One of the recurrent features of the Anglo-Saxons' sense of space is their constant fear of invasion. The outside is always a threat and, as Jennifer Neville demonstrates in her study of the representations

---

[82] Hans-Werner Goetz, 'Concepts of Realm and Frontiers from Late Antiquity to the Early Middle Ages: Some Preliminary Remarks', in Pohl, Wood, and Reimitz, *The Transformation of Frontiers from Late Antiquity to the Carolingians*, 73–82.
[83] W. G. Hoskins, *English Landscapes* (London: British Broadcasting Corporation, 1973), 38.
[84] See Mary P. Richards, 'Anglo-Saxonism in the Old English Laws', in Allen J. Frantzen and John D. Niles (eds.), *Anglo-Saxonism and the Construction of Social Identity* (Gainesville: University Press of Florida, 1997), 40–59 (49); James Campbell, Eric John, and Patrick Wormald, *The Anglo-Saxons* (London: Penguin, 1991; first publ. London: Phaidon, 1982), 160, and *Alfred the Great: Asser's* Life of Alfred *and Other Contemporary Sources*, ed. and trans. by Simon Keynes and Michael Lapidge (London: Penguin, 1983), 171.
[85] 'This is the peace that King Alfred and King Guthrum and the councillors of all the English people and all the people who are in East Anglia have resolved and have secured with oaths for themselves and their followers' (*The Laws of the Earliest English Kings*, ed. and trans. by F. L. Attenborough (New York: Russel and Russel, 1922; repr. 1963), 98).
[86] 'First about our boundaries', (*Laws of the Earliest English Kings*, 98).

of the natural world in Old English poetry: 'the Anglo-Saxons viewed their society both as a necessary defence for individuals and as a fragile structure always under attack'.[87] The opposition inside/outside is foregrounded and, with it, an almost infinite series of related contrasts, such as here/elsewhere, open/closed, etc.[88] The manifestations of this metaphorical way of thinking may vary: inside/outside the land of a kingdom, inside/outside a city or a palace, inside/outside an imaginary space, such as a religious community, Christianity for instance.

The concept of frontier is central to such an outlook, since it marks the separation between an enclosed and bounded place—the 'inside'—and the 'outside'. Unsurprisingly, therefore, the measure of a leader's power may be gauged by his capacity to deal with people from elsewhere, with foreigners and enemies, regardless of whether they attack from the outside—as Grendel in *Beowulf*, are part of the community and rebel against their ruler—as Satan in the *Genesis* poems, or are distant visitors, peaceful strangers arriving at a foreign court.[89] Yet the notion of the limit is always ambiguous, for it not only defines the 'inside' and the 'outside', but it is also the place where the two come into contact. Is the limit an obstacle or a passage way? Consequently, the basic opposition of inside and outside is rarely clear-cut and unproblematic; repeatedly blurred, it constantly needs to be reasserted.

Enclosure is an essential component in the emergence of a sense of place and it is necessary for human beings to locate themselves in the cosmos.[90] It can be a loving shelter as well as a binding punishment, such as hell to which Satan is confined and which he has to measure at the end of *Christ and Satan*. The opposition inside/outside culminates in architectural metaphors, in particular in the image of the building. Zumthor notices that an edifice's first function is to introduce order into spatial chaos; it fulfils a protective role for human beings.[91] Heorot is, of course, the first example to come to mind, and not only because of its obvious sheltering function. The hall organizes space in the land of the Danes; it marks the boundary dividing the outside darkness and the

---

[87] Neville, *Natural World*, 88.
[88] See Zumthor, *Mesure du Monde*, 58–62, and Le Goff, 'Qu'est-ce que l'histoire de l'imaginaire?', 233.
[89] Helms, *Ulysses' Sail*, 152.
[90] See Ruth Wehlau, *'The Riddle of Creation': Metaphor Structures in Old English Poetry*, Studies in the Humanities: Literature–Politics–Society, 24 (New York: Lang, 1997), 133.
[91] Zumthor, *Mesure du Monde*, 91.

light inside, and it is also the point where they come into contact. The door of the hall is the gateway through which one passes from one world to the other. Boundaries therefore have to do with separation, but also with liminality: they are the point where 'us' becomes 'not us'. Grendel in *Beowulf* and the saint in *Andreas* only need to touch them for the doors of Heorot or of the prison where Matthew is captive to collapse. The boundary between two worlds is permeable and never secure.

Boundaries and liminality inevitably evoke the notion of the centre because they conjure up another important opposition: centre/periphery. These two elements are inseparable and are part of the same mental structure. The centre is not a fixed point in space, but it is the place in relation to which periphery and decentring are located.[92] Never situated at random, the centre is invested with meaning. To borrow Zumthor's words, it is the 'fondement métaphysique et mystique de tout ordre du monde'.[93] Different types of centres can coexist, and political or geographical focal points do not always coincide with imaginary and mental pivots. The chapters that follow identify literary devices which articulate the opposition centre/periphery and which are operative in constructing and locating a middle point. As boundaries always need to be re-traced, centres cannot be firmly established. In *Beowulf*, for instance, the world of monsters mirrors the civilized heart of the realm, especially in the second part of the poem where the establishment of a spatial focus poses problems: is it the old king's hall, the dragon's barrow, or the dead hero's funeral mound?

Centrality and marginality define the position of an individual, that is, the portion of space s/he occupies. A place is not simply a point in space: 'Le lieu d'un être', says Zumthor, 'non moins que celui d'un objet, est perçu comme une qualité propre de cet objet ou de cet être.'[94] A location in space is not merely a topographical accident, but it is an essential ingredient in a process of self-definition. These reflections on centres and peripheries, on boundaries and place introduce the third issue raised by the notion of the mental map: identity.

The question of identity is as inscribed in space as political or religious ideologies are. Le Goff reminds us that 'pour les hommes, pour les peuples, les pays, l'espace sont un lieu de recherche consciente ou inconsciente de pouvoir et d'identité'.[95] The early Middle Ages see peoples in search of land, of an area where they can establish their

---

[92] Ibid., 21.   [93] Ibid., 21.   [94] Ibid., 53.
[95] Le Goff, 'Discorso di chiusura', 835.

jurisdiction. They institute a link between political rule and the lands they inhabit in order to create their own territory. The notion of territory is important because it unites a people and a tract of land; it designates the area over which a given community has rights.[96] Le Goff stresses this association between space and identity: 'Recherche de l'identité: il s'agit ici de l'identité des peuples à la recherche de leur territoire.... La *localisation* est un *processus d'identification*.'[97] The Anglo-Saxons therefore unsurprisingly opposed the marginal situation to which classical learning confined them and they developed numerous strategies of recentring. For instance, the narratives of Ohthere and Wulfstan, interpolated at the beginning of the vernacular translation of Orosius's *Historiarum adversum Paganos Libri Septem*, redefine King Alfred's court and pull it away from the margins.[98] The two travellers' accounts present it as an attractive centre of power and culture, as a place where the explorers find an audience and where the information they gathered in the course of their expeditions will be preserved.

Possession and control of space are crucial issues in a mental outlook in which land grounds not only claims to power but also lays the foundations of a sense of identity. As a consequence, invasion—in all its forms—is the greatest threat: it entails loss of land, negation of power, and annihilation of one's sense of identity. Old English texts are populated by characters deprived of their original home; the pervasive theme of exile testifies to the persistence of this motif. Adam and Eve, Guðlac, Andrew, Grendel and Satan, Helen, the apostles, but also Beowulf, the migrating Israelites, Ohthere and Wulfstan, and the Germanic tribes crossing from the Continent, all have somehow left their original homes and are in search of a new land. Even the *Maxims*, especially the *Cotton Maxims*, can be understood along similar lines. They echo this motif of dislocation not by presenting people looking for an ideal dwelling but, on the contrary, by obsessively assigning everything and everybody to its proper place. The verses recreate the original, natural order of the world thanks to language which links one thing to one place: a hawk must be on a glove, a wolf in the wood, a boar in the grove, and so forth.[99]

[96] See Zumthor, *Mesure du Monde*, 78–80.
[97] Le Goff, 'Discorso di chiusura', 836. Emphases in Le Goff.
[98] *The Old English Orosius*, ed. by Janet Bately, EETS ss. 6 (Oxford: Oxford University Press, 1980), 13–18.
[99] *The Anglo-Saxon Minor Poems*, 55–7. For a detailed discussion of the maxims, see Carolyne Larrington, *A Store of Common Sense: Gnomic Theme and Style in Old Icelandic*

In these maxims, making poetry clearly entails creating a new mental world. Their ideal portrayal of nature attempts to counterbalance the constant displacement that affects the fallen world's population following the original banishment from Eden. It betrays an omnipresent anxiety about spatial location and possession of land. Let me now turn my attention to the three strategies that help to secure control over space: knowledge, 'othering' processes, and narratives.

A ruler has to have a good knowledge of the lands and peoples under his jurisdiction. Dicuil, for instance, mentions several times the holy emperor Theodosius who orders a survey of the whole world.[100] Similarly, the interpolation of Ohthere's and Wulfstan's accounts in the vernacular translation of Orosius highlights King Alfred's glory through his familiarity with distant lands, just as the mention of table maps in Charlemagne's testament reveals the political ambitions of the emperor.[101] In all these examples, the equation is clear: to know is somehow also to dominate. In another ninth-century treatise, the anonymous *De Situ Orbis*, the plea for geographical learning is grounded on actual political circumstances. The prologue explains that the Norman raids and invasions, whose progress and course were not known, call for a better, more accurate geographical knowledge. In this instance, actual solicitations and external influences affect the development of spatial knowledge.[102] Learning is implicitly linked to spatial control, for it comes as a reaction, and possibly as a solution, against terrifying invasions.[103]

To secure control over a given tract of land, one possibility is to define its previous inhabitants or rival pretenders as wild, outlandish, or monstrous. These creatures are uncivilized and they are denied enjoyment of a territory because they are unable to enforce laws and rule over an area. Through this process of 'othering', opponents are

---

and Old English Wisdom Poetry (Oxford: Clarendon Press, 1993) and Nicholas Howe, *The Old English Catalogue Poems*, Anglistica, 23 (Copenhagen: Rosenkilde and Bagger, 1985), ch. 4.

[100] *Dicuili Liber de Mensura Orbis Terrae*, ed. and trans. by J. J. Tierney, Scriptores Latini Hiberniae, 6 (Dublin: Dublin Institute for Advanced Studies, 1967), prologue 1, p. 44; v. 4, pp. 56–8.

[101] Le Goff, 'Discorso di chiusura', 836 and Eginhard, *Vie de Charlemagne*, ed. and trans. by Louis Halphen, 4th edn. (Paris: Belles Lettres, 1938, repr. 1967), 98–100.

[102] On this point, see Gautier Dalché, *Conférence...8 janvier 2001*, 46–7, and Gautier Dalché, 'Principes et modes', 142–3.

[103] *Anonymi Leidensis De Situ Orbis Libri Duo*, ed. by Ricardo Quadri (Padua: Antemore, 1954), 3.

deprived of their rights to the land. Saints' lives make extensive use of this strategy when tracing the progress of a holy man or a holy woman's mission of conversion: saints tend to reach lands populated by demons. Likewise, the *Beowulf* poet's depiction of monsters, in particular of Grendel and his mother, undermines the claims they could have on part of the Danish realm. A similar strategy also operates in Bede's *Ecclesiastical History*. The historian insists that the Britons, who inhabited the British Isles before the Anglo-Saxon tribes migrated from the Continent, dwell on the very outskirts of the world. Geographical distance is used as evidence against their religious practices: because they are remote from Rome, the heart of Christendom, their peculiar rites must be flawed, and they should therefore adopt the correct Roman ceremonial.[104] Such a stance at the same time recasts the Anglo-Saxons as orthodox Christians, as the champions of proper religious observances. It deprives the Britons of their privilege of seniority and suggests that the descendants of the Germanic tribes truly deserve to rule over Britain.

Narratives play a central role in securing control of space. The seizure of land is always an event of the past: it has always already taken place and it is commemorated in a story recounting this primordial episode. Accounts of the initial appropriation of a territory are a privileged place to investigate the relationships between narrative and control of space because they simultaneously mirror an ideal state of the world and they betray current concerns about spatial organization and domination. They also follow a pattern of national mythmaking by projecting a nation's identity onto the past.[105] The texts discussed in this book are all, to some degree, narratives of origin and can be divided in two subgroups: creation and migration narratives.

Creation narratives are accounts of cosmogonic myths which explain how the world and its existing structures first came into being. They tend to validate the state of the universe as it is.[106] These texts shed light on spatial issues, not only because they describe the creation of the cosmos, but also because they reflect the world's original spatial organization.

---

[104] *Bede's Ecclesiastical History*, ed. Colgrave and Mynors, iii. 25, p. 300.
[105] Davis, 'National Writing', 611.
[106] Lars Lönnroth, 'Iörð fannz æva né upphiminn: A Formula Analysis', in Ursula Dronke and others (eds.), *Speculum Norænum: Norse Studies in Memory of Gabriel Turville-Petre* (Odense: Odense University Press, 1981), 310–27 (323). See also Paul Ricoeur, 'Mythe: l'Interprétation Philosophique', *Encyclopaedia Universalis*, xv (1989), 1041–8.

Acknowledging their close ties with myths of origin, Neville points out that these accounts of creation 'claim to look back to a time at which the essential nature of the structure in question came into being unqualified and uncorrupted, in order to provide a point of comparison with a later time'.[107] Yet if these narratives recall a lost ideal, a closer analysis reveals that they often also represent an aspiration for the future, a desired state of the world. They present an ideal version of power, one that controls and organizes space in the best possible way.

Narratives of migration and subsequent conquest raise similar issues. They also foreground the question of origin, and they link it either with a territory that has been left behind or with a land to be conquered. They tell how ancestors mastered distance and controlled space. The Anglo-Saxons, for instance, kept the memory of their migration from the Continent vividly alive. Howe identifies this episode as a fundamental event in their history, and he argues convincingly that 'the Anglo-Saxons honored the ancestral migration as the founding and defining event of their culture. They turned to it so that they might identify their common nature as a people and understand their religious history.'[108] The memory of the original migration from the Continent helped to connect the Anglo-Saxons to the land they conquered and to strengthen their claim to it.

Creation and migration narratives both fuse temporal and spatial elements. In migration narratives, geographical distance is also a lapse of time, and 'far-away', the land of origin, is equated with 'in the past', the time of the forefathers. A similar displacement takes place in creation narratives; for, the first, ideal state of the world is not only situated in the past, but also in the distance. Paradisiacal life, after all, can be enjoyed only in Eden, itself placed in the Far East. This fusion of time and space grants authority to one's vision of power and of spatial distribution. In his study of the chronotopes, Mikhail Bakhtin reminds us that: 'in order to endow any ideal with authenticity, one needs only conceive of its once having existed in its "natural state" in some Golden Age, or perhaps existing in the present but somewhere at the other end of the world, east of the sun and west of the moon.'[109] The temporal and

---

[107] Neville, 'Natural World', 57.
[108] Nicholas Howe, *Migration and Mythmaking in Anglo-Saxon England* (New Haven: Yale University Press, 1989), p. ix.
[109] Mikhail Bakhtin, *The Dialogic Imagination: Four Essays by M. M. Bakhtin*, trans. by Caryl Emerson and Michael Holquist (Austin: University of Texas Press, 1981), 147–8.

spatial distances that are at the core of migration and creation narratives should not obscure their relevance for Anglo-Saxon England: these texts shed light on its sense of space.

Heroic poetry also partakes in this spatial and temporal dynamics. It recounts past events usually situated in a distant land. *Beowulf*, for instance, stages heroes from the time of the Germanic migrations; the action takes place in Scandinavia and is geographically remote from the British Isles. Yet despite a geographical and temporal distance, the subject matter of heroic poetry reflects a civilization's analysis of its own origins. It participates in the formation of social, cultural, and political communities,[110] by telling how hostile forces were originally defeated, be they threatening neighbours or terrifying monsters. The information transmitted by heroic poems is fluid and is modified according to particular circumstances. But it always says something about the present state and concerns of the community since, as Zumthor notes in his *Introduction à la poésie orale*: 'Ne reste en mémoire que ce qui est socialement utile.'[111]

Narratives of origin therefore tell of the appropriation of a given territory, describing either its coming into being through a divine act of creation or its conquest as a result of a past migration. The original land seizure remains a founding event constantly remembered and deeply inscribed in a people's memory. The narrative commemorating it thus clearly articulates a spatial claim.

This survey of the culture of space and of space as a mental structure in Anglo-Saxon England suggests that these two levels of analysis share a number of fundamental characteristics. The idea that the world is closed, finite, that one is either inside or outside the bounds of a community, is central to Old English authors' spatial imagery, to the terminology they used, as well as to medieval views of the world. The concept of frontiers is vital, and an anxiety always surrounds the establishment of secure boundaries. A natural fear of invasion follows, and the irruption of the foreign often means complete annihilation. A religious and symbolic view of the world is reflected in medieval mapping practices, as well as in Old English authors' affective evaluation of distance and in the significance they grant to the various places of their poetic geography. The quest for geographical and cosmological knowledge betrays a desire to control space and to strengthen one's own identity. Conceiving

---

[110] On this point, see Zumthor, *Mesure du Monde*, 383.
[111] Paul Zumthor, *Introduction à la poésie orale* (Paris: Seuil, 1983), 109.

of outsiders as 'constituting others', pushing them to the periphery, and describing them as wild and untamed, reassure a people about both its own place in the universe and its civilized nature. Spatial organization supports territorial possession and self-definition; it is articulated in narratives which, looking to the past, justify the current spatial distribution or depict a lost ideal which in fact gestures toward a hoped-for, desirable state of the world.

The evaluation of the specifically Anglo-Saxon character of the spatial features outlined above is a complex question. Although I am reluctant to argue for a strict correspondence between the spatial constructs found in Old English literature and the Anglo-Saxons' historical circumstances (namely, the Viking raids and invasions which started at the end of the eighth century and lasted throughout the period, seriously challenging Anglo-Saxon rule over England), it is necessary to address the question of the relation between the history of knowledge and of ideas, and their wider historical context.[112] In this respect, the convergence between anxieties linked to the actual survival of the Anglo-Saxons' territorial rule and concerns about spatial integrity as expressed in their works of literature is striking. However, external influences are not sufficient to explain either the evolution of medieval thinking about the world or its changing representations, and the complex interplay between historical events, scientific discoveries, and mental structures is a study that remains to be undertaken.[113]

Commenting on methodological problems, Le Goff points out that: 'l'information sur les réalités géographiques "objectives" et sur les réalités mentales est très mêlée. Si l'on veut distinguer les documents qui renseignent malgré eux et ceux qui ont été faits pour renseigner sur l'espace on constate que les documents du premier type sont majoritaires.'[114] The historian warns his reader against a restrictive understanding of what constitutes geographical evidence; he encourages

---

[112] Danielle Jacquart, 'Conférence de Mme Danielle Jacquart, Directeur d'études', in *Conférence d'Ouverture de M. Patrick Gautier Dalché: 8 janvier 2001*, École Pratique des Hautes Études: Sections des Sciences Historiques et Philologiques (Paris: La Sorbonne, 2002), 25–33 (29–30).

[113] On this point, see Jacques Verger, 'Conférence de M. Jacques Verger, Correspondant de l'Institut', in *Conférence d'Ouverture de M. Patrick Gautier Dalché: 8 janvier 2001*, École Pratique des Hautes Études: Sections des Sciences Historiques et Philologiques (Paris: La Sorbonne, 2002), 11–24 (20).

[114] Le Goff, 'Discorso di chiusura', 813.

us to gather information widely and to treat it wisely. Old English geographical documents are indeed very rare and do not really include more than the beginning of the *Old English Orosius* and the Cotton Map. Maps are always shaped by a pre-existing ideology and the Cotton Map, the only one that survives from the Anglo-Saxon period, is no exception. It informs us as much about the Anglo-Saxons' ideology—their own sense of self—as about the geography of the northern European shores. Geographical sources are moreover influenced by the expectations inherent to the very genre they belong to. They cannot dispense with a call to past authorities, for this is how they assert their own validity. Historical texts, such as Bede's *Ecclesiastical History* or the Anglo-Saxon Chronicle, may claim to represent an outside reality more accurately than Old English poems do. But a close analysis reveals that they too are dependent on tradition and shaped by narrative strategies.

To this first group of geographical evidence, Le Goff adds another one which he calls 'les documents indirects, inconscients, ou involontaires'.[115] Attention is drawn to a corpus that is not primarily geographical, but that should be taken into account when reconstructing a society's sense of space; for artistic creations, and especially works of literature, constitute a privileged documentation for critics interested in exploring the *imaginaire*—in the present case, a spatial *imaginaire*.[116] Critics are thus faced with a twofold difficulty: how to understand geographical evidence and how to use indirect documents.

The heterogeneous nature of the corpus examined in the following chapters attempts to answer this double challenge. It includes both testimonies from the Old English poetic corpus and documents of a more historical nature. Three points need clarification here. First, although much of the poetry is conventional, Old English verse nevertheless sheds light on the Anglo-Saxons' outlook on the surrounding world. Ruth Wehlau reminds us that 'it is these conventions, these same formulae and topoi, that call for analysis'. And she concludes with this happy turn of phrase: 'Poetry, after all, is a way of thinking.'[117] Secondly, it is sometimes difficult to distinguish clearly between poetic and historico-geographical documents since some Old English poems, *Exodus* or *Beowulf*, for instance, may also be considered to be historical

---

[115] Le Goff, 'Discorso di chiusura', 813. On this point, see also Gautier Dalché, *Conférence . . . 8 janvier 2001*, 60.
[116] Le Goff, *L'Imaginaire médiéval*, p. iii.
[117] Wehlau, *'Riddle of Creation'*, 128.

records memorializing past events. But despite this ambiguity, I believe that Bede's *Ecclesiastical History* or the *Old English Orosius* make a more serious claim to represent an external, tangible reality than *Andreas* does, for example. Thirdly, the texts discussed in *Creation, Migration, and Conquest* are all familiar to Anglo-Saxonists: they are sources which occupy a prominent position in tradition. As such, they not only shaped the contemporary reading conventions of Old English texts, but they also have a higher paradigmatic value. It is obvious that the approach developed in this book, as well as the questions addressed to the corpus under consideration here, could be extended to historical or literary evidence not included in the present study. And yet, the close reading in which this study engages sheds new light on and offers innovative interpretations of well-known Old English texts. The aim of the chapters that follow is not therefore a complete inventory of spatial imagery in the Old English corpus. Quite the contrary, this book's ambition is exemplification, and not exhaustiveness.

Paul Zumthor remarks that 'toute appropriation d'espace comporte un aspect irrationnel et fantasmatique... Les civilisations, au cours des siècles, ont varié à l'infini les modalités et le vocabulaire des antiques rituels de prise de possession'.[118] Unable to do justice to the 'infinite variations' with which civilizations commemorate the appropriation of their territory, I nevertheless hope, in bringing together poetic and historical documents and in reading across the various genres which traditionally organize the vernacular literary corpus of Anglo-Saxon England, to reflect the Old English authors' various mental outlooks on spatial questions and to highlight similarities between them. More generally, this book invites the exploration of new correspondences between texts. Its ambition is to identify the writing strategies which underlie the political implications of spatial representations and which articulate any sense of self in geographical terms.

Creation, Migration, and Conquest progresses in three loose steps. Part I is devoted to narratives of creation. Chapter 2 analyses poems accounting for the genesis of the world, such as the *Genesis* poems, *Christ and Satan*, Cædmon's *Hymn*, *Widsiþ*, *Riddles 40* and *66*, and various creation scenes scattered in other texts. The struggle for the control of land appears as a major concern in these lines. This part also examines the parallels uniting creation and poetry or rhetoric, for the interactions between making poetry and making worlds are complex and numerous.

[118] Zumthor, *Mesure du Monde*, 17.

Heroic verse, which constitutes the subject matter of the next chapter, relates the legendary appropriation of a communal space and can therefore be understood as a particular instance of creation narratives. With special attention to *Beowulf* and *Judith*, these pages address questions of centrality and marginality, of limits and boundaries, and discuss the ambiguous nature of the centre. Chapter 4 focuses on descriptions of Britain in classical and Anglo-Saxon texts, especially in Bede's *Ecclesiastical History*, Gildas's *De Excidio Britonum*, the *Old English Orosius*, Dicuil's *De Mensura Orbis*, and medieval maps. The identification of various strategies of recentring points to the Anglo-Saxons' current concerns about situation and self-definition, and this chapter traces the emergence of a new mental world in which the British Isles are no longer peripheric.

The other two terms guiding my reflection, namely migration and conquest, are introduced in Chapter 5. Engaging in a close reading of saints' lives (mainly *Guthlac A*, *Elene*, *Andreas*, and *The Fates of the Apostles*), it examines in detail the missionary travels the protagonists undertake and it identifies various devices aimed at securing land appropriation, devices which announce the motif of conquest. Chapter 6, which completes Part II, devoted to migration, focuses on scriptural poems (*Genesis A*, *Exodus*, and occasionally *Daniel*), and more precisely on the spatial questions they raise, such as the motif of the quest for land or the vital importance of land ownership. *Creation, Migration, and Conquest* closes on an analysis of historical documents (Gildas's *De Excidio Britonum*, Bede's *Ecclesiastical History*, and the Anglo-Saxon Chronicle), paying particular attention to the notion of migration and to the various strategies these texts develop to justify territorial claims.

PART I

CREATION

2

Ordering the World: Creation Narratives and Spatial Control

IN chapter 24 of the fourth book of his *Ecclesiastical History of the English People*, Bede tells the story of Cædmon, who becomes the first Anglo-Saxon poet to compose religious verse in the vernacular. Cædmon, embarrassed because he cannot sing, leaves the feast he is attending when he sees the harp approaching and his turn to contribute to the entertainment drawing near. He goes to his shed, falls asleep, and is visited in a dream by someone who enjoins him to recite poetry. The cowherd asks his supernatural visitor what he should sing about, and the answer is: 'Canta... principium creaturarum'.[1] This first injunction to tell of the origins of creatures has been heard by many of Cædmon's followers, and it has left a considerable legacy in the Old English poetic corpus.

Cædmon's *Hymn*, *Genesis A*, *Riddle 40*, *Riddle 66*, *The Order of the World*, *Beowulf* with Hroðgar's building of Heorot or Scyld's coming, as well as *Widsiþ* and the openings of *Elene*, *Guthlac A*, *Andreas*, *Juliana*, *The Fates of the Apostles*, all reflect on the genesis of the world they depict, and most include scenes of creation, a literary topos in Old English poetry.[2]

Stories of origins, a desire to discover the beginnings of the world and of mankind are recurrent concerns to Anglo-Saxon poets. Knowledge of the creation process yields information on an original act which is the model for all subsequent undertakings. At the time of creation, nothing had yet been altered or defaced; the world was as it should be, in its

---

[1] 'Sing... about the beginning of created things' (*Bede's Ecclesiastical History of the English People*, ed. and trans. by Bertram Colgrave and R. A. B. Mynors (Oxford: Clarendon Press, 1969; repr. 1991), iv. 24, p. 416). For the translation, see the same volume. Unless otherwise indicated, further Bede citations are from this edition.

[2] See Malcom Godden, 'Biblical Literature: the Old Testament', in Malcolm Godden and Michael Lapidge (eds.), *The Cambridge Companion to Old English Literature* (Cambridge: Cambridge University Press, 1991; repr. 1994), 206–26 (210).

first, ideal, and perfect state. 'The creation of the world is the exemplar for all constructions', Mircea Éliade notes, 'every new town, every new house that is built, imitates afresh, and in a sense repeats, the creation of the world'.[3] It is the archetype that inspires every succeeding founder or creator, and narratives of the birth of the universe allegedly expose an original, 'right' order of the world.

Even though creation narratives recount a past event, they clearly also say something about the contemporary world. They hardly ever focus on the first cause of things, that is, they are not interested in knowing the power behind the making of the material world. Rather, they concentrate on the state of the universe as it is, the present-day order of things, and their aim is to validate it.[4] A study of narratives that conjure up an idyllic, forever lost past may thus divulge something of their authors' frame of mind. Jennifer Neville values the information that can be deduced from these texts, because 'such accounts [of creation]... can reveal what a writer considers to be the central issues of his text, or, at least, their underlying assumptions'.[5] These descriptions should be recognized for what they are: namely, representations of a desirable organization of the world, of order, and of fitness as the Anglo-Saxons conceived of it. Being projected on to the past grants them legitimacy, for they are not merely contemporary fantasies of how the world should be, but they become insights into how the world has always been or should always have been.

The present chapter examines episodes dealing with the shaping of the universe, with Satan's rebellion and with the fall of mankind. Depicting how the cosmos first came into being, creation narratives reflect on the world's original configuration. They betray special concerns with questions of space and spatial organization: how was the world originally set up? How should it be now? Who should rule where? Over which subjects? How can one assert one's right over a portion of land? The following pages pay particular attention to these issues.

Crucial to any creation narrative is the role of language, whose function it is to memorialize, to recreate, and to 'justify' an original

---

[3] Mircea Éliade, *Patterns in Comparative Religions*, trans. by Rosemary Sheed (London: Sheed and Ward, 1958), 379.
[4] Jonathan Z. Smith and Richard G. A. Buxton, 'Myth and Mythology', in *The New Encyclopaedia Britannica* (Chicago, 2003), xxiv, 715–32 (723).
[5] Jennifer Neville, *Representations of the Natural World in Old English Poetry*, Cambridge Studies in Anglo-Saxon England, 27 (Cambridge: Cambridge University Press, 1999), 57.

state of the world. Profound and complex links unite poetic and material creations. Cædmon's *Hymn* and *Widsiþ* will illustrate this interplay between the making of poetry and the making of worlds. The *Hymn*, embedded in a narrative framework that casts it into a Christian context, understands poetic composition as the result of divine inspiration to sing about creation. *Widsiþ* is a catalogue poem which, by rehearsing traditional Germanic knowledge, conjures up a lost heroic world.

I will identify two different modalities of creation—transformation and expansion, before analysing in more detail the main characteristics of these newly shaped spaces. A discussion of Satan's fall and of Adam and Eve's expulsion from Paradise, together with the spatial issues these episodes raise, will conclude this chapter. The present inquiry into the genesis of numerous territorial spheres (the cosmos, poetic worlds, Paradise, the earth, physical and political dominions, and so on) will foreground questions of spatial configuration, of demarcation of territory, and of control over a given tract of land, all of which are central features of the Anglo-Saxons' conceptions of space, and which bear on the contours of their mental maps.

'CANTA...PRINCIPIUM CREATURARUM'

Poetic Beginnings—Poems about Beginnings

The night of the miracle, the apparition visiting Cædmon orders him to sing about 'the beginning of created things'. Bede tells his reader that, in answer to this command, the cowherd 'statim ipse coepit cantare in laudem Dei Conditoris uersus quos numquam audierat'.[6] Ordered to compose poetry about creation, Cædmon praises the Creator. Moreover, the *Hymn* opens with an invitation to glorify the Lord: 'Nu scylun hergan hefaenricaes Uard'.[7] According to Bede, the very first line of Old English religious verse is a tribute to the Guardian of heaven.

The Guardian of heaven is identified with the Creator in the subsequent lines of the *Hymn*: He is called *metud* (l. 2), the Creator, and

---

[6] 'thereupon Cædmon began to sing verses which he had never heard before in praise of God the Creator' (*Bede's Ecclesiastical History*, iv. 24, p. 416).

[7] 'We should now praise the Guardian of heaven' (Cædmon's *Hymn*). I use the Moore Version of the *Hymn* edited in *Sweet's Anglo-Saxon Reader*, rev. Dorothy Whitelock, 15th edn. (Oxford: Clarendon Press, 1967; repr. 1988), 181.

Cædmon enjoins his audience to praise *uerc Uuldurfadur*.[8] It is of course fitting that the poem's beginning should allude to the Creator and should thus somehow coincide with the origin of the world. Referring to Mircea Éliade's *Myth of the Eternal Return*, Carolyne Larrington notices that 'before something new is undertaken . . . the original creative act must be rehearsed'.[9] Divine creation becomes a model both for the fictional world set up by the poem and for the human process of poetic composition. Bede presents Cædmon's *Hymn* as the very first instance of religious verse in Old English: because this poem refers to God the Creator, it blurs the line between divine and human, material and linguistic creations.

Widsiþ can be compared to the *Hymn* in this regard. Adopting the form of the catalogue, it appeals to writers 'who value plenitude over other considerations'.[10] Because the catalogue has no inherent force of closure, it fosters the illusion that it can contain all there is to know. Clearly of an encyclopaedic nature, *Widsiþ* conveys this sense of comprehensiveness. Joyce Hill situates the fascination for the poem in its totalizing effect with regard to the Germanic past, and not, as was traditionally the case among critics, in the informative content of the allusions.[11] The lists of tribes and leaders it includes conjure up a defunct, lost world. Yet, the very naming process of the enumeration actualizes and creates the past and its space anew, just as the *Hymn* generates the world as it existed at the time of creation. Moreover, a parallel can be drawn between the encyclopaedist's and God's knowledge. As Northrop Frye points out, in the compositions of the medieval minstrel or the clerical poet, 'the encyclopaedic knowledge . . . is regarded sacramentally, as a human analogy of divine knowledge'.[12] *Widsiþ* therefore is also a creation poem, because it linguistically fashions a past, ideal universe, and because its *scop* becomes another creator figure. Both in Cædmon's *Hymn* and in *Widsiþ*, language shapes the material world.

---

[8] 'the work of the Father of glory' (Cædmon's *Hymn* 3ª).
[9] Carolyne Larrington, *A Store of Common Sense: Gnomic Theme and Style in Old Icelandic and Old English Wisdom Poetry* (Oxford: Clarendon Press, 1993), 172.
[10] Nicholas Howe, *The Old English Catalogue Poems*, Anglistica, 23 (Copenhagen: Rosenkilde and Bagger, 1985), 28.
[11] Joyce Hill, '*Widsið* and the Tenth Century', *Neuphilologische Mitteilungen*, 85 (1984), 305–15 (305). On the Anglo-Saxon audience's reception of this poem, see Roberta Frank, 'Germanic Legend in Old English Literature', in Godden and Lapidge, *Cambridge Companion to Old English Literature*, 88–106, esp. 101–6.
[12] Northrop Frye, *Anatomy of Criticism: Four Essays* (Princeton: Princeton University Press, 1957), 57.

Cædmon is a precursor: he is a unique figure in the history of the development of religious vernacular composition. In Bede's anecdote, an analogy connects Cædmon as a poet to God as a creator: for, just as the first material creation stimulates the future builder, similarly the cowherd provides a divinely inspired model for subsequent poets. Of course, it is not the Lord Himself, nor one of His angels, who recites the *Hymn*, but the cowherd's inspiration is otherworldly. The paradigmatic nature of Cædmon's verses is again stressed when Bede insists that none of the cowherd's heirs could compare with him: 'Et quidem et alii post illum in gente Anglorum religiosa poemata facere temtabant, sed nullus eum aequiperare potuit.'[13] The *Hymn* and Cædmon's other lost poems represent an ideal that can never be equalled, just as God's creation represents the world in its pristine state.

Right from the start, the speaker of *Widsiþ* is characterized as someone 'se þe monna mæst mægþa ofer eorþan, | folca geondferde'.[14] A fiction is thus established which alleges that the *scop* will recount his own experiences, that he will tell of peoples and places of which he has first-hand knowledge. Moreover, the excellence of his song, mentioned on lines 105–8, together with the meaning of the name *widsiþ*, a likely nickname for 'far traveller', reinforce the exemplary quality of the speaker.[15] Like Cædmon, the *Widsiþ scop* is a pioneer. Disregarding chronology, he claims to have personally visited all the great rulers and tribes he mentions and to have gathered all the tales which poets after him sing, thus casting himself as the founder of a Germanic poetic tradition.

Both Cædmon and the *Widsiþ* speaker are sources of inspiration for future minstrels. Their artistic compositions shape a poetic world and, at the same time, mark the birth of a literary tradition. The relationship the poets entertain with the first creative act is thus twofold: they sing it, keeping its memory alive, and they mimic it when they compose new verse. Ruth Wehlau has this happy phrase about Cædmon's *Hymn*: 'placed at the beginning of the canon', she says, 'the hymn is both a

---

[13] 'It is true that after him other Englishmen attempted to compose religious poems, but none could compare with him' (*Bede's Ecclesiastical History*, iv. 24, p. 414).

[14] 'who among men had travelled to most tribes and peoples on earth' (*Widsiþ* 2–3ᵃ). *The Exeter Book*, ed. by George Philip Krapp and Elliott van Kirk Dobbie, Anglo-Saxon Poetic Records, 3 (New York: Columbia University Press, 1936; repr. 1966), 149–53.

[15] For parallels with Old Norse analogues of supernatural travellers, see *Old English Minor Poems*, ed. by Joyce Hill, Durham and St Andrews Medieval Texts, 4 (Durham: Durham and St Andrews Medieval Texts, 1983), 14 and 102.

poetic beginning and a poem about beginnings'.[16] I argue the same status for *Widsiþ*.

'Heaven as a roof for the children of men': Creation's Anthropocentric Perspective

Creation narratives have a didactic purpose: they are meant to instruct. Bede specifies that the *Hymn* and Cædmon's subsequent poems, beautiful and moving, influenced many people, encouraging them to amend their lives and to turn to God.[17] Cædmon's poetry serves a missionary ambition: it promotes the audience's religious education.

The catalogues in *Widsiþ* also have an informative content. The poem commemorates a past world; it rehearses the temporal and geographical ancestry of the audience. Its gnomic element is important: the speaker says, for instance, that he has met many leaders, but that Hwala was the best and Alexander the mightiest of them all. As a result, he sets them up as examples.[18] *Widsiþ* is not a random enumeration, but it enlightens its listeners on who was a great leader and why.[19] The *scop* is not merely memorializing for the sake of his poetic followers; he reaches a wider audience, to whom he teaches something about its origins and about its past and present leaders.

In their ambition to instruct, these two poems mirror the processes of creation they recount; for, if verse is composed to benefit the public, similarly the shaping of the world profits mankind. In Cædmon's *Hymn*, human beings find shelter in the newly created universe. The poet says that God 'aerist scop aelda barnum | heben til hrofe',[20] and that: 'Tha middungeard moncynnæs Uard, | eci Dryctin, æfter tiadæ | firum foldu'.[21]

The two dative forms, *barnum* and *firum*, indicate that the divine creative act is undertaken for mankind.[22] Christopher Manes recognizes

---

[16] Ruth Wehlau, 'Rumination and Re-Creation: Poetic Instruction in the *Order of the World*', *Florilegium*, 13 (1994), 65–77 (67).

[17] *Bede's Ecclesiastical History*, iv. 24, p. 418.   [18] *Widsiþ* 14–16ª.

[19] For instance, the speaker values generosity above all else in the rulers he visits. *Widsiþ* 3ᵇ–4ª, 56, 65ᵇ–67, 73–4, 90–8, 129–30, and 138–9.

[20] God 'first created heaven as a roof for the children of men' (Cædmon's *Hymn* 5–6ª).

[21] 'Then afterwards, the Guardian of mankind, the eternal Lord, arranged the earth for men' (Cædmon's *Hymn* 7–9ª).

[22] For a different view on this point, see Charles Abbott Conway, 'Structure and Idea in "Cædmon's Hymn" ', *Neuphilologische Mitteilungen*, 96 (1995), 39–50.

in this anthropocentric perspective a characteristic element of Old English—or, more widely, of Germanic—creation scenes. The critic understands it as 'a distinctive feature of the Cædmonian religious manner. It identifies humanity as the reason for some of God's creative activities much more directly than does the biblical account'.[23] This outlook singles out human beings as those who benefit from the coming into being of the world.

In *Genesis A* the account of Adam and Eve's expulsion from Paradise replays the shaping of the world as depicted in creation narratives. For the vernacular poet adds to his biblical source and specifies that as soon as the first human beings find themselves in the world, God alleviates their punishment.[24] As a consolation, He settles them comfortably in their new environment: 'ac he him to frofre let hwæðere forð wesan | hyrstedne hrof halgum tunglum | and him grundwelan ginne sealde'.[25]

Widsiþ betrays 'a geographical sense of the past'.[26] Its aim is neither precisely to depict the geography of continental Germania, nor accurately to situate the boundaries of each tribe's territory. The poem evokes a world, it lists its main centres of power, but it never describes it. Paul Zumthor's comments on travel narratives should help us here to understand what is at stake in this poetic practice; the historian notes that the 'récit... reste accroché à des lieux successifs, série de toponymes jalonnant le discours, comme pour signifier une appropriation symbolique de territoire plutôt que pour opérer une projection dans l'étendue'.[27] Zumthor equates toponymic catalogues with a symbolic appropriation of territory. Listing peoples and places is indeed an ancient motif of world domination that can be traced to antiquity.[28] Such a strategy

---

[23] Christopher Manes, 'The Substance of Earth in *Beowulf*'s Song of Creation', *English Language Notes*, 31/4 (1994), 1–5 (2). See also Ute Schwab, *Einige Beziehungen zwischen altsächsischer und ängelsächsischer Dichtung*, Centro italiano di studi sull'alto medioevo, 8 (Spoleto: Centro Italiano di Studi Sull'Alto Medioevo, 1988), 68. For further examples of this anthropocentric bias, see *Beowulf* 94–5, *Maxims I* 15ᵃ–16, and *The Order of the World* 59ᵃ.

[24] Genesis 3: 24.

[25] 'but as a consolation to them, he nevertheless let the roof decorated with holy stars stand and he gave them abundant earthly wealth' (*Genesis A* 955–7).

[26] Nicholas Howe coins this expression when discussing *Beowulf*, but it can obviously also be used when thinking about *Widsiþ*. Nicholas Howe, *Migration and Mythmaking in Anglo-Saxon England* (New Haven: Yale University Press, 1989), 176.

[27] Paul Zumthor, *La Mesure du Monde* (Paris: Seuil, 1993), 302.

[28] Christian Hänger, *Die Welt im Kopf: Raumbilder und Strategie im Römischen Kaiserreich*, Hypomnemata, 136 (Göttingen: Vandenhoeck and Ruprecht, 2001), 236. Hänger refers to the *Aeneid* VI. 792–800.

operates in *Widsiþ*: naming is not only a creative or memorializing act; it is also an essential element in an appropriation process, for the vernacular text linguistically seizes a geographical extension, an imaginary continental home.

Cædmon's *Hymn* and *Widsiþ* both foreground the notion of creation, in the shaping of a new world as well as in the coming into being of a novel poetic convention. These verses also address territorial issues: they depict the appearance of a pre-lapsarian world in the *Hymn* and a lost, distant home to which return is impossible in *Widsiþ*. In both cases, the audience can imagine itself as the first, rightful occupiers of these newly shaped expanses. Language is indispensable to validate a new material creation: it defines the space that has just been formed and it claims it for oneself, in the present case for mankind or for an Anglo-Saxon audience. To combine words and to construct worlds are analogous activities.

TYPES OF CREATION

Broadening my corpus beyond *Widsiþ* and Cædmon's *Hymn*, I would like now to examine the creation process in more detail. Various types of accounts of the world's genesis can be distinguished according to how they conceive of creation, that is, whether they see this original act as a transformation or as an expansion. In both cases, architectural metaphors are pervasive; they are crucial elements in an analysis of how creation narratives speak about space. Also central to every model used to represent the coming into being of a new world is their obsession with territorial possession and control of space, a question with which the present chapter will conclude.

Creation as Transformation

Cædmon tells his audience that God formed heaven and earth, but he does not specify where the material the Lord had at his disposal came from. More precisely, he does not account for the creation of primordial matter. Mentioning the creation of heaven, the poet says that God shaped 'heben til rofe'.[29] The function attached to this new component of the material world is determined: it is to protect mankind. What

---

[29] 'heaven as a roof' (Cædmon's *Hymn* 6ª).

comes into being at that very moment is therefore a function, and not a new object. For Ruth Wehlau, 'Old English poetry always presents the Creation as an arranging and a construction rather than a creation *ex nihilo*'.³⁰ The idea that the material world could result from a creation *ex nihilo* was in fact foreign to the traditional Anglo-Saxon way of thinking, as it is, more generally, to myths of origin whose function is to recount the initial ordering of the world, the founding episodes of civilization.³¹

In the Cædmon anecdote, not only material, but also poetic creation amounts to a transformation of pre-existing material. The cowherd starts his career by devising elegant verses on the topic the apparition gives him. Later, when the abbess Hild recognizes the holiness of his gift, she orders him to be instructed in sacred history. The cowherd then, 'at ipse cuncta, quae audiendo discere poterat, rememorando secum et quasi mundum animal ruminando, in carmen dulcissimum conuertebat'.³² Bede compares Cædmon to a ruminant, thereby stressing the fact that the poet 'digests' what he has been fed. Cædmon never independently composes verse on a topic of his choice; for his entire career, he transforms what he learns.³³ Neither cosmic creation nor artistic composition produces something from nothing, and both stress rearrangement and modification of pre-existing material.

---

³⁰ Ruth Wehlau, *'The Riddle of Creation': Metaphor Structures in Old English Poetry*, Studies in the Humanities: Literature–Politics–Society, 24 (New York: Lang, 1997), 40.

³¹ Wehlau, *'Riddle of Creation'*, 40, and Neville, *Natural World*, 62. On the numerous parallels existing between the Anglo-Saxon and other Germanic accounts of creation, see Jacob Grimm, *Deutsche Mythologie*, 4th edn. by Elard Hugo Meyer, 3 vols. (Berlin: Dümmlers, 1875–8), I, 463–76. See also Laura Morland, 'Cædmon and the Germanic Tradition', in J. M. Foley (ed.), *De Gustibus: Essays for Alain Renoir* (New York: Garland, 1992), 324–58; Schwab, *Einige Beziehungen*, 66–7; Constance B. Hieatt, 'Cædmon in Context: Transforming the Formula', *Journal of English and Germanic Philology*, 84 (1985), 485–97; Lars Lönnroth, 'Iörð fannz æva né upphiminn: A Formula Analysis', in Ursula Dronke and others (eds.), *Speculum Norænum: Norse Studies in Memory of Gabriel Turville-Petre* (Odense: Odense University Press, 1981), 310–27; *Genesis A: A New Edition*, ed. by A. N. Doane (Madison: University of Wisconsin Press, 1978), 73–4; J. B. Bessinger, Jr., 'Homage to Cædmon and Others: A Beowulfian Praise Song', in Robert B. Burlin and Edward B. Irving, Jr. (eds.), *Old English Studies in Honour of John C. Pope* (Toronto: University of Toronto Press, 1974), 91–106; and Paul Beekman Taylor, 'Heorot, Earth and Asgard: Christian Poetry and Pagan Myth', *Tennessee Studies in Literature*, 11 (1966), 119–30.

³² 'He learned all he could by listening to them and then, memorizing it and ruminating over it, like some clean animal chewing the cud, he turned it into the most melodious verse' (*Bede's Ecclesiastical History*, iv. 24, p. 418).

³³ Leonore Abraham discusses this aspect of Cædmonian creativity in terms of *inventio* and *dispositio*, pointing out that Bede clearly indicates that Cædmon lacked the first. Leonore Abraham, 'Cædmon's *Hymn* and the 'geþwærnysse' (Fitness) of Things', *American Benedictine Review*, 43 (1992), 331–44.

Genesis A offers a detailed yet incomplete account of the world's beginnings; it is a fairly close paraphrase of the Book of Genesis, chapters 1 to 22, although the hexameral opening is one of the most conspicuous of the poet's additions. Only the first three days of creation are preserved before a first gap occurs in the manuscript. One or two leaves might have been lost and the poem resumes with the creation of Eve.[34] *Genesis A* begins with the traditional call to praise God. The poet then reports Lucifer's fall, the rebellious angels' banishment to hell, and God's subsequent creation of human beings. The revolt and fall of Lucifer and his followers precede the accounts of the world's and mankind's creations. When God contemplates how to respond to the angels' apostasy, the *Genesis A* poet says: 'Ne wæs her þa giet nymþe heolstersceado | wiht geworden, ac þes wida grund | stod deop and dim, drihtne fremde, | idel and unnyt'.[35] These lines render Genesis 1: 1–2: 'In principio creavit Deus caelum et terram. Terra autem erat inanis et vacua.'[36] A comparison of the biblical and the Old English passages indicates that there is no account of the creation of matter in the vernacular text, for the poet does not translate 'creavit Deus caelum et terram'. When nothing existed but the shadow of darkness, the matter of the earth was already there, useless but nevertheless present. Commenting on these lines, Neville distinguishes between an uncreated world on the one hand, and a void or a neutral chaos on the other.[37] These very lines describe the latter, namely a primordial and shapeless world that is *dreama leas* and 'idel and unnyt'.[38] The critic summarizes this point when she notices that creation 'in the Old English *Genesis* is more an act of transformation from dark, hostile uselessness to bright, safe fruitfulness than creation *ex nihilo*'.[39]

---

[34] *Genesis A*, ed. Doane, 8–10.

[35] 'Nothing had yet been created here, except the shadow of darkness, but the wide earth stood mysterious and obscure, desolate and useless, estranged from the Lord' (*Genesis A* 103–6a).

[36] 'In the beginning God created heaven and the earth. And the earth was without form'. The Latin text is from: *Biblia Sacra iuxta Vulgatam Versionem*, ed. by Bonifatius Fischer and others, rev. by Robert Weber, 3rd edn. (Stuttgart: Deutsche Bibelgesellschaft, 1969; repr. 1983). The English translation is from *The Holy Bible Containing the Old and New Testaments: Translated out of the Original Tongues: and with the Former Translations Diligently Compared and Revised by His Majesty's Special Command* (New York: Nelson, [n.d.]).

[37] Neville, *Natural World*, 57–9.   [38] *Genesis A* 108ᵃ and 106ᵃ.

[39] Neville, *Natural World*, 62. On this point, see also Lönnroth, 'Formula Analysis', 316.

The words *idel* and *unnyt* call for further comments, for a close examination of the occurrences of this pair in the Old English corpus suggests that the status of the land and the transformation of a wasted space are controversial issues. In *Genesis A*, the earth is 'idel and unnyt', 'wonn and weste',[40] until God's word shapes this world: 'oðþæt þeos woruldgesceaft | þurh word gewearð wuldorcyninges'.[41] Here, the poet focuses interest on how, from a vague expansion, the world comes to be a place where human beings can dwell comfortably. As this chapter will subsequently show, this adaptation of a wasteland for the use of mankind constitutes a bone of contention between God and Satan.

These two words appear in other creation scenes, namely in *Beowulf* and *Guthlac A*. In the hagiographic poem, the wilderness in which the saint settles is 'idel ond æmen, eþelriehte feor' and it 'bad bisæce betran hyrdes'.[42] The saint converts this useless expanse into a home for himself. He is the better guardian who is awaited and whose presence will alter the nature of the wasteland. This transformation is a gradual process completed toward the end of the poem when the devils carry him back from his last temptation at the doors of hell. The poet describes the *beorg* thus: 'Smolt wæs se sigewong ond sele niwe, | fæger fugla reord, folde geblowen'.[43] The holy man's fortitude has metamorphosed the contested dwelling place, and a new stretch of land has been gained for mankind.

The description of Heorot's destruction at the hands of Grendel in *Beowulf* makes use of similar terms. The monster's repeated attacks plunge the royal hall in a state of aporia; it is raided 'oð þæt idel stod | husa selest'.[44] The word *idel* also appears in Beowulf's speech to Hroðgar when the hero first arrives in Denmark. The Geatish warrior says that he has heard that the best of halls stands 'idel ond unnyt'.[45] The regal building has become useless to mankind, just as in *Genesis*

---

[40] 'dark and desolate' (*Genesis A* 110ª).
[41] 'until the creation of this world happened through the word of the King of glory' (*Genesis A* 110ᵇ–111).
[42] 'desolate and deserted, the distant ancestral domain' *Guthlac A* 216 and 'it awaited the visit of a better guardian' (*Guthlac A* 217). *The Exeter Book*, 49–88.
[43] 'The plain of victory was calm and the dwelling new, the voice of the birds pleasant, and the earth blossoming' (*Guthlac A* 742–3).
[44] 'until the best of houses stood desolate' (*Beowulf* 145ᵇ–146ª). *Beowulf and the Fight at Finnsburg*, ed. by F. Klaeber, 3rd edn. (Lexington, MA.: Heath, 1922; repr. 1950).
[45] 'desolate and useless' (*Beowulf* 413ª).

A the earth lacks a function after the fall of the rebellious angels and before the creation of the human race.

Because it echoes the episode of the shaping of the earth in *Genesis A*, the use, in *Beowulf,* of the word *idel* to depict Heorot suggests that the hero's defeat of Grendel amounts to a creation scene. Futher lexical analysis reinforces this postulate. Earlier in the poem, the song about the genesis of the earth that the *scop* performs in the hall obviously echoes the creation motif underlying Heorot's construction. The two are not merely associated because they are juxtaposed: the link is also semantic, since the words *gefrætwian* and *gefrætwan* occur in both passages.[46] Hroðgar orders the builder of the hall *folcstede frætwan* and, at creation, God 'gefrætwade foldan sceatas | leomum ond leafum'.[47] Significantly, the verb *gefrætwian* resurfaces after Grendel's defeat. To prepare the feast celebrating the hero's victory in Heorot, 'þa wæs haten hreþe Heort innanweard | folmum gefrætwod'.[48] A close reading of these passages therefore suggests that when he overcomes Grendel, Beowulf refashions a world for the Danes, a space where they can live and prosper. He mirrors Hroðgar's building of the royal hall, thus becoming another creator figure.

Scyld Scefing's mysterious arrival in Denmark is a complex scene which deserves attention in the context of the present discussion. Scyld comes from beyond the seas, a destitute young boy who subsequently rises to great glory and power. When he dies, the survival of his dynasty is secured by his son, Beow. Scyld's coming transforms the land of the Danes and gives it a new political organization. This episode is clearly a story of beginnings, 'the mythical foundation of civilization itself'.[49] Scyld's achievement unites control of space and the genesis of human society; both Beowulf and Scyld transform the Danish realm and offer a rejuvenated homeland to its people.

A land put to bad use, or worse, to no use at all, is *idel* in *Guthlac A, Beowulf,* and *Genesis A*. In all these examples, an area is transformed; a wilderness is tamed and civilized. A new space thus comes into

---

[46] Wehlau, *'Riddle of Creation',* 18–19. See also Robert E. Bjork, 'Speech as Gift in *Beowulf', Speculum,* 69 (1994), 993–1022 (1003); and Taylor, 'Poetry and Myth', 121.

[47] 'to adorn the dwelling-place' (*Beowulf* 76[a]) and God 'adorned the corners of the earth with branches and leaves' (*Beowulf* 96–7[a]).

[48] 'Then it was quickly ordered that Heorot should be adorned within by hands' (*Beowulf* 991–2[a]).

[49] James W. Earl, *Thinking about Beowulf* (Stanford, CA: Stanford University Press, 1994), 46.

being, a land human beings can enjoy. Creation becomes the seemingly unproblematic metamorphosis of unused expanses into new spaces, the positioning of mankind in a given place.

Creation as Expansion

Transformation and expansion, the two modalities accounting for the genesis of a new space, are not mutually exclusive. A closer reading of the opening lines of *Beowulf* for instance reveals that even though Scyld's arrival transfigures the Danish kingdom and its political structures, this episode also conceives of the coming into being of a new world as a progressive expansion. Scyld arrives destitute. He subsequently strengthens his kingdom, he rules the Danes 'oð þæt him æghwylc ymbsittendra | ofer hronrade hyran scolde'.[50] His dominion grows and it gradually incorporates neighbouring tribes. He controls an ever increasing stretch of land.

At first sight, Scyld is a godsend to the people; he relieves the lordless Danes from their misery. God: 'fyrenðearfe ongeat, | þe hie ær drugon aldorlease | lange hwile'.[51] But Joyce Tally Lionarons has pointed out that these lines apply not to Scyld himself, but to his son.[52] The divine sanction is accorded to Beow only and it is *not* Scyld whom God sends 'folce to frofre'.[53]

Because he juxtaposes the first political takeover and the divinely sanctioned succession of Beow, the poet suggests that Scyld's accession to power was peaceful and beneficent. And yet, his reign was stained by violence. Lines 4–6ª tell that: 'Oft Scyld Scefing sceaþena þreatum, | monegum mægþum meodosetla ofteah, | egsode eorlas'.[54] This description of Scyld's behaviour, to follow Lionarons further, 'paints a somewhat darker picture by refusing to specify just who Scyld's enemies were, just whose mead-benches he took away, just which nobles he terrified'.[55] Scyld is a complex figure: does he

---

[50] 'until each neighbouring people across the sea had to obey him' (*Beowulf* 9–10).
[51] God 'perceived the great distress which they had suffered when they were without a lord for a long time' (*Beowulf* 14ª–16ᵇ).
[52] Joyce Tally Lionarons, '*Beowulf*: Myth and Monsters', *English Studies*, 77 (1996), 1–14 (6).
[53] 'as a comfort to the people' (*Beowulf* 14ª).
[54] 'Scyld Scefing often deprived troops of enemies, many tribes of their hall-seats, he terrified the noblemen' (*Beowulf* 4–6ª).
[55] Lionarons, '*Beowulf*: Myth and Monsters', 7.

really rescue the lordless Danes? Or does he on the contrary invade and conquer their court, their land, and eventually the territory of their neighbouring tribes?[56] The ambiguity surrounding the status of the Danish dynasty before Scyld's arrival, his own violent reign, and a divine blessing granted not to him but to his son undermine the positive bias which characterizes the creation of the new lineage.

Scyld's ambiguous status—is he a saviour or an invader?—is echoed by the foundational act of Hroðgar's kingship, the building of Heorot. If the erection of the hall is praised within the discourse of the text, that is, if it is represented as a univocally positive event, the appearance of a wicked enemy nevertheless calls into question the spatial distribution set up in this creation scene. Grendel is called 'se þe moras heold, | fen ond fæsten', which means that he is in command of his own territory, the marshland.[57] Similarly, his mother controls the waters of the mere; she is 'se ðe floda begong | heorogifre beheold hund missera'.[58] Grendel and his mother form a small community and they dwell in their own province. Hroðgar's adversary is not a perpetually wandering exile; the *Beowulf* poet places him in a wasteland within earshot of Heorot, where the beauties of creation are celebrated in a song that the monster resents. But I would like to suggest that what the monster really opposes may be Hroðgar's territorial organization in Denmark, rather than the *scop*'s performance. The fact that the king's dominion impinges on areas where Grendel rules cannot be excluded, especially not when one bears in mind that Beowulf purges both Heorot and the mere of hostile presences, thereby extending Hroðgar's authority over areas previously under Grendel's control. The struggle between the king and the monster may well be territorial at heart.

An analysis of the opening of *Elene* reveals troubling similarities with the beginning of *Beowulf*. Constantine's empire grows steadily and it gradually incorporates neighbouring lands. Cynewulf says that:

---

[56] The Danes' previous king, the one who left his people leaderless, may have been Heremod. The fact that he became a wicked ruler in his old age and that his people suffered under his rule could explain the ensuing dynastic void. This would also explain why Heremod precedes Scyld in Anglo-Saxon genealogies. See Heather O'Donoghue's note 31 in *Beowulf*, trans. by Kevin Crossley-Holland (Oxford: Oxford University Press, 1999), 113 and *Beowulf and the Fight*, ed. Klaeber, 162–4.

[57] 'he who ruled the moors, the fens, and the stronghold' (*Beowulf* 103^b–104^a).

[58] 'she who, fiercely ravenous, had guarded the expanse of the water for fifty years' (*Beowulf* 1497^b–1498).

'Æðelinges weox | rice under roderum.'⁵⁹ As a consequence, the emperor's power increases so that: 'he manegum wearð | ... mannum to hroðer, | werþeodum to wræce'.⁶⁰ In her edition of the poem, Pamela Gradon notes the similarities between this passage and *Beowulf*, line 5. She observes that 'the functions of the good king are the consolation of the people and the confusion of their foes'.⁶¹ But the points of contact between these two poems are more numerous than this passing observation suggests. Verbal echoes abound and these two texts use similar wording to describe the growth of the good leader. Line 8ᵃ of *Beowulf* says that Scyld 'weox under wolcnum', repeating the lexical construction that juxtaposes the verb *weaxan* and the preposition *under* introducing a term referring to the sky. In both cases, the hero expands his realm under the vault of heaven to the distress of his neighbours. Scyld prospers and secures his power over his own kingdom and its vicinity until he rules over surrounding areas. In *Elene* too, the emperor has to confront his neighbours. The poet calls the king of the Huns who gather on the boundaries of Constantine's empire *cyning ymbsittendra*.⁶² Both Scyld and Constantine challenge and subdue their neighbours. And in both cases, this is positively connoted. Of Constantine, the poet says: 'he wæs riht cyning'; the lines devoted to Scyld conclude thus: 'þæt wæs god cyning!'⁶³

In *Elene* and in *Beowulf*, the creation of a new space is presented as the expansion of an original place, be it the Roman Empire or the Danish realm. In this model, territorial growth develops from a location occupied by the hero and aspires to universal dominion. Although the discourse of the text presents these instances of creation as beneficent events, Grendel's appearance, the violence of Scyld's rule, and the opposition to Constantine's reign question the spatial constitution of kingly domains. They cast a shadow over these accounts of creation and they suggest that these tales might obliterate the darker aspects of territorial rule. For instance, one might wonder whether the land on which these new dominions develop is really empty. Strategies

---

⁵⁹ 'The empire of the prince grew under the sky' (*Elene* 12ᵇ–13ᵃ). *The Vercelli Book*, ed. by George Philip Krapp, Anglo-Saxon Poetic Records, 2 (New York: Columbia University Press, 1932; repr. 1961), 66–102.

⁶⁰ 'he became a comfort to many men, a misery to the nations' (*Elene* 15ᵇ–17ᵃ).

⁶¹ *Cynewulf's 'Elene'*, ed. by P. O. E. Gradon (Exeter: University of Exeter, 1977; first publ. London: Methuen, 1958), 26.

⁶² 'the king of the neighbouring peoples' (*Elene* 32ᵇ–33ᵃ).

⁶³ 'he was a righteous king' (*Elene* 13ᵇ); 'that was a good king!' (*Beowulf* 11ᵇ).

of dispossession, which motivate the depiction of the space that is appropriated as empty or as populated by monsters or enemies, silence possible challenges to this new territorial organization and pass over the enmity and the outbreaks of violence it causes.

Creation and Architectural Metaphors

The third model of creation brings together the genesis of a new world and the construction of a new building. Vernacular poets often use scenes recounting the setting up of an edifice to signal the coming into being of an original space. The association between building imagery and the creation of the world is omnipresent in the Old English corpus. Ruth Wehlau, in her detailed study of this question, acknowledges that such parallels are not specific to Old English literature, but that they have roots in the Bible as well as in other literary traditions.[64] *Genesis A* describes the creation of the firmament thus: 'Heht þa lifes weard | on mereflode middum weorðan | hyhtlic heofontimber.'[65] The same image also appears in connection with the earth when, at the end of the first day, 'seo tid gewat ofer timber sceacan | middangeardes'.[66] In the present context, I translate *timber* as 'structure' but BT gives two additional meanings for this particular use of the word, namely, 'building, edifice'. The expression *timber middangeardes* in these lines thus draws a parallel between creation and construction.

Commenting on the notion of the building, Zumthor reminds his readers of its primary function: 'donner ce signal indubitable, qui introduit l'ordre dans le chaos spatial'.[67] Fittingly therefore, creation is often equated with the making of a new edifice. *Beowulf* most clearly illustrates this point, since the construction of Heorot is a cosmological act which represents the establishment of a new political authority. The story of the hall's making is a narrative of origin which is mirrored in the first entertainment the *scop* performs in the newly constructed building: the song of creation.

[64] Wehlau, '*Riddle of Creation*', 17. See also Jan T. Nelis and Antoon Schoors, 'Creation', in *Dictionnaire Encyclopédique de la Bible*, ed. by Centre: Informatique et Bible, Abbaye de Maredsous, resp. scient. Pierre-Maurice Bogaert and others ([Turnhout]: Brepols, 1987), 310–13, and Job 38: 1–11.

[65] 'The Guardian of life ordered that a pleasant heavenly structure be upon the middle of the sea' (*Genesis A* 144^b–146^a).

[66] 'time passed, hurried off over the structure of the earth' (*Genesis A* 135–136^a). See also *Christ I* 1–17. *The Exeter Book*, 3–49.

[67] Zumthor, *Mesure du Monde*, 91. See also Wehlau, '*Riddle of Creation*', 13.

The first poem of the 'Advent Lyrics' that constitute *Christ I* develops an extended metaphor that combines architecture, building, and creation.[68] It is based on Matthew 21: 42 and it presents Christ as a *weallstan*, a stone for building that is first rejected by the workers but that later becomes the cornerstone holding the wide walls together. The poet says that it is fitting that He: 'gesomnige side weallas | fæste gefoge'.[69] In this passage, Christ is the keystone holding together the hall and preventing its collapse. When Christ is called *heafod... healle mærre* therefore, and when, later in the poem, He is begged to come again and restore his work that has been defiled, He is cast in the role of the Creator, whose Second Coming would revitalize our post-lapsarian, corrupted world.[70] The architectural image elaborated in these lines thus alludes to the whole cosmos.

Architectural metaphors also resurface in saints' lives. Guðlac and his virtuous living transform the *beorg* where he resides, for the poet says that, when the saint returns to his dwelling after having been tempted at the doors of hell, the plain is calm and the *sele niwe*: a new building has appeared.[71] With his *beorg*, the saint creates a rejuvenated space, and the poet resorts to building imagery to express it.

Elene offers its own version of this topos.[72] The queen's mission to the land of the Jews comes to a conclusion when she builds a church on Calvary 'þær sio halige rod | gemeted wæs'.[73] This sanctuary is more than a commemorating sign in the landscape. *Elene* specifically mentions the construction, not just of any building, but of a *church*, which confers additional relevance to the queen's adventures in Jerusalem. A church is a special edifice; reiterating its cosmological implications, Zumthor points out that it 'englobe... et délimite l'espace privilégié des rapports de l'homme avec le cosmos, et de tout enseignement sur celui-ci. Le visible s'y marie à l'invisible; le Ciel, la Terre et le monde souterrain

---

[68] *The Advent Lyrics of the Exeter Book*, ed. by Jackson J. Campbell (Princeton: Princeton University Press, 1959), 11.

[69] he 'should bring together the wide walls with firm joints' (*Christ I* 5–6ª).

[70] 'the head... of the glorious hall' (*Christ I* 4). Representations of Christ as the Creator were current in patristic and medieval times. For further references, see Charles R. Sleeth, *Studies in 'Christ and Satan'* (Toronto: University of Toronto Press, 1982), 11–12.

[71] 'the dwelling [was] new' (*Guthlac A* 742ᵇ).

[72] See Earl R. Anderson, *Cynewulf: Structure, Style and Theme in his Poetry* (Rutherford, NJ: Fairleigh Dickinson University Press, 1983), 120–1 on the construction of the church in *Elene* as a type-scene.

[73] 'where the holy rood was found' (*Elene* 1011ᵇ–1012ª).

y coïncident'.⁷⁴ In *Elene*, the temple memorializes the discovery of the cross and the narrative brings together hell, this transitory world, and heaven. The parallels between Judas's torture in the pit before he agrees to co-operate with the queen, the cross's confinement before Helen retrieves it from under the earth, and Christ's descent into Hell before the Resurrection have long been recognized.⁷⁵ A human society constituted by Helen and the crowd surrounding her on the one hand, infernal regions where the cross and Judas are locked up on the other, and finally the celestial kingdom which Christ's Crucifixion has opened for mankind, intersect on Calvary. Moreover, this church locates Christendom's new centre and becomes a point of attraction for people dwelling in distant lands who travel there to find healing and consolation.⁷⁶ The church figures the broad compass of an enlarged Christian world and it localizes the heart of this new expansion: the place of the Crucifixion. Building a church there, Helen, and through her Constantine, the Roman Emperor, produce a Christian model of the cosmos. This creation scene seals Constantine's achievement: he has produced a new world order.

An important linguistic element often appears in creation scenes permeated by architectural imagery. The connexion between the genesis of a new world and language discussed above in connection with *Widsiþ* and Cædmon's *Hymn* continues here, and it strengthens the analogy between the construction of buildings and the birth of the cosmos. For instance, in *Genesis A* the earthly creation comes into being 'þurh word ... wuldorcyninges', thus echoing the opening of the Gospel of John.⁷⁷ More interestingly, in *Elene*, Cynewulf adds an apparently insignificant detail to his source when he recounts the building of the church: he specifies that it is Constantine who orders its construction. This modification might seem irrelevant at first sight but, in the present context, it makes of the episode of the Church's construction at Calvary a complete creation scene, which results from the emperor's linguistic input.

In *Beowulf*, a number of speech acts are necessary for Heorot to be raised at the beginning of the poem. It first comes into Hroðgar's mind

---

⁷⁴ Zumthor, *Mesure du Monde*, 101.
⁷⁵ Thomas D. Hill, 'Sapiential Structure and Figural Narrative in the Old English *Elene*', in R. E. Bjork (ed.), *Cynewulf: Basic Readings* (New York: Garland (rev. version), 1996), 207–28 (first publ. in *Traditio*, 27 (1971) 159–77); Daniel G. Calder, *Cynewulf* (Boston: Twayne, 1981), 124. See also Anderson, *Cynewulf*, 161.
⁷⁶ *Elene* (1212ᵇ–1217ᵃ).
⁷⁷ 'through the word ... of the King of glory' (*Genesis A* 111) John 1: 1.

that he 'healreced hatan wolde, | medoærn micel men gewyrcean'.[78] The building originates in an order uttered by the sovereign to his subjects, for he commands, *hatan*, the edifice to be built. Hroðgar's architectural enterprise is also linguistically validated in the *scop*'s song of creation. Finally, when the hall is completed, the king gives it its name: 'scop him Heort naman'.[79] Naming Heorot is an adamic gesture: as the first man named the things of creation, the Danish king gives Heorot its name.[80] The construction of the hall thus figures the beginning of human society. But in this scene, the king is also a divine figure who uses speech to fashion a world: the poet describes Hroðgar as 'se þe his wordes geweald wide hæfde'.[81] Language secures territorial rule here, and the *Beowulf* poet repeatedly associates Heorot, language, and the creation of a new space.

In Old English poetry, creation is a process of transformation or of expansion, and it is often equated with the construction of a building. New worlds provide a shelter for mankind, and in all cases, the creation process brings together material and linguistic components. Consequently, these scenes exemplify the crucial role language plays in the shaping of a new space, a role that will resurface later in this study, namely in Chapters 4 and 7, which are devoted to poetico-historical documents. This time, emphasis will be put on the symbolic appropriation of new mental spaces through language and narratives. The coming into being of a new space is never a neutral and inoffensive event. For, just as creation scenes silence or 'other' those who might object to the new spatial distribution, territorial appropriations are challenged and need justification. In both cases, strategies of dispossession operate through language.

CHARACTERISTICS OF CREATION

Enclosures, Boundaries, and Knowledge of Space

The creative act is a process that unfolds in time: it is because God keeps intervening that the world endures. Old English poets resort to images of enclosure to verbalize this divine intercession. In *Christ and Satan*, we

---

[78] 'that he would order men to construct a building, a great mead-hall' (*Beowulf* 68–9).
[79] 'he created for it the name Heorot' (*Beowulf* 78ᵇ).
[80] See Genesis 2: 19–20.
[81] 'he who ruled widely with his word' (*Beowulf* 79).

read that 'deopne ymblyt clene ymbhaldeð | meotod on mihtum, and alne middangeard'.[82] God holds lands and waters, that is, the whole of creation, in his embrace. The Lord's clasp is the source of his power over the universe. In *Riddle 40*, God 'eorþan ond heofones, | healdeð ond wealdeð, swa he ymb þas utan hweorfeð'.[83] The pair *healdan* and *wealdan* suggests that to hold is somehow to rule. The mention of God wandering around creation further emphasizes the idea of enclosure, for this image materializes the sky as a vault on which one can walk. These elements all have biblical roots; in Isaiah 40: 12 for example, the Lord holds the waters in his hand; in Job 38: 1–11, He locks up the waters and the winds; and in Job 22: 14, He walks on the firmament. These images are of course also echoed in Cædmon's *Hymn*, where heaven is indeed a roof.[84]

This divine force surrounds not only the whole cosmos: smaller entities too are encompassed by fixed boundaries. Dry lands, the home of men, need to be enclosed and protected against external assaults. *Maxims I* say that: 'Storm oft holm gebringeþ, | geofen in grimmum sælum; onginnað grome fundian | fealwe on feorran to londe... | Weallas him wiþre healdað'.[85] In the present case, walls defend homelands against the attack of the storm. Cliffs fulfil a similar function. Towering high in Old English descriptions of the natural world, they fence in a definite space and protect it from the outside, from the sea. When these defences fail, destruction ineluctably follows. *Christ I* exploits this imagery when describing Doomsday:

> Hreosað geneahhe
> tobrocene burgweallas. Beorgas gemeltað
> ond heahcleofu, þa wið holme ær
> fæste wið flodum foldan sceldun,

---

[82] 'the Creator entirely embraces in his might the deep expanse and all the world' (*Christ and Satan* 7–8). *The Junius Manuscript*, ed. by George Philip Krapp, Anglo-Saxon Poetic Records, 1 (New York: Columbia University Press, 1931; repr. 1964), 135–58. For a discussion of these lines, see *Christ and Satan: A Critical Edition*, ed. by Robert Emmett Finnegan (Waterloo, Ontario: Laurier University Press, 1977), 91 and Thomas D. Hill, 'Apocryphal Cosmography and the "stream uton sæ": A Note on *Christ and Satan*, lines 4–12', *Philological Quarterly*, 48 (1969), 550–4.
[83] 'He holds and rules earth and heaven, just as He wanders about around them' (*Riddle 40* 4^b–5. *The Exeter Book*, 200–3).
[84] Morland, 346. This imagery brings to mind Old Icelandic cosmology which traces the origins of the sky to the skull of a primeval giant.
[85] 'Often the sea shall bring a storm, the flood in severe seasons; fiercely they, grey, will go far on the land... Walls will hold strongly against them' (*Maxims I* 50^b–53^a. *The Exeter Book*, 156–63).

stið ond stædfæst,   staþelas wið wæge,
wætre windendum.⁸⁶

The collapse of boundaries constituted by walls, mountains, or cliffs marks the beginning of the utter destruction that will take place at the end of times. A fatal return to the primordial chaos which existed before the creative act of transformation, a chaos where elements mingle, where the world exists as an undifferentiated expansion, is a constant danger.[87] External forces, such as the storm or the waves in the passage just quoted, threaten to violate established boundaries and to cause the dissolution of the world.

Destruction can also originate from within an enclosed and well-defined space; for, creation as presented in Old English verse is the union of contrary components. In *The Order of the World*, toward the end of the text, the poet says that God brings together day and night, depth and height, air and water, land and sea... These elements stay together because God holds them *miclum meahtlocum*, with a great belt of might.[88] The world does not dissolve and each constituent go its own way precisely because God girdles creation.

The divine *meahtloc* marks the separation between the visible, material and the invisible, celestial creations. The poet of the *Order of the World* further mentions the limit dividing the worlds of men and of angels when he says that the *dryhtnes duguþe*, the Lord's host: 'in þam frumstole þe him frea sette, | hluttor heofones weard, healdað georne | mere gemære'.[89] Bernard Huppé offers a translation of this poem in the *Web of Words* and he freely renders the second part of the above quotation as follows: the legions 'hold gladly the sublime course'.[90]

---

[86] 'City-walls, broken, shall abundantly fall. Mountains and high cliffs shall melt, which earlier protected the earth from the ocean, firm and immovable bulwarks against the waves, the heaved waters' (*Christ III* 976ᵇ–981ᵃ).
[87] On the links between the creation and the destruction of the world, see Lönnroth, 'Formula Analysis', 322–3.
[88] *The Order of the World* 88ᵃ. *The Exeter Book*, 163–6. Note that this image unavoidably brings to mind the World Serpent of Old Icelandic mythology. On this motif, see Preben Meulengracht Sørensen, 'Thor's Fishing Expedition', in Gro Steinsland (ed.), *Words and Objects: Towards a Dialogue between Archaeology and History of Religion*, Institute for Comparative Research in Human Culture. Serie B; Skrifter, 71 (Oslo: Norwegian University Press, 1986), 257–78.
[89] 'in the thrones that the Lord, the bright Guardian of heaven, set up for them, they zealously keep the famous boundary' (*The Order of the World* 51–53ᵃ).
[90] Bernard F. Huppé, *The Web of Words: Structural Analysis of the Old English Poems* Vainglory, The Wonders of Creation, The Dream of the Rood and Judith (Albany: State University of New York Press, 1970), 31.

According to him, this passage means that the angels keep the correct course of the stars in heaven and thus obey the word of God. Yet BT does not support the translation of *gemære* as 'course', but give 'end, boundary, termination, limit'. The dictionary indicates that the term is used to refer to landed property where it designates a boundary, and that it can also mark English political divisions. This lexical evidence suggests that the phrase *mere gemære* should be translated as the 'famous boundary' and be understood as referring to the idea of a precise limit between the angelic realm in heaven and the human sphere on earth. It may be equated with the enclosure that holds the material creation together and prevents its contrary elements from separating.

Images of God encircling creation suggest that, to Him at least, the cosmos is an expanse that can be grasped. In *The Order of the World*, He holds all the creation 'in his anes fæþm',[91] and in *Riddle 40*, creation says that: 'folm mec mæg bifon ond fingras þry | utan eaþe ealle ymbclyppan'.[92] The Creator holds the universe, He controls it. He is at the same time granted intimate knowledge of its every detail. In *Christ and Satan*, we read that 'He selfa mæg sæ geondwlitan, | grundas in geofene, godes agen bearn, | and he ariman mæg rægnas scuran, | dropena gehwelcne'.[93] Christ's grasp of the world is exhaustive, so much so that He can count every single drop of rain. This ability to reckon and to specify characterizes in fact divine power.[94] Christ's control of creation lies in his panoramic, detailed, and extensive vision of the earth. Knowledge of space, figured by an encompassing embrace and a totalizing vision, grounds and secures territorial authority.

Creation is conceived as an enclosed and limited area only when examined from God's point of view, and *Christ and Satan* sharply contrasts the figures of Satan and of Christ on this point. After the devil's last attempt to lead him into temptation, Christ banishes his opponent to the underworld and condemns him to measure hell with

---

[91] 'in His embrace only' (*The Order of the World* 56ᵃ).

[92] 'a hand may surround me and three fingers easily encompass me completely from the outside' (*Riddle 40* 52–3). For the image of the three fingers used to measure, see Isaiah 40: 12.

[93] 'He Himself, God's own child, may see through the sea, the bottom of the ocean, He may count the showers of rain, each one of the drops' (*Christ and Satan* 9–12ᵃ). See Finnegan (ed.), 91, and Hill, 'Apocryphal Cosmography', for arguments against the emendation of *heofene* to *geofene*.

[94] Constance Harsh, '*Christ and Satan*: The Measured Power of Christ', *Neuphilologische Mitteilungen*, 90 (1989), 243–53 (243). See also Ruth Wehlau, '*Riddle of Creation*', 29. For similar biblical images, see Job 28: 24 and Baruch 3: 32.

his hands: 'Wite þu eac, awyrgda, hu wid and sid | helheoðo dreorig, and mid hondum amet'.⁹⁵ He orders the devil to do so 'oððæt þu þone ymbhwyrft alne cunne'.⁹⁶ This passage indicates that Satan does not yet know the dimensions of his new abode. Christ further tells his adversary that he should determine: 'hu heh and deop hell inneweard seo'.⁹⁷ The word that interests me here is *inneweard*, for it indicates that Satan is *in* hell when he gauges its extent. Unlike Christ, Satan does not behold his dwelling place from the outside; he does not encompass and control it.

The poet mentions the fallen angel's perception of the distance that separates him from the doors of hell: 'Þa him [Satan] þuhte þæt þanon wære | to helleduru hund þusenda | mila gemearcodes'.⁹⁸ Here, *hund þusenda* may well be a general term indicating a great distance, rather than denoting precisely a hundred thousand miles. However that may be, for Satan, hell is a vast region indeed. The poem's conclusion, reporting the fallen angel's punishment, is a precise reversal of Christ's power as depicted at the beginning.⁹⁹ His figure contrasts with Christ's: he is confined to hell, forced to measure it with his hands and he perceives his new residence as a very extensive place. His adversary, on the other hand, observes the whole of creation from the outside, he surveys and encompasses it with his gaze and knows it intimately.

Similarly with mankind: it does not share God's omniscient viewpoint. In *Genesis A*, the land and the waters that God creates for men after the fall of the angels are *rum* and *sid*, and the expression *widlond* designates the earth's inhabitable expanse.¹⁰⁰ *Christ II* resorts to the metaphor of the sea-journey to describe human condition in the world, and it says that we toss over *yða ofermæta*, measureless waters.¹⁰¹ Unlike Christ, human beings in this transitory world cannot know the extent of the sea or the precise dimensions of the world. Both the abodes created for mankind and the ocean surrounding them are vast. As hell appears

---

⁹⁵ 'Know also, accursed one, how broad and wide the bloody vault of hell is and measure it with your hands' (*Christ and Satan* 698–9).
⁹⁶ 'until you know all the extent' (*Christ and Satan* 701).
⁹⁷ 'how high and deep the inner part of hell is' (*Christ and Satan* 706).
⁹⁸ 'It seemed to him that from that place to the doors of hell there were a hundred thousands measured in miles' (*Christ and Satan* 719–21ᵃ).
⁹⁹ For a different reading of this passage, see Ruth Wehlau, 'The Power of Knowledge and the Location of the Reader in *Christ and Satan*', *Journal of English and Germanic Philology*, 97 (1998), 1–12 (5–6).
¹⁰⁰ On these three terms, see lines 114ᵇ, 123ᵃ, 134ᵇ, 156ᵃ, 162ᵃ, and 167ᵇ.
¹⁰¹ *Christ II* 854ᵃ.

immense to Satan, creation seems wide to men. Only God therefore can mentally or physically comprehend the whole of creation; his omnipotent and all-encompassing gaze will be reflected in the mapping practices discussed below in Chapter 4.

Occupation of Space and Transgression

Riddle 66 is a short poem revolving around the notion that the world is an enclosed area: it is encompassed by a speaker who says that all the seas and the green plains are in his or her encircling arms: 'Sæs me sind ealle | flodas on fæðmum ond þes foldan bearm, | grene wongas'.[102] The narrator further contains the invisible universe by sinking under hell, flying above the heavens, and stretching out over the angels' dwellings. Creation is personified as a presence outside what is created, a presence that holds it together. Yet, at the same time, it is also inside the created world. The riddle closes on these lines: 'eorþan gefylle, | ealne middangeard ond merestreamas | side mid me sylfum. Saga hwæt ic hatte'.[103] Here, the speaker fills creation and the text insists that the universe must be inhabited. In this particular poem, the world exists because it is at the same time encircled and filled.

The notion that space has to be settled and populated is pervasive in the Old English corpus, and it has wide-reaching consequences for the mental map the Anglo-Saxons elaborated. For a given area has to be occupied. Just as the emphasis placed on boundaries reflects the idea that space is a bounded extension, the stress put on the occupation of land is again congruent with general medieval notions of space. As Zumthor observes: 'L' "espace" médiéval est...ce qui est entre deux: un vide à remplir. On ne le fait exister qu'en le parsemant de sites.'[104] The necessity for space to be filled raises the question of land distribution and land control, a preoccupation that permeates not only accounts of creation, but also narratives of the fall of the angels and of Adam and Eve's first sin.

Genesis A specifies that the rebellious angels left empty seats in heaven when they fell: 'Him on laste setl, | wuldorspedum welig, wide stodan

---

[102] 'The sea, the waters, and the inside of the earth, the green fields are all in my embrace' (*Riddle 66* 3^b–5^a). *The Exeter Book*, 230–1.

[103] 'I fill the earth, the whole world, and the wide waters with myself. Say what I am called' (*Riddle 66* 8^b–10).

[104] Zumthor, *Mesure du Monde*, 51.

| gifum growende on godes rice, | beorht and geblædfæst, buendra leas'.[105] The banishment from heaven of Lucifer and his followers leaves gaps in the celestial dwellings. These voids prompt God to create mankind, for He considers: 'hu he þa mæran gesceaft, | eðelstaðolas eft gesette, | swegltorhtan seld, selran werode'.[106] The fall of the angels depletes the citizenship of heaven which must be made whole again,[107] and deserving human beings will contribute to heaven's replenishment when they inherit a place in the celestial realm after their death.

Augustine was the first to formulate this idea: according to him, the number of spiritual beings inhabiting heaven is perfect and should remain stable.[108] Bede introduces this 'doctrine of replacement' to Anglo-Saxon England, a doctrine espoused by Ælfric and Wulfstan. These two authors do however adapt the concept to their own concerns. Dorothy Haines notes that Ælfric, in his 'Sermo de Initio Creaturae', speaks of 'wununga on heofonan rice' that man should earn.[109] Later on in the homily, Ælfric calls them *stede*, 'seats'.[110] In this respect, Ælfric's account is close to that of *Genesis A*, where the poet uses terms such as *setl, seld*, and *eðelstaðolas*.[111] BT translates this precise instance of *setl* as 'a seat, place where one abides, an abode, a residence, dwelling', and this occurrence of *seld* as 'a seat, residence, mansion, hall'. *Eðelstaðolas* compounds *eðel*, the native land, with the action of establishing, founding, settling, and fixing derived from *staþolian*. Consequently, both Ælfric and *Genesis A* deal with places to be settled, with residences to be occupied. The Anglo-Saxons thus had a particular understanding of Augustine's doctrine of replacement. They were original in stressing that 'God's purpose in creating mankind was not just to complete numbers,

---

[105] 'Behind them, the seats, rich with abundance of glory, increased with gifts, radiant, and prosperous, stood widely deprived of their inhabitants in the kingdom of God' (*Genesis A* 86ᵇ–89).

[106] 'how He may again settle the excellent creation, the settlements, the heavenly bright houses, with a better company' (*Genesis A* 93ᵇ–95).

[107] See also *Genesis B* 395–7ᵇ.

[108] On the 'doctrine of replacement', see David F. Johnson, 'The Fall of Lucifer in *Genesis A* and Two Anglo-Latin Royal Charters', *Journal of English and Germanic Philology*, 97 (1998), 500–21; Dorothy Haines, 'Vacancies in Heaven: The Doctrine of Replacement and *Genesis A*', *Notes and Queries*, 44 (1997), 150–4; *The Saxon Genesis*, ed. by A. N. Doane (Madison: University of Wisconsin Press, 1991), 132–3, and B. Lohse, 'Zu Augustins Engellehre', *Zeitschrift für Kirchengeschichte*, 70 (1959), 278–91.

[109] Haines, 'Vacancies in Heaven', 153. 'dwellings in the kingdom of heaven'. *Ælfric's Catholic Homilies. The First Series Text*, ed. by Peter Clemoes, EETS ss. 17 (Oxford: Oxford University Press, 1997), 181.

[110] *Ælfric's Homilies*, ed. Clemoes, 181.   [111] *Genesis A* 86ᵇ, 94ᵃ, and 95ᵃ.

but to settle residences'.[112] What matters here is to occupy a certain territory, and not to leave it empty. These accounts of the creation of mankind betray an urge not to leave empty places vacant, but to people them with worthy occupants.

Places cannot be settled at random and the distribution of the population in space remains under God's control. He appoints an appropriate place to everyone and everything. For instance, the angels first remain 'in þam frumstole þe him frea sette', they occupy the site that God allotted to them.[113] When one of them rebels, a new place is created especially for him: God, angry, 'sceop þam werlogan | wræclicne ham weorce to leane'.[114] Hell did not exist before Lucifer's fall, because there was no need then for a place of punishment. Mankind undergoes a similar change of location after original sin is committed. Human beings are first assigned their proper position in creation; they dwell in Paradise where God 'let heo þæt land buan'.[115] After the first couple eats the forbidden fruit, God punishes the tempter and the sinners: He tells Adam: 'Þu scealt oðerne eðel secean, | wynleasran wic'.[116] Once they have disregarded God's command, the first humans are no longer worthy of remaining in Paradise. Place and identity are linked: because their crime has altered their nature, Satan, Adam, and Eve have to occupy a place that corresponds to their new status. The Lord controls the spatial organization of both the visible and the invisible creations. He sets up thrones for the righteous angels, hell for the wicked ones, He orders Adam and Eve to dwell in Paradise, He expels them from Eden when they are no longer worthy of it. He devises a place for everything material or immaterial.

God's power is therefore a power over space and Satan, as well as the first human beings, acknowledges this aspect of divine authority. When he laments his fate in hell, the devil says that he and his followers should abandon any hope of ever occupying a better dwelling: 'Ne ðurfon we ðes wenan, þæt us wuldorcyning | æfre wille eard alefan, | æðel to æhte, swa he ær dyde'.[117] Satan admits that it was the Lord who granted

---

[112] Haines, 'Vacancies in Heaven', 153.
[113] 'in the throne that the Lord set up for them' (*The Order of the World* 51).
[114] 'created a miserable home for that faith-breaker as a reward for his deed' (*Genesis A* 36^b–37).
[115] 'let them inhabit that land' (*Genesis B* 239^b).
[116] 'You shall seek another home, a dwelling place more deprived of joy' (*Genesis A* 927–8^a).
[117] 'Because of this, we need not hope that the King of glory will ever grant [us] an estate, a home as a possession, as He previously did' (*Christ and Satan* 114–16).

him a home in heaven in the first place. He was allowed to occupy a celestial throne because it agreed with God's will, not because he himself was powerful enough to do so. And his enforced confinement to the nether regions demonstrates that divine power exceeds his own. This idea resurfaces at the end of the poem, when Satan is condemned to measure hell; for, Christ tells his enemy that his punishment will teach him something: 'Wast þu þonne þe geornor þæt þu wið god wunne, | seoððan þu þonne hafast handum ametene | hu heh and deop hell inneweard seo'.[118] Satan will discover both the configuration of his place of banishment and the nature of his adversary, that is, he will face both new and unfamiliar surroundings and the greater power of God. There is something to be learnt from space.

After the fall, Adam bemoans his new condition. He wishes to amend his ways and to deserve divine mercy. He says that he would not hesitate to fulfil God's will,

> þeah me on sæ wadan
> hete heofones god   heonone nu þa,
> on flod faran...
> ac ic to þam grunde genge,   gif ic godes meahte
> willan gewyrcean.[119]

Doane reads these lines typologically: he understands this trial by sea punishment as announcing baptism, the remedy to original sin.[120] Yet this passage could also indicate that Adam has realized that the true nature of God's power is a power over space. He therefore expresses his newly acquired obedience in spatial terms and says that he would go wherever the Lord ordered, even if it were a place as hostile as the bottom of the sea.

The original space of creation is enclosed, properly filled, and settled. But this arrangement is constantly challenged and is never allowed to endure. The sense of space that can be reconstructed from creation scenes as narrated in Old English verse suggests an insecurity about boundaries, a constant fear of the outside (considered as a threat), and an anxiety to secure every thing in its proper place. For, when enclosures

---

[118] 'You will then know more exactly that you struggled against God after you have measured with your hands how high and deep hell is inside' (*Christ and Satan* 704–6).

[119] 'even if heavenly God now ordered me to walk into the sea from here, to go into the water... but I would go to the bottom [of the sea] if I could perform God's will' (*Genesis B* 830ᵇ–835ᵃ).

[120] *The Saxon Genesis*, ed. Doane, 152–3.

and limits weaken, chaos prevails and the world is eventually destroyed, invaded from the outside or dissolving as a result of internal antagonism.

CONTROL OF SPACE AND THE FALL OF THE ANGELS

The Bible offers no account of the creation and of the rebellion of the angels. Tradition has identified pride as the first transgression, on the ground that before the fall, the angels could not have been enticed to sin for the possession of a material good, but that they could have refused to follow God's rule.[121] Anglo-Saxon poets were aware of this conventional understanding of the cause of Lucifer's downfall and they mention it in their accounts of the angel's disobedience. In *Genesis A*, Lucifer errs *for oferhygde*, 'because of pride'.[122] The poet repeats the term on line 29, and together with 'þæs engles mod', 'the angel's pride', identifies them as the spur of the rebellion. *Genesis B* says that the Lord realizes 'þæt his engyl ongan ofermod wesan' and *Christ and Satan* that the rebellious angels had forsaken God's light *for oferhygdum*.[123]

Yet, Old English versions of the angelic fall are more complex than appears at first sight. In the introduction to his edition of *Genesis B*, Doane says that Satan's *ofermod* 'consists in his notion that "þurh his anes cræft" he can make a more splendid throne ("stenglicran stol") higher in Heaven somewhere to the west and north'.[124] Anglo-Saxon poets, echoing Isaiah 14: 12–14, consistently link Satan's fall with his wish to set up his own throne in the north part of heaven.

Pride was a laudable attribute of Germanic heroes and ranked high in the traditional Anglo-Saxon scale of values. In itself, it was not a sufficient argument to exile Satan. Old English poets therefore resort to the heroic ethos upon which the relationship between the lord and

---

[121] T. Deman, 'Orgueil', in *Dictionnaire de Théologie Catholique*, ed. by A. Vacant and others, 21 vols (Paris: Letouzey et Ané, 1903–72), xi (1931), 1410–34.

[122] *Genesis A* 22ᵇ.

[123] 'that his angel began to be proud' (*Genesis B* 262 and *Christ and Satan* 69ᵃ). René Derolez raises the question of the 'true nature' of *Genesis B* and he asks whether the Old Saxon interpolation should be treated as Old English poetry *tout court*. I do not intend to address this issue here, but I would like to point out that my analysis of the poem's spatial imagery has found it remarkably congruent with that of other Old English accounts of the fall. René Derolez, '*Genesis*: Old Saxon and Old English', *English Studies*, 76 (1995), 402–23 (402).

[124] *The Saxon Genesis*, ed. Doane, 121.

the retainer is based to condemn the devil's rebellious thoughts. When they relate this episode, they use heroic imagery to tell of Lucifer's desire to have his own throne. God becomes a Germanic ruler and Satan a rebellious follower who is exiled.[125] The mutinous thane strives to establish his own domain within his lord's realm and, as a result, spatial issues are foregrounded. Doane points out that 'to fall, Satan must struggle against things as they naturally are'.[126] While the critic goes on to discuss the devil's opposition to language, I would like to suggest that it is also a spatial arrangement that Lucifer rejects. His contention with God has to do with control of space, and the rebellious angel refuses to recognize God's greater spatial mastery. His revolt begins when, in *Genesis A*, he says 'þæt he on norððæle | ham and heahsetl heofena rices | agan wolde'.[127] From wanting his own throne in heaven, Satan's ambition rapidly entices him to compete for the control of the entire celestial kingdom. After claiming ownership of a *ham* or a *heahsetl*, the rebellious angels boast that they could easily possess *rice*.[128] The word may mean either 'kingdom' or 'power'; in either case, it indicates that the devil's followers no longer intend to share it with God, but that they think they can enjoy it in its entirety.

Genesis B is structured around a similar gradation. The poet first mentions that Lucifer is the most beautiful angel God created. This outstanding being rebels 'wið þone hehstan heofnes waldend, þe siteð on þam halgan stole'.[129] This passage marks the beginning of the enmity between God and Satan, and the wording of the line is striking. The audience is reminded that God occupies 'þam halgan stole', the blessed throne, and that He rules heaven, that He is *heofnes waldend*. These are precisely the divine attributes that Satan tries to appropriate. He first thinks that he can build a home for himself that would be more glorious than God's: 'Þohte þurh his anes cræft | hu he him strenglicran stol

---

[125] P. J. Lucas, 'Genesis', in Michael Lapidge and others (eds.), *The Blackwell Encyclopaedia of Anglo-Saxon England* (Oxford: Blackwell, 1999), 200–1; *The Saxon Genesis*, ed. Doane, 116–38, and R. E. Woolf, 'The Devil in Old English Poetry', *Review of English Studies*, NS 4 (1953), 1–12 (1–2). For the military undertones of the relationship between God and Satan, see Maria Vittoria Molinari, 'La caduta degli angeli ribelli: considerazioni sulla *Genesis B*', *Annali, Istituto Orientale di Napoli (AION)*, Filologia Germanica, 18–19 (1985–6), 417–40.

[126] *The Saxon Genesis*, ed. Doane, 119.

[127] 'that he wanted to possess a home and a high throne in the north part of the kingdom of heaven' *Genesis A* 32^b–34^a.

[128] *Genesis A* 33^a and 47^a.

[129] 'against the highest ruler of heaven who sits on that holy throne' (*Genesis B* 260).

geworhte, | heahran on heofonum'.¹³⁰ He then persuades himself that he can be the lord of the rebellious angels, that he can 'rædan on þis rice'.¹³¹ His dream of a seat in the celestial realm swells and becomes a yearning for the lordship over the whole of heaven.

Once cast in hell, Satan accuses the Lord of his failure. He says that 'we hine for þam alwaldan agan ne moston, | romigan ures rices'.¹³² The translation of 'romigan ures rices' is disputed; according to Alain Renoir, the phrase is generally translated as 'must cede our realm', on the grounds that the basic meaning of *romigan*, 'to strive for', would not make sense in this context. Since Satan refers back to a time when he had a place in heaven, it would be illogical for him to desire something he already possesses. Yet Renoir, and following him Doane, argues for the retention of the verb's original meaning.¹³³ The former points out that Satan does not claim a place he already has in heaven but, more drastically, that he wants to overthrow God and to become the new ruler of the celestial regions. I agree with this interpretation and I would like to insist on the use of the possessive pronoun *ures*. At this point, Satan is made to allude to the whole of heaven—not just to his own seat—and it is significant that he should refer to it as *ures*.¹³⁴ For, when he first contemplates his coup against the Lord, he speaks of *þis rice*, thereby suggesting that the kingdom of heaven is a new territory to be conquered. But later, when his attempt has failed and he is confined to hell, he speaks of *ures rices*; the possessive pronoun indicates that he does not abandon his claim. On the contrary, from his point of view, heaven was rightly his and God wrongly deprived him and his followers of it. This celestial domain, and not hell, is what he thinks he is entitled to. Interestingly, he does not consider himself sovereign in hell, although he is surrounded by faithful followers who carry out his orders when they cause the fall of the first human beings. Satan still says: 'Ic eom rices leas'.¹³⁵ Lucifer first desires to control *þis* kingdom of heaven where he first had his appointed place. After his rebellion, the celestial realm from which he has been banished becomes *ures rices*

---

¹³⁰ 'He thought how, by means of his own ability, he might construct a stronger throne, higher in heaven' (*Genesis B* 272ᵇ–274ᵃ).
¹³¹ 'rule over this kingdom' (*Genesis B* 289ᵃ).
¹³² 'we could not possess it [a home in heaven], strive for our kingdom, because of the Almighty' (*Genesis B* 359–60ᵃ).
¹³³ *The Saxon Genesis*, ed. Doane, 270–1 and Alain Renoir, '"Romigan ures rices": A Reconsideration', *Modern Language Notes*, 72 (1957), 1–4.
¹³⁴ On the use of *ures*, see *The Saxon Genesis*, ed. Doane, 271.
¹³⁵ 'I am bereft of [my] kingdom' (*Genesis B* 372ᵇ).

for him and his followers. And finally, Satan, bound in hell, complains that he has been deprived of his own kingdom. The more the devil is proved wrong in his ambition to take over control of heaven, the more obstinate he becomes about his alleged right to it.

Elene mentions the fight opposing God and Satan in similar terms. After the discovery of the cross, the fallen angel appears and delivers a passionate speech. Such devilish tirades are typical of the lamentations Satan utters after his fall. He usually deplores his fate and rehearses the wrongs that he has suffered from the time of the Incarnation. At one point in *Elene*, he says, talking of the Saviour: 'Is his rice brad | ofer middangeard. Min is geswiðrod | ræd under roderum.'[136] This passage clearly states that the growth of one realm, namely, of Christendom's dominion, entails the decrease of another, that is, of Satan's earthly rule: the fallen angel challenges God over territorial control.

In *Christ and Satan*, Satan reviews the events that led to his ruin and he says that he wanted to 'agan me burga gewald | eall to æhte'.[137] This passage is striking because of its concentration of words denoting possession and control: *agan*, *æhte*, and *gewald*. *Genesis A* puts a similar emphasis on the fallen angel's craving to own the whole of heaven, for the expression *agan wolde* or *agan woldan* occurs twice when the causes of Lucifer's fall are rehearsed.[138] Charles Sleeth notices that *agan* is one of Satan's favourite words and that he thus 'shows that he regards his estate in heaven as a property'.[139] Old English poets describe the feud between God and his devilish enemy not simply as the revolt of a retainer against his lord or against the place assigned to him in the social hierarchy. More concretely, what is at stake in this struggle is the appropriation and the control of space.

Satan's claim to rule heaven is a motif that resurfaces at other points in the Old English corpus, for instance in the episode of the devil's temptations of Christ as recounted in *Christ and Satan*. After having taken Jesus to a mountain top and shown him the surrounding lands, the devil says: 'Ic þe geselle on þines seolfes dom | folc and foldan. Foh hider to me | burh and breotone bold to gewealde, | rodora

---

[136] 'His kingdom is wide over the earth. My authority has dwindled under the sky' (*Elene* 916^b–918^a).

[137] 'to possess for myself control over the cities, to have all as a possession' (*Christ and Satan* 86^b–87^a).

[138] *Genesis A* 34^a and 48^a.   [139] Sleeth, *Studies in 'Christ and Satan'*, 17.

rices'.[140] Satan traditionally rules over the earth, he is the prince of this world,[141] and he logically offers Christ power over 'folc and foldan'. It is more surprising, however, that his snare should include 'burh and breotone bold... rodora rices', domains pertaining to the kingdom of heaven. This particular element is added by the Old English poet and is necessary to make the meaning of the poem complete; for 'as Satan fell in the beginning by grasping covetously for the highest possession, so he tempts Christ to fall to hell by grasping covetously for a rule and a possession, and this too must be nothing less than the highest possession.'[142] This modification of the biblical account supports my claim that territorial struggle plays a key role in the depiction of the relationships between God and Satan. In the Old English version of Christ's temptations, Satan usurps his adversary's position in pretending to have authority over both heaven and earth. In mentioning the celestial domain, he presents Christ with a snare that strongly echoes the one that caused his own downfall: to rule in heaven. Had Christ succumbed, He would at the same time have admitted that Satan was in a position to grant those areas to someone else and that he effectively had authority over them. In this scene again, Satan strives for control of heaven.

Christ's answer to Satan's offer coincides with the particulars of the temptation, for the Saviour says: 'Gewit þu, awyrgda, in þæt witescræf'.[143] This line renders Matthew 4: 10 and the Old English poet once more elaborates on his model.[144] In the vernacular text, Christ does not merely dismiss the tempter, He orders him to return to hell, a detail not found in the biblical passage. In response to the devil's suggestion that he might be in a position to distribute lands to others, including Christ, the Saviour confines his enemy to his appropriate abode, thereby asserting His own control of space. The exact wording of both the devil's temptation and of Christ's reply underlines the nature of the bone of contention opposing them: who controls space, and especially who rules over the kingdom of heaven?

---

[140] 'For your honour, I give you people and land. Receive here from me to rule a city and a spacious dwelling of the kingdom of heaven' (*Christ and Satan* 684–7ª).
[141] Neville, *Natural World*, 43, esp. n. 102.
[142] Sleeth, *Studies in 'Christ and Satan'* 26. See also 65–6.
[143] 'Accursed one, go to that cavern of torments' (*Christ and Satan* 690).
[144] 'tunc dicit ei Iesus vade Satanas' (Matthew 4: 10). See also Luke 4: 13.

CONTROL OF SPACE AND THE FALL OF MANKIND

Once Satan has failed in his attempt to gain control of heaven and realizes that his rebellion is vain and hopeless, he directs his animosity against Adam and Eve. This shift is best observed in *Genesis B*. Confined to hell, the devil says: 'Þæt me is sorga mæst, | þæt Adam sceal, þe wæs of eorðan geworht, | minne stronglican stol behealdan'.[145] As Satan referred to the kingdom of heaven as *ures rices*, he speaks here of *minne stol*. From his point of view, the first man has been granted something that is not his. The devil finds it unacceptable that 'his' own place in heaven should be occupied by someone else. As a consequence, the feud opposing him to his creator is displaced and redirected against Adam, and the object of the enmity between the fallen angel and the first human beings is once again occupation of space.

Satan realizes that, as long as Adam and Eve are dear to God, they: 'moton him þone welan agan | þe we on heofonrice habban sceoldon, | rice mid rihte'.[146] He again uses the term *agan*, to possess, and he contests Adam's possession and enjoyment of a seat in heaven, thus repeating his conflict against God. The phrase 'rice mid rihte' suggests that Satan considers that he has a valid claim to the kingdom of heaven, that he should possess it 'by right'. It recalls a passage in *Christ and Satan* where Satan and his followers 'woldon benæman nergendne Crist | rodera rices, ah he on riht geheold'.[147] The pair *rice* and *riht* occurs in both poems; in *Christ and Satan*, it is Christ who rightly rules over heaven, whereas in *Genesis B*, it is the devil who attempts to assert his right to the celestial kingdom against Adam. In both cases however, what matters is who possesses heaven and who is entitled to it.

The devil thinks that the pains he suffers in hell would become more bearable if only he could expel Adam and Eve from the kingdom of heaven.[148] He therefore decides to deprive human beings from the enjoyment of their celestial home: 'Uton oðwendan hit nu monna

---

[145] 'It is my greatest anxiety that Adam, who was made of earth, should hold my strong seat' (*Genesis B* 364ᵇ–366).
[146] They 'may possess the riches, the kingdom that we should by right have in heaven' (*Genesis B* 422ᵇ–424ᵃ).
[147] They 'wanted to deprive Christ the Saviour from the kingdom of heaven, but He held it by right' (*Christ and Satan* 345–6). See also Sleeth, *Studies in 'Christ and Satan'*, 65–6.
[148] See *Genesis B* 433ᵇ–434.

bearnum, | þæt heofonrice, nu we hit habban ne moton'.[149] Satan's envoy, the tempter who leads the first individuals astray, knows that his success will please his master. Right after Adam and Eve have eaten the apple, he gives a speech and, addressing Satan, says: 'Swa þu his sorge ne þearft | beran on þinum breostum... |... þæt her men bun | þone hean heofon'.[150] Satan is still confined to hell, but to know that Adam and Eve are banished from heaven consoles him, for if he cannot enjoy his celestial throne, neither can they. If he failed in his territorial struggle against God, against the first human beings he has been rather more successful.

Logically therefore, when the tempter entices Adam and Eve to eat the forbidden fruit, he should promise them possession of heaven. This argument is indeed found in *Christ and Satan* but not in the context of the fall. When Christ descends to hell, Eve utters a speech in which she admits that Adam and she fell because the devil's messenger promised them ownership of the celestial kingdom. She says: 'Gelærde unc se atola... |... þæt wit blæd ahton, | haligne ham, heofon to gewalde'.[151] Once again, the tempter uses words denoting control and possession, such as *agan* or *gewald*, at least according to Eve. In this account of original sin, human beings commit the same offence as Satan, that is, they believe that they can own heaven.

The tempter of *Genesis B* mentions possession of space neither to Adam nor to Eve. To lure the first man away from God's command, he says that his spiritual understanding and his intelligence will be increased, that his body will become more beautiful, and that he will be wiser, if only he eats the apple.[152] The devil's envoy adopts a different strategy with Eve; he attempts to frighten her, for he says that God will be angry with them when He discovers that Adam has scorned the command of his alleged messenger. In neither case therefore does the tempter promise control of a certain portion of space. At one point however, he tells Eve that she will be able to see throughout the world and to contemplate God on His throne.[153] The promise is fulfilled when the first woman eats the forbidden fruit, and she says: 'Ic mæg heonon

---

[149] 'let us take it away from the children of men, this kingdom of heaven, now that we cannot have it' (*Genesis B* 403^b–404^a).

[150] 'Thus you need not endure sorrow in your breast,... that men here occupy the high heaven' (*Genesis B* 733^b–736^a).

[151] 'The terrible one persuaded us... that we may have joy, the holy home, heaven in our possession' (*Christ and Satan* 411–13).

[152] *Genesis B* 500–4^a.   [153] See *Genesis B* 564^b–567.

geseon | hwær he sylf siteð, (þæt is suð and east)'.[154] The vision quickly vanishes when Adam sins too, and it is replaced by a more appropriate vision of hell.[155]

Eve's vision marks a clear departure from the biblical account. Although Doane sees here a possible echo of Genesis 3: 4–6—where the serpent promises Eve that if she eats the fruit, her eyes will open and she will know good and evil—the critic nevertheless recognizes that the use of the episode is peculiar to the Old English poet, for the vision does fulfil the tempter's promise.[156] What exactly Eve sees is not entirely clear, and lines 666–71 are not without ambiguities. John Vickrey has pointed out that they might mean that she only thinks she beholds God, but that she in fact sees where He sits, the Lord himself remaining hidden by the surrounding angels.[157] In this case, this passage implies that Eve is confused and cannot recognize her vision for what it is, namely, God judging men at the end of time. She does not realize that she witnesses the consequence of her and Adam's sin.

I would like to suggest a different reading of this scene, and I contend that Eve thinks she contemplates God the Creator. She says that she sees 'se ðas woruld gesceop'.[158] This allusion to the beginning of times reveals that the first woman believes that she is granted insights into the divine process of creation and into the world's original spatial disposition. This hypothesis is supported by the observation, a few lines below, that she can gaze far and wide *ofer heofonrice*, across the kingdom of heaven.[159] Her visual powers are suddenly enhanced and she enjoys a panoramic view of the celestial domains. She echoes the figure of Christ in *Christ and Satan* to whom a similar all-encompassing gaze is granted. The mention both of God the Creator and of an extraordinary visual power bestowed on Eve implies that the tempter's allurements include the illusion that if one eats the forbidden fruit, one will know the world as it was when it first came into being. In other words, one will be like the Christ of *Christ and Satan*, beholding the newly formed creation in one glance and having authority over it. And is this not what Satan

---

[154] 'I can see from here where He Himself sits, that is south and east' (*Genesis B* 666^b–667).
[155] *Genesis B* 770^b–774 and 792^b–793^a.
[156] *The Saxon Genesis*, ed. Doane 145–6.
[157] John F. Vickrey, 'The Vision of Eve in *Genesis B*', *Speculum*, 44 (1969), 86–102 (97).
[158] 'He who created this world' (*Genesis B* 668^b). [159] *Genesis B* 609^a.

desired, to become like God, to set up his own throne in heaven, and to know, to control the whole of creation?

Spatial issues are a driving force behind Satan's thirst for revenge; they operate in the tempter's strategy to cause the fall of the first human beings and they render Adam and Eve vulnerable to the tempter's words. A close reading of the temptation scene in *Genesis B* reveals that even if Eve's downfall is caused by her fear of God's anger, the episode nevertheless echoes Satan's first crime: in both cases, the sinners are seduced by their desire to know and control space.

CONCLUSION

Narratives play a pivotal role in the elaboration of a given spatial order and the accounts of creation examined in this chapter yield information about space and its organization. They look to the past and depict an ideal, pre-lapsarian world which, because of its antiquity and perfection, becomes a model. An analysis of these narratives illuminates the connection existing between creation and poetry, for language is essential in shaping, establishing, and legitimizing the existence of a poetic and mental world.

A close reading of creation narratives brings to light anxieties linked to control of space. It is indeed essential to master distance and spatial distribution, and such issues are a bone of contention between God and Lucifer, and between Satan and the first human beings. Accounts of the genesis of the world stress that it is God who ultimately rules over space, and Old English poets modify their biblical sources to indicate that the very first crime, that which causes Lucifer's downfall and his resentment of Adam and Eve, is a territorial transgression.

Divine power is spatial: the Lord knows creation intimately and He decides who dwells where. Knowledge is equated with power and the Lord's familiarity with the universe contrasts with Satan's ignorance of hell's dimension and with mankind's alienation from its environment—Adam, after having eaten the forbidden fruit, wonders how he and Eve are to live in this world.[160] The notion of the boundary, which limits newly created areas, is necessary to think space, for it defines a given extension. In the vernacular poems analysed above,

---

[160] 'Hu sculon wit nu libban oððe on þys lande wesan' (*Genesis B* 805).

frontiers hold the world together; they prevent its dissolution into chaos. This conception of space culminates in the image of the building, an enclosed and protected sphere which will be examined in more detail in the following chapter. In this logic, the exterior is either a threat, for instance the place where destructive storms originate before attacking the fortifications protecting mankind's dwelling places, or a place of banishment, as is the world for Adam and Eve after their expulsion from Paradise.

A close analysis of these tales of origins recalls contemporary spatial notions as outlined in the preceding chapter. For instance, although God is omnipotent and his power is spatial, these texts present space as a finite extension. Cosmographic imagery reflects this sense of enclosure: it represents heaven as a roof or the Lord's spatial control as an embrace. Localization, always a process of identification, sheds light on these texts' insistence that every creature should occupy its proper place in the general economy of creation. Accounts of how the cosmos and the earth came into being conjure up an ideal state of the world, that is, a world where everyone has its proper place and where attempts to possess more than what one has been granted are equivalent to a revolt against God.

And yet spatial transgression, feared and hauntingly present, has always already taken place. Lucifer in creation narratives, but also civilizing heroes or monstrous enemies in the chapters that follow, all gesture toward the past and recall the initial break away from an undifferentiated space. Significantly, the *Genesis B* poet evokes this time of spatial indistinctiveness when he specifies that before they broke God's command, Adam and Eve 'næfdon on þam lande þa giet | sælða gesetena'.[161] Whether *þam lande* refers back to Eden, or announces the first humans' residence outside Paradise, this passage indicates that to have an appointed dwelling belongs to the world after the fall. It suggests therefore that before original sin, space is not divided and compartmented as it is afterwards. Both a curse and a conquest, this original spatial rupture is fundamental to the constitution of human society, for it marks the emergence of culture.[162] An essential tool to enable a society to think about itself, transgression in the last resort defines and consolidates a community's identity.

---

[161] 'They did not yet have fixed dwellings on this land' (*Genesis B* 784^{b}–785^{a}).
[162] On this point, see Marc Augé, 'Eroi', in *Enciclopedia Einaudi*, ed. Giulio Einaudi, 16 vols. (Turin: Einaudi, 1977–82), v. 636–56 (637–8).

3

The Centres of *Beowulf*: A Complex Spatial Order

THE creation topos, examined in the previous chapter, is again pervasive in *Beowulf*—in the Scyld episode, in the building of Heorot, in the song of creation, in the consequences of the hero's victory over Grendel. Investigating questions of creation and beginnings, the poem betrays a special interest in the genesis of kingdoms, in how they are formed and how they can ensure their survival. This attention to origins raises a number of questions linked to spatial organization and territorial authority, for epic poems bring together two closely related issues: control of space and the coming into being of a given society.[1] Paul Zumthor relates these texts to processes of territorialization; he says that 'nos épopées doivent être considérées dans la perspective de la formation de communautés sociales et culturelles au moment où s'amorce le procès d'où sortiront les nations modernes: phase de "territorialisation" où, dans l'imaginaire, dans les discours, non moins que sur le terrain, exister c'est occuper, délimiter, défendre.'[2] To occupy, to delimit, to defend: this is precisely what is at stake in *Beowulf*, where communities first have to exist in space. Peter Clemoes reminds us that, from an institutional point of view, the kings depicted in *Beowulf* rule over peoples and not countries.[3] And yet, to secure a territory and to prosper is a recurrent

---

[1] The notion that *Beowulf* is an epic has been challenged by Tolkien and, more recently, by Stanley. See J. R. R. Tolkien, 'Beowulf: The Monsters and the Critics', in R. D. Fulk (ed.), *Interpretations of Beowulf: A Critical Anthology* (Bloomington: Indiana University Press, 1991; first publ. in *Proceedings of the British Academy*, 22 (1936), 245–95), 14–44 (34) and Eric G. Stanley, *In the Foreground:* Beowulf (Cambridge: Brewer, 1994), 64.

[2] Paul Zumthor, *La Mesure du Monde* (Paris: Seuil, 1993), 383. On this point, see also James W. Earl, *Thinking about Beowulf* (Stanford, CA: Stanford University Press, 1994), 38.

[3] Peter Clemoes, *Interactions of Thought and Language in Old English Poetry*, Cambridge Studies in Anglo-Saxon England, 12 (Cambridge: Cambridge University Press, 1995), 4–5.

concern of the *Beowulf* poet, thus testifying to the importance of spatial control and of land possession. To occupy a tract of ground literally means to exist as a group. The first task of the good leader is to protect the homeland, and epic poetry preserves the memory of its original conquest from monsters or hostile neighbours.

To define its own space, a society needs to organize itself around a focal point: the centre is an essential element in any actual or imaginary spatial configuration. But, as Zumthor points out, 'à cette perpétuelle re-centration, à cette saturation de l'espace, s'oppose et se combine une tendance à sans cesse frôler une limite'.[4] The epic genre is thus doubly polarized, for the establishment of a centre allows, and even inevitably entails, the construction of the periphery and the margins. *Beowulf*'s geography combines these two impulses: a continual attempt at localizing the centre and a perpetual anxiety about the precise situation and the maintenance of a frontier dividing 'us' from 'them'.

This chapter focuses mainly on *Beowulf*; when relevant, it alludes to *Judith*, a poem that, with the emphasis it places on transgression and on the confrontation of two hostile enemies, echoes many of the issues raised by the epic. My reading will pay particular attention to these two texts' spatial constructs and it will analyse their geographical organization. More precisely, it will examine the poems' various places and their notions of centre and periphery. My discussion of *Beowulf*'s loci will in particular challenge any clear-cut division between the realms of the 'civilized' and the 'monstrous'; it will lead me, in a second moment, to call into question the very notion of the centre. What constitutes a centre? Can a 'civilized' centre survive? The motif of invasion is closely linked to these issues; for, centres are always under threat. The foreign is constantly irrupting at the heart of the familiar, both in the main body of the poem, that is, in the account of Beowulf's fights against the monsters, and in the more historical material included in the text. My reflections on how the rulers in *Beowulf* deal with the foreign will introduce the notion of the gaze, a means to assimilate and tame alien visitors. The present chapter will close on a discussion of a cluster of images used to signal territorial appropriation, such as treading and stepping on the earth. The ambiguity intrinsic to the landscape of *Beowulf*, a fantasy construct, the complex links between monstrosity and periphery, as well as the problematic drawing and establishment of boundaries point to the fundamental ambiguity inherent in the idea of territorial sovereignty.

[4] Zumthor, *Mesure du Monde*, 384.

One should always be aware, when reading *Beowulf*, of an important temporal displacement: the poem tells us as much, if not more, about the poet's contemporary period as about a distant past. This idea is implicit in Zumthor's first quotation, with its recognition that epic narratives encompass a formative process uniting past and present. James W. Earl clearly spells out this dual aspect when he says that the past is idealized in heroic literature; that it is 'not exactly a reconstruction of earlier history, but a narrative representation of contemporary social concerns, energies, and ideals, projected onto the past'.[5] Aware of these difficulties, I will not focus on spatial questions of the Migration Age, that is, on the geographical situation of the Geats and the Danes on the Continent during the fifth and the sixth centuries. I shall on the contrary concentrate on the information that can be gathered from the poem about the Anglo-Saxons' spatial *imaginaire* and on patterns of thought recurrent in the way they talked about and represented space. In what follows, questions dealing with centre and periphery, with invasion and integration, and with the problematic establishment of boundaries will be foregrounded.[6]

THE PLACES OF *BEOWULF*

Kings' Hall and Monsters' Dens: Opposition?

Scholars often organize *Beowulf*'s geography around two opposite poles: the realms of good governance and that of monstrosity.[7] To the former belong Heorot, the hero's hall in the land of the Geats, and his burial

---

[5] Earl, *Thinking about Beowulf*, 34.

[6] Note that it is not my intention here to discuss the controversial dating of the poem, a disputed question not only for *Beowulf*, but for many of the texts under consideration in this book. My aim is rather to understand how they each contribute to produce, to define, and constantly to reshape a particular spatial *imaginaire*.

[7] See e.g. Nicholas Howe, 'The Landscape of Anglo-Saxon England: Inherited, Invented, Imagined', in John Howe and Michael Wolfe (eds.), *Inventing Medieval Landscapes: Senses of Place in Western Europe* (Gainesville: University of Florida Press, 2002), 91–112 (106); Marie-Françoise Alamichel, 'Voyage dans les paysages du *Beowulf*', in Marie-Françoise Alamichel (ed.), *Beowulf: Symbolismes et interprétations* (Paris: Éditions du Temps, 1998), 87–106 (88); Victor Schreb, 'Setting and Cultural Memory in Part II of *Beowulf*', *English Studies*, 79 (1998), 109–19 (111); Jan Čermák, '*Hie dygel lond warigeað*: Spatial Imagery in Five Beowulf Compounds', *Linguistica Pragensia*, 1 (1996), 24–34 (27); and John Halverson, 'The World of *Beowulf*', *Journal of English Literary History*, 36 (1969), 593–608 (601). For the first half of the poem, Daniel G. Calder, 'Setting and Ethos: The Pattern of Measure and Limit in *Beowulf*', *Studies in Philology*, 69 (1972), 21–37 (22).

mound; to the latter, Grendel's mere and the dragon's lair. In this binary layout, two clearly defined spheres defy and complement each other.

On the side of orderly rule, Heorot and the hero's funeral pyre mirror one another. Hroðgar erects a high and lofty hall that towers over many lands,[8] similarly, the Geats build for their dead leader: 'hlæw on hliðe, se wæs heah ond brad, | wægliðendum wide gesyne'.[9] The hero's burial mound rises high; seen from afar, it guides seafarers sailing on the ocean. Heorot fulfils a comparable function at the beginning of the poem when the coastguard watching over the Danish shores accompanies the Geats on land 'oþ þæt hy sæl timbred | geatolic ond goldfah ongyton mihton'.[10] He ensures that the newcomers will follow the right road, led as they are by the view of the regal palace.

When he recounts Heorot's construction, the poet also announces its eventual destruction. The building: 'heaðowylma bad, | laðan liges'.[11] Beowulf's stronghold meets the same fate: it is wrecked by the dragon's fire. On the morning following the monster's punitive expedition, the king learns that: 'his sylfes ham, | bolda selest brynewylmum mealt'.[12] Contrary to what happens with Heorot—which is damaged during the fight between Grendel and Beowulf and is later renovated[13]—the hero's hall is not rebuilt. Instead, a burial mound is erected to receive the champion's dead body. Fire reappears in this new construction, this time displaced unto the hero's corpse which is cremated before finding its place in the barrow. Like his own hall and Heorot, Beowulf's body meets its end in fire.[14]

As long as they can fulfil their function, both Heorot and Beowulf's hall constitute a communal space for the people. Hroðgar heads various feasts in Heorot, and if the poet never shows Beowulf presiding over a banquet in his own home, the speech Wiglaf delivers before helping the

---

[8] *Beowulf* 81^a–82^b. *Beowulf and the Fight at Finnsburg*, ed. by F. Klaeber, 3rd edn. (Lexington, MA: Heath, 1922; repr. 1950).
[9] 'a barrow on the cliff, which was high and large, visible from afar to seafarers' (*Beowulf* 3157–8).
[10] 'until they could see the timbered hall, splendid and decorated with gold' (*Beowulf* 307^b–308).
[11] 'awaited the hostile flame, the hateful fire' (*Beowulf* 82^b–83^a).
[12] 'his own home, the best of halls, melted in the surge of fire' (*Beowulf* 2325^b–2326).
[13] *Beowulf* 991–1002^a.
[14] On the analogy the poet establishes between the poem's significant places and bodies, see Alamichel, 'Voyage', 103. More generally, see also Joyce Tally Lionarons, 'Bodies, Buildings and Boundaries: Metaphors of Liminality in Old English and Old Norse', *Essays in Medieval Studies*, 11 (1994), 43–50.

hero in his fight against the dragon clearly indicates that such ceremonies did take place in his lord's hall. The warrior says:

> Ic ðæt mæl geman, þær we medu þegun,
> þonne we geheton ussum hlaforde
> in biorsele, ðe us ðas beagas geaf,
> þæt we him ða guðgetawa gyldan woldon[15]

The lords—Beowulf or Hroðgar—give out treasure, so that their warriors stand by them in times of need. Discussing the concept of the hall in Old English poetry, Kathryn Hume points out that 'what the poem celebrates is, of course, not simply the hall as a building, but the social system associated with it'.[16] In the hall, ties are created between the king and his retainers that ensure the good functioning of society, and Heorot and Beowulf's palace are places of social bonding.

Grendel's attacks upset this harmonious balance and plunge Heorot in a state of aporia. They paralyse the Danish social system: Hroðgar's followers cannot fight for their lord and no pledges are exchanged in a hall which no longer grants protection to the warriors. Beowulf's stronghold becomes similarly useless as a result of the dragon's raid. The monster's assaults wreck not only the hero's hall, but also, as the poet specifies, the *gifstol Geata*.[17] The Geats' throne is destroyed, that is, the place where regal authority is exercised, the seat of power of a particular tribe. Interestingly, the poet also mentions the *gifstol* during Grendel's incursion in Heorot, to say that 'no he þone gifstol gretan moste'.[18] Even though this passage is difficult to interpret, it nevertheless suggests that the monster cannot go near the throne, either to attack it or simply to approach it.[19] These lines bring to mind Henri Lefebvre's comments

---

[15] 'I remember the time when we drank mead, when, in the beer-hall, we promised our lord, the one who gave us rings, that we would repay him for the war-equipment' (*Beowulf* 2633–6).

[16] Kathryn Hume, 'The Concept of the Hall in Old English Poetry', *Anglo-Saxon England*, 3 (1974), 63–74 (64). See also Hugh Magennis, *Images of Community in Old English Poetry*, Cambridge Studies in Anglo-Saxon England, 18 (Cambridge: Cambridge University Press, 1996), 35.

[17] 'the throne of the Geats' (*Beowulf* 2327ª).

[18] 'he could not approach the throne' (*Beowulf* 168).

[19] For a discussion of these lines, see *Beowulf: A Student Edition*, ed. by George Jack (Oxford: Clarendon Press, 1994), 38, and *Beowulf and the Fight at Finnsburg*, ed. Klaeber, 134. Heaney, Mitchell and Robinson, Jack, Donaldson, Bradley, and Klaeber all take the pronoun *he* to refer to Grendel. *Beowulf*, trans. by Seamus Heaney (London: Faber and Faber, 1999); *Beowulf: An Edition with Relevant Shorter Texts*, ed. by Bruce Mitchell and Fred C. Robinson (Oxford: Blackwell, 1998); *Beowulf*, trans. by E. T. Donaldson,

on monumental space, a space that organizes its texture around relevant points such as a sanctuary or a throne. Defined by what can, and consequently what cannot and should not, happen in it, it becomes the metaphorical, almost metaphysical support of a society.[20] When Grendel or the dragon destroy the regal seat therefore, their actions affect the whole of society. As conquerors or revolutionaries do, they attack monuments in order to obliterate a community.[21] In raiding Heorot and the hero's stronghold, they challenge a space that offers to each of its members the image of his or her belonging, and that erases the violence inherent in its establishment.[22] Once the *gifstol* is wrecked, the Danes or the Geats can no longer weave their social bonds. This is the root of the monsters' terrifying power, 'because they destroy the hall and with it all possibility of communal life'.[23] Their attacks annihilate the very possibility for a community to conceive of itself as a unified whole, and they thus announce a people's ultimate dispersion and destruction.

Towering high in the landscape, seen from afar, linked to fire: Heorot, Beowulf's hall and his funeral pyre form a cluster of analogous places. A likeness can also be detected between Grendel's mere and the dragon's cave. Both are for instance located underground. Beowulf dives into the lake to find the enemy hall, and when Grendel's mother notices the foreign visitor, she grasps him and: 'Bær þa seo brimwylf, þa heo to botme com, | hringa þengel to hofe sinum'.[24] The hostile creature's home is situated at the bottom, *to botme*, of the pond. The way to the dragon's lair also lies underground; beneath the stone barrow, 'stig under læg'.[25] The poet often places this cave 'under' another geographical feature: 'under harne stan', 'under eorðweall', 'under inwithrof'.[26] And when the dragon returns home after his attack, he flies down toward his lair:

---

in *The Norton Anthology of English Literature*, ed. by M. H. Abrams and others, 6th edn., 2 vols. (New York: Norton, 1962; repr. 1993), i. 27–68; and *Anglo-Saxon Poetry*, trans. by S. A. J. Bradley (London: Dent, 1982). For a different view, see Stanley B. Greenfield, ' "Gifstol" and Goldhord in *Beowulf* ', in *Hero and Exile: The Art of Old English Poetry* (London: Hambledon, 1989), 33–42 (esp. 36–7).

[20] Henri Lefebvre, *La Production de l'espace* (Paris: Anthropos, 1974), 258–9.
[21] Lefebvre, *Production de l'espace*, 254.   [22] Ibid, 253.
[23] Nicholas Howe, *Migration and Mythmaking in Anglo-Saxon England* (New Haven: Yale University Press, 1989), 162.
[24] 'When she came to the bottom, the she-wolf of the water bore the ring-mailed prince to her house' (*Beowulf* 1506–7).
[25] 'a path lay underneath' (*Beowulf* 2213^b).
[26] 'under a grey rock', 'under a mound', 'under an evil roof' (*Beowulf* 2744^b, 3090^a, 3123^b).

'nyðer eft gewat | dennes niosian'.[27] In her essay on the landscapes of *Beowulf*, Marie-Françoise Alamichel observes that the monsters are situated under the earth and she adds: 'à cet *infernum* ('le lieu d'en-bas') s'opposent les hautes falaises, les promontoires et collines, les palais du pays des hommes, majestueux et élancés: le Haut est refusé aux monstres'.[28] A high/low dichotomy contrasts human and monstrous dwellings: while the latter are confined to the lower regions, the former tower over many lands (Heorot) or are seen from afar (Heorot and Beowulf's barrow).

Grendel's mere and the dragon's lair are mysterious places; they are hidden away underground and their positions in the geography of the poem pose problems. When the poet first relates Grendel's attacks on Heorot, he specifies that 'men ne cunnon, | hwyder helrunan hwyrftum scriþað'.[29] The paths the demons tread are unknown to men, and so is the location of their abode. After Grendel's mother avenges her son's death in Heorot, the king says that he does not know where she has fled.[30] He adds that the two monsters 'dygel lond | warigeað'.[31] It thus seems that the Danes, and Hroðgar in particular, do not know where the mere lies and where the two fiends dwell. And yet, contradicting this conclusion, the king provides Beowulf with a detailed description of the enemy lake after specifying that: 'Nis þæt feor heonon | milgemearces, þæt se mere standeð'.[32] The mere would then not be far from Heorot and not so secret after all.

On the morning of Beowulf's victory over Grendel, people come from afar to look at the enemy's severed arm hanging in Heorot. Some of them also travel to the shores of the monsters' lake. At this point, the poet uses a subtle narrative device to transport his audience, together with the warriors who look at the hand, from the hall to the mere. The demon's footsteps provide the spatial transition between the two places:

> No his lifgedal
> sarlic þuhte   secga ænegum
> þara þe tirleases   trode sceawode,
> hu he werigmod   on weg þanon,

---

[27] 'he went back down to seek out his lair' (*Beowulf* 3044ᵇ–3045ᵃ).
[28] Alamichel, 'Voyage' 96.
[29] 'men did not know where the demons move on in circles' (*Beowulf* 162ᵇ–163).
[30] *Beowulf* 1331ᵇ–1333ᵃ.
[31] 'inhabit a secret land' (*Beowulf* 1357ᵇ–1358ᵃ).
[32] 'Measured in miles, it is not far hence that the mere lies' (*Beowulf* 1361ᵃ–1362).

> niða ofercumen, on nicera mere
> fæge ond geflymed feorhlastas bær.
> Ðær wæs on blode brim weallende³³

The warriors look at Grendel's tracks in Heorot and, in the following line, they are standing on the shore of the lake. Such a literary construction suggests that the characters have followed the monster's trail to the pool. In a similar fashion, when, after the avenging raid of Grendel's mother, Hroðgar sets out for the mere with Beowulf and a company of retainers, the poet says: 'Lastas wæron | æfter waldswaþum wide gesyne, | gang ofer grundas'.³⁴ Here again, the warriors retrace the monstrous woman's bloody footprints. The Danes, and Hroðgar in particular, are presented as ignorant of the whereabouts of the Grendelkin, of the nature of their shelter, to which they cannot travel unless there is a path leading to it. The king and his men have to follow the tracks the monsters leave behind to go to the mere. Yet they know about Grendel and his mother, about the mere; they are aware that it does not lie far away and they can even describe it. There is therefore a fundamental ambiguity surrounding the location and the nature of the monsters' lake: it is at the same time alien and familiar, hidden from men and near Heorot.

A similar ambiguity is attached to the position of the dragon's lair. The way there is 'eldum uncuð'.³⁵ Yet the last survivor who buries his people's treasure finds a barrow ready to shelter it: 'Beorh eallgearo | wunode on wonge wæteryðum neah, | niwe be næsse'.³⁶ Later in the poem, Beowulf's instructions concerning his burial mound echo this passage: the hero's tomb should be erected near the sea, 'æt brimes nosan'.³⁷ It should be a memorial to Beowulf and it should 'heah hlifian on Hronesnæsse'.³⁸ These two barrows—the hero's and the dragon's—are situated by the sea and they commemorate either a dead leader or an extinct people. The similarities connecting Beowulf's tomb to the mound the last survivor finds for the treasure suggest that the

---

³³ 'His death did not seem grievous to any of the warriors who looked at the tracks of the vanquished one, how he, disheartened, overcome by battle, doomed to die, and put to flight, left bloody tracks away from there to the lake of monsters. There the water surged with blood' (*Beowulf* 841ᵇ–847).
³⁴ 'Footprints were visible far and wide along the forest paths, tracks over the earth' (*Beowulf* 1402ᵇ–1404ᵃ).
³⁵ 'unknown to men' (*Beowulf* 2214ᵃ).
³⁶ 'A cave quite ready was situated on a plain near the waves of the sea, new by the headland' (*Beowulf* 2241ᵇ–2243ᵃ).
³⁷ 'near a sea promontory' (*Beowulf* 2803ᵇ).
³⁸ 'tower high over Hronesness' (*Beowulf* 2805).

latter may also, at one point, have stood out in the countryside and have been visible from afar. When it receives the dead people's gold, the barrow 'wunode on wonge', it is not yet secret and concealed beneath the earth.[39] By the time the dragon occupies the cave, it is unknown to men, hidden underground. As if by magic, the barrow is now difficult of access; it may have been openly visible, but it has become hard to locate. Like Grendel's abode, the dragon's cave occupies a shifting and ambiguous place in *Beowulf*'s poetic geography.

Enigmatic and uncertain locations are also found in *Judith*. The Assyrian leader Holofernes, the heroine's enemy, can be equated with the monsters of the epic poem, with the hostile presences which lurk in the vicinity and threaten an established community (the Danes, the Geats, or, in this case, the Hebrews). The inmost part of Holofernes's pavilion, his bed, is one of the poem's significant places and it is enveloped in a halo of mystery. Surrounded by a marvellous curtain which functions as a two-way mirror, it allows the ruler to look outside toward his retainers but hides him from their view. This artefact transforms the bed into a mysterious site; like Grendel's mere and the dragon's cave, it is a place that is near at hand and yet invisible. Thus, when Judith ventures to the enemy camp, she penetrates a strange and alien space imitating Beowulf when he fights Grendel's mother or Wiglaf when he enters the dragon's barrow.

The apparent dichotomy opposing royal halls (centres of power towering high in the countryside, reduced to a state of aporia by hostile onslaughts, eventually destroyed by fire) and monsters' abodes (mysterious places, hidden away and yet near at hand) invites the classification of the settings of *Beowulf* into two neatly distinguishable categories: the world of men on the one hand and that of monsters on the other. And yet this conclusion, seemingly so simple, deserves futher attention.

Kings' Halls and Monsters' Dens: Similarities?

A second look at the categories outlined above calls them into question, for parallels can be drawn between Heorot and Grendel's mere on the one hand, and between the dragon's cave and the hero's hall or his burial mound on the other. Heorot and Grendel's lake are for instance situated close to one another and each has its own ruler: Hroðgar controls the Danish kingdom while the monster and his mother exercise authority

---

[39] The barrow 'was situated on a plain' (*Beowulf* 2242^a).
[40] *Beowulf* 103–104^a and 1497^b–1499^a.

over the fenland and the pond.[40] Heorot and the mere are conflicting centres of power in the land of the Danes. One regulates the world of men while the other dominates the monsters' domain.

These two provinces do not coexist peacefully side by side, for each impinges on the other's territorial sphere. Uninvited guests or avenging strangers penetrate both Grendel's and Hroðgar's halls.[41] The hero, the monster, and his mother all travel to a foreign stronghold to redress their wrongs and to retaliate against their enemies. Grendel, disturbed by the noise of feasting in Heorot, or, as suggested in Chapter 2, enraged by the new territorial organization following the building of Heorot, first requites his grudge on human society in Hroðgar's hall. Subsequently, his mother avenges his death by raiding the Danish palace, and Beowulf retaliates against the monstrous woman on her own ground, in her underwater cave.

These intrusive raids unfold following a comparable sequence of events. During their visit, the uninvited guests all attack someone lying down on a bench. When in Heorot, Grendel seizes and kills Hondscioh, a Geatish warrior: 'he gefeng hraðe forman siðe | slæpendne rinc'.[42] On the night he meets his death, before he faces the Geatish hero, the hostile visitor first kills a man asleep in the hall. In the underwater den, during his second fight, Beowulf defeats the monster's mother and then beheads Grendel. The hero sees his former opponent lying on a bed:

> he [Beowulf] on ræste geseah
> guðwerigne Grendel licgan,
> aldorleasne...
> ...
> ... ond hine þa heafde becearf.[43]

Both in Heorot and in Grendel's hall, a sleeping or a dead warrior is the victim of the invading stranger's violence.

Further echoes resonate between these two scenes: Beowulf beheads the monster in his own home, just as the latter attacked the Geatish champion in Heorot,[44] which, one remembers, the king had entrusted

---

[41] On the reversals of the host and guest relationships in the poem, see Joyce Tally Lionarons, '*Beowulf*: Myth and Monsters', *English Studies*, 77 (1996), 1–14 (7–11).
[42] 'at the first occasion, he quickly seized a sleeping warrior' (*Beowulf* 740–1ᵃ).
[43] 'he saw Grendel, worn out by war, lie dead on a bed... and he cut off his head' (*Beowulf* 1585ᵇ–1590).
[44] On this point, see Edward B. Irving, Jr., *Rereading Beowulf* (Philadelphia: University of Pennsylvania Press, 1989), 150.

to the hero.⁴⁵ Moreover, these two encounters between Grendel and Beowulf are prefaced by a fight opposing one of the enemy's companions: Hondscioh and the monster's mother. The Danish hall and the mere therefore witness similar fighting episodes and the poem thus builds an analogy between these two locations.

From Grendel's cave, Beowulf brings back a giant sword-hilt which he gives to Hroðgar. Runes are engraved on it:

>   on ðæm wæs or writen
> fyrngewinnes,   syðþan flod ofsloh,
> gifen geotende   giganta cyn,
> frecne geferdon⁴⁶

The king looks at the writing and learns about the giants' history; for, the hilt tells of the beginning of the *fyrngewinnes*, the ancient strife: it is a tale of origin which preserves the monsters' own history. Heorot fulfils a similar mnemonic function for mankind: it provides a place where poems are recited. These songs tell of creation and of significant episodes in the subsequent history of the Danes: the genesis of the earth (lines 90–8), Beowulf's victory over Grendel (lines 867^b–74^a), Sigemund (lines 874^b–915), Finn and Hnæf's enmity (lines 1063–159^a), or some unspecified elegy commemorating past times (lines 2105–14). The poems performed in Heorot keep alive in the audience the memory of Danish history; in Grendel's mere, runes commemorate the giants' past. Human beings and monsters value and remember their own history, especially tales of their origin. Grendel's hall cannot therefore be reduced to the mere negation of Hroðgar's stronghold: on the contrary, it is the focal point of a social system which is in competition with the Danish kingdom.

In her reflections on the concept of the hall, Kathryn Hume contends that 'when chaos and violence take the form of a definite antagonist, a malignant being, its dwelling becomes an anti-hall'.⁴⁷ She distributes the core conceits of the hall-cluster in two separate categories: 'gift-giving, loyalty and *wynn* on the one hand, and strife, storm and the anti-hall on the other'.⁴⁸ And yet Grendel's cave includes some of the elements that Hume assigns to the hall. For instance, the fact that the monster's death is avenged suggests that loyalty is valued and that its duties are

---

⁴⁵ *Beowulf* 655–61.
⁴⁶ 'on it, the origin of the ancient strife was written when, after the flood, the rushing sea killed the race of giants, they fared terribly' (*Beowulf* 1688^b–1691^a).
⁴⁷ Hume, 'Concept of the Hall', 68.   ⁴⁸ Ibid.

taken seriously in this other realm. The idea that Grendel's grotto, as an anti-hall, would not offer protection against storm is also open to question; for, when Beowulf arrives in Grendel's hall, he notices that he is in a place:

> þær him nænig wæter wihte ne scepede,
> ne him for hrofsele hrinan ne mehte
> færgripe flodes[49]

The monsters' cave keeps the hostile flood away. And to the wounded troll, his den represents a desirable and welcoming place. After fighting Beowulf in Heorot, he flees to his grotto and: 'in fenfreoðo feorh alegde'.[50] The compound *fenfreoðo*, with the element *freoðo*, 'peace, security, protection, a refuge' decidedly indicates that the underwater cave shelters and protects its inhabitants.[51] In it, a brilliant light, a *blacne leoman* shines.[52] This hostile place therefore becomes 'a circle of light and peace enclosed by darkness, discomfort and danger', which is precisely how Hume defines the hall.[53] The monsters' cave offers protection against hostile natural elements; it is a place of security and comfort. It is associated with light, just as Heorot is said to radiate over many lands.[54] The lake dwelling can therefore be compared to a royal hall, and as Irving sums up, 'we see one hall pitted against another'.[55] A close analysis of the Danish kingdom's main places demonstrates that Heorot and Grendel's mere, far from being opposite sites, are in fact mirrors of each other.

The preceding chapter has analysed the close links existing between the opening of *Beowulf* and creation narratives. The spatial situation prevailing in Hroðgar's realm after Grendel's apparition in fact strongly echoes *Genesis B*'s depiction of the world after the fall. The biblical poem ironically describes Satan's rule in hell as that of a lord surrounded by his followers.[56] Immediately after his banishment from heaven, the fallen

---

[49] 'where no water could harm him at all, nor could the sudden attack of the flood reach him because of the roofed hall' (*Beowulf* 1514–1516ª).
[50] 'gave up his life in the fen-refuge' (*Beowulf* 851).
[51] For a different reading of this passage, see Magennis, *Images of Community*, 132.
[52] *Beowulf* 1517ª.   [53] Hume, 'Concept of the Hall', 64.
[54] *Beowulf* 311.   [55] Irving, *Rereading Beowulf*, 150.
[56] See Peter J. Lucas, 'Loyalty and Obedience in the Old English *Genesis* and the Interpolation of *Genesis B* into *Genesis A*', *Neophilologus*, 76 (1992), 121–35; *The Saxon Genesis*, ed. by A. N. Doane (Madison: University of Wisconsin Press, 1991), 123; Maria Vittoria Molinari, 'La caduta degli angeli ribelli: considerazioni sulla *Genesis B*', *Annali, Istituto Orientale di Napoli (AION), Filologia Germanica*, 18–19 (1985–6), 417–40; and R. E. Woolf, 'The Devil in Old English Poetry', *Review of English Studies*, NS 4 (1953), 1–12 (8).

angel is called 'se ofermoda cyning', an expression which suggests that he may not have lost all his power.[57] He asks his followers to bring about the fall of mankind and here is the promise he makes to the successful devil: 'sittan læte ic hine wið me sylfne'.[58] As a reward, Satan offers what he and his companions have forfeited when they rebelled, that is, a place of honour next to the ruler of the kingdom. In this passage, Satan furthermore echoes Christ announcing that righteous human beings shall sit with him in heaven.[59] Although he considers himself bereft of his proper dominion, Satan nevertheless assumes that he can grant places in hell. He thinks that he exercises spatial power over the nether regions, an assumption that turns him into a contrasting image of God ruling in heaven and on earth. His infernal kingdom is a distorted reflection of the celestial domain, a relationship analogous to the one uniting Grendel's mere and Heorot.

In *Beowulf* the relationships between the world of humans and of monsters become more complex as the narrative progresses; for, in the poem's second part, the spatial layout is organized around three focal points: the royal palace, the monster's cave, and the hero's tomb. Let us first consider Beowulf's hall and the dragon's lair. The monster's fire destroys the *gifstol* of the Geats in retaliation for the cup a slave steals from the dragon's hoard. Without a throne from which to distribute treasure, the hero can no longer be a king to his people and his hall ceases to be a communal place of exchange. The dragon's barrow also eventually becomes useless and the monster, when dead, can of course no longer enjoy it. The *Beowulf* poet specifically says that the beast: 'hæfde eorðscrafa ende genyttod'.[60] Once the dragon is dead, its lair is repeatedly invaded and its treasure thoroughly plundered. The barrow is left empty and useless, no longer fulfilling its original function, that is, no longer sheltering a treasure. Both Beowulf's hall and his enemy's den are utterly destroyed and they become purposeless ruins.

While correspondences between these two locations are indisputable, it is more rewarding, in thinking of the poem's geography, to focus on the dragon's lair and the hero's burial mound. In keeping with the elegiac tone that characterizes the second part of the poem, it is the

---

[57] 'the proud king' (*Genesis B* 338ª).
[58] 'I will let him sit beside me' (*Genesis B* 438ª).
[59] See for instance Luke 22: 28–29 and Matthew 19: 28.
[60] 'he had used his earthly caverns to the end' (*Beowulf* 3046). Klaeber quotes Earle's translation for this line: 'he had made his last use of earth(ly) caverns'. *Beowulf and the Eight*, ed. Klaeber, 225. John Earle, trans., *The Deeds of Beowulf* (Oxford: Clarendon Press, 1892), 100.

latter that most clearly echoes the monster's cave. The *Beowulf* poet, for instance, links the motif of the last survivor to both these places. The gold the dragon appropriates is first buried by an anonymous character who has outlived his entire people and who is referred to as 'se ðær lengest hwearf, | weard winegeomor'.[61] He is the one who remains alive when everybody else has passed away. As for Beowulf, just before dying, he gives all the necessary recommendations about how to build his burial mound. He addresses Wiglaf one last time and tells him that he is the ultimate representative of their race:

> Þu eart endelaf   usses cynnes,
> Wægmundinga;   ealle wyrd forsweop
> mine magas   to metodsceafte[62]

Subsequently, Wiglaf conducts Beowulf's funeral, he watches over the construction of Beowulf's barrow, and he buries the treasure and his lord's body in the same tomb. Beowulf's last words to him further suggest that his own death will eventually mark the extinction of the Wægmundings. Wiglaf becomes another last survivor figure.

The motif of the complete destruction of a people resurfaces again when the Geats' destruction is announced. Wiglaf addresses reproachful words to the timorous retainers who fled to the wood instead of helping their lord in his fight against the dragon. He says that when their enemies hear of their cowardice, they will attack and send the Geats in exile:

> londrihtes mot
> þære mægburge   monna æghwylc
> idel hweorfan,   syððan æðelingas
> feorran gefricgean   fleam eowerne[63]

Similarly, the messenger who informs Beowulf's people of the death of its leader tells the Geats that warriors and beautiful women will have to tread the paths of exile, deprived of gold.[64] Both Wiglaf and the Geats are therefore unhappy survivors to Beowulf. They reflect the figure of the last survivor as only exile, death, and destruction await them. This motif tightly links the dragon's barrow to Beowulf's burial mound and it confers to the latter great prominence in the poem's geography.

---

[61] 'the one who lived longest, the guardian mourning for his friends' (*Beowulf* 2238ᵇ–2239ᵃ).

[62] 'You are the last remnant of our race, the Wægmundings; fate swept off all my kinsmen to death' (*Beowulf* 2813–15).

[63] 'each man of your clan must go deprived of land-privileges, when the men from afar have heard of your flight' (*Beowulf* 2886ᵇ–2889).

[64] *Beowulf* 3017ᵇ–3019.

Geographical ambiguity

Under closer scrutiny, an analysis grouping together the relevant places of the first part of the poem, the part set in Denmark on the one hand, and that of the second half, located in the Geatish homeland, on the other, is not satisfactory, for it does not account for the echoes and similitudes that exist between all of *Beowulf*'s loci. Architectural elements connect the dragon's lair, Heorot, and Grendel's cave, for instance. As he approaches the enemy's den for his third fight, Beowulf notices stone-arches, features which are mentioned again when the hero is about to die:

> seah on enta geweorc,
> hu ða stanbogan stapulum fæste
> ece eorðreced innan healde.[65]

The presence of pillars and arches indicates that the dragon's abode consists of an edifice that has been built. Moreover, when the poet tells of the origins of the treasure, he says that the last survivor who buried it found a *beorh eallgearo, nearocræftum fæst*, as if waiting to receive the precious rings.[66] The barrow is ready and protected by mysterious powers: somebody must therefore have prepared it for subsequent use. I do not wish to come back here in any great detail to the account of Heorot's construction, a topic which has been dealt with in the preceding chapter. Let me just mention that the hall is secured with iron bonds, just as the dragon's barrow is reinforced by strong pillars.[67] As to Grendel's hall, called a *hrofsele*, it has a roof or a ceiling.[68] Again, Heorot's roof is mentioned after the fight opposing Grendel and Beowulf: it is the only part of the building that escapes undamaged.[69] All these various halls, Hroðgar's palace, Grendel's den, and the dragon's barrow have been built; they are not natural refuges found in an untamed countryside.

The significant places of the poem all shelter two important things: treasure and a dead or sleeping body. Precious weapons must have hung on the walls of Grendel's abode, since the hero kills the monster's mother with a sword found in the enemy hall; he says: 'ic on wage geseah wlitig hangian | ealdsweord eacen'.[70] On a nearby bed, Grendel's

---

[65] '[he] saw the work of giants, how the age-old earth-hall contained stone-arches secured by pillars' (*Beowulf* 2717^b–2719).

[66] 'a cave quite ready', 'secured by skill in enclosing' (*Beowulf* 2241^b, 2243^b).

[67] *Beowulf* (773^b–775^a). [68] 'a roofed-hall' (*Beowulf* 1515^a).

[69] *Beowulf* (999^b–1000^a).

[70] 'I saw hanging on the wall a beautiful mighty ancient sword' (*Beowulf* 1662–3^a).

corpse rests. Heorot presents a similar picture: helmets, mail-coats, and spears are clearly visible at the heads of the sleeping warriors on the night of the she-monster's attack.[71] In the second part of the poem, the runaway slave angers the dragon because he steals a cup from the treasure while its guardian is sleeping: 'he [the dragon] slæpende besyred wurde | þeofes cræfte'.[72] This image is echoed by the poet's description of the funeral barrow Beowulf's followers build to shelter the remains of his cremated body:

> Hi on beorg dydon   beg ond siglu,
> eall swylce hyrsta,   swylce on horde ær
> niðhedige men   genumen hæfdon[73]

The dead hero buried with the treasure he has retrieved for his people duplicates the figure of the dragon guarding the hoard. The beast sleeps on his hoard; Beowulf lies dead on a pile of treasures; Grendel's body rests near the giant-sword; and the Geatish warriors sleep in Heorot surrounded by their weapons. *Beowulf*'s places all contain a treasure and, as Alamichel points out, 'chacun des espaces structurants du poème est un lieu double, une coque dissimulant un trésor'.[74] Heorot is decorated with precious tapestries, Hroðgar and Wealhþeow distribute gifts in the hall, tombs contain piles of gold, Grendel's cave houses valued weapons, among which an ancient sword, and the dragon's lair is a treasure-cache. In all these sites, there is a sleeping—or dead—creature with precious war-gear hanging on a wall near the bed.

These comments on *Beowulf*'s places bring to mind the beheading scene in *Judith*, a moment in which the points of contact between the two poems are particularly striking. Holofernes falls dead drunk on his bed, an unconscious body lying down. Near his reclining figure hangs the magical net, which the poet describes as *eallgylden*, all golden.[75] Moreover, Judith must have found the sword with which she kills the Assyrian ruler in his tent: the poet does not mention where it comes from, nor could one imagine that the heroine would have been allowed to carry a weapon to her meeting with Holofernes. In this

---

[71] *Beowulf* 1242–6ª. On this point, see Andy Orchard, *Pride and Prodigies: Studies in the Monsters of the Beowulf-Manuscript* (Cambridge: Brewer, 1995), 30 n. 13.

[72] '[while] sleeping, he was tricked by the cunning of a thief' (*Beowulf* 2218–19ª).

[73] 'They placed in the mound rings and jewels, all such ornaments that the hostile men had previously taken from the hoard' (*Beowulf* 3163–5).

[74] Alamichel, 'Voyage', 104.

[75] *Judith* 46ᵇ. *Beowulf and Judith*, ed. by Elliott van Kirk Dobbie, Anglo-Saxon Poetic Records, 4 (London: Routledge and Kegan Paul, 1953), 101–9.

scene, therefore, the scriptural poem brings together all the ingredients pertaining to significant places in *Beowulf*: an unconscious body, gold, and valuable objects and weapons.

The motif of the dead leader buried with great riches invites us to extend our horizon and to consider other places of *Beowulf*'s poetic geography, like Scyld's funeral vessel, for instance. During the funeral, the leader's corpse is committed to *bearm scipes*, the bosom of the ship.[76] Scyld is placed in the middle of the boat and treasure is piled up on his chest. In this programmatic episode, a now familiar spatial construct can be discerned; and Scyld's funeral ship becomes the very first of the poem's significant locations: a cache hiding a treasure and its dead guardian. Similarly, one thinks also of Finn's hall, for the Finnsburh episode opens with the cremation of Hnæf and his nephew: dead bodies are burned inside the hall, surrounded by precious weapons.[77]

These various episodes, both in *Beowulf* and in *Judith*, depict places where extraordinary events happen which, it should be noticed, all involve a specific body part: the head. This is most clearly the case in the scriptural poem when the heroine beheads Holofernes and in *Beowulf* when the hero brings back the monster's head from his expedition to the underwater hall. But this body part is also associated with the other poetic places under consideration here. The dragon is roused by the slave's intrusion and, crucially, the stolen cup lies by the beast's head. The intruder stepped 'dyrnan cræfte dracan heafde neah'.[78] Is it because the slave ventures so close to its head that the hoard's guardian is furious? When the Geats settle for the night in Heorot, they 'setton him to heafdon hilderandas, | bordwudu beorhtan'.[79] Heads and precious objects are again collocated. In the Scyld episode, attention is also drawn to the Danish king's head when the poet mentions that his followers place 'segen gyldenne | heah ofer heafod'.[80] All these scenes are built on a cluster of images including a reclining figure, weapons, and precious objects, and something happening to the head.

Grendel and the dragon, monstrous though they may be, are not merely wild creatures confined to natural shelters. Discussing places of community in Old English poetry, Hugh Magennis states that, in *Beowulf*, 'the symbol of its [humankind's] life of civilization is not

---

[76] *Beowulf* 35ᵇ.   [77] *Beowulf* 1107–13.
[78] 'with secret cunning near the dragon's head' (*Beowulf* 2290).
[79] They 'placed their battle-shields, their bright wooden shields at their heads' (*Beowulf* 1242–3ᵃ).
[80] 'a high, golden standard over his head' (*Beowulf* 47ᵇ–48ᵃ).

"domesticated" landscape, but the hall building in the stronghold, withstanding both human enemies and the menace of the wilderness'.[81] He adds that 'Grendel and his mother are associated with the wilderness, the unknown and threatening world beyond the stronghold and its environs... and the dragon which afflicts Beowulf's people lives "on þære westenne".'[82] Although such a reading cannot be denied, I believe that the opposition monstrous/civilized could be overemphasized and could consequently overshadow the fact that the three monsters are consistently associated with a hall that has been built and that offers them protection, which shelters history and precious artefacts, which, in short, contains many elements pertaining to 'civilization', as Hroðgar's hall embodies it.[83]

Because of the numerous parallels, reversals, and correspondences that exist between all the places constitutive of the poem's geography, the world of *Beowulf* cannot be schematized as a sphere of human glory and order threatened by dark, destructive forces to be kept at bay. On the contrary, the various domains are intimately connected and the only clear distinction established between chaos and order is that made by the characters themselves.[84] The similarities and overlaps between the abodes of kings and of their enemies must be recognized and investigated, for they prevent a dualistic reading of the poem's geography. They invite the audience to acknowledge the text's own ambiguity with regard to its spatial organization. It discloses an anxiety about where exactly the civilized and the monstrous, the friendly and the threatening are located. In the last instance, it raises fundamental questions such as: where is the centre situated? Or what exactly is a centre? I now turn my attention to these interrogations.

CENTRES AND INVASIONS

Attempts at Definition

As I hope the preceding section has made clear, a careful study of *Beowulf*'s geography invites questions about what lies at the heart

---

[81] Magennis, *Images of Community*, 128.
[82] 'in the wasteland' (*Beowulf* 2298ᵃ). Magennis, *Images of Community*, 130.
[83] For a different view, see Jennifer Neville, *Representations of the Natural World in Old English Poetry*, Cambridge Studies in Anglo-Saxon England, 27 (Cambridge: Cambridge University Press, 1999), 70–4.
[84] S. L. Dragland, 'Monster-Man in *Beowulf*', *Neophilologus*, 61 (1977), 606–18 (615).

of both human realms and monstrous domains. Following on these observations, I would like here to focus on the location and description of the poem's centres. In the first part of the text, the focal point for mankind clearly seems to be Heorot. Every movement converges towards the royal hall and, inside the building, toward Hroðgar: 'the centrality of his [Hroðgar's] position is implied in Beowulf's first approach to him, from sentinel to Heorot to the King's intermediary . . . to the King himself: Beowulf moves in definite stages from the periphery to the center'.[85] The hero's journey is over not when he lands in Denmark, but only when he is face to face with the king.

But the text contradicts this simple geography: it problematizes the notion of the centre and more precisely the question of who exactly occupies it. When the monsters attack, the king is not physically present in Heorot: he spends the night with his wife in her bower. Neither do his warriors sleep in the hall; afraid of Grendel's hatred, they prefer to rest somewhere else:

> Þa wæs eaðfynde   þe him elles hwær
> gerumlicor   ræste sohte,
> bed æfter burum[86]

One may wonder how many Danes guard their hall once the sun sets. A tentative explanation of this desertion of Heorot could be that at night the king is metaphorically present in his stronghold through the *gifstol* the monster cannot approach. But this optimistic reading is undermined by the poet's assertion that, since Hroðgar's warriors seek shelter away from the hall at the end of the day, Grendel 'swa rixode . . . | ana wið eallum'.[87] At night, Hroðgar and his warriors are absent from the hall, and the monster takes control.

The situation in Heorot changes with Beowulf's arrival. Before retiring for the night, Hroðgar entrusts the hall to the Geatish hero. He wishes him *winærnes geweald*,[88] and tells him:

> Næfre ic ænegum men   ær alyfde,
> . . .

---

[85] Halverson, 'World of *Beowulf*', 595. On the various steps Beowulf goes through when landing in Denmark, see also Teresa Pàroli, 'La soglia come cronotopo narrativo ed esistenziale nel medioevo germanico', in Paola Cabibbo (ed.), *Sulla soglia: questioni di liminalità in letteratura* (Rome: Il Calamo, 1993), 37–65 (48–50).

[86] 'It was easy to find one who tried to find for himself a resting place elsewhere, further away, a bed among the dwellings' (*Beowulf* 138–40ᵃ).

[87] 'Thus he [Grendel] ruled . . . alone against all' (*Beowulf* 144ᵃ–145ᵃ).

[88] 'control of the hall' (*Beowulf* 654ᵃ).

> ðryþærn Dena   buton þe nu ða.
> Hafa nu ond geheald   husa selest[89]

The king surrenders his control of Heorot to Beowulf, a gesture necessary for the hero to secure victory over the monster. For, if the Geatish champion is in control of the hall, consequently Grendel's attack becomes a transgression challenging his own authority, and Beowulf exercises a just vengeance when he kills his opponent.[90] 'Who holds what and on what legal basis,' David D. Day sums up, 'who exercises *mund* over a particular physical space and with what justification, seems a great concern to the poet in the Grendel section.'[91] But the credibility of this gesture is again undermined by the poet's assertion that it is Grendel, and not Hroðgar or Beowulf, who rules there at night.

The geography of the poem's second part is no longer polarized between the king's hall and the monster's cave. Identifying a centre becomes therefore all the more complicated. In Beowulf's kingdom, a human being invades the serpent's barrow and the beast retaliates for the intrusion and the theft of the cup. Does this sequence of events echo Grendel's attacks on Heorot and Beowulf's punitive expedition to the mere? If this is the case, it suggests that toward the end of the text, the spatial focal point shifts from the regal hall to the dragon's lair which in turn becomes another Heorot. The barrow is after all an attractive place for the slave who is in need of a dwelling,[92] and who fetches there an object that could enable him to re-integrate human society.[93] It is moreover a place that is invaded and from which a retaliatory expedition is launched. The barrow finally appeals to the Geats and they enter it several times when its guardian is dead: Beowulf sends Wiglaf to the cave to bring back gold and Wiglaf and other Geatish warriors subsequently plunder the hoard.[94] The dragon's cave is therefore the place to which,

---

[89] 'Never before have I entrusted . . . the Danes' splendid hall to any man but to you now. Hold and guard the best of houses now' (*Beowulf* 655–8).

[90] On this point, see David D. Day, 'Hands across the Hall: The Legalities of Beowulf's Fight with Grendel', *Journal of English and Germanic Philology*, 98 (1999), 313–24 (324).

[91] Day, 'Legalities', 322. He defines *mund* as the Germanic legal concept of control or guardianship over persons and places, a term which, in addition to its specialized legal signification, has the primary meaning of 'hand' (p. 315).

[92] 'ærnes þearfa' (*Beowulf* 2225ª). Please note that the manuscript is damaged at this point and that this reading is conjectural. Most editors, however, adopt it.

[93] *Beowulf* 2281ᵇ–2283ª.   [94] *Beowulf* 2743ᵇ–6, 3120–31ª.

in the main action of the poem's second part, most people converge. In this respect, it recalls Heorot.

As the poem draws to a close, its geography becomes increasingly unsettled. The centre shifts away from the barrow and a new focal point emerges: Beowulf's tomb. The hero's pyre reflects and repeats the dragon's lair, since the gold buried in the monster's dwelling has been transferred there. In the closing lines of the poem, the tomb remains the only outstanding feature in the countryside, seen from afar by seafarers, and a point of attraction both for the warriors riding around it and for the mourning woman standing nearby. The centre of the poem's second part is therefore a barrow sheltering gold and watched over by a sleeping or a dead guardian, be it Beowulf or the dragon. It is a site that signals the dispersion and destruction of a people, of the last survivor's tribe as well as of the leaderless Geats.

How can one define and locate the focal points of the text's geography? If they are understood as places around which society is organized, one must then postulate the presence of several of them, such as Heorot or Beowulf's hall. But Grendel's cave would also fit this definition, as the monster and his mother do form a 'civilized' community. Moreover, this definition of the centre complicates the localization of a focal point in the poem's second part. There, noticeable places commemorate a people's extinction; they are signs of an absence. Resorting to another criterion, it could be said that a centre is a place occupied by a powerful ruler. But such a definition overlooks the complex issue of who rules in Heorot and in Beowulf's hall: the legitimate king or the invading monster? Similar doubts arise when considering Grendel's cave and the dragon's barrow. I would like to contend that the most rewarding way to think about the centre is to consider it as a place constantly threatened by the outside world, as a place that is in fact always invaded and violated. The notion of invasion is crucial to conceptualize centre and periphery, for before transgression, only undifferentiated space existed, as the preceding chapter has shown. Extending this argument further, I speculate that the spaces *Beowulf* depicts also need transgression to exist. The various invasions recounted in the epic do not therefore challenge an established spatial order, but they are dynamic forces that call it into being.

The spheres occupied by mankind are obviously invaded by enemies: Grendel raids Heorot, the dragon irrupts in Beowulf's hall and destroys it. Furthermore, Hroðgar, recalling his feud against Grendel, says that when he ruled the Danes in his youth, he thought that he had no enemy: 'ic me ænigne | under swegles begong gesacan ne tealde'.[95] But Grendel's appearance proves him wrong, he who interestingly calls the monster *ingenga min*, my invader.[96] He thus establishes a special connection between himself, his realm, and Grendel: the Danish kingdom does not, cannot exist without its monster.

Grendel's cave and the dragon's barrow are also violated by a foreign visitor. Beowulf enters the underwater hall when he seeks Grendel's mother on her own ground. And if, for his last battle, the hero does not go into the dragon's barrow—the fight takes place outside—the lair is nevertheless invaded, first by the runaway slave and then, after its guardian's death, by Wiglaf and his companions who plunder the hoard. To think about *Beowulf*'s places in terms of invasion shows that no unambiguous distinction can be established between the world of men and that of monsters: none is immune from the disruption caused by the sudden intrusion of a hostile stranger.

These reflections can be developed further and a close reading of the poem reveals that the notion of invasion deeply infuses the whole of the text's geography. Other episodes are modelled on this pattern, that is, they depict a visitor entering or invading someone else's sphere. Beowulf's expedition to Heorot is, for instance, structured in this way. Even though Beowulf, and especially his father Ecgþeow, are not strangers in Denmark, the poet nevertheless insists that the hero comes as a foreigner to the realm of the Danes.[97] The coastguard identifies Beowulf and his men as coming from afar. He addresses the visitors as *feorbuend* and *mereliðende*: he is immediately aware of their distant origins.[98] When addressing his king, Wulfgar announces the presence of the Geats, *feorran cumene*, and Beowulf later urges Hroðgar to grant him his request 'nu ic þus feorran com'.[99] More significantly still, the poet himself acknowledges that Beowulf is a stranger in Hroðgar's kingdom at crucial moments in the unfolding of events, such as after the hero's victory over Grendel. He says: 'Hæfde þa gefælsod se þe ær feorran com,

---

[95] 'I did not consider that I had any adversary under the expanse of the sky' (*Beowulf* 1772[b]–1773).

[96] *Beowulf* 1776[b].

[97] Hroðgar says that he knew Beowulf as a child and that he settled his father's feud: *Beowulf* 372–6 and 459–72.

[98] 'far-dwellers' and 'seafarers' (*Beowulf* 254[b], 255[a]).

[99] 'coming from afar' (*Beowulf* 361[b]); 'now that I have come from afar' (*Beowulf* 430[b]).

| . . . sele Hroðgares', calling Beowulf 'the one who came from afar'.[100] Similarly, after the hero kills Grendel's mother, he beheads the monster in his lair and the waters of the mere become gory. Danish and Geatish warriors waiting by the pond witness this phenomenon and deduce that their champion has been defeated. The Danes return to Heorot, but the Geats stay by the lake; the text reads: 'gistas setan | modes seoce ond on mere staredon'.[101] Immediately after Beowulf's second victory, therefore, the poet again reminds his audience that the Geats, and consequently their leader, are foreigners—*gistas*—in Denmark.

Moreover, when the Geats land near Heorot and proceed to the hall, the coastguard says that he will ask a young retainer to watch over their ship:

                      oþ ðæt eft byreð
ofer lagustreamas   leofne mannan
wudu wundenhals   to Wedermearce[102]

Not for one moment does he envisage that Beowulf might stay in Denmark: the Geats are foreigners who come to do whatever business they have in the realm of the Danes and then leave. They are not meant to stay.

Since Hroðgar leaves Heorot at night, since Grendel is said to rule in the hall and Beowulf to come from afar, who are therefore the opponents who fight in Heorot? The battle against the monster is given a double twist. It is not only a savage enemy—Grendel—attacking a king—Hroðgar. Rather, the fiend usurps the royal position and is destroyed by a hero who mirrors his own initial deadly invasion. The question of who has authority in Heorot (Hroðgar, Grendel, or Beowulf?) and who raids the heart of the Danish kingdom (the Geatish warrior? The monster from the fens?) remains open. The centre is an ambiguous spot: similarly, the identity and status of its leader (Who is he? Is he dead? Is he asleep?) is debatable. But what is certain is that the centre is permanently threatened by hostile invasions and that its possession is never completely secured.

---

[100] 'The one who had previously come from afar... had cleansed Hroðgar's hall' (*Beowulf* 825–6[b]).
[101] 'the strangers, sick at heart, sat down and looked at the mere' (*Beowulf* 1602[b]–1603).
[102] 'until the ship with a curved prow carries back the dear men over the sea to the land of the Weder-Geats' (*Beowulf* 296[b]–298). On the motif of a ship standing on a shore, awaiting the outcome of an adventure as topos of 'sea-voyage' type-scenes, see Earl R. Anderson, *Cynewulf: Structure, Style and Theme in his Poetry* (Rutherford, NJ: Fairleigh Dickinson University Press, 1983), 120.

The text seems to hesitate about the status and the location of its geographical focal points, for are Heorot raided by the Grendels and the dragon's barrow plundered by the Geats still strong spatial pivots in the realm? This spatial indecision is especially striking when contrasted with the pervasive creation motif which permeates the beginning of the poem. The initial geographical certainty that these scenes seemed to outline, that is, the depiction of the stage on which subsequent action will take place, is repeatedly questioned. What is at stake is and remains therefore the establishment of a lasting territorial rule and of a secure realm.

Centres and Invasions in the Poem's Historical Material

So far, I have focused on Beowulf's encounter with monsters and on the places where these battles take place. But *Beowulf* contains other loci that deserve attention, namely those in which the so-called 'historical episodes' unfold.[103] I am thinking in particular of the dynastic troubles awaiting the Danes, of the Geatish–Swedish wars, and of the battle at Finnsburh, stories in which the 'invasion motif' is of course pervasive. As a way into this material, I will consider first the two queens, Wealhþeow and Hygd, and their interventions in the process of royal succession.

During the banquet following Beowulf's victory over Grendel, Wealhþeow advises the king against leaving his kingdom to the Geatish hero. She says:

> Me man sægde,   þæt þu ðe for sunu wolde
> hererinc habban. . . .
>   . . .þinum magum læf
> folc ond rice,   þonne ðu forð scyle,
> metodsceaft seon.[104]

The queen maintains that she trusts Hroðulf will be faithful to her children, should Hroðgar die when they are still too young to rule. She objects to the accession of a foreigner to the Danish throne: she wants the kingdom to remain in the care of Hroðgar's *magum*. Like the coastguard

---

[103] I am well aware that it is impossible to establish a clear distinction between what is 'historical' and what is 'legendary' in *Beowulf*. I do, however, use terms such as 'historical material' or 'historical episodes' to distinguish the story of the hero's fights against the monsters from a wider background retracing the fates of the various tribes mentioned in the poem.
[104] 'I have been told that you wished to have the warrior as your son . . . leave your people and your kingdom to your kinsmen when you are to go forth, to meet death' (*Beowulf* 1175–80ª).

at the beginning of the poem, she is aware that foreigners should not remain in Denmark after they have successfully fulfilled their mission.

Unlike Wealhþeow, Hygd offers Beowulf the Geatish throne when Hygelac falls in Frisia, because she does not think that her son Heardred is strong enough to hold on to power:

> þær him [Beowulf] Hygd gebead   hord ond rice,
> beagas ond bregostol;   bearne ne truwode,
> þæt he wið ælfylcum   eþelstolas
> healdan cuðe,   ða wæs Hygelac dead.[105]

Beowulf refuses the Geatish queen's offer and instead acts as a guardian to the young king. He does not want to succeed to the throne while a legitimate heir can be secured. Hygd's fears are eventually proved right when Onela kills her son. The Swedish king takes revenge on Heardred because the latter offered shelter to his two rebellious nephews, Eanmund and Eadgils, in his court:

> Him þæt to mearce wearð;
> he þær for feorme   feorhwunde hleat,
> sweordes swengum,   sunu Hygelaces[106]

Heardred's death is the consequence of his hospitality: he dies *for feorme*. The arrival of foreigners at the court causes its leader's fall.

Nicholas Howe argues that in contrasting Heardred (killed in the Geatish *eþel*) with Hygelac (who meets his end in Frisia), the poet alters the geographical focus of the text by 'depicting the outside world as a threat to the homeland rather than as a proving ground for the hero'.[107] Yet, my analysis of the poem's places has indicated that the outside world is always a menace, that every centre (Heorot, the Geatish *eþel*, the monsters' abodes) is constantly threatened by invasion. When the hero proves himself in the outside world, he becomes a foreigner entering and assuming authority in somebody else's sphere of influence. Both queens are aware of the peril the outside represents for their realms. Hygd perceives that her own son is not powerful enough to repel his enemies, and she attempts to preserve the safety of the kingdom by entrusting it to

---

[105] 'there Hygd offered him [Beowulf] treasure and the kingdom, rings, and the throne; she did not trust that her son would be able to hold the ancestral throne against foreign people, now that Hygelac was dead' (*Beowulf* 2369–72).

[106] 'That was his death; Hygelac's son got there his mortal wound, a stroke of the sword, because of his hospitality' (*Beowulf* 2384ᵇ–2386).

[107] Howe, *Migration and Mythmaking*, 160.

the king's nephew, Beowulf. She thus repeats Wealhþeow's gesture who entreats Hroðgar to leave the Danish throne to his nephew, Hroðulf. The Danish queen bars the hero, a foreigner, from succeeding to power, just as Hygd attempts to keep the outside at bay when offering Beowulf the Geatish succession.

Although the threat of invasion by foreign tribes is subdued during Beowulf's reign, the circumstances in which Hæðcyn and Heardred, respectively Hygelac's brother and son, die foreshadow the annihilation of the Geatish realm. In the first instance, Hæðcyn is killed avenging previous attacks on the homeland; in the second, strangers arrive at the court and eventually cause Heardred's fall. In both cases, foreigners trespass on the kingdom's boundaries. Significantly, Beowulf's fall against the dragon leaves his realm open and vulnerable to alien threats. The messenger who announces the hero's death also says that time of war against the Franks and the Frisians is near, for these tribes have not forgotten Hygelac's raid in Frisia and their hostility remains intact. Nor are the Swedes oblivious of the battle at Ravenswood and of Ongenþeow's killing. They too represent a serious danger to the Geatish kingdom.[108] Even if these prophecies of destruction are uttered by a coward and are thus potentially open to question, they nevertheless introduce a note of territorial loss and exile at a time when the Geatish kingdom is left leaderless. Beowulf kills the dragon but he cannot secure his kingdom against foreign threats. The Geatish king dies fighting a monster which was lurking in his realm; his people will be annihilated by surrounding tribes.

The presence of foreign warriors at an enemy court is the central motif of the Finn episode. This story, sung by the *scop* in Heorot, recounts how Finn, a Frisian king married to the Danish princess Hildeburh, welcomes to his court a group of Danes led by Hnæf, his brother-in-law. A fight breaks out between the two parties and the conflict reaches a stalemate after Hnæf's death. A peace treaty is agreed upon and, the freezing cold and bad weather preventing them from returning home, the Danes spend the winter in Frisia. The following spring, battle is renewed and Hnæf's followers avenge their leader's killing.

During the winter separating the two phases of the conflict, the Danes and their enemies are forced to cohabit in Frisia. The poet says that oaths are sworn to ensure peace, and

---

[108] *Beowulf* 2910^b–3007^a.

>   þæt hie him oðer flet   eal gerymdon,
>   healle ond heahsetl,   þæt hie healfre geweald
>   wið Eotena bearn   agan moston[109]

This difficult passage has given rise to comments and discussion: the moot point is whether or not the Danes and the Jutes cohabit in the same stronghold. Klaeber admits that it is not clear whether a new hall is meant here, a reading which would make sense if the edifice in which the battle took place had been badly damaged. The critic however asserts that: 'whether another hall was meant or not, it is shared by the two parties'.[110] George Jack disagrees; he rejects the idea that the Danes could dwell in the same building as their enemies. To make sense of the passage, he follows Tolkien in presuming that there were Jutes fighting on both sides of the conflict: 'those with whom they [the Danes] are to share a hall can hardly be Jutes among Finn's followers, against whom they have been fighting, and must presumably be Jutes from the retinue of Hnæf'.[111] In this case, the text suggests that the Danes were granted a hall for themselves. Be that as it may, and however we choose to understand these lines, the Danes remain a problematic presence in Frisia. If they have their own building, the centre of power is duplicated. If they have to share the Frisians' stronghold, two competing troops are forced to find shelter in the same hall. This would echo Eadmund and Eadgils's presence at Heardred's court: the two fugitive warriors flee their enemies and have to remain at the Geatish court, a situation metaphorically recalled by Hnæf's followers needing protection against the winter cold. The Danes cannot be integrated in the Frisian realm; they remain a threatening presence whether they share a hall with their enemies or are granted their own place.

Finn's defeat is ultimately caused by his inability to eliminate all the Danish warriors, and in particular Hengest who assumes command of the survivors, during the first phase of the battle:

>   ... he ne mehte   on þæm meðelstede
>   wig Hengeste   wiht gefeohtan,

---

[109] 'that they cleared entirely another hall for them, a hall and a high-seat, so that they might possess control over half of it with the sons of the Jutes' (*Beowulf* 1086–8).

[110] *Beowulf and the Fight*, ed. Klaeber, 173.

[111] *Beowulf: Student Edition*, ed. Jack, 92. See also J. R. R. Tolkien, *Finn and Hengest: The Fragment and the Episode* (London: Allen and Unwin, 1982).

> ne þa wealafe   wige forþringan
> þeodnes ðegne¹¹²

He cannot *forþringan* his hall of the presence of the enemy. Klaeber glosses *forþringan* as rescue, protect.[113] Tolkien discusses this interpretation; he disagrees with Klaeber and concludes that 'the natural sense—in view of the uses of the prefix *for-* and *þringan* trans.—would be "thrust forcibly away", and so it appears to have been'.[114] What is at stake here is that Finn must 'purify' his hall, that is, dislodge the outsiders who dwell in it. This episode presents a king, Finn, who cannot properly deal with foreigners: because of his actions—his aggressive behaviour—they become hostile. And once the conflict has broken out, the Frisian ruler is unable to control the outsiders, either by destroying them or by securing a lasting peace. He loses control over the strangers at his court, he cannot ensure the integrity of his realm, and his forthcoming destruction therefore becomes unavoidable.

Similarly, when Beowulf narrates his adventures in Denmark to Hygelac, he tells the king about Hroðgar's daughter, Freawaru, who is promised to Ingeld as a peace-pledge. The hero predicts that the truce between the two tribes, the Danes and the Heathobards, will not hold. Hostility will break out when Ingeld and his followers will behold Danish warriors in their hall. The appearance in the hall, *on flett*, of Freawaru's retainer displeases Ingeld and his followers.[115] Furthermore, the old Heathobard warrior who sparks off fighting resorts to the same argument in his whetting speech, in which he calls young thanes into action. He enjoins them to look at their enemies in the hall. He says: 'Nu her þara banena byre nathwylces | frætwum hremig on flet gæð'.[116] Here again, it is the presence of the foreign that cannot be tolerated; the queen's thane is eventually killed and the alien element is eliminated from the hall.

---

[112] 'he could not fight the battle to the end in this meeting-place against Hengest, the prince's thane, nor dislodge the survivors by fighting' (*Beowulf* 1082–5ª).

[113] See also *Beowulf and the Fight*, ed. Klaeber, 172.

[114] Tolkien, *Finn and Hengest*, 100.

[115] *Beowulf* 2034ª. These lines are ambiguous and, following Klaeber and Jack, I take the pronoun *he* (l. 2024) to refer to Freawaru's wedding-attendant. A case can be made for understanding the pronoun as designating Ingeld (see *Beowulf*, ed. Mitchell and Robinson, 117 n).

[116] 'Now the son of one of the slayers walks about the hall, exulting in weapons' (*Beowulf* 2053–4).

In *Beowulf*, a comparable spatial *imaginaire* informs both the hero's fights against monsters and the various 'historical episodes'. Leaders are never able to prevent the outside world's catastrophic invasion.

Taming the Foreign: The Gaze

How should a good leader deal with the foreign that intrudes into his court? When possible, the external world should be kept at bay—as Wealhþeow intimates. But once it has entered the sphere of the familiar, it needs to be either completely eradicated or thoroughly tamed. Commenting on Beowulf's victory over Grendel, Jennifer Neville says that the hero 'transforms Grendel's intractable threat into a dismembered corpse. His efforts end when Grendel is fully integrated into human society... That is, Grendel... becomes... an object defined by society.'[117] Beowulf is successful because he manages metaphorically to blend the monster into Danish society, an operation signalled by the placing of the defeated enemy's arm under Heorot's roof where everyone can see it.[118] I contend that the notion of the gaze plays an important role in this process, for it offers a means to integrate an unfamiliar presence and to subdue its disruptive potential. It transforms what is being looked at into a passive object.

At the end of Beowulf's first fight, the poet insists that the hero has put an end to the Danes' affliction. Grendel's arm is there to prove it:

> Þæt wæs tacen sweotol,
> syþðan hildedeor   hond alegde,
> earm ond eaxle —þær wæs eal geador
> Grendles grape—   under geapne hrof.[119]

Beowulf needs a sign of his victory because Hroðgar and most of the Danes did not witness the battle and its outcome.

After his second fight, Beowulf brings back two things from the mere: Grendel's severed head and the giant sword hilt. The monstrous body part is carried into the hall:

---

[117] Neville, *Natural World*, 80–1.   [118] *Beowulf* 834–6 and 982–90.
[119] 'That was a clear sign when the one brave in battle placed the hand, the arm and the shoulder under the broad roof—there was Grendel's grasp all together' (*Beowulf* 833b– 836).

> Þa wæs be feaxe   on flet boren
> Grendles heafod
> ...
> wliteseon wrætlic;   weras on sawon.[120]

Not only is Grendel's head a *wliteseon*, a sight, a spectacle, but the poet also specifies that men looked at it: 'men on sawon'. After the arm, the head is offered to public scrutiny. It becomes a thing defined by the onlooker whose gaze marks a distance between the observer and what s/he scrutinizes. The arm and the head, successively displayed in Heorot, metonymically represent the monster's entire body. More generally, they gesture toward the hostile presence which was lurking in the periphery and which has become part of the Danish world, that is, something shaped, limited, and located by the Danes.[121]

When he lands in Hroðgar's kingdom, Beowulf is not identified as a threatening presence because he accepts being looked at and he does not move stealthily in Denmark. The coastguard notices that the Geats come to shore openly: 'No her cuðlicor cuman ongunnon | lindhæbbende'.[122] The hero and his followers do not hide their arrival. They also remain clearly visible during the banquets held in Heorot, Beowulf either accepting the cup from Wealhþeow or receiving treasures from Hroðgar.[123] Furthermore, when the hero travels to Heorot, to Grendel's pond, or to his ship, his movements are always public: he never journeys alone or secretly.

The gaze also contributes to the intelligibility of the giant sword Beowulf brings back from Grendel's mere. Two things are engraved on the hilt: the origin of the *fyrngewinnes*, the ancient strife, and the name of the maker or the owner of the sword.[124] Exactly what this ancient strife refers to is open to speculation: Cain's murder of Abel? The Flood?[125]

---

[120] 'Then Grendel's head was carried into the hall by the hair, the wondrous sight... men looked at it' (*Beowulf* 1647–50).

[121] It might be worth noting here that this is precisely what is at the heart of Modþryðo's rebellion: she refuses to be looked at and thus to be confined to the traditional role of peace-weaver assigned to women in heroic society. On this point, see Gillian R. Overing, 'The Women of *Beowulf*: A Context for Interpretation', in P. S. Baker (ed.), *Beowulf: Basic Readings*, Basic Readings in Anglo-Saxon England, 1 (New York: Garland, 1995), 219–60.

[122] 'Never have shield-bearers undertaken to come here more openly' (*Beowulf* 244–5^a).

[123] *Beowulf* 623–31, 1023–4^a, 1190^b–1191.   [124] *Beowulf* 1689^a, 1694–8^a.

[125] Klaeber suggests that the origin of the *fyrngewinnes* was the ungodly acts that preceded the Flood, according to Genesis 6: 4–6. Jack opts for Cain's fratricide, but

Hroðgar reads the runes on the hilt; more precisely, the poem says that he *hylt sceawode*.[126] The sword hilt brought to him at the end of the second fight, commemorating the destruction of the giant kin, indicates that victory has now been achieved over the entire monster race. No unexpected avenger will come to retaliate against Hroðgar and his men. With his gaze, the king symbolically integrates his enemies within his kingdom, first Grendel, then the whole of his race; they become part of it, from their origins to their final destruction.

> Bio nu on ofoste, þæt ic ærwelan,
> goldæht ongite, gearo sceawige
> swegle searogimmas[127]

These words, uttered by the wounded hero after his confrontation with the dragon, puzzle readers of the poem. How are we to understand the dying hero's wish to look at the treasure he has just won in battle? Is old Beowulf becoming greedy? The emphasis put on looking and on the gaze at this point suggests a different reading of the passage.[128] A few lines above, Beowulf orders Wiglaf to go and *hord sceawian*.[129] When he enters the cave, the hero's companion sees glittering gold and a golden standard sheds light 'þæt he þone grundwong ongitan meahte, | wræte giondwiltan'.[130] The dragon's den is illuminated so that men entering it may see—*ongitan, giondwlitan*—what lies around them. From the cave, Wiglaf brings back precious objects and Beowulf looks at them.[131] Significantly, in his subsequent speech to the cowardly retainers, when Wiglaf informs them that their lord has won the treasure, he says: 'hord

---

Mitchell and Robinson claim that it is the biblical story of the Deluge, in which God destroyed giants and Cain's descendants. Dennis Cronan favours a shift in significance and he argues that by the time the hilt passes into Hroðgar's possession, it is no longer a memorial of the origins of God's enemies, but a token of their defeat. The weapon, first crafted to celebrate God's enemies, becomes a trophy of God's justice and Beowulf's valour. See *Beowulf*, ed. Mitchell and Robinson, 103; Dennis Cronan, 'The Origin of Ancient Strife in *Beowulf*', *Germanic Studies in Honour of Anatoly Liberman: North-Western European Language Evolution (NOWELE)*, 31–2 (1997), 57–68 (65–6); and *Beowulf and the Fight*, ed. Klaeber, 189–90.

[126] 'looked at the hilt' (*Beowulf* 1687b).
[127] 'Make haste now so that I may see the store of gold, look at the ancient riches' (*Beowulf* 2747–9a).
[128] On the image of looking and treasure, see Edward B. Irving Jr., *A Reading of Beowulf* (New Haven: Yale University Press, 1968), 206.
[129] 'look at the hoard' (*Beowulf* 2744a).
[130] 'so that he may see the surface of the floor, look over the ornate objects' (*Beowulf* 2770–1a). See also *Beowulf* 2756–62a and 2767–9a.
[131] *Beowulf* 2793b, 2796b.

ys gesceawod, | grimme gegongen'.¹³² The treasure, not a monster's bodily part, is here the token of victory, since the dragon, once dead, is pushed into the sea. Moreover, the very wording of the above quotation suggests that to examine the treasure and to acquire it are the same thing, that these two actions are equivalent. The hero's companion then tells the Geatish warriors that he too has seen the gold and he declares that they all should enter the dragon's barrow and take a look at it.¹³³ The treasure is the object of an intense and repeated gaze; it is thus appropriated first by the hero and then by the Geatish warriors: it becomes part of Beowulf's kingdom. And one should only remember at this point that the gold is eventually placed into the dead hero's tomb.

In his reading of *Beowulf*, Edward Irving contrasts a passive vision in part II of the poem, a vision which does not entice the onlooker to act, with a more active one in part I. The view of a sword in the Heathobard episode, for instance, is a provocation calling for an immediate reaction.¹³⁴ Yet even what Irving labels 'passive vision' does not remain without effects: in Beowulf's realm, it serves to include the alien, represented by the hoard, within the familiar, the dead man's barrow. The power of the gaze counterbalances the threat of the foreign: it establishes who the onlooker and who the object of the gaze are, and where both are located. If a clear boundary cannot be drawn between the worlds of monsters and of humans, the gaze helps repeatedly to distinguish between 'them' and 'us'. Where geography remains vague, the direction of the gaze dispels ambiguity.

A similar dynamics of seeing and being seen shapes *Judith*. The net surrounding Holofernes's bed symbolizes the power relationships between the poem's various characters; for, before the visit of the Hebrew woman, the magical curtain is the means through which Holofernes rules over his retinue. His ability to see without being seen exemplifies the control he exercises over his men and foregrounds the power of his gaze. But Judith's coming reverses the situation, for while the heroine does look at him, the Assyrian leader presumably never sees her.¹³⁵ Because of its visual properties, the net shields Judith from Holofernes

---

[132] 'the hoard is examined, grimly won' (*Beowulf* 3084ᵇ–3085ᵃ).
[133] *Beowulf* 3087–90ᵃ, 3101–5ᵃ.   [134] Irving, *A Reading*, 206.
[135] Karma Lochrie, 'Gender, Sexual Violence, and the Politics of War in the Old English *Judith*', in Britton J. Harwood and Gillian R. Overing (eds.), *Class and Gender in Early English Literature: Intersections* (Bloomington: Indiana University Press, 1994), 1–20, (9). For Bernard Huppé, the net suggests the mysterious presence of a god-like figure. Bernard F. Huppé, *The Web of Words: Structural Analysis of the Old English Poems*

and it also protects her from the drunken guests. As we will see below, the curtain signals within the Assyrian camp a boundary that is not easy for the general's men to cross. The heroine's invisibility further allows her to leave the Assyrian camp after having killed Holofernes and she successfully resists being merged into the society of her enemies.

Conversely, Judith's victory over Holofernes is complete only when she brings back and displays his head to her people in Bethulia. The scene in which the enemy body part is presented to the Hebrews is infused with terms denoting seeing and looking. The heroine orders her servant to *ætywan*, display, the head to the crowd.[136] She then addresses her people and says:

> Her ge magon sweotole. . .
> . . . on ðæs laðestan
> hæðenes heaðorinces   heafod   starian.[137]

Holofernes's head is offered to public scrutiny as Grendel's is in Heorot. And if displaying the head may be a necessary token of victory, the physical proof that the enemy has been vanquished, it also signals its integration within the home society and the circumventing of its disruptive potential. Publicly to exhibit (part of) the defeated enemy, that is, to objectivize it through one's gaze, is one of the ways in which a ruler can deal with the foreign at his court. In this case, the outsider loses its dangerous potency; it no longer threatens the survival of the centre and its effective neutralization is confirmed by its actual dismemberment.

MONSTERS AND BOUNDARIES

Setting the Limits

Monsters are commonly associated with the limits of civilization. Cast as belonging to 'them', as fundamentally different from 'us', they are assigned a radically alien nature. They usually dwell on the confines of society: their difference is thus expressed in spatial terms.[138] They are a

---

Vainglory, The Wonders of Creation, The Dream of the Rood *and* Judith (Albany: State University of New York Press, 1970), 163–4.

[136] *Judith* 174^b.

[137] 'Here you can clearly gaze on the head of this most hateful heathen warrior' (*Judith* 177–9).

[138] See e.g. Jeffrey Jerome Cohen, 'Old English Literature and the Work of Giants', *Comitatus*, 24 (1993), 1–32 (24).

menace: lurking on the other side of the border, they constantly threaten to cross it and to blur the demarcation between culture and nature, between tamed and wild. When they do overstep the mark, monsters perform an action whose significance is twofold: they challenge the difference between civilized and monstrous realms on the one hand, while on the other revealing, crystallizing, and possibly redefining the boundaries of the territory they invade. Grendel for instance does both: with his mock hall, he mirrors Hroðgar's court, thus questioning the precise location of the centre of power and, with his intrusion into the royal stronghold, he draws attention to the border separating the king's realm from his own wasteland. The monster's threat therefore points to the limits of Danish society, limits which concern both its civilized status and its territorial integrity.

My contention here is that a frontier that is transgressed is not always necessarily abolished. Quite on the contrary, attention is drawn to a limit violated by a trespasser. Let us consider Grendel and his mother: they are able to cross the border separating Heorot from their own dominion. Grendel repeatedly does so and is thus paradoxically instrumental in establishing the limits of the Danish kingdom. The poet grants the monster and his mother control over the wasteland.[139] Quite logically therefore, they are called *mearcstapan*, those who wander in the borderland.[140] This phrase calls to mind the image of Grendel's roaming the marshes and thus physically drawing boundaries on the soil of Denmark. His wanderings trace the line where the king's rule stops and where his own begins. Neville articulates these two aspects when she claims that Grendel and other terrifying outsiders 'define the limits of society, both by stalking around the boundaries and by threatening its existence'.[141] The monster's presence bears upon both the nature and the extent of the civilized world. As invasion is necessary to think about the centre, trespassers are useful to reflect on the frontiers of society.

Examining bodies, buildings, and boundaries, Joyce Tally Lionarons notes that medieval stories telling of the eradication of monsters and giants 'tend to emphasize the setting and maintenance of limits and borders; the hero is one who often by virtue of his own marginal status can define and enforce those societal boundaries'.[142] According to the critic therefore, transgressions call attention to the status and

---

[139] *Beowulf* 102–4^a and 1497^b–1499^a.   [140] *Beowulf* 103^a and 1348^a.
[141] Neville, *Natural World*, 73.
[142] Lionarons, 'Bodies, Buildings and Boundaries', 49.

location of the boundary, while the hero's actions aim at reasserting and strengthening the border. But as I hope to have demonstrated, *Beowulf* seriously challenges the distinction between what is monstrous and what is human. An analysis of the various journeys that the characters undertake and that criss-cross the poem's geography reveals that these movements not only violate and challenge frontiers, but that they at the same time define and draw territorial boundaries.

Grendel is not the only figure who haunts the periphery: so does the hero, especially in his youthful swimming contest against Breca. Beowulf tells how he ventured his life in the sea and came back unharmed and victorious. In the waves, he enters the sphere of the water-monsters. They attack the intruder who defends himself successfully. Beowulf uses the image of the feast to describe the outcome of his struggle: he says that he denies his enemies a joyful feast at the bottom of the sea and that when daylight comes, many fiends lie dead by the shore. The scene is a clear reiteration of Grendel's attack on Heorot: a solitary invader enters a hostile territory at night, he deprives the inhabitants of their banquet, he decimates his opponents, and he escapes unscathed. Beowulf's expedition also involves a spatial component, for the hero kills so many sea-monsters 'þæt syðþan na | ymb brontne ford brimliðende | lade ne letton'.[143] The hero's expedition secures a new route for sailors. It thus redefines part of the maritime territory as being under men's control. As Grendel's roaming outlines the boundaries of mankind's dominion, Beowulf's swimming determines the limits of the lands the monsters rule.

When he realizes that a cup has been stolen from his treasure, the dragon circles his barrow: 'hat ond hreohmod hlæw oft ymbehwearf | ealne utanweardne'.[144] At first sight, it seems that the monster is looking for his thief, for tracks that could lead him to his lost cup. But the circular motion also indicates that the dragon attempts to re-establish his cave's boundaries, the limits that have just been violated. The verb *ymbehweorfan*, 'to go round', echoes the wanderings of the Grendelkin; for, when he first introduces the monster and his mother, the poet says that men did not know: 'hwyder helrunan hwyrftum scriþað.'[145] The

---

[143] 'so that they afterwards did not at all hinder the seafarers' passage across the high sea' (*Beowulf* 567ᵇ–569ᵃ).

[144] 'hot and fierce [he] repeatedly circled the whole barrow outside' (*Beowulf* 2296–7ᵃ).

[145] 'where the demons wandered' (*Beowulf* 163). On this line, see Thomas D. Hill, 'Hwyrftum scriþað: *Beowulf*, line 163', *Medieval Studies*, 33 (1971), 379–81.

term *hwyrft* implies the idea of a circular movement; it often designates an orb, a circle, or the course of the stars. The dragon around his barrow, as well as Grendel and his mother around the Danish kingdom, moves in circles through the countryside.

Finally, the most conspicuous circles depicted in *Beowulf* are the ones the warriors trace around their leader's tomb which, I suggest, circumscribe a new space in the devastated kingdom. Confined to the barrow's immediate surroundings, they indicate that this is all that remains of Beowulf's sphere of power. The circling movements of Grendel, of Beowulf, of the dragon, and of the Geatish warriors retrace boundaries that have been crossed and to which attention is directed: the frontiers of the Danish kingdom, the domain of mankind at sea, the barrow sheltering a treasure, or the hero's funeral pyre. In all these cases, an outstanding being (re)defines territorial boundaries. The recurrence of this image in *Beowulf*'s poetic geography betrays a wider anxiety about the establishment and maintenance of borders, a concern which, in the epic poem, affects not only kings, but also monsters who are likewise compelled to secure their own territory.

Treading the Ground and Territorial Control

Borders are literally traced by the strides with which various characters travel through *Beowulf*'s poetic geography and recurrent images of stepping and treading in the poem call for closer analysis. Terms such as *tredan*, 'to tread, to walk upon', *steppan*, 'to stride, to march', *mætan*, 'to measure, to traverse', *stræt*, 'street', and *last*, 'track, footprint' foreground the action of walking, of stepping on the ground, an image which supports territorial claims and signals spatial appropriation.[146]

The poet's very choice of words underlines the complex relationship uniting Hroðgar and Grendel. On the night he encounters Beowulf in Heorot, the monster enters the hall, and the poet says: 'on fagne flor feond treddode'.[147] This line occurs before Grendel's defeat in battle, that is, at a moment when, as we have seen, he might control the hall at night. The representation of the monster stepping on Heorot's floor is a further indication that he does indeed rule the stronghold. This scene is

---

[146] For an analysis of individual landscape terms, see Margaret Gelling, 'The Landscape of *Beowulf*', *Anglo-Saxon England*, 31 (2002), 7–11 (7).

[147] 'the enemy walked upon the decorated floor' (*Beowulf* 725).

echoed later in the poem, namely when the Danish king re-enters Heorot after the first fight. The *Beowulf* poet depicts Hroðgar and Wealhþeow coming out of the queen's bower, and he says that the king *tryddode*, 'stepped', with a troop of retainers.[148] Hroðgar, at that very moment, may symbolically be regaining possession of his hall. The repetition of the image of stepping which uses closely related verbs (*tredan* and *treddian*), contrasts these two moments in the poem. It suggests that spatial authority pertains once to Grendel and once to Hroðgar.

Many characters travel between Heorot and the mere and the descriptions of the roads they follow deserve attention. Grendel's years-long expeditions to Heorot leave bloody tracks in the landscape and on the morning of Beowulf's victory, people come from afar to see the *laþes lastas*.[149] The footprints of Grendel's mother are also visible on the ground when the king and his warriors travel to the mere after the she-monster: 'Lastas wæron | æfter waldswaþum wide gesyne | gang ofer grundas'.[150] Moreover, as discussed earlier in this chapter, the Danes are unable to travel to the mere unaided, ignorant as they seem to be of its precise location. Significantly, it is their enemies' traces that they follow to go there. Travelling back and forth between their underwater cave and Heorot therefore, the Grendelkin leave their mark in the hall as well as on the countryside, thus demonstrating that they are in control of both.

Journeying to the enemy lake is difficult not only because its location is ambiguous, but also because the paths leading there are unpleasant, steep, narrow, and unknown.[151] But the return from the mere is a very different journey; for, the *Beowulf* poet markedly modifies his text's imaginary geography when he depicts Danish and Geatish retainers going back to the royal stronghold, either after Beowulf's victory over Grendel or after his successful raid to the monsters' lair. On the morning following the hero's first fight, some warriors journey to the lake's shore. Coming back from the mere, they race their horses and they 'fealwe stræte | mearum mæton'.[152] Beowulf and the Geatish warriors carrying Grendel's head after the second fight return to Heorot on foot. They 'foldweg mæton, | cuþe stræte'.[153] In both cases, the poet uses the terms

---

[148] *Beowulf* 922ᵃ.
[149] 'the footprints of the hateful one' (*Beowulf* 841ᵃ). See also *Beowulf* 132.
[150] 'the footprints were clearly visible on the forest-paths, the tracks over the plain' (*Beowulf* 1402ᵇ–1404ᵃ).
[151] *Beowulf* 1408–11.
[152] 'they traversed the dusky road with their horses' (*Beowulf* 916ᵇ–917ᵃ).
[153] 'they came upon the path, the known road' (*Beowulf* 1633ᵇ–1634ᵃ).

stræt and *mæton*. The change from *last*—used when warriors travel to the mere—to *stræt*—used when human beings journey back from the enemy lake after Beowulf's victory over Grendel first, and over his mother then—indicates that Beowulf's military success leaves its mark on the countryside. The hero and the warriors who come back from the mere appropriate the territory over which the monsters formerly ruled. The hero's victories are consequently reflected in the affective depiction of the natural world: steep and unfamiliar paths are transformed into a *cuþe stræte*, well-known road.[154]

The account of Beowulf's contest against Breca echoes this motif, for Unferð asks the newcomer about his swimming contest. He calls this experience a *sorhfullne sið*, undertaken 'on sidne sæ', thus implying that the two young men engage in a dangerous venture in a hostile environment.[155] But he also says that once in the water, Beowulf and Breca *mæton merestræta*.[156] The very wording used by the Danish retainer at this point—the use of the verb *metan*, 'to measure, to traverse', and of the element *stræt* in the compound—suggests that the hero, when venturing in the ocean, seizes an alien domain, that he tames and gains it for the world of human beings.

The dragon's wrath is roused by a slave who breaks into the hoard and steals a precious cup. Interestingly, the treasure's guardian is further angered when he discovers the *feondes fotlast*.[157] The poet adds that the runaway slave 'to forð gestop | ... dracan heafde neah'.[158] The causes of the dragon's rage are thus twofold: the theft on the one hand and the spatial transgression which leaves traces in the barrow on the other. Read in the context of the present discussion, the terms *fotlast* and *gesteppan* suggest that the intrusive slave challenges the monster's authority over his own realm. And when the monster subsequently circles his barrow, he attempts to negate the new territorial distribution evidenced by the slave's incursion into the hoard.

The *Judith* poet, by ironically playing on the motif of warriors stepping into combat, also makes use of this cluster of images.[159] The vernacular author brings a number of changes to his biblical source:

---

[154] *Beowulf* 1634ª.
[155] 'a perilous expedition' (*Beowulf* 512ª); 'in the broad sea' (*Beowulf* 507ª).
[156] 'traversed the sea-ways' (*Beowulf* 514ª).
[157] 'the enemy's footprint' (*Beowulf* 2289ª).
[158] he 'had stepped forth too ... close to the dragon's head' (*Beowulf* 2289ᵇ–2290).
[159] On this point, see *Judith*, ed. by Mark Griffith (Exeter: University of Exeter Press, 1997), 66.

he reduces the number of characters that appear in the text and he omits figures like Achior, the good Assyrian, Ozias, the chief nobleman of Bethulia, and Bagoas, Holofernes's eunuch.[160] Griffith observes that the latter who, in the apocryphal text, leads Judith to Holofernes's tent, disappears and is replaced by an armed band who 'bearhtme stopon | to ðam gysterne'.[161] The verb *stepan* is repeated later in the poem in the context of the Hebrew attack on the Assyrian camp.[162] In this case, the advancing march precedes an expected and violent encounter between two enemy forces. 'The Hebrews' speedy advance to battle (l. 200–212b *stopon*)', Griffith says, 'in retrospect makes the Assyrian "advance" on Judith's guest-house and their "retreat" from Holofernes' tent appear absurd (l. 39b, 69b, *stopon*).'[163] And yet, in the scene in which the Assyrians lead Judith to their captain's tent, the verb *stepan* also precedes a bloody and destructive encounter which incidentally foreshadows the Assyrians' military defeat. But the main difference between these two moments is that the Bethulians march against an enemy camp while the Assyrians remain within their own compound. Their martial steps take them from Judith's chamber to Holofernes's bed and the Assyrians do not assert their control of space behind the limits of their own camp.

In the case of the Assyrians, transgression and venture into an enemy space take place in fact inside the camp, in Holofernes's tent which is the hostile locus of the camp. During the Bethulian onslaught, the Assyrians do not dare enter the pavilion and wake their chieftain. Instead, they congregate outside the magical curtain and desperately clear their throat in a vain attempt to get Holofernes's attention.[164] Finally, as the situation becomes critical, one warrior is bold enough and 'he in þæt burgeteld | niðheard neðde'.[165] Only when forced by circumstances to do so does this warrior risk entering the tent. In this scene, the net represents a boundary difficult to cross. The poet's use of the verb *stepan* when describing the Assyrians leading Judith to Holofernes's bed is thus explained, for entering the leader's tent is a daring expedition indeed, for the heroine of course, but also for Holofernes's own men. Even though it is the Assyrians who are besieging Bethulia, the space that is being transgressed and conquered is Holofernes's tent and encampment.

---

[160] *Judith*, ed. by B. J. Timmer (London: Methuen, 1952), 13–14.
[161] 'stepped noisily to the guest-chamber' (*Judith* 39^b–40^a).
[162] ll. 200^b and 212^b.   [163] *Judith*, ed. Griffith, 66.
[164] *Judith* 267^b–273^a.
[165] 'daring, he ventured into the tent' (*Judith* 276^b–277^a).

Another instance of the stepping motif occurs when the two women return to Bethulia. They leave the Assyrian camp and they see the city's shining walls. At that point, Judith and her maid hasten forward, they 'feðelaste forð onettan' until they reach the city.[166] The two women's *feðelaste*, their quick steps, mark out the track that the Hebrews will follow later in the poem when they rush into battle against the Assyrian camp. With their footprints, Judith and her servant reclaim the ground on which they walk, thus indicating that Holofernes's death marks the beginning of the Bethulians' military triumph.[167]

CONCLUSION

A study of *Beowulf*'s poetic geography reveals a number of ambiguities inherent in the poem's spatial organization. Its settings resist being classified as belonging either to the world of civilization or to the world of monstrosity. The text's different places ultimately all reflect one another and blur the division between the human and the inhuman, between 'us' and 'them'.

The poem also questions the notion of the centre. The features characterizing *Beowulf*'s significant places include the presence of a leader who is either dead or asleep, reclining on a bed surrounded by treasure. More importantly still, all these places are threatened by the outside and are eventually invaded. According to these criteria, not only Heorot or Beowulf's hall, but also Grendel's mere and the dragon's barrow are centres in the poem. From the attacks by Grendel and his mother to the wars the Franks and the Swedes wage against the Danes, the alien is represented as a transgressive force that cannot be kept at bay. The invasion motif, on which the preceding lines have shed light, coupled with the spatial component inherent in the notion of transgression, on which Chapter 2 concluded, are both necessary to objectivize and delimit a given area; in short, they are both indispensable to think about space.

---

[166] 'they hastily stepped forward' (*Judith* 139). For an analysis of these lines as an instance of the 'Hero on the Beach' type-scene, see Donald K. Fry, 'The Heroine on the Beach in *Judith*', *Neuphilologische Mitteilungen*, 68 (1967), 168–84.

[167] Note that in *Exodus*, the sea that drowns Pharaoh's army is called *fah feðegast* (*Exodus* 476ª). The enemy of the Egyptians crushes them down under its feet, a striking image when applied to the sea. For a discussion of this passage, see Karin E. Olsen, 'The Dual Function of the Repetitious in *Exodus* 447–515', in L. A. J. R. Houwen and A. A. MacDonald (eds.), *Loyal Letters: Studies on Medieval Alliterative Poetry and Prose* (Groningen: Egbert Forsten, 1994), 55–70 (61).

Beowulf articulates the relationship between centre and margins as a threat of invasion from the outside. This spatial tension inevitably focuses attention on the notion of the boundary; for, repeated spatial transgressions not only question an established territorial order, but they also bring it to light. Hroðgar's dominion seemed boundless during his glorious, youthful days, when Heorot was being built. Grendel's intrusion quickly dispels this illusion and reveals that the royal rule has its limits, that it stops where the monster's control of the periphery starts. Treading and stepping imagery signals territorial authority, an imagery to which the poet resorts to indicate who rules where and when.

The uncertain nature of its various places and the problematic status of the centre characterize *Beowulf*'s poetic geography and shape the poet's reflections on what is central and what is marginal. They preclude any clear-cut correspondence between these two terms, and between notions of civilization and monstrosity. The spatial ambiguity which lies at the heart of the epic poem also points to the difficulties, already discussed in relation to creation narratives, of establishing a well-defined, stable, and lasting dominion. The pervasive presence of the motif of invasion and the importance granted to boundaries already mentioned in Chapter 2 are complexified by the *Beowulf* poet. Transgression here is no longer identified as a past rupture necessary to the emergence of a human community; but, endlessly multiplied, it reflects, in the epic's many subtleties, a permanent interrogation about the relation between 'us' and 'them', an interrogation about the very nature of civilization which is expressed in terms of spatial integrity and territorial rule.

4

Localization and Remapping: Creating a New Centrality for Anglo-Saxon England

In his *Geography*, the Greek scholar Strabo (63 BC–AD 21) offers a description of Britain. He mentions its location, size, and natural resources, before turning his attention to the island's inhabitants. He notices that the Britons are taller than the *Celti* and he adds: 'the following is an indication of their size: I myself, in Rome, saw mere lads towering as much as half a foot above the tallest people in the city, although they were bandy-legged and presented no fair lines anywhere else in their figure.'[1] If the Britons stand out in the crowd, it is not simply because of their size: it is above all because Strabo portrays them as ugly and misshapen. Proceeding with his unflattering portrayal of the Britons, the Greek geographer stigmatizes their customs when he declares that 'their habits are in part like those of the *Celti*, but in part more simple and barbaric'.[2] In this ethnographic account therefore, the Britons' physical alterity is reflected in their primitive behaviour.

A few lines below, the geographer comments further on the British Isles: he locates Ierne (Ireland) beyond Britain and notes that its inhabitants are even less civilized than the Britons.[3] There is a gradation toward savageness in Strabo's text: the further north the lands he describes lie, the wilder they become. Britain, though not the very last land toward the north, is remote from Rome; the people who live there are ugly and their barbaric customs are outdone only by those of Ierne's inhabitants. The islanders are portrayed as unattractive brutes and they do not compare favourably with the Romans.

---

[1] Strabo, *The Geography of Strabo*, ed. and trans. by H. L. Jones, 8 vols. (London: Heinemann, 1917–32; repr. 1966–70), ii (1969), 4. 5. 2, p. 255.
[2] Strabo, *Geography*, ii. 4. 5. 2, p. 255.   [3] Ibid., ii. 4. 5. 4, p. 259.

Seven centuries later, the Anglo-Saxon historian Bede gives, in his *Ecclesiastical History of the English People*, another account of the impression Britain's inhabitants make in Rome: he tells of angelic slave boys who catch Gregory's eye in a Roman market. This encounter will spur this same Gregory, when Pope, to launch a conversion mission to the Anglo-Saxons. Like the Britons described by Strabo, the slave boys are conspicuous in the crowd. Bede notes that in the market place: '[Gregory] uidisse inter alia pueros uenales positos candidi corporis ac uenusti uultus, capillorum quoque forma egregia. Quos cum aspiceret, interrogauit, ut aiunt, de qua regione uel terra essent adlati; dictumque est quia de Brittania insula, cuius incolae talis essent aspectus.'[4] Bede's insular boys also stand out in a Roman crowd, but this time it is their fairness that draws attention. Gregory inquires further about who these youths are. More precisely, he wants to learn the name of their people, of their king, and their place of origin. These questions are the occasion for Gregory's famous puns which transform the *Angli* into angels, their kingdom *Deiri* into 'de ira', the divine wrath from which they are snatched, and the name of their king, *Ælle*, becomes 'alleluia', an injunction to sing God's praise. Bede thus reads in the answers given to his questions God's plan for the Anglo-Saxons in Britain: their beauty reveals that they are in fact proleptic Christians, and it announces the special role they have been granted in religious history.

These anecdotes present two radically different pictures of Britain and its inhabitants. Yet this discrepancy is not surprising as it reflects their authors' respective positions. The former account is the work of someone from the Mediterranean world who situates Britain in the distance and who links it to the wildness traditionally associated with the periphery. The author of the latter episode is a native of the British Isles who was probably reluctant to place his countrymen on the fringes

---

[4] Gregory 'saw some boys put up for sale, with fair complexions, handsome faces, and lovely hair. On seeing them he asked, so it is said, from what region or land they had been brought. He was told that they came from the island of Britain, whose inhabitants were like that in appearance' *Bede's Ecclesiastical History of the English People*, ed. and trans. by Bertram Colgrave and R. A. B. Mynors (Oxford: Clarendon Press, 1969; repr. 1991), ii. 1, p. 132. The translations are from the same edition. Please note that since the Old English version of Bede's *Ecclesiastical History* follows its Latin original very closely, at least for the passages on which I comment, I have chosen not to include it in my discussion. *The Old English Version of Bede's Ecclesiastical History of the English People*, ed. and trans. by Thomas Miller, EETS os. 95 and 96, 2 vols. (London: Oxford University Press, 1890–1; repr. 1997).

of the known world. Moreover, Strabo speaks of the Britons and Bede of the Anglo-Saxons. The medieval historian identifies himself with the race of the Angles and writes his history in praise of Britain's Germanic conquerors.[5] Bede rewrites his homeland as a significant place in Christendom. Curiously, however, and I will come back to this point below, the Anglo-Saxon historian does not negate the distance separating his island from the Continent, for the Gregory he puts on stage does not know who the slave boys are, where they come from, and who their king is.

Despite their idiosyncrasies, these two anecdotes share an important feature: they both associate identity with localization. They also contain in embryo the main questions addressed in this chapter. Where is Britain located on the map of the oecumene in classical and Anglo-Saxon worldviews? Does its situation change in the course of time? What remapping processes do the Anglo-Saxons elaborate to reposition themselves? And why is geographical localization so important? Surveying a sample of texts from antiquity to Anglo-Saxon England, as well as a selection of early medieval maps, I will trace Britain's metamorphosis from a savage and foreign land into a new political, cultural, and religious centre. In all probability, the Anglo-Saxons did not experience the liminal position which classical learning assigned to their island, and they do not, in their mental map, confine their homeland to the periphery. Supplementing and when necessary correcting their authorities with first-hand information, Anglo-Saxon authors remap the contours of northern Europe and redefine the location of Britain and of the ends of the earth.

This chapter examines the situation that a number of classical authors (mainly Caesar, Tacitus, and Strabo) attribute to Britain in their geography, before turning to native sources, such as Bede's *Ecclesiastical History*, the Old English rendering of Orosius's *Historiarum adversum Paganos Libri Septem*, and Dicuil's *Liber de Mensura Orbis Terrae*. Texts such as these are usually classified as 'historical' works. They often foreground questions of space and geography since, as Monika Otter points out, 'spatial references are... one of the most important

---

[5] In the preface to the *Ecclesiastical History*, Bede identifies himself as one of the *Anglorum* whose history is being recorded. He rejoices that King Ceolwulf wants to know more about 'nostrae gentis uirorum inlustrium'. *Nostra* includes Ceolwulf and Bede, as well as the medieval audience. Bede writes its own history to his own people. Bede, *Ecclesiastical History*, preface, 2.

guarantors of the referentiality of historical narrative'.[6] The critic further observes that the very importance granted to spatiality makes historical narrative an interesting place to disturb referentiality. But the (un)faithful relationships historico-geographical documents entertain with the reality they claim to represent is not the object of the following lines. Discussing the development of geographical knowledge, Patrick Gautier Dalché questions, as a matter of principle, any strict correspondence between reality and its representation. He no longer deems it possible today 'de s'en tenir à une histoire de la géographie fondée sur la croyance en l'adéquation entre la réflexion sur l'espace réel, et sa représentation figurée. Comme le montre aussi l'évolution récente de la géographie, celle-ci, aujourd'hui comme au moyen âge, est toujours affaire de concepts, non de "réalités".'[7] The concepts informing geographical reports and their spatial representations will be examined as narrative constructs endowed with an ideological function, that is, as tools shaping the audience's perception of its localization and hence of itself. In addition to the various strategies to which Old English authors resort to recentre their island on the map of the world, I will pay particular attention to what is at stake in geographical descriptions, such as the links uniting spatial knowledge and power, or localization and sense of self.

Unlike Chapters 2 and 3, which dealt mainly with space as a mental structure, this new chapter proceeds to address the Anglo-Saxons' culture of space. Adopting a more historical perspective, it traces the evolution of a given body of knowledge, namely of geographical learning, from antiquity to Anglo-Saxon England. The present chapter expands on a number of issues central to the poetic representations of space studied so far, such as the localization and the definition of the centre and the periphery, the characterization of the spheres of civilization and wilderness, and finally the link between spatiality and a community's sense of itself, thus bringing to light the spatial *imaginaire* which permeates historico-geographical documents.

[6] Monika Otter, *Inventiones: Fiction and Referentiality in Twelfth-Century English Historical Writing* (Chapel Hill: University of North Carolina Press, 1996), 9.

[7] Patrick Gautier Dalché, 'De la glose à la contemplation. Place et fonction de la carte dans les manuscrits du haut Moyen Age', in *Géographie et culture: La représentation de l'espace du VIe au XIIe siècle* (Aldershot: Ashgate, 1997; first publ. in *Testo e immagine nell'alto medioevo*, Settimane di studio del Centro italiano di studi sull'alto medioevo, 41 (Spoleto: Centro Italiano di Studi sull'Alto Medioevo, 1994)), viii. 693–771 (771).

CLASSICAL VIEWS OF BRITAIN'S GEOGRAPHICAL LOCATION

Britain in the Distance

Classical learning traditionally locates Britain in the distance and stresses the gap separating it from continental Europe. In his *Natural History*, Pliny the Elder (*c.* AD 23–79) places the island far away from the Continent. In this standard work of reference, Anglo-Saxon scholars found their homeland lying to the north-west facing Germany, Gaul, and Spain 'magno intervallo adversa'.[8] Solinus (third century AD), another major source for Old English authors, discusses the location of the island in his *Collectanea Rerum Memorabilium*. He clearly sets it apart from the rest of Europe: 'finis erat orbis ora Gallici litoris, nisi Brittania insula non qualibet amplitudine nomen paene orbis alterius mereretur'.[9] Solinus expresses Britain's alterity by comparing it to another world set beyond the limit of the oecumene. This image draws attention to the island's size, but it also suggests that Britain is separated from the rest of Europe, not only geographically, but also by its very nature: it is a radically different place.

That Britain is an isolated and remote land is an enduring notion. It resurfaces for instance several centuries later in Isidore of Seville's geography. The encyclopaedist (570–636) states that 'Brittania Oceani insula interfuso mari toto orbe divisa'.[10] This time, the island is opposed to the whole world and the limit between the two is a stretch of water.

Against this background of distance and otherness, I would like to discuss in more detail the accounts that Caesar, Strabo, and Tacitus provide about Britain. This sample of texts demonstrates that, although their authors follow the tradition briefly sketched above in mentioning

---

[8] 'across a great distance' (Pliny the Elder, *Natural History*, 4. 16. 102, p. 348. *C. Plini Secundi: Naturalis Historiae: Libri* XXXVII, ed. by Charles Mayhoff, 5 vols. (Leipzig: Teubner, 1892–1909; repr. 1967–70), i (1967).

[9] 'The sea coast of Gaul was the end of the world except that the island of Britain, of whatever size it be, almost deserves the name of another world' (Solinus, *Collectanea Rerum Memorabilium* 22. 1, pp. 99–100). *C. Iulii Solini: Collectanea Rerum Memorabilium*, ed. by T. Mommsen (Berlin: Weidmann, 1895; repr. 1958).

[10] 'Britain is an island on the Ocean divided from the whole world by the sea lying in between' (Isidore, *Etymologies* 14. 6. 2. *Isidori Hispalensis Episcopi: Etymologiarum Sive Originum: Libri* XX, ed. by W. M. Lindsay, 2 vols. (Oxford: Clarendon Press, 1911; repr. 1985), ii.

the island's remoteness, they do not all adopt a similar attitude toward distance. Tacitus's *Agricola*, for instance, elaborates a complex articulation of proximity and distance. Moreover, these writers all reflect on the general state of knowledge about Britain and the north, thus inevitably questioning the origin of their information: is it first-hand knowledge? Or does it derive from oral reports that travellers to distant lands tell? These problems combine with the evaluation of distance and they implicitly bear both upon the nature of these outlying regions (are they remote, unknown, and mysterious, or are they accessible and already mapped?) and upon the explorer who describes them.

Caesar (100–44 BC) speaks extensively about Britain in his *Gallic Wars*. The Roman author thinks that it would be useful for his future military campaigns to know more about the Britons' customs and about their island's geography because 'omnibus fere Gallicis bellis hostibus nostris inde subministrata auxilia intellegebat'.[11] The Romans are not familiar with Britain; they are no exception, since Caesar says that merchants know only its southern shores, for almost no one travels there: 'neque enim temere praeter mercatores illo adiit quisquam'.[12] Moreover, those who do journey to Britain have nothing to say about it. Although Caesar questioned them, he learned almost nothing about this distant island which is therefore presented as a mysterious place escaping Roman control.[13]

In the *Gallic Wars*, Caesar develops the notion that the further north one goes, the wilder the world becomes. He plays on the opposition between the centre and the periphery, between the known and the unknown which is equated with the opposition between civilization and barbarism. In his world-view, the centre is obviously in Rome, capital of the civilized world, and Britain is on the outskirts. Caesar develops this dichotomy within Britain itself when he implies that the further away one goes from the island's southern shores, the more savage its inhabitants become. The most civilized people among the Britons are

---

[11] 'He understood that in almost all the Gallic wars help had been furnished for our enemies from there' Caesar, *The Gallic Wars* 4. 20, p. 110. César, *Guerre des Gaules*, ed. and trans. by L.-A. Constans, rev. A. Balland, 2 vols. (Paris: Belles Lettres, 1995–6), i (1996); all page references are to this edition.

[12] 'In fact, nobody except traders dares journey there' Caesar, *Gallic Wars*, 4. 20, p. 110.

[13] 'Itaque uocatis ad se undique mercatoribus neque quanta esset insulae magnitudo, neque quae aut quantae nationes incolerent, neque quem usum belli haberent aut quibus institutis uterentur, neque qui essent ad maiorum nauium mutitudinem idonei portus reperire poterat' (Caesar, *Gallic Wars*, 4. 20, pp. 110–11).

found in the south, in Kent: 'ex his omnibus longe sunt humanissimi qui Cantium incolunt'.[14] They are influenced by the lifestyle of the Gauls, which is not the case of those dwelling further inland. Distance is here the mark of what is wild and outlandish.

The opening lines of the present chapter have demonstrated that Strabo too assumes that remote regions are uncivilized. He fixes the northern limits of the populated world in Ierne, the island beyond Britain. It marks the point where inhabitable lands come to an end: 'For modern scientific writers are not able to speak of any country north of Ierne, which lies to the north of Britain and near thereto, and is the home of men who are complete savages and lead a miserable existence because of the cold; and therefore, in my opinion, the northern limit of our inhabited world is to be placed there.'[15] The Greek scholar again voices the widespread idea that the periphery is the home of savage and barbarous creatures. In this geography, beastly people live in Ierne, the last populated island, and the inhabitants of neighbouring Britain are not much more civilized.[16]

When Strabo extends his anthropological description to Ierne, he says: 'concerning this island I have nothing certain to tell, except that its inhabitants are more savage than the Britons'.[17] This quotation is remarkable. First, the author recognizes the doubtful character of his report when he says that he has 'nothing certain' to say about Ierne. Secondly, the only thing that escapes this general uncertainty is the barbarous character of its inhabitants. This conviction rests on a geographical certitude which implicitly suggests that since Ierne lies further away than Britain, it must inevitably be wilder than its southern neighbour.

Caesar and Strabo link distance and barbarism: the periphery is wild and savage. Moreover, remote lands are badly known: it is difficult to gather information about them, for few people travel there and those who do have nothing of note to report.

The life of Agricola that Tacitus (55–117) writes at the end of the first century markedly contrasts with the schema outlined above. Unlike Caesar, Tacitus himself cannot claim first-hand knowledge of the land he describes. But the protagonist of his text, Agricola, did journey to Britain, and the panegyrist underlines this fact in order

---

[14] 'Of them all, those who dwell in Kent are by far the most civilized' (Caesar, *Gallic Wars*, 5. 14, ii (1995), p. 141.
[15] Strabo, *Geography*, i (1966), 2. 5. 8, p. 443.   [16] Ibid., ii. 4. 5. 2, p. 255.
[17] Ibid., ii. 4. 5. 4, p. 259.

to establish the validity of his report. He distances himself from previous writers on the subject and says that his text will report facts faithfully: 'Britanniae situm populosque multis scriptoribus memoratos non in comparationem curae ingeniiue referam, sed quia tum primum perdomita est; ita quae priores nondum comperta eloquentia percoluere, rerum fide tradentur'.[18] Previous accounts of Britain are ornate and inaccurate, and although Tacitus claims not to challenge them, in fact, he does. He opposes the rhetoric inherent in older narratives to the factuality characterizing his own. The Roman author says that Agricola did not merely travel to the island: he was the first thoroughly to survey and to control it. The military power he gained over this remote region vouches for the accuracy of the information he reports.

Tacitus follows the convention that confines Britain to the periphery: he implies that there is no land to the north of it when he says: '... septentrionalia eius, nullis contra terris, uasto atque aperto mari pulsantur'.[19] A few lines below, he adds that Agricola was the first to circumnavigate Britain and to discover its insularity: 'hanc oram [north of Scotland] nouissimi maris tunc primum Romana classis circumuecta insulam esse Britanniam adfirmauit'.[20] In Tacitus's European geography, Britain is the remotest of all lands, it lies in the 'last sea' (the *novum mare*) and has remained, until Agricola's coming, uncharted and unknown. Its northern borders were not precisely defined until the Roman governor's expedition surveyed this outlying corner of the world. The mapping of a mysterious land counts as one of the great deeds of the illustrious man and it provides Agricola with an occasion to win fame. Distance becomes something positive: the testing-ground of great men. The mention of the circumnavigation of Britain moreover indicates that Agricola literally encompasses and symbolically appropriates the island. Tacitus's narrative therefore claims the whole of Britain for the known world, an interpretation that is supported by the name the British chief Calgacus

---

[18] 'The geographical position of Britain and its people have been recorded by many writers; I record them not to challenge comparison in the matter of accuracy or talent, but because for the first time it was thoroughly subdued: thus, those things, which earlier writers, not yet informed, have adorned with their stilted eloquence, these will be faithfully exposed' (Tacitus, *Agricola* 10. 1) Tacite, *Vie d'Agricola*, ed. and trans. by E. de Saint-Denis (Paris: Belles Lettres, 1942; repr. 1967), 8.

[19] 'its [Britain's] northern parts have no lands opposite them, but are beaten by a vast and open sea' (Tacitus, *Agricola* 10. 2, p. 8).

[20] 'for the first time, the Roman fleet sailed round the shore of the last sea and established that Britain was an island' (Tacitus, *Agricola*, 10. 5, p. 8).

later gives his Roman enemies: *raptores orbis*.[21] Agricola's journey explores a distant land and in so doing annexes it to the Roman sphere of control.

Britain's remoteness is again foregrounded in the speech Tacitus attributes to Calgacus. Interestingly, in these lines, distance becomes something positive, for the insular leader declares that isolation has preserved the island's freedom and independence, that it has for a long time 'defended' the Britons and protected the island from invaders.[22] Although the British ruler praises the independence granted by distance, he is also aware that the periphery is at the same time a place that invites exploration and invasion. Remote regions may appeal to some, for, as Calgacus notes, 'omne ignotum pro magnifico est'.[23] The distance that is usually a mark of barbarism signals here the last free corner of the world: at the same time, it invites exploration and conquest.

This brief survey indicates that classical learning traditionally places Britain on the outskirts of the known world. But it also demonstrates that the evaluation of distance does not rely solely on scientific measurement: its appreciation varies depending on the context and on the author's particular agenda. Throughout the *Agricola* for instance, Tacitus plays with the topos that views Britain as a remote land. He uses it to enhance the achievements of his hero who has mapped an outlying island. Furthermore, by investing with positive meaning the distance separating Britain from a Roman centre of civilization, the historian suggests that his protagonist took control over the desirable home of proud and sovereign warriors, over the last free corner of the world. Although remoteness is usually suspect, always a place of possible monstrosity and savageness, it can also shelter freedom and marvels.

Britain and the Finis Terrae

If the quality of the distance separating Britain from the Continent may fluctuate, so does the precise location of the island. For is Britain really the last land toward the north? Or is it not quite the last? The island's

---

[21] Tacitus, *Agricola*, 30. 6, p. 24.
[22] 'Nos terrarum ac libertatis extremos recessus ipse ac sinus famae in hunc diem defendit' (Tacitus, *Agricola* 30. 4, p. 24).
[23] 'all that is unknown is magnified' (Tacitus, *Agricola*, 30. 4, p. 24). On this point, see also M. Gorrichon, 'La Bretagne dans la "Vie d'Agricola" de Tacite', in R. Chevallier (ed.), *Littérature Gréco-Romaine et Géographie Historique: Mélanges offerts à Roger Dion*, Caesarodunum, 9bis (Paris: Picard, 1974), 191–205 (204).

geographical situation is often articulated in relation to the fringes of the earth: it is depicted sometimes as the ultimate, sometimes as the penultimate land toward the north. This distinction, together with the localization of the ends of the world, is not immaterial, because it affects the characterization of the island, of its nature, and of its inhabitants.

In Caesar's geography, Britain is the last land toward the north. Having specified that it is shaped like a triangle, Caesar says: 'Tertium est contra septentriones; cui parti nulla est obiecta terra'.[24] There is nothing north of Britain, only the open sea: the island lies on the edge of the world. But compared with other antique world-views, Caesar's geographical picture lacks a crucial element in the depiction of the far north, namely Thule.

When reporting on Britain's geographical situation, Tacitus declares that there is no land north of it.[25] But he contradicts this assertion in his account of Agricola's journey round the island and this sailing expedition is the occasion for the Roman historian to mention another island in the ocean. He says: 'dispecta est et Thyle, quia hactenus iussum; et hiems adpetebat.'[26] Tacitus mentions Thule as a land Agricola has seen from afar. Whereas Britain is claimed as part of the Roman world, Thule is only surveyed at a distance. Yet this brief allusion links the two islands since the latter is only to be seen from the northern shores of the former. By calling 'Thule' the isolated land the Roman governor catches sight of when circumnavigating Britain, Tacitus conjures up the legendary limit of discovery and ensures that his hero, Agricola, has travelled as far north as possible. Crucially, therefore, once Thule is mentioned, the ends of the world are pushed beyond Britain, unfamiliar expanses open up, and Britain, no longer a terminus, becomes a last outpost before plunging into the unknown.

The first intelligence about Thule reached the Mediterranean world around 300 BC with Pytheas of Massalia, a navigator and a geographer, the first Greek to visit and describe Britain and the Atlantic coast of Europe. He claimed to have explored a large part of Britain on foot, and he was the first to mention Thule. Pytheas's work, *On the Ocean*, is lost, but his account is known through the writings of subsequent historians

---

[24] 'The third side faces north and has no land facing it' (Caesar, *Gallic Wars* 5. 13, ii. 141).
[25] '...septentrionalia eius, nullis contra terris, uasto atque aperto mari pulsantur' (Tacitus, *Agricola* 10. 2, p. 8).
[26] 'Thule was also seen, because their orders stopped there: winter was approaching' (Tacitus, *Agricola* 10. 6, pp. 8–9).

and geographers.²⁷ According to Strabo, Pytheas says that it takes six days to sail from Britain to Thule and that this remote island lies near the frozen sea.²⁸ In these regions, Pytheas declares, land, sea, and air are indistinguishable: the elements remain in suspension together and the result is a substance resembling sea-lungs, on which one can neither sail nor walk.²⁹

On the Ocean has often been quoted by later authors, and some of its content has thus been preserved through the ages. Strabo figures prominently in the transmission of Pytheas's text; he mentions Thule, the last land that bears a name: 'for Thule, of all the countries that are named, is set farthest north'.³⁰ Although Strabo seems to admit the presence of the island in this passage, he nevertheless endeavours to prove that it does not exist and that Pytheas lied in his account of the far north. He heavily attacks the ancient explorer's findings and says that he has found him, 'upon scrutiny, to be an arch-falsifier'.³¹ In fact, Strabo is unhappy with Pytheas because he does not think that the earth could be inhabited as far north as Thule. When he discusses this distant island, he tends to focus on the question of the ends of the earth, which, as we have seen, he situates in Ierne.³² But whether the Greek geographer chooses Ierne or Thule as the ends of the world, one should notice that he clearly places yet another land beyond Britain.

The link between Thule and Britain, on the one hand, and between Thule and the ends of the world, on the other, is also drawn by Pliny the Elder in his *Natural History*. The Roman author mentions Thule as the most distant of all the islands surrounding Britain: 'ultima omnium quae memorantur Tyle'.³³ Britain lies in the distance, but further away there is Thule, the 'ultima' island.³⁴

Classical tradition generally places another island beyond Britain, be it Thule or Ierne. Consequently, even though Britain is far away from Rome, the distance separating these two geographical locations does not necessarily imply that the northern island lies on the edge of the world. Thule, glimpsed from afar, marks the ends of the earth. Being further

---

[27] On the surviving fragments and testimonies of Pytheas's work, see Christina Horst Roseman, *Pytheas of Massalia: On the Ocean: Text, Translation and Commentary* (Chicago: Ares, 1994).
[28] Strabo, *Geography of Strabo* i. 1. 4. 2, p. 233.
[29] Strabo, *Geography* i. 2. 4. 1, p. 399.   [30] Ibid., ii. 4. 5. 5, p. 261.
[31] Ibid., i. 1. 4. 3, p. 235.   [32] Ibid., i. 2. 5. 8, p. 443, and i. 2. 5. 14, p. 457.
[33] 'the last of all those recorded is Thule' (Pliny, *Natural History* 4. 16. 104, p. 349).
[34] See also Solinus, *Collectanea Rerum Memorabilium* 22. 9, pp. 101–2.

away than Britain, Thule pulls it away from the margins and places it on the dividing line between the familiar and the mysterious. Britain mediates between a civilized world centred on Rome and the wilderness lurking beyond its shores: it fully belongs to neither of them.

In the picture emerging from this quick survey of classical views of Britain and of the location of the *finis terrae*, the distance between the Mediterranean centre of civilization and these northern lands is never downplayed. But the meaning assigned to distance may vary, depending on the general intent of the text, as the *Life of Agricola* demonstrates. Moreover, the association of Britain with Thule complexifies the location of the former island: it sits uneasily between the familiar vicinity and the misty and inscrutable margins of the world.

ANGLO-SAXON VIEWS OF BRITAIN'S GEOGRAPHICAL LOCATION

Textual Evidence

From the classical tradition, Anglo-Saxon authors inherit a geography wherein their island lies in the distance and they write against a background which confines them to the fringes of the world: from Pytheas to Isidore, Britain belongs to the periphery. But how do Old English authors receive this spatial layout? How do they perceive the geography of northern Europe, and especially Britain's position in it? The classical outlook, which defines the Anglo-Saxons as outsiders, was likely to pose a problem to the inhabitants of the British Isles; for, centre and periphery, distances and boundaries are relative concepts that are a function of the subject's point of view, and insular authors most probably did not feel themselves to be marginal and peripheric. Experience contradicted, and thus challenged traditional geographical scholarship.

Moreover, geography was never immune to the promptings of contemporary events. For instance G., the anonymous author of the *De Situ Orbis*, a Carolingian scientific treatise, testifies to the influence of worldly affairs on spatial knowledge. In his Prologue, he declares that he has been spurred to write his geographical text not simply by the demands of his pupils, but more urgently by the Norman incursions into Gaul.[35] The impending danger caused by northern raiders calls

---

[35] 'studio quorundam fratrum nostrorum admonitus, immo ob utriusque maris aliquantulum ignotos navigationis excursus, discipulorum mitissima deprecatione accensus,

for a better geographical knowledge and motivates the exploration and (re)mapping of the shores of northern Europe: historical circumstances occasion a re-evaluation of traditional learning.

In 'Of Myths and Maps: the Anglo-Saxon Cosmographer's Europe', Margaret Bridges reflects on Old English authors' response to this classical inheritance and she wonders at their late reactions against this marginal position. She says: 'it does seem suspicious, however, that English cosmographers should have continued for so long to transmit and translate works in which they are thus marginalized, until such time, well into the thirteenth century, as they develop strategies for recuperating *auctoritas*'.[36] But do the Anglo-Saxons really wait until the thirteenth century to develop such strategies? A careful reading of Bede, of the *Old English Orosius*, of geographical treatises by natives of the British Isles, such as Dicuil, together with an analysis of early medieval maps, will suggest that the Anglo-Saxons are not content to repeat and faithfully to transmit their sources: they transform them into original narratives in which they redefine the northern confines of the continent and recentre themselves on the map of the world.

Bede

In the writings of the Northumbrian historian there are two moments relevant for an investigation of the position vernacular authors assign to their island: the first is the opening of the *Ecclesiastical History*, where the Anglo-Saxon scholar describes Britain and situates it in a wider European geography, and the second are the allusions to Thule scattered in his scientific and exegetical texts.

The *Ecclesiastical History* opens with a description of Britain. This passage is a mosaic of quotations from Pliny, Gildas, Solinus, and Orosius.[37] Bede follows Pliny when he situates Britain opposite Germany, Gaul, and Spain, and when he specifies that the island is located at a great distance—'multo interuallo aduersa'[38]—across from continental Europe. He literally echoes Orosius when he says that Britain's northern coast has the Orkney Islands behind it: 'A tergo autem, unde

---

hunc de situ orbis libellum ex multorum praecedentium qui hinc tractaverunt dictis excerptum componere studui' *Anonymi Leidensis De Situ Orbis Libri Duo*, ed. by Riccardo Quadri (Padua: Antemore, 1954), 3.

[36] Margaret Bridges, 'Of Myths and Maps: the Anglo-Saxon Cosmographer's Europe', SPELL, 6 (1992), 69–84 (72).

[37] Bede, *Ecclesiastical History* i. 1, p. 14, note 1.   [38] Ibid., i. 1, p. 14.

Oceano infinito patet, Orcadas insulas habet.'[39] Bede does not mention Thule: the legendary island is not part of the *Ecclesiastical History*'s geography. The allusion to the *Oceanus infinitus* bathing Britain's northern coast and the absence of reference to Thule, which would have pushed the ends of the earth further north, suggest that Britain is far away from the European mainland. Britain, together with the Orkney Islands, is confined to the boundless ocean that surrounds the land masses.

In his scientific writings Bede develops another kind of geography which extends further north beyond Britain. In *De Temporum Ratione*, he discusses the length of the day at the summer solstice: he traditionally resorts to the theory of the five climatic zones and mentions the number of hours of daylight from Meroe (located near the sources of the Nile) to Britain: 'Sic fit, ut uario lucis incremento in Meroe longissimus dies xii horas aequinoctiales et octo partes unius horae colligat, Alexandriae uero xiiii horas; in Italia xv, in Britannia xvii, ubi aestate lucidae noctes haud dubie repromittunt... subiecta terrae continuos dies habere senis mensibus'.[40] Bede then alludes to Pytheas's travel to Thule—six days' sail north of Britain—and quotes what Pliny and Solinus say about the island, namely, that there is no day during the winter solstice and no night during the summer one. He relies on classical sources at this point and does not claim any first-hand knowledge of Thule. What matters here is that the Anglo-Saxon author acknowledges the existence of a last land beyond his own, thus contradicting his own report on Britain's geography found at the beginning of the *Ecclesiastical History*.

Bede again mentions Thule and the solstice phenomenon in an exegetical text: *In Regum xxx Quaestiones*. He identifies the origin of his information: it derives from 'ueterum historiae et nostri homines aeui qui illis de partibus adueniunt'.[41] At this point, the Anglo-Saxon scholar

---

[39] 'Behind the island, where it lies open to the boundless ocean, are the Orkney islands' Bede, *Ecclesiastical History*, i. 1, p. 14. See also Orose, *Histoires (Contre les Païens)*, ed. and trans. by Marie-Pierre Arnaud-Lindet, 3 vols. (Paris: Belles Lettres, 1990–1), i. 31.

[40] 'So it happens that by the variable increase of light in Meroe the longest day counts twelve equinoctial hours and a little more, in Alexandria fourteen hours; in Italy fifteen, in Britain seventeen, where in the summer clear nights without doubt promise... that the regions of the earth lying under have continuous day for six months' *Bedae Venerabilis: Opera: Pars vi: Opera Didascalica*, ed. by C. W. Jones, Corpus Christianorum Series Latina, 123 B (Turnhout: Brepols, 1975), 378–9. Please note that I discuss only *De Temporum Ratione* ch. 31, since it combines material on Thule and the length of the days found at other points in Bede's scientific writings, namely *De Temporum vii* and *De Natura Rerum ix*.

[41] 'the stories of the elders and the men of our time who come from these regions' *Bedae Venerabilis: Opera: Pars ii: Opera Exegetica 2*, ed. by D. Hurst, Corpus Christianorum Series Latina, 119 (Turnhout: Brepols, 1962), 317.

complements classical reports with testimonies of actual travellers. The allusion to people from those regions visiting Britain implies that these lands are inhabited and that it is possible to journey to and fro between them. The historian hesitates about Thule's precise location, for he says of the solstice that 'hoc qui in insula Thule quae ultra Brittanniam est uel in ultimis Scytharum finibus degunt . . . fieri uident'.[42] This physical phenomenon is seen either in Thule, beyond Britain, or on Scythia's outermost borders. Bede might at this point be referring to reports about northern European or Asiatic regions. The historian could have heard about them either from people dwelling there or from occasional travellers to these areas, one thinks of Wulfstan or Ohthere, for instance. If this is the case, the Anglo-Saxon author might be attempting to reconcile tradition about Thule and first-hand accounts about northern lands. Be that as it may, what matters here is that Bede is caught in a tension between the contrasting views of Thule and the far north found in classical authorities on the one hand and in reports of real travellers on the other.

There is a surprising discrepancy within Bede's geographical writings. In his scientific and exegetical works, Thule lies north of Britain and the author alludes to reports of people who have travelled to these northern lands. The mention of actual journeys taking place between these two locations demystifies the far north, and all the more Britain. In the *Ecclesiastical History*, the Anglo-Saxon historian constructs his geographical section on previous authorities: Britain is the last land toward the north, facing the boundless ocean. It decidedly lies in the periphery.

I opened this chapter with Bede's anecdote of the Anglo-Saxon slave boys, an episode to which I would like to return now. I suggested above that the fact that the Northumbrian historian was himself a native of the British Isles accounted for the positive picture of the insular youths and their homeland these lines present. And yet, even though he discards here the traditionally negative view of his island and thus seems to retrieve his homeland from the misty confines of the earth, Bede nevertheless locates Britain in the distance. Gregory, for instance, does not know anything about the slave boys: he does not know who they are, where they come from, who their king is. For him, Britain is a complete *terra incognita*. A few lines below, the distance separating Britain from Rome is again foregrounded. For, as soon as he sees the Anglo-Saxon youths, Gregory

---

[42] 'those who live in the island of Thule which is beyond Britain or in the last regions of the Scythians . . . see it happen' (*Bedae Venerabilis: Opera: Pars* II: *Opera Exegetica 2*, 317).

wants to set out to their island on a mission of religious conversion. But Bede specifies: 'Quod dum perficere non posset quia, etsi pontifex concedere illi quod petierat uoluit, non tamen ciues Romani, ut tam longe ab urbe secederet, potuere permittere'.[43] Britain is presented as remote and difficult of access, and the journey there is perilous.

Even though he clearly writes this episode in praise of his homeland and of his fellow countrymen, Bede nevertheless retains some of the topoi which locate Britain in the periphery. The way the historian articulates centrality and distance is a question of special significance in a work which, like the *Ecclesiastical History*, is focused on Rome in its defence and promotion of orthodox religious observances. Although he does not play down the distance separating his island from Rome, Bede linguistically redeems it with the puns he attributes to Gregory. For they rehabilitate another crucial element constitutive of Britain's alterity, namely language. The initial incomprehension that necessitated a translator mediating between Gregory and the slave boys vanishes when the vernacular names *Angli*, *Deiri*, and *Ælle* become the portents of the Anglo-Saxons' extraordinary religious destiny.[44] The puns are more than a movement of cultural appropriation; they are linguistic and creative acts that conjure up a new mental space, the homeland of 'angelic' inhabitants. As such, they influence the perception of Britain's location and of the character of its inhabitants, and they testify to the power of language to characterize, define, and locate.

In the anecdote of the slave boys, Bede transforms distance into something positive and appealing; he transcends it by inscribing his homeland and its inhabitants in a religious frame of reference. Consequently, the evaluation and perception of distance vary depending on the narrative context. The last chapter of this study will return to this contrast when examining the description of Britain found at the beginning of the *Ecclesiastical History* and when analysing the various rhetorical devices which make of Britain a special land reserved for a special people.

---

[43] 'But he was unable to perform this mission, because although the pope was willing to grant his request, the citizens of Rome could not permit him to go so far away from the city' (Bede, *Ecclesiastical History*, ii. 1, p. 134).

[44] On this point, see also Nicholas Howe, *Migration and Mythmaking in Anglo-Saxon England* (New Haven: Yale University Press, 1989), 18–19, and Nicholas Howe, 'An Angle on this Earth: Sense of Place in Anglo-Saxon England', *Bulletin of the John Rylands University Library of Manchester*, 82 (2000), 3–27 (4–5).

Ælfric

Bede's cosmological comments in the *De Temporum Ratione* are the source of a closely related passage in Ælfric's *De Temporibus Anni*.[45] Ælfric also discusses the length of the day at the summer solstice and he repeats the same four landmarks that his predecessor mentions: Meroe, Alexandria, Italy, and Britain. About Britain, he says: 'On Engla lande hæfð se lengsta dæg seofontyne tida; On ðam ylcan earde norðeweardan beoð leohte nihta on sumera swilce hit ealle niht dagige swa swa we sylfe foroft gesawon.'[46] Ælfric departs from his source when he adds a reference specifically to the north of Britain where, he says, summer nights are clear. This allusion gestures toward northern lands, more precisely toward Thule, which the insular author introduces in the following lines, and it diminishes the gap separating the two islands. In this geography, lands and islands extend toward the north in a continuum. More importantly still, Ælfric evokes direct knowledge of the solstice phenomenon he describes and he supports his assertion with the phrase: 'swa swa we sylfe foroft gesawon'. The meteorological events so typical of Thule can also be observed in Britain. Thule can no longer therefore be depicted as another world of wonder and marvel, and its radical otherness is undermined. Finally, when he talks about the last island toward the north, Ælfric does not quote any authority. He simply says: 'Thile atte an igland benorðan þisum iglande six daga fær on sæ'.[47] He does not base his report on previous sources and the information he provides is no longer mediated by classical learning. As Bede before him, Ælfric supports his scientific writings on the characteristics of the north with direct experience; and he moves from the oral reports the Northumbrian scholar heard second-hand to the assertion that 'we' witness the phenomena described. These two insular authors signal a change of attitude not only toward traditional knowledge, but more importantly toward the reality being described; for, Britain and other northern lands become places where people actually live and to which one can travel: they are no longer inaccessible reaches lost in the periphery.

---

[45] Ælfric, *De Temporibus Anni*, ed. by Heinrich Henel, EETS os. 213 (London: Oxford University Press, 1942), 6. 14–20, pp. 48–50.

[46] 'In England, the longest day has seventeen hours; in that same land toward the north, the nights are clear in the summer, as if it was dawn all night long, just as we ourselves very often saw' (Ælfric, *De Temporibus Anni* vi. 17–18, pp. 48–50).

[47] 'There is an island called Thule to the north of this land, six days' sail on the sea' (Ælfric, *De Temporibus Anni* vi. 19, p. 50).

The Old English Orosius

During the reign of King Alfred, an ambitious translator rendered Orosius's *Historiarum adversum Paganos Libri septem* into Old English. This translator took many liberties with his source text, especially in his depiction of northern Europe and of the fringes of the world. The *Old English Orosius* innovates in its approach to these questions: it presents a view of the septentrional end of the continent based on actual exploratory travels and it attempts to provide an accurate geography of these regions. The report of Ohthere's journey, for instance, may be understood as an effort to clarify the exact location of various northern lands and people. But the translator's geographical innovations have a wider impact and in the opening pages of the vernacular rendering it is the geography of the whole of Europe that is modified according to better, more precise spatial information. As a consequence, Britain's place on the map of the world is redefined.

The provenance of the translator's better geographical knowledge is a moot question. In an article on 'The Relationship between Geographical Information in the *Old English Orosius* and Latin Texts other than Orosius', Janet Bately calls for the study of the text's first chapter as an independently rewritten section.[48] Most of the additions to Orosius's Latin original, both to the opening pages and to the subsequent body of the text, can be traced back to Latin sources. But the new material concerning continental Europe is an exception. It does not derive from classical texts and no definite alternative authority has been found for it. Several options have been put forward to explain its origins: oral reports from travellers, first-hand knowledge, Latin or vernacular texts, or a world map. In the introduction to her edition of the *Old English Orosius*, Bately summarizes the critical debate that has developed around the provenance of this new geographical learning and the possible use of a *mappa mundi*, and she concludes:

> The author of Or. [Old English Orosius], then, in his revising of OH [Latin Orosius], may have had at his disposal a *mappa mundi*, though there is no conclusive evidence that this was actually the case. He was quite possibly aided by an annotated or glossed Latin manuscript or by a commentary on OH,

---

[48] Janet M. Bately, 'The Relationship between Geographical Information in the *Old English Orosius* and Latin Texts other than Orosius', *Anglo-Saxon England*, 1 (1972), 45–62 (45).

though this too is a matter of conjecture. What cannot be disputed is that he had access to a considerable body of geographical information in addition to that provided by OH.[49]

The sources of the translator's intelligence cannot be identified with certainty, but the additions certainly betray a concern for geographical information. They aim at presenting a more accurate picture of Europe than that found in the Latin Orosius.

The present discussion will address three aspects of the *Old English Orosius*'s opening section: what the vernacular text has to say about Britain; its review of the frontiers of the European continent; and finally the nature of the additions about northern lands that the translator inserts in his report.

About Britain, the *Old English Orosius* says: 'Brittannia þæt igland, hit is norðeastland, 7 hit is eahta hund mila lang 7 twa hund mila brad. Þonne is be suðan him on oðre healfe þæs sæs earmes Gallia Bellica, 7 on westhealfe on oþre healfe þæs sæs earmes is Ibærnia þæt igland, 7 on norðhealfe Orcadus þæt igland.'[50] This passage is based on Orosius I. 2. 76–7, and the Old English text abridges it.[51] It is remarkably brief and the geographical information it conveys scant given that the translation was after all made in Britain. Various critics, from Malone to Bately, have noted the scarcity of details the translator provides about the island.[52] Bately says: 'Most surprising of all is what seems to be a total lack of interest in the history and geography of Britain. Nothing is added to the sketchy and inaccurate description of Britannia in the first chapter'.[53] The meagre part allotted to Britain's history and geography is indeed striking. For instance, although he translates a universal history, the vernacular author does not hint at the political situation prevailing

---

[49] *The Old English Orosius*, ed. by Janet Bately, EETS ss. 6 (Oxford: Oxford University Press, 1980), p. lxvii.
[50] 'The island of Britain extends toward the north-east and is eight hundred miles long and two hundred miles broad. Then to the south of it on the other side of the arm of the sea is Gallia Bellica and toward the west on the other side of the arm of the sea is the island of Ibærnia, and toward the north the island of Orkney' *The Old English Orosius*, 19.
[51] 'Britannia oceani insula per longum in boream extenditur; a meridie Gallias habet. Cuius proximum litus transmeantibus ciuitas aperit quae dicitur Rutupi portus; unde haud procul a Morinis in austro positos Menapos Batauosque prospectat. Haec insula habet in longo milia passuum DCCC, in lato milia CC.' Orose, *Histoires (Contre les Païens)*, 2. 76–7, i. 31.
[52] Kemp Malone, 'King Alfred's North: a Study in Medieval Geography', *Speculum*, 5 (1930), 139–67 (142).
[53] *The Old English Orosius*, p. xcvii.

at the time of composition, and especially not at the Viking attacks afflicting Anglo-Saxon England. Regarding this paradox, it might be argued that since the digest of world history found in the *Old English Orosius* complements that of other texts translated as part of King Alfred's scheme to revive learning in his kingdom, such as the Anglo-Saxon Chronicle and the Old English version of Bede's *Ecclesiastical History*, the *Old English Orosius* need not repeat information about Britain already provided by these two narratives.[54]

My discussion of the centres of *Beowulf*, and especially the ambiguity surrounding the location and the establishment of the text's focal points could suggest another possible explanation for the absence of any detailed reports about Anglo-Saxon England in this translation. The silence surrounding the island from which the work originates could be part of a narrative strategy aiming at establishing the centre as a special place, the point around which neighbouring lands are organized. The rest of the translation revolves around Rome, cradle of the Incarnation and middle point of the Christian view of history Orosius adopts. The opening section of the Old English rendering does not directly contradict this geographical perspective, but Ohthere's and Wulfstan's reports, together with the description of continental Europe, by implication designate Britain as the pivotal point in this world-view: instead of a terminus, the island becomes a spatial pivot, the place from which the rest of the world is surveyed. According to this hypothesis, therefore, the *Old English Orosius*'s first chapter constructs a poetic geography that purposely recoils from defining its own heart unless by implication. In this logic, Britain does not need to be commented upon: as it is the place where 'we' are, it is part of the familiar sphere. It is thus 'the world' that needs to be described, a perspective that subtly calls into question Rome's obvious centrality.

The *Old English Orosius* also radically reorganizes Europe's boundaries. In the introduction to her edition of the vernacular text, Janet Bately contends that 'in the section dealing with the geography of continental Europe, 12/14–19/10, changes are so radical that it is possible to consider the whole section as rewritten to conform to the ninth-century situation as known to the author of Or. [the *Old English Orosius*] or his

---

[54] This hypothesis implies that some at least of the prose texts translated or composed during the Alfredian period were part of a coherent plan and were thought of as a whole. There is, however, no conclusive evidence to support this hypothesis. I am indebted to Professor Malcom Godden who first suggested this idea to me.

immediate source.'⁵⁵ It would be beyond the scope of the present discussion to provide an exhaustive account of all of the translator's additions. I shall therefore limit my observations to the modifications brought to the northern and western frontiers of Europe on the one hand, and to the new depiction of the continent that emerges as a result of these changes, in particular as a result of Ohthere's report, on the other.

Passing in review the continent's western boundaries, the translator mentions Spain in the south-west and Ireland in the west. He says: 'Se westsuþende Europe landgemirce is in Ispania westeweardum et ðæm garsecge 7 mæst æt þæm iglande þætte Gaðes hatte . . . 7 hire on westende is Scotland.'⁵⁶ Later in the text, the vernacular author completes this picture toward the north saying that 'þonne be westannorðan Ibernia is þæt ytemeste land þæt man hæt Thila'.⁵⁷ The translator follows his source for the south-western and north-western limits, which were already set in Spain and Thule. But when he places Ireland west of Britain, he modifies Europe's occidental boundary, since the Latin Orosius placed it in the ocean beyond Spain and situated Ireland between Britain and Spain.⁵⁸ In her commentary, Bately points out that a translator working in England could be drawing on his personal experience when placing Europe's western extremity in Ireland.⁵⁹ Although this hypothesis cannot be proved, it is reinforced by the numerous recourses to experience found in other insular geographical descriptions. Examples of this practice have been found in Bede and Ælfric, to which one should add Ohthere's and Wulfstan's reports as well as Dicuil's *De Mensura Orbis*.

Interestingly, when the translator recapitulates Europe's frontiers, he does not clearly name any northern boundary for the continent. The closest he comes to doing so is when he delimits the extent of the *Germania* and mentions the *Cwensæ*. In this passage, the *Germania* is a region which extends 'norþ oþ þone garsecg þe mon Cwensæ hæt'.⁶⁰ In her notes, Bately says that the translator here renders 'per litus septentrionalis

---

⁵⁵ *The Old English Orosius*, p. lxvii.
⁵⁶ 'The south-western boundary of Europe is in Spain in the western part, at the ocean and especially at the island that is called Gades . . . and Europe's western extremity is in Scotland [that is, Ireland]' (*The Old English Orosius*, 9).
⁵⁷ 'Then to the north-west of Ibernia is that furthest land that is called Thule' (*The Old English Orosius*, 19).
⁵⁸ 'Europae in Hispania occidentalis oceanus termino est' Orose, *Histoires (Contre les Païens)*, 2. 7, i. 14; 'Hibernia insula inter Britanniam et Hispaniam sita longiore ab africo in boream spatio porrigitur' Orose, *Histoires (Contre les Païens)*, 2. 80, i. 32.
⁵⁹ *The Old English Orosius*, 159.
⁶⁰ 'north until the ocean that is called *Cwensæ*' *The Old English Orosius*, 12.

oceani' of the Latin Orosius, which is 'the extreme northern limit of the *oikoumene*, the known land mass'.[61] The actual location of the *Cwensæ* has given rise to numerous discussions; after summarizing them, the editor concludes by suggesting that the *Cwensæ* should be identified with 'a (known or unknown) stretch of water forming the northernmost boundary of *Germania* and taking its name from the people living, or believed to live, in that area, the *Cwenas*'.[62] I would like to stress here that the *Cwensæ* does indeed signal the frontier of the *Germania*; it is the northern limit of a territory about which the translator says: 'hit mon hæt eall Germania'.[63] The *Old English Orosius* mentions *Cwenland* and the *Cwenas* at other points, but these two terms always appear in connection with people of the *Germania*.[64] The *Cwensæ* is thus mentioned in connexion with a particular area and not when the translator rehearses the boundaries of the whole of Europe or of the oecumene. In fact the Old English author never sets a specific northern boundary to Europe. Thus he invites the inclusion of Ohthere's voyage and of his account of the far north. The presence of the traveller's report in the *Old English Orosius* may thus be understood as an attempt to clarify northern Europe's geography: once again, experience would be preferred to traditional knowledge.

Ohthere's Report

Ohthere is a Norwegian explorer whose travel account is found in the opening chapter of the *Old English Orosius*. This report (together with that of Wulfstan, another traveller) contains a unique description of northern Europe: when Ohthere sets out to travel, he goes due north. His journey may have been motivated by interesting trading opportunities. Bately reminds us in her notes that 'archaeological evidence appears to suggest that Norsemen were very active in the Arctic regions beyond the North Cape in the second half of the ninth century'.[65] Ohthere was thus perhaps involved in some mercantile activities and he could have travelled to England to find new markets for the goods he praises in his report.[66] But Ohthere himself suggests another reason for his journey:

---

[61] *The Old English Orosius*, 166.   [62] Ibid., 166.
[63] 'it is all called Germania' (*The Old English Orosius*, 12).
[64] On page 13, *Cwenland* is situated north of the Swedes, and on page 15, Ohthere reports on the attacks the Norwegians suffer at the hands of their northern neighbours, the *Cwenas*.
[65] *The Old English Orosius*, 180.
[66] See Jacqueline Simpson, *Everyday Life in the Viking Age* (London: Batsford, 1967), 97.

he says that he 'wolde fandian hu longe þæt land norþryhte læge, oþþe hwæðer ænig mon be norðan þæm westenne bude. Þa for he norþryhte be þæm lande'.⁶⁷ Even though the traveller was probably not the first to undertake this journey, he nevertheless presents himself as an explorer, as someone who intends to discover unknown territories. Consequently, his expedition amounts to a mapping enterprise, and the report of his exploration preserved at the court of King Alfred testifies to a symbolic control and appropriation of distant lands.

In accordance with the trope that links distance and savageness, Ohthere decidedly heads toward wild lands; for, he says that north of where he lives, the land 'is eal weste, buton on feawum stowum styccemælum wiciað Finnas, on huntoðe on wintra 7 on sumera on fiscaþe be þære sæ'.⁶⁸ The Finns the explorer mentions have a primitive lifestyle: they do not till the land, that is, they lack this early sign of civilization which marks the transition from nomad to settler. This is also the case of the Terfinnas, their neighbours, whom he meets further north. The description of their land echoes that of the Finns': it 'wæs eal weste, buton ðær huntan gewicodon, oþþe fisceras, oþþe fugeleras'.⁶⁹ Earlier in this chapter, the sections devoted to Caesar's and Strabo's views of northern Europe have shown that their accounts evoke an untamed wilderness peopled by savage creatures. As the boundaries of the familiar world are pushed further and further away, disparaging terms are used to describe distant regions. At first sight, Ohthere's account seems to be modelled on this trope. Yet, a different picture of the north emerges under closer analysis; for, beside the Terfinnas dwell the Beormas, who 'hæfdon swiþe wel gebud hira land'.⁷⁰ The Beormas are remarkable, because in addition to adapting their environment to their needs, they are also knowledgeable and they preserve some form of learning. Thus they inform Ohthere on a number of subjects: 'fela spella him sædon þa Beormas ægþer ge of hiera agnum lande ge of þæm landum þe ymb hie

---

[67] '[he] intended to explore how long that land stretched toward the north, or whether any man lived to the north of the wilderness. Then he went directly north along that land' (*The Old English Orosius*, 14).

[68] the land 'is all waste, except on a few places here and there [where] Finns camp, hunting in the winter and fishing at sea in the summer' (*The Old English Orosius*, 14).

[69] it 'was all waste, except where hunters camp, or fishermen, or fowlers' (*The Old English Orosius*, 14).

[70] who 'had cultivated their land very well' (*The Old English Orosius*, 14).

utan wæron'.⁷¹ The Beormas speak of their own land and of the territories surrounding them, thus indicating that they are familiar with these regions and that their spatial knowledge extends beyond their immediate environment. Even though Ohthere does not vouch for the truthfulness of these stories (this is the reason why he does not repeat them) and thus casts a doubt on their reliability, nevertheless in this account of the Beormas, distance no longer entails a plunge into barbarism. The explorer's report attests that civilized people dwell in the periphery.

Reflecting on the surprising absence of bitterness against the Danes in the *Old English Orosius*, R. Hodgkin points out that Alfred was especially concerned with barbarous people—not really with the Vikings: 'it was the outlandish, the abnormal, peoples—the Finns, the Beormas, and the Esti—who interested him [Alfred]'.⁷² But if the Finns are not a very 'advanced' people inasmuch as they do not cultivate the land, and if the Esti (who are mentioned in Wulfstan's report) have strange funerary customs, it is difficult to describe the Beormas as 'outlandish' or 'barbarous'. On the contrary, Ohthere's account, and in particular his description of this people, sketches a new centrality located toward the north. In the land of the Beormas, Ohthere arrives at a place where culture and knowledge coexist. Crucially, the inclusion of the Norwegian's report in the *Old English Orosius* affects Britain's geographical situation, and the Beormas function as a mirror image reflecting Alfred's own court. For, having demonstrated that it is possible to discover alternative centres of power and knowledge beside the obvious one in Rome (the focal point of Orosius's *Historiarum* and of its vernacular rendering), this travel narrative recasts the royal court as a new central point. The translator establishes several focal points in his text—Rome, Alfred's court, the Beormas; in so doing, he echoes *Beowulf* in questioning the status and the location of a civilized centre.

Before concluding on the *Old English Orosius*, a few words on the question of the textual status of Ohthere's and Wulfstan's reports. These two narratives, introduced by *Ohthere sæde* and *Wulfstan sæde*, are the most conspicuous of all the additions to the Latin Orosius.⁷³ They are testimonies of ninth-century (or possibly early tenth-century) travellers and they convey contemporary knowledge about northern

---

⁷¹ 'the Beormas told him many stories, both about their own land and about the lands that were round about them' (*The Old English Orosius*, 14).

⁷² R. H. Hodgkin, *A History of the Anglo-Saxons*, 3rd edn., 2 vols. (Oxford: Clarendon Press, 1935; repr. 1952), ii. 646.

⁷³ *The Old English Orosius*, 13 and 16.

Europe. These two reports in their entirety might well be later scribal interpolations, in which case they would not originally have been part of the vernacular translation. In 'Old English Prose before and during the Reign of Alfred', Bately convincingly argues that they have been interpolated.[74] In support of her argument, she notices the absence of transition between the geographical account that precedes and follows Ohthere's and Wulfstan's sections and their own narratives. There is no attempt to link the first and last words of the reports to the rest of the text. In a note, she concludes that 'all the signs are that the passages were added after the translation and rewriting of Orosius, *Historiarum Libri Septem* I, ii, was completed and that the *terminus ad quem* is the date of the Lauderdale ms'.[75] She explains the reports' stylistic peculiarities by suggesting that they record the replies given by Ohthere and Wulfstan to a series of unreported questions.[76] But even if the two narratives are scribal interpolations, they indicate that, in the England of Alfred's time — if the reports are contemporary with the translation of Orosius's text — or of Edward's time — if the interpolations shortly predate the composition of the Lauderdale manuscript, there was an extraordinary interest in geography, and especially in the geography of northern and continental Europe.

Dicuil

Dicuil's geographical treatise, the *Liber de Mensura Orbis Terrae* (*c*.825) echoes the opening section of the *Old English Orosius* in two respects: the author includes information from actual travellers in his account of the north and he depicts Britain as a starting point for exploratory travels.

Dicuil belongs to a tradition of Irish scholars who travelled to the Frankish kingdom. As a native of the British Isles, his perception of centrality and marginality is obviously not that of somebody from the Mediterranean region, and his own geographical expertise comes into play when he describes the northern and western limits of Europe. About the islands north-west of Britain, he says: 'in aliquibus ipsarum habitaui,

---

[74] Janet M. Bately, 'Old English Prose before and during the Reign of Alfred', *Anglo-Saxon England*, 17 (1988), 93–138.
[75] Bately, 'Old English Prose', 117. The manuscript is dated from the tenth century; see *The Old English Orosius*, p. xxiii.
[76] Bately, 'Old English Prose', 119.

alias intraui, alias tantum uidi, alias legi'.[77] He is familiar with these places and his account includes some that he visited personally. The author also resorts to what he has heard from travellers: when he talks of unknown islands around Britain, he bases his account on the testimony of a priest who sailed to one of them.[78] Dicuil further mentions islands to which Irish hermits used to journey and live before Norsemen started raiding these areas. Interestingly, the Carolingian author talks about these places even though he says that 'numquam eas insulas in libris auctorum memoratas inuenimus.'[79] Dicuil frees himself from classical learning: not content with modifying his sources, he also transmits some geographical knowledge that has not been mediated by tradition at all.

Discussing the islands around Britain, Dicuil mentions Thule. After the classical period, as perceptions of Britain's location on the map of the world change, so do ideas about this distant land and the ends of the earth. The Carolingian geographer reviews what classical authors say about Thule and he mentions Pliny, Isidore, Priscian, and Solinus.[80] But against them, he sets reports of real travellers: 'Trigesimus nunc annus est a quo nuntiauerunt mihi clerici qui a kalendis Febroarii usque kalendas Augusti in illa insula manserunt'.[81] Dicuil opposes experience to learned authorities, and he resorts to the former to correct what tradition says about the location of the frozen sea: 'Et idcirco mentientes falluntur qui circum eam concretum fore mare scripserunt'.[82] Dicuil does not reverently follow his sources and he considers actual travelling experiences to be valid testimonies. He grants them enough authority to modify traditional accounts of the far north on the basis of what this new intelligence reports.

The Carolingian author claims that, during his lifetime, clerics were living in Thule part of the year, and that he talked to some

---

[77] 'among these I have lived in some, and have visited others; some I have only glimpsed, while others I have read about' *Dicuili Liber de Mensura Orbis Terrae*, ed. and trans. by J. J. Tierney, Scriptores Latini Hiberniae, 6 (Dublin: Dublin Institute for Advanced Studies, 1967), vii. 6, pp. 72–4. The translations are from this edition.

[78] 'Aliquis presbyter religiosus mihi retulit' Dicuil, *De Mensura Orbis*, vii. 14, p. 74.

[79] 'I have never found these islands mentioned in the authorities' (Dicuil, *De Mensura Orbis*, vii. 15, p. 76).

[80] Dicuil, *De Mensura Orbis*, vii. 7–10, p. 74.

[81] 'It is now thirty years since clerics, who had lived on the island from the first of February to the first of August, told me...' (Dicuil, *Liber de Mensura Orbis*, vii. 11, p. 74).

[82] 'Therefore those authors are wrong and give wrong information, who have written that the sea will be solid about Thule' (Dicuil, *Liber de Mensura Orbis*, vii. 13, p. 74).

of them. These people have been identified with Irish hermits and Dicuil's Thule with Iceland. Icelandic historical sources mention the presence of anchorites from Ireland on the island when the Norwegians first arrived.[83] With Dicuil's account, Thule's history takes a new turn; for the island is no longer a concept—the 'last land'—but it becomes a real region, pinned down on the map and to which one can actually journey. The exploration of the far north transforms Thule, this distant place only vaguely known, into Iceland, an existing island, thus having experience confirm learned authorities. Traditional descriptions of Thule may not conform to Iceland's geographical reality in every particular, but the fundamental question of the existence of this distant island was resolved. Consequently, the ends of the world recede further away and, with them, the strangeness and barbarism attached to these unfamiliar areas. As the world opens up toward the north, the periphery retreats in the distance and Britain is gradually recentred. These vast northern regions eventually form a world of their own and its inhabitants situate themselves at the heart of this new geographical construct.

A fundamental shift of perspective characterizes both Dicuil's geographical treatise and the opening section of the *Old English Orosius*: Britain becomes a focal point from which exploratory travels originate and to which they return. The island's position is consequently redefined: it becomes a centre around which the periphery is distributed. In Dicuil's text, Britain is the standpoint from which neighbouring lands are viewed. Its classical portrayal as a remote land is silenced, and the island is now placed at the centre of a new spatial organization.

---

[83] 'En áðr Ísland byggðisk af Nóregi, váru þar þeir menn, er Norðmenn kalla papa; þeir váru menn kristnir, ok hyggja menn, at þeir hafi verit vestan um haf, því at fundusk eptir þeim bœkr írskar, bjǫllur ok baglar ok enn fleiri hlutir, þeir er þat mátti skilja, at þeir váru Vestmenn. Enn er ok þess getit á bókum enskum, at í þann tíma var farit milli landanna.' (But before Iceland was settled from Norway there were other people there, called *Papar* by the Norwegians. They were Christians and were thought to have come overseas from the west, because people found Irish books, bells, croziers, and lots of other things, so it was clear that they must have been Irish. Besides, English sources tell us that sailings were made between these countries at the time.) *Íslendingabók: Landnámabók*, ed. by Jakob Benediktsson, Íslenzk Fornrit, 1 (Reykjavík: Hið Íslenzka Fornritfélag, 1968), 31–2. See also the parallel account found in the *Íslendingabók*, 5 in this same volume. For the translation, see *The Book of Settlements: Landnámabók*, trans. by Herman Pálsson and Paul Edwards, Icelandic Studies, 1 (Winnipeg: University of Manitoba Press, 1972), 15. To my knowledge, the equation of Iceland with Dicuil's Thule has never been seriously questioned. Christina Horst Roseman says that by Dicuil's time the identification is 'almost certain': Roseman, *Pytheas*, 157.

142 Creation

In both texts, Britain also becomes a pole where scientific knowledge is gathered and preserved. With Ohthere's and Wulfstan's reports, the royal court of Wessex welcomes foreigners and stores new geographical information. Alfred, the Anglo-Saxon king, benefits from this spatial reorganization: it grants him the aura of prestige and power attached to one in contact with and in control of distant regions—Chapter 7 will come back to these issues at more length. It also casts his court as a place where strangers are received, and their reports contribute to the general increase of learning.[84] According to this outlook, Britain is a centre of knowledge and, as geographical knowledge signals power, the West Saxon court also symbolically extends its control over the various lands that have been surveyed and mapped in the course of these journeys.

Cartographic Evidence

In addition to scientific treatises, contemporary *mappae mundi* constitute another body of evidence which provides precious information when studying geographical constructs and medieval views of the world. I shall examine below a selection of early *mappae mundi*, that is, representations of the entire oecumene on which Britain's depiction and position is of special interest. Other types of maps produced during the Middle Ages, such as regional plans or portolan charts, as well as later, more famous, and more artistically accomplished cartographic representations, such as the Hereford or the Ebstorf maps, will not be commented upon at any length. More specifically, the present section will trace Britain's changing localization from the depiction of the world found in Manuscript 29 of the Albi library to the Cotton Map, the only map surviving from the Anglo-Saxon period. It will contrast continental and insular geographic depictions.

When thinking about medieval *mappae mundi*, some important qualifications should be kept in mind. First, although these maps offer a digest of what was known about the Christian world, they do not aim at geographical accuracy and do not attempt to gather and present the latest spatial knowledge of the day. But they fulfil various other functions. Mere diagrams, they could help to clarify some of the ideas developed by the accompanying texts or assist in the teaching

---

[84] Mary W. Helms, *Ulysses' Sail: An Ethnographic Odyssey of Power, Knowledge, and Geographical Distance* (Princeton: Princeton University Press, 1988), 5 and 63.

of geography. Thanks to their schematic nature, they were mnemonic tools which attached lists of names to particular geographical regions represented on the map,[85] whereas more elaborate *mappae mundi*, in recording significant events in world history, betray an exegetical or philosophical ambition. Secondly, a map is not an ahistorical and transcultural entity. It is a graphic representation mediating between the world and the viewer, and even if this mediation vanishes from sight, the *mappa mundi*'s apparent transparency is misleading.[86] For the map always conveys more than purely geographical information: it betrays its maker's cosmological, symbolic, political, or religious view of the world.[87] Because they prevent us from viewing maps as reliable depictions of an external reality, these reservations invite an examination of *mappae mundi*—and, in the present case, of Britain's position on them—as symbolic and ideological acts of representation. In an attempt to address the ideological implications inherent in any mapping process, the *mappae mundi* discussed here will be considered as instruments both of power and of (self-) representation.

Maps are objects of power. The world picture that the *mappa mundi* presents is beyond perception: no human being will ever be granted this two-dimensional and globalizing view from above. Unsurprisingly, therefore, cartography has for a long time remained a divine privilege, for only the gods can enjoy such an encompassing view of the world.[88] This notion permeates Roman imperial ideology, and one of the characteristics of the good leader becomes his knowledge and (symbolic) domination of the world, that is, his ability to map and represent it.[89] This tradition associates cartographic enterprises with ideal rulers, be they Caesar, Augustus, or Theodosius; for only the ideal ruler is granted the privilege to rank with the divinity.[90] A topos thus appears that links the good emperor to the cadastration of the totality of the world and

[85] Gautier Dalché, 'De la glose à la contemplation', 736.

[86] Christian Jacob, *L'Empire des cartes: approche théorique de la cartographie à travers l'histoire* (Paris: Albin Michel, 1992), 29–30.

[87] Jacob, *Empire des cartes*, 36.

[88] Pascal Arnaud, 'L'Affaire Mettius Pompusianus ou le crime de cartographie', *Mélanges de l'École Française de Rome. Antiquité*, 95 (1983), 677–99 (691).

[89] Patrick Gautier Dalché, 'Tradition et renouvellement dans la représentation de l'espace géographique au XIe siècle', in *Géographie et culture: La représentation de l'espace du VIe au XIIe siècle*, (Aldershot: Ashgate, 1997; first publ. in *Studi Medievali*, 24 (1983)), iv. 121–65 (125). See also Helms, *Ulysses' Sail*, 5.

[90] Arnaud, 'Affaire Pompusianus', 693–4. See also Patrick Gautier Dalché, *La 'Descriptio Mappae Mundi' de Hugues de Saint-Victor* (Paris: Études Augustiniennes, 1988), 89.

FIG. 1. Lambert of Saint Omer, *Liber Floridus*, depicting Augustus as a cartographer. Paris, Bibliothèque Nationale, MS Lat. 8865, fo.45. Bibliothèque Nationale photo.

to the subsequent establishment of a *mappa mundi*.[91] An illustration contained in a manuscript of the *Liber Floridus* of Lambert of Saint Omer, for instance, exemplifies this traditional motif: it represents the Emperor Augustus as a cartographer holding the terrestrial globe in his hand with an inscription indicating that he has issued an edict ordering the universe to be surveyed (Fig. 1).[92] At the beginning of the *De*

---

[91] Arnaud, 'Affaire Pompusianus', 694.
[92] The inscription in the circle around Augustus reads: 'Exiit edictum a Cesare Augusto ut describeretur universus orbis'. Marcel Destombes dates the manuscript from

Mensura Orbis, Dicuil inscribes himself within this same tradition when he declares that he will follow the authority of the envoys sent by the Emperor Theodosius to measure the world. For the Carolingian author, their account will prevail over that of Pliny.[93] Later in the Middle Ages, the thirteenth-century *mappa mundi* preserved at Hereford Cathedral illustrates this traditional notion.[94] At the bottom left-hand corner of the map the author, Richard of Holdingham, places the Emperor Augustus who hands a Latin decree to three surveyors, ordering them to 'go into the whole world and report back to Senate on every continent' (Fig. 2).[95] All these examples testify to the role attributed to sovereigns in the discovery, exploration, and appropriation of new territories. They express more clearly than narrative geographical treatises could the prestige attached to mapping enterprises as they figure the rights and control that are symbolically claimed over the spaces thus represented.[96]

Maps are also objects of representation and self-representation. Christian Jacob observes that the map reflects one of the constitutive features of any scientific activity, namely that 'connaître, c'est s'approprier, se représenter, se donner soi-même à voir'.[97] What is being displayed is not only a picture of the world, but more interestingly *soi-même*, that is, the very instance of knowledge. Drawing a map inevitably entails the

around 1260; for a description of the manuscript, see Marcel Destombes, *Mappemondes: AD 1200–1500* (Amsterdam: Israel, 1964), 115. See also Arnaud, 'Affaire Pompusianus' 695–6.

[93] 'cogitaui ut liber de mensura prouintiarum orbis terrae sequeretur secundum illorum auctoritatem quos sanctus Theodosius imperator ad prouintias praedictas mensurandas miserat; et iuxta Plinii Secundi praeclaram auctoritatem ipsarum dimensionem uolo supplens ostendere' (Dicuil, *De Mensura Orbis*, prologue, 1, p. 44).

[94] On this map, see Evelyn Edson, *Mapping Time and Space* (London: British Library, 1997), 139 ff., and P. D. A. Harvey, *Mappa Mundi. The Hereford World Map* (London: British Library, 1996).

[95] 'Ite in orbem vniu*er*sum · *et* de omni eius continencia referte ad senatum · *et* ad istam confirmandam Huic scripto sigillum meu*m* apposui ·' For the transcription and the translation: Harvey, *Mappa Mundi*, 54. This geographical project is reiterated in the pentagonal frame surrounding the picture, where one reads: 'A Iulio Cesare orbis terrarum metiri cepit. A Nicodoxo omnis oriens dimensus est. A Teodoco septemtrion et occidens dimensus est. A Policlito meridiana pars dimensus est'. See Naomi Reed Kline, *Maps of Medieval Thought: The Hereford Paradigm* (Woodbridge: Boydell and Brewer, 2001), 58, and Scott D. Westrem, *The Hereford Map: A Transcription and Translation of the Legends with Commentary*, Terrarum Orbis, 1 (Turnhout: Brepols, 2001), 3.

[96] Jacob, *Empire des cartes*, 44–5. See also Jacques Le Goff, 'Discorso di chiusura', in *Popoli e paesi nella cultura altomedievale*, 2 vols, Settimane di studio del Centro italiano di studi sull'alto medioevo, 29 (Spoleto: Centro Italiano di Studi sull'Alto Medioevo, 1983), 805–38 (836).

[97] Jacob, *Empire des cartes*, 44.

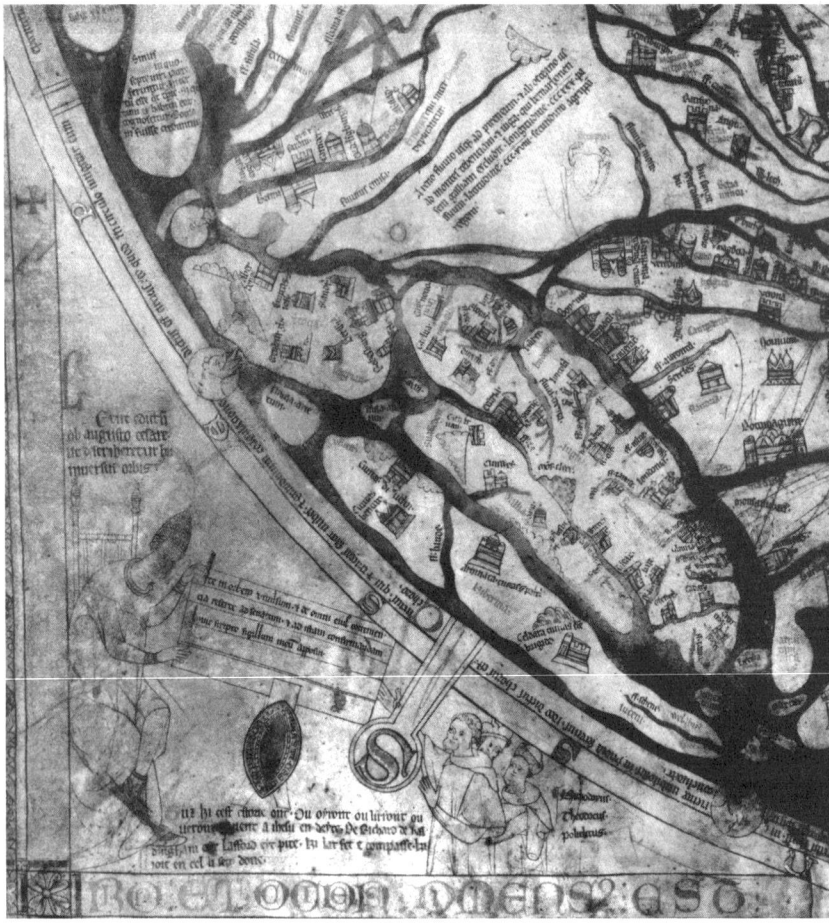

Fig. 2. The Hereford *mappa mundi* (detail). Parchment size 158 × 133 cm. Courtesy of the Dean and Chapter of Hereford and the Herford Mappa Mundi Trust.

staging of a cultural imagery. Where is the centre located? How does it relate to the periphery and to the ends of the world? For, a *mappa mundi* always addresses the question of where 'we' are and where 'they' dwell, that is, of what is central and what is marginal.

Britain is unmistakably on the edge of the world in one of the earliest medieval representations of the oecumene: the rough map found on folio 57ᵛ in Manuscript 29 of the Médiathèque Pierre Amalric (Fig. 3).[98] The manuscript is an eighth-century miscellanea originating from Spain or south-western France, and the map precedes geographical extracts. (The clarified sketch of it (Fig. 4) is taken from Konrad Miller's study of *mappae mundi*.) The Albi mapmaker shaped the earth like a horseshoe surrounded by the Outer Ocean. The map is oriented toward the east with Asia at the top, Europe on the left, and Africa on the right. The Mediterranean Sea is the extent of water reaching within the semicircle of lands. *Britania* is placed in the Ocean, opposite to *Ispania*, at the very bottom left-hand corner of the map. It is alone in lying in the Outer Ocean; all the other islands that are depicted on the map, such as *Corsica, Sardinia, Sicilia, Creta*, and *Cyprus*, are situated in the Mediterranean Sea and are enclosed in the land masses.

If the actual geography of Europe and its islands is reflected in this spatial organization (Britain is situated toward the north-west and islands such as Corsica, Sardinia, etc. in the Mediterranean), the map nevertheless stresses Britain's isolation, for it is the only place lying beyond the circle of lands represented by the horseshoe. Moreover, neither the shape of the island nor that of the European coastline suggests any relationship between the two places. The northern shores of the continental land masses are not indented in accordance with the shape of the island facing it, since the mapmaker adopts a conventional rounded or oval shape when drawing coastlines. Visually therefore, the Albi map clearly isolates Britain from the rest of the world.

The situation of Britain is more ambiguous on the Ripoll map, contained on fols. 143ᵛ–144ʳ of Manuscript 123 of the Queen of Sweden at the Vatican Library.[99] This map dates from the eleventh

---

[98] For a reproduction of the map and a descrpition of the manuscript, see *Catalogue général des manuscripts des bibliothèques publiques des départements*, i (Paris: Imprimerie Nationale, 1849), 486–7. See also Edson, *Mapping*, 32–3; Gautier Dalché, 'De la glose à la contemplation', 758–9; *Itineraria et alia geographica*, ed. by F. Glorie, Corpus Christianorum Series Latina, 175 (Turnhout: Brepols, 1965), 467–71, and Konrad Miller, *Mappae Mundi: die ältesten Weltkarten*, 6 vols. (Stuttgart: Roth'sche, 1895–98), iii (1895), 57–60.

[99] The map is discussed in Edson, *Mapping*, 80–5; Patrick Gautier Dalché, 'Notes sur la "carte de Théodose II" et sur la "mappemonde de Théodulf d'Orléans" ', in *Géographie et Culture: La représentation de l'espace du VIe au XIIe siècle* (Aldershot: Ashgate, 1997; first publ. in *Geographica Antiqua*, 3–4 (1994–5)), ix. 91–107; Gautier Dalché, 'De la glose à la contemplation', 761–2; Destombes, *Mappemondes*, 48; and A. Vidier, 'La Mappemonde de Théodulfe et la mappemonde de Ripoll', *Bulletin de géographie historique et descriptive*, 26 (1911), 285–318.

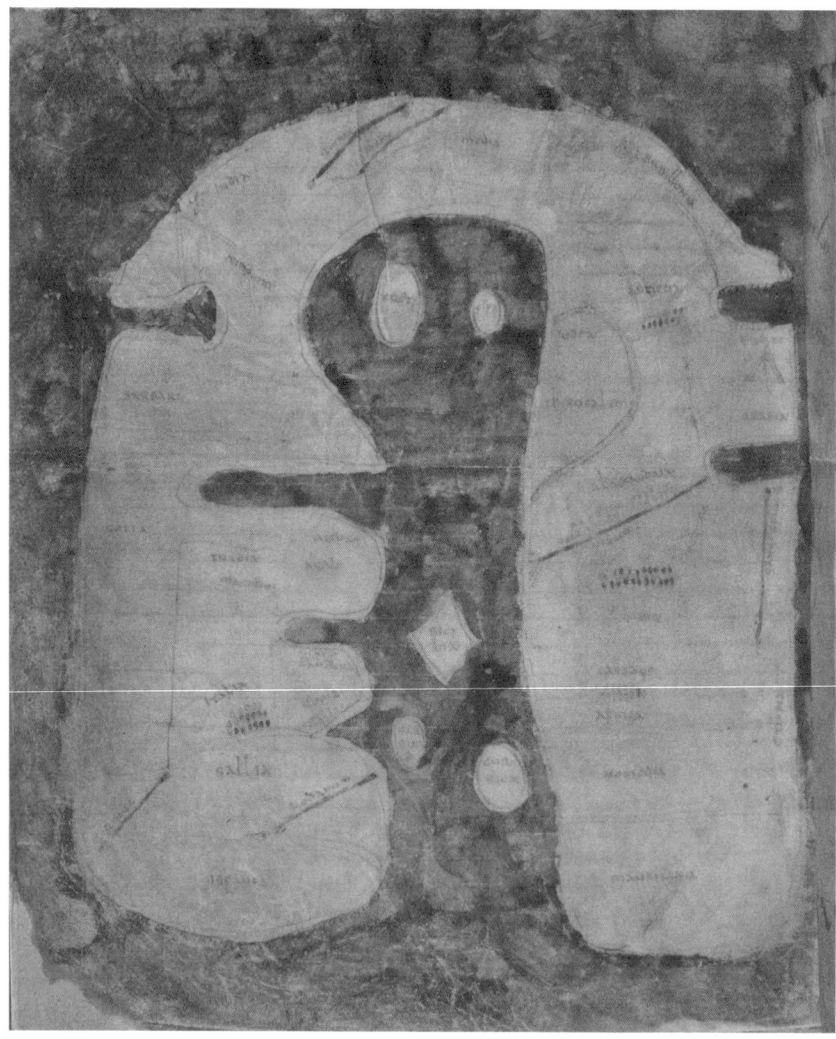

FIG. 3. The Albi *mappa mundi*. Map size 29 × 23 cm. Albi, Médiathèque Pierre-Amalric Rés. MS 115 (29), fo.57ᵛ.

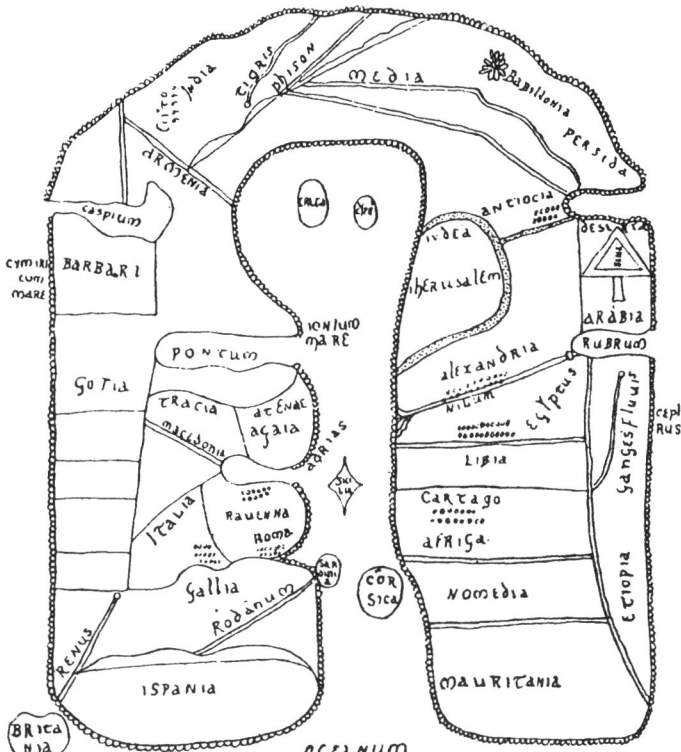

Fig. 4. Sketch of the Albi *mappa mundi*, from Konrad Miller, *Mappae Mundi: die ältesten Weltkarten*, 6 vols. (Stuttgart: Roth'sche, 1895-8, iii (1895), 58.

century and originates from Spain (Fig. 5). It is circular and joins the tripartite and the zonal mapping models. Oriented toward the east, it is surrounded by the Outer Ocean in which the twelve winds are represented. The left half of the circle depicts the world, following a TO structure; the disc is divided in two by an inscription explaining that the equator marks the limit of human knowledge about the earth. Logically, therefore, nothing is represented in the other half of the circle: the space remains free to contain textual inserts. Of special interest in this map is its depiction of the north, where one finds an inscription explaining that there is an uninhabitable zone toward the north and

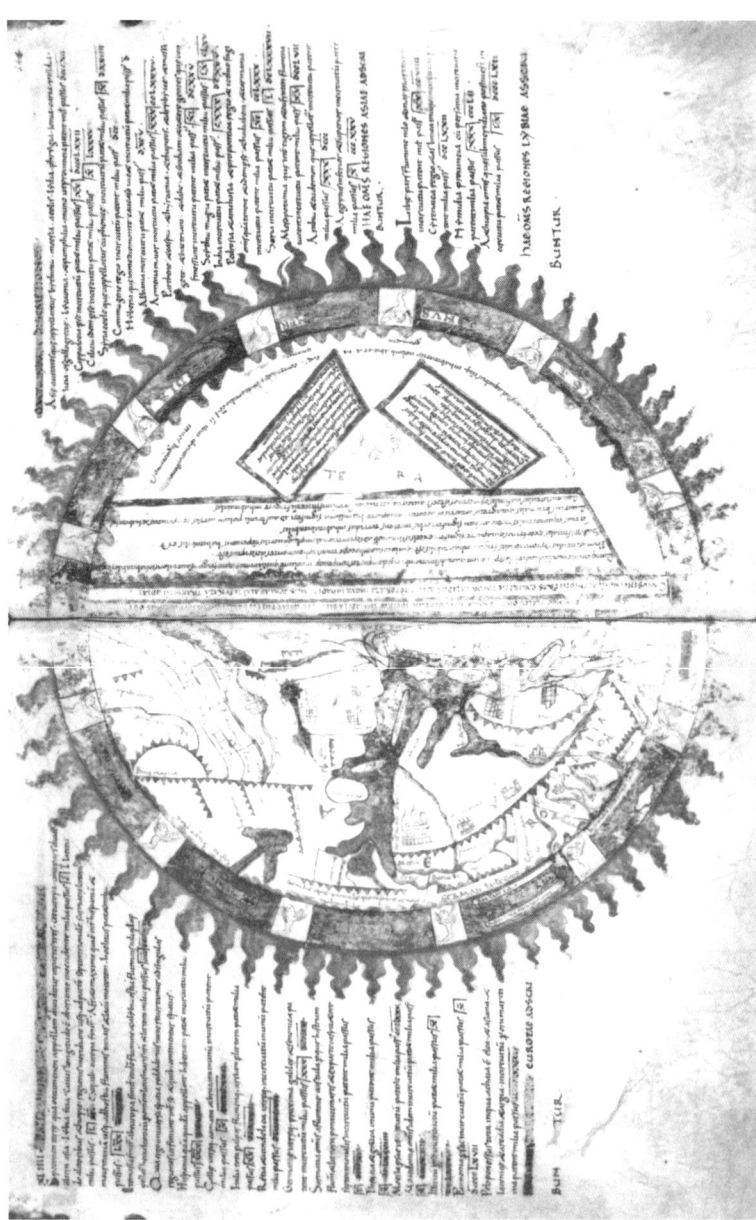

Fig. 5. The Ripoll Map. Diameter 33.8 cm. Biblioteca Apostolica Vaticana, Reg. Lat. 123, fos. 143ᵛ–144ʳ. © Biblioteca Apostolica Vaticana (Vatican).

Localization and Remapping 151

that the Greeks call it the Arctic.¹⁰⁰ This zone is located between a range of mountains and the Outer Ocean; *mappae mundi* do not usually represent this unknown region. Britain figures on the Ripoll Map: in the Outer Ocean are two islands, *Britania* and *Hibernia Scontorum* (Fig. 6). They are situated precisely beyond the range of mountains previously mentioned, the mountains that signal the division between the inhabited and uninhabited worlds. Thus, strictly speaking, Britain is located beyond the expanse of familiar and populated regions. But as Britain and Ireland are placed in the Ocean and not exactly on the strip of lands bearing the inscription, it is possible that the scribe who devised the map did not want to imply that Britain was uninhabitable. He might rather have located Britain close to these remote lands to convey the idea that it lies as far away as possible from the Mediterranean world.

The maps found in the manuscripts of Beatus of Liebana's *Commentary on the Apocalypse of St John* are, like the Albi *mappa mundi*, early testimonies of medieval world-views, since of the fourteen surviving full-page maps, four can with certainty be traced back to the tenth century.¹⁰¹ The largest and most detailed of the Beatus maps is the Saint-Sever exemplar, held in Paris, at the Bibliothèque Nationale, fonds latins 8878, between folios 45 and 46 (Fig. 7).¹⁰² It originates from Gascony and it was devised between 1028 and 1072, the dates of Abbot Gregory to whom the scribe, Stephanus Garsia, dedicates his work.¹⁰³ My comments here are based on this exemplar. The Saint-Sever map is oval and follows the traditional tripartition of the world between Asia, Europe, and Africa. It is oriented toward the east, where Adam and Eve are represented in Paradise, Eve picking the apple. Compared with the two preceding examples, the number of islands situated in the Outer Ocean toward the *septentrio* multiplies; one finds: *Insula Tile, Insula Briter, Insula Brittannia*, and *Insula Hibernia*. The size of these islands varies, but they all have the same oval outline and there is no attempt to differentiate them according

---

¹⁰⁰ 'circulus septentrionalis quem Grecis articos uocantur inabitabilis'. See the reproduction of the map in Vidier and the transcription of the text of the map in Gautier Dalché, 'Notes sur la "carte de Théodose II" et sur la "mappemonde de Théodulf d'Orléans" ', 97.
¹⁰¹ For a general stemma of the large Beatus maps, see *The History of Cartography*, ed. by J. B. Harley and David Woodward, 6 vols. (Chicago: University of Chicago Press, 1987), i. 305.
¹⁰² On the Beatus maps, see Edson, *Mapping*, 149–59.
¹⁰³ Edson, *Mapping*, 155.

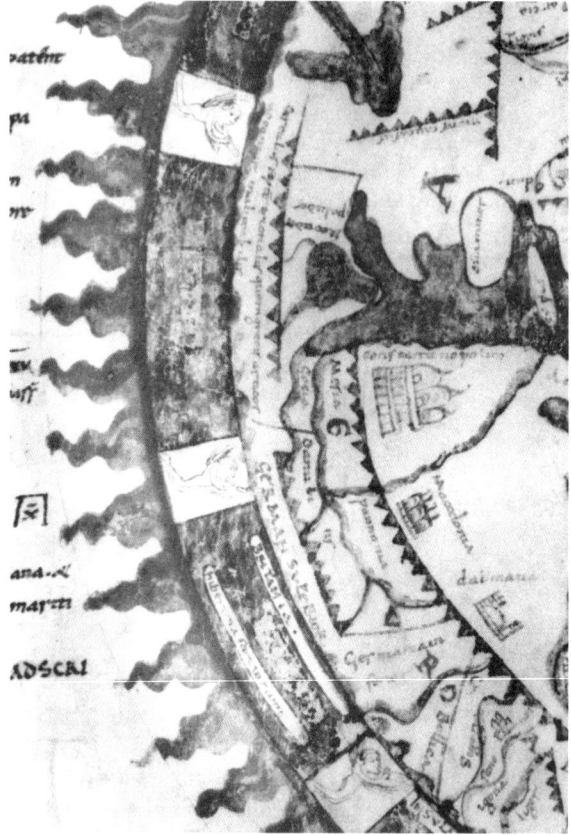

FIG. 6. The Ripoll Map (detail). Biblioteca Apostolica Vaticana. Reg. Lat. 123. fo. 143ᵛ. © Biblioteca Apostolica Vaticana (Vatican).

to their shapes. Britain stands out among them because it is by far the largest, and because five cities are depicted on it: *Lindino, Lindo, Uirigonio, Moriduno,* and *Condeaco* (Fig. 8). On this map, Britain lies once more in the periphery, in the Outer Ocean. But this representation differs from those found in the Albi or the Ripoll maps, for Britain is no longer isolated in the Ocean but is surrounded by three other islands. Moreover, its cities are pictured and this suggests that Britain is a familiar territory which has been mapped (even if only

Localization and Remapping 153

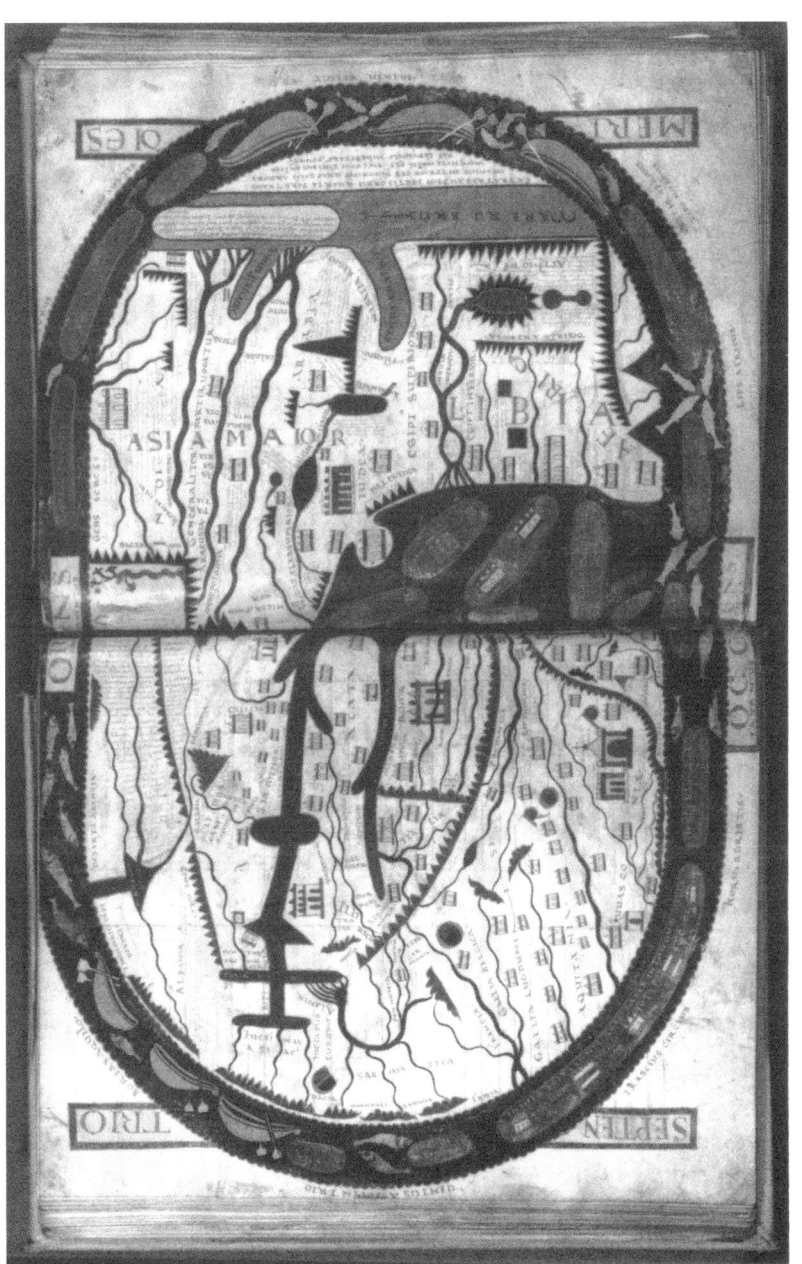

FIG. 7. The Saint-Server *mappa mundi*. Paris, Bibliothèque Nationale, MS Lat. 8878, fos. 45bis^v–45ter. Map size 57 × 37 cm. Bibliothèque Nationale photo.

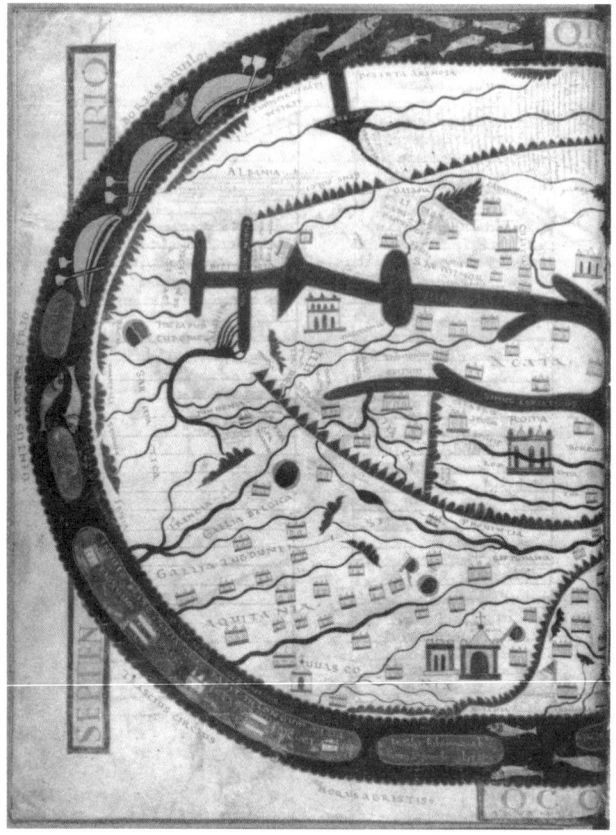

Fig. 8. The Saint-Server *mappa mundi* (detail). Paris, Bibliothèque Nationale, MS Lat. 8878, fo. 45bis^v. Bibliothèque Nationale photo.

roughly) and that its inhabitants are civilized, since they are able to build cities.

These three cartographic instances not only situate Britain in the margins, they also tend to isolate it from the Continent. As such, they display a view of the world, and especially of northern Europe, that accords with their southern origins.

Contrasting with these three southern maps, the Cotton Map was produced in England before the Conquest (Fig. 9). Preserved in British

Localization and Remapping 155

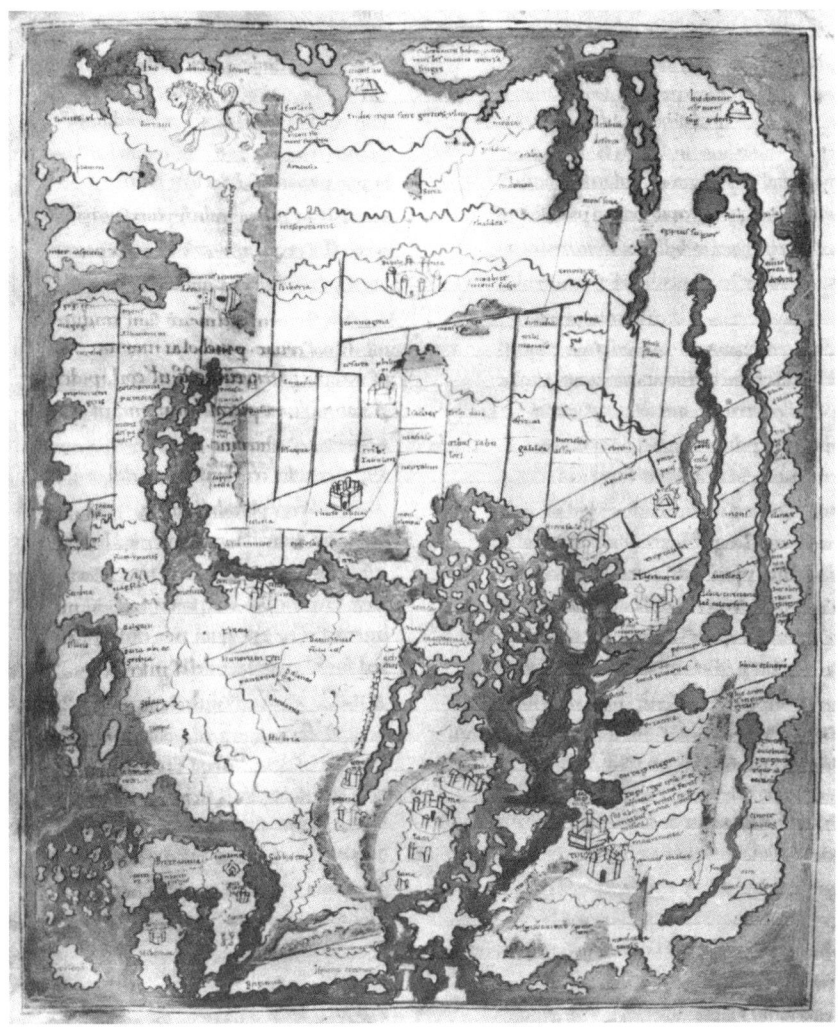

FIG. 9. The Cotton *mappa mundi*. British Library, Cotton Tiberius B. v. 1, fo.56ᵛ. Map size 21 × 17 cm. By permission of the British Library.

Library Cotton Tiberius B. V. 1, fo. 56ᵛ,[104] a bilingual manuscript containing writings in both Latin and Old English, this map is remarkable because it is the only one surviving from the Anglo-Saxon period, probably dating back to the tenth century. It is still unclear whether it was attached to a particular text.[105]

The Cotton *mappa mundi* displays a unique representation of northern Europe. The British Isles take up a large portion of the map, much larger than their actual size—when measured against the oecumene—would allow for. The map is striking because it radically differs from the representations of the British Isles discussed above: it offers a fairly accurate portrayal of this part of the world. This may be due to the rectangular shape of the map which facilitates the drawing of this 'corner' of the world. More probably however, it was drawn on better, more precise geographical information about north-western Europe.[106] Commenting on this *mappa mundi*, Patrick McGurk observes that the extra space granted by the rectangular shape of the map was used to depict not land masses, but seas and inlands.[107] In this novel representation of the world, Britain is surrounded by various islands: the *Orcades* toward the north, *Tylen* toward the north-west, and *Island* toward the east.[108] *Hibernia* (Ireland) is correctly placed toward the west. The Cotton Map therefore does not situate Britain on the edge of the world: it is on the contrary completely surrounded by other islands and it correctly relates to the Continent. Although the uneven outline adopted by the mapmaker in his depiction of the coastlines is as much a convention as the geometrical shapes found in other *mappae mundi*,[109] the indentation of Britain's seashores matches that of the corresponding continental littoral. The British Isles are shown in their correct position opposite the French coast.[110]

---

[104] The map is discussed in Edson, Mapping, 74–80, and in P. McGurk, 'The Mappa Mundi', in *An Eleventh-Century Anglo-Saxon Illustrated Miscellany*, ed. by P. McGurk and others, Early English Manuscripts in Facsimile, 21 (Copenhagen: Rosenkilde and Bagger, 1983), 79–86. See also David Hill, *An Atlas of Anglo-Saxon England* (Oxford: Blackwell, 1981).

[105] Edson, *Mapping*, 75, suggests that the map accompanied Priscian's *Periegesis* whereas McGurk, 'Mappa Mundi', 79, thinks that the map was not attached to any particular text.

[106] McGurk, 'Mappa Mundi', 80.   [107] Ibid., 83.

[108] *Island* could be identified with the Scandinavian peninsula, for it was one of the places that tended to be confused with Thule.

[109] McGurk, 'Mappa Mundi' 82.   [110] Ibid., 80.

Just as Old English authors are reluctant to confine their island to the periphery when setting out the geography of northern Europe, similarly Anglo-Saxon mapmakers do not situate Britain on the fringes of the world. The Cotton *mappa mundi* is an explicit testimony to the fact that the Anglo-Saxons did not perceive themselves as isolated and peripheric, for their homeland is assigned a new location on the map of the world. In the Cotton Map, Britain is granted pre-eminence because it is allowed to occupy so much space in this representation of the world. Moreover, by including Britain within the broad outline of the land masses and by enclosing it in a cluster of islands, the Anglo-Saxon mapmaker grants his own country a new, regional centrality.[111]

A comparison of the Albi, the Ripoll, and the Saint-Sever maps on the one hand, and of the Cotton Map on the other, demonstrates that the location of the instance of knowledge influences mapping practices. These observations echo the conclusions reached when reading Anglo-Saxon texts against their classical authorities. Bede, Dicuil, and the Old English Orosius reorganize their sources to convey a different sense of place: from an Anglo-Saxon perspective, the ends of the world are pushed further away and the position of the subject becomes a new focal point around which proximity and distance are organized.

CONCLUSION: RELIGIOUS RECENTRING

The promise of a religious centrality for Anglo-Saxon England implicit in the founding anecdote of the slave boys is echoed at other points in the Old English corpus, for instance in the version of the settlement of Britain found in the *Ecclesiastical History* and discussed in the last chapter of this book. Two examples of this recentring are examined here, because by linking Britain with Europe's intellectual and religious destiny, they remap Christendom and firmly anchor Anglo-Saxon England in this new religious geography.

The entry for the year 891 of the Anglo-Saxon Chronicle reports that three Irishmen arrive at Alfred's court: 'þrie Scottas comon to Ælfrede cyninge on anum bate butan ælcum gereþrum of Hibernia . . . þa comon hie ymb vii niht to londe on Cornwalum 7 foron þa sona to

---

[111] For a different view of Britain's position on the Cotton Map, see Howe, 'An Angle on this Earth', 12.

Ælfrede cyninge'.[112] Even though this incident may well be 'thoroughly characteristic and genuine' in its depiction of pious Irish exiles, as Plummer and Earle's notes to their edition of the Chronicle point out, it nonetheless affects the audience's view of the royal court.[113] For, in this anecdote, it is the place to which God directs his followers who trust in his judgement and who let providence guide their journey, thus implying that Anglo-Saxon England is a significant site in Christendom. The transformation of the island into an outstanding landmark in a religious geography is even more conspicuous in Æthelweard's *Chronicle*.[114] Æthelweard translates the Anglo-Saxon Chronicle into Latin towards the end of the tenth century, and he includes this episode in his text. But, according to him, the Irish exiles who stop at King Alfred's court later continue their travels to Rome and, he adds, they intend to go as far as Jerusalem.[115] Because these three locations are juxtaposed, England is implicitly put on an equal footing with Rome and Jerusalem: it is transformed into a major religious site.

Anglo-Saxon authors also use theological concepts to attest the importance of their homeland in Christian history. They resort, for instance, to the theory of the four world empires which originates in the biblical Book of Daniel.[116] A form of political eschatology based on the vision of Daniel, it organizes world history around the succession of four universal empires, with Rome as the last one. A spatial element is added to this temporal sequence, for it always follows an east–west course. This doctrine, in the elaboration and transmission of which Jerome and Orosius figure prominently, was current in Anglo-Saxon England. It is clearly spelled out in the *Old English Orosius*, and for the translator the four empires stand 'on feower endum þyses middangeardes'.[117] Crucially, this teleological outlook situates salvation in the west. King Alfred remembers it when he composes his Preface to the Old English

---

[112] 'Three Irishmen came from Ireland to King Alfred in a boat without oars ... then after seven nights they landed in Cornwall and they immediately went to King Alfred' *The Anglo-Saxon Chronicle: A Collaborative Edition: III MS A.*, ed. by Janet Bately (Cambridge: Brewer, 1986), 54.

[113] *Two of the Saxon Chronicles Parallel*, ed. by Charles Plummer and John Earle, reissued by Dorothy Whitelock, 2 vols. (Oxford: Clarendon Press, 1892–9; repr. 1980), ii. 103.

[114] *The Chronicle of Æthelweard*, ed. by A. Campbell (London: Nelson, 1962).

[115] 'Deinde Romam uestigia legunt ut soliti crebro Christi magistri petitum. Mentes ab inde Hierosolimis ire prætendunt' (*Chronicle of Æthelweard*, 48).

[116] Daniel, 2: 31–43.

[117] 'in the four corners of the world' (*The Old English Orosius*, 36). See also Orose, *Histoires (Contre les Païens)*, ii 1. 4–6, ii. 84–5.

translation of Gregory's *Pastoral Care*. He first deplores the decay of learning in his kingdom and then recollects how the Law was first composed in Hebrew and how the Greeks 'ða wendon hie hie on heora agen geðiode ealle'.[118] After the Greeks, the Romans did the same: 'Lædenware swæ same, siððan hie hie geliornodon, hie hie wendon ealla ðurh wise wealhstodas on hiora agen geðiode'.[119] The King concludes by observing that all the other Christian nations have done the same. Mentioning in turn Greece, Rome, and Britain, Alfred gestures toward the theory of the *translatio studii*, a variant of the more general theory of the four world empires.[120] In this case, the centre of learning and culture is thought to pass from one place to another following an east–west course, that is, to travel from Athens to Rome.[121] In Alfred's Preface, it goes one step further, from Rome to Anglo-Saxon England. In adding his own island as the last of these cultural and religious landmarks, the King implies that it is on a par with Jerusalem, Athens, and Rome. Britain's geographical situation near the western ends of the world is fully accepted. It is even turned to the Anglo-Saxons' advantage thanks to the role it was to play at the end of time, according to a universal historiography that expects the Roman Empire—or its renovated versions—to stand until Christ's Second Coming. Here again, Britain, critically situated toward the west, claims for itself a major role in Christian history.

An analysis of Britain's location on the map of the world demonstrates that insular authors resort to various strategies to re-situate their island in a wider European geography. In their scientific writings, they modify their learned sources and base their accounts of the lands that lie north of Britain on experience, either their own or that of actual travellers. Remapping the continent's northern shores, both the translator of the *Old English Orosius* and the Cotton mapmaker minimize their island's marginality: they make of their homeland an integral part of

---

[118] The Greeks 'then translated it all into their own language' 'On the State of Learning in England', in *Sweet's Anglo-Saxon Reader*, rev. Dorothy Whitelock, 15th edn. (Oxford: Clarendon Press, 1967; repr. 1988), 4–7 (6).

[119] 'similarly the Romans, after they had learned it, translated it all by means of learned interpreters into their own language' ('On the State of Learning in England', 6).

[120] Kathleen Davis, 'National Writing in the Ninth Century: A Reminder for Postcolonial Thinking about the Nation', *Journal of Medieval and Early Modern Studies*, 28 (1998), 611–37 (615).

[121] On the concept of the *translatio studii*, see J. Verger, 'Translatio studii', in *Lexikon des Mittelalters*, ed. by Robert Auty and others (Munich: Lexma, 1980–99), viii (1997), 946–7.

the continent. With Ohthere's account, as well as with the travellers' reports mentioned by Dicuil, the island becomes a point of departure for exploratory travels toward distant regions. Bede and his slave boys transcend Britain's remoteness by inscribing it in a religious frame of reference, transforming isolation into election. Yet, despite their idiosyncrasies, insular authors adopt a new perspective on centrality and periphery and organize their geographical outlook around their island.

Negotiating between the culture of space they receive from tradition and their own understanding of what is at stake in localization, Anglo-Saxon authors elaborate a new geography to accommodate their own sense of identity. As they did not experience the liminal place assigned to them in classical geographical accounts, they had to redefine their position in relation to continental Europe. Critics, Davis for instance, recognize that the concept of national identity is not given but created, and that it contains an important spatial component. Discussing Alfred's Preface to his translation of the *Pastoral Care* and the King's construction of the *Angelcynn*, Davis observes that this text 'presupposes both the unity of this people and their belonging to the physical land, each of which depends on the other for definition'.[122] People and place are brought together and are imagined at the same moment. This chapter has investigated the relationships existing between the characterization of a people and its spatial localization.

Mental maps are not faithful transcriptions of an outside 'reality', but they are manifestations of a particular spatial *imaginaire*. Negating or reinvesting distance, mapping out a new centrality toward the north, insular authors move from 'them' to 'us', thus challenging the role of 'constituting other' which classical tradition attributed to them. By refusing to be confined to a remote location, they contest a negative vision of themselves. By modifying their geographical position, they reinterpret themselves. They become a powerful people—when geographical knowledge, for instance Ohthere's report, signals territorial control; they become a civilized people—when the Alfredian court preserves the new spatial information gathered by northern explorers; and they become an elected people—when religious predestination promises them a crucial role in Christianity's intellectual and eschatological future.

[122] Davis, 'National Writing', 620.

PART II

MIGRATION

5

Integrating New Spaces: Saint's Lives and Missions of Conversion

GUTHLAC A, the Old English poetic life of St Guðlac, recounts how the holy man settles in the wilderness to lead a life of prayer and worship. He chases out hostile fiends who constantly harass him and trouble his solitary retreat, and who want him to leave the *beorg* where he at present dwells. They enjoin him to find another home where he has friends, an injunction to which the saint answers: 'Wid is þes westen, wræcsetla fela, | eardas onhæle earmra gæsta'.[1] He points out that the wasteland is vast and he advises them simply to move further away. But the demons cannot follow his advice: a close reading of the text reveals that the fiends in fact lose their homes as a consequence of the holy man's settlement in the desert. The poet himself recognizes that the demons 'ne motun hi on eorðan eardes brucan'.[2] In this poem, the *beorg* functions as a metonymy for the wilderness and the saint gains control of the entire wasteland. The demons understand what is at stake in their conflict against Guðlac along similar lines. According to them, their opponent wants to make them homeless. They tell him: 'Ðu þæt gehatest þæt ðu ham on us | gegan wille'.[3]

In *Guthlac A*, the saint and the fiends are clearly fighting for a piece of land. This motif is central to a poem which revolves around the question of who possesses the *beorg*. The saint unambiguously declares his right to the mound he settles in one of his dialogues with his enemies. He says: 'Her sceal min wesan | eorðlic eþel, nales eower leng'.[4] This claim is

---

[1] 'This wilderness is vast, many the places of exile, the secret regions of the wretched spirits' (*Guthlac A* 296–7). *The Exeter Book*, ed. by George Philip Krapp and Elliott van Kirk Dobbie, Anglo-Saxon Poetic Records, 3 (New York: Columbia University Press, 1936; repr. 1966), 49–88.
[2] 'they cannot enjoy an abode on earth' (*Guthlac A* 220).
[3] 'You have vowed that you will conquer a home from us' (*Guthlac A* 271–2ᵃ).
[4] 'Here my earthly dwelling shall be, no longer yours' (*Guthlac A* 260ᵇ–261).

later backed by Bartholomew, who rescues Guðlac from his temptation at the doors of hell. He orders the demons to carry the holy man back to his retreat and he declares that 'he [Guðlac] sceal þy wonge wealdan, ne magon ge him þa wic forstondan'.[5] Bartholomew's declaration marks the end of the conflict and Guðlac's victory over the evil spirits. The hermit has dislodged the creatures that used to dwell in the wilderness and he now controls it. Guðlac's fight against the demons is territorial at heart and the motif of land possession is of paramount importance in the poem.

Guðlac is not the only saintly figure whose actions are motivated by a desire to control a piece of land; for this motif resurfaces in all the hagiographic poems this chapter analyses. A close reading of *Elene* reveals that the stimulus for the queen's travels goes beyond a mere retrieval of the Holy Cross and involves the geographical extension of Constantine's authority. Similarly, *Andreas* and the *Fates of the Apostles* follow the journeys of Christ's disciples into distant countries, a narrative pattern that betrays the poet's interest in mapping or in symbolically appropriating remote regions of the oecumene. A thematic unity connects all the vernacular hagiographic poems under consideration here and, as Alvin Lee observes, each of these texts is 'an extension of the heroic actions described briefly in the *Fates of the Apostles*'. He further notes that 'Andrew, Helena, Juliana, and Guðlac are all engaged in extending the dryht of Christ into territories where it has not previously been known'.[6] In order to fulfil their missions, saints have to travel to distant lands. As a result, Old English hagiographic poems create a vast imaginary geography and, as I hope to demonstrate, they foreground spatial and territorial issues.

This chapter, divided into four parts, addresses first the question of limits and borders; for, in representing saints who wander near the margins of the familiar world, vernacular hagiographic poets foreground the notion of frontiers. As the preceding chapters have shown, boundaries are essential to the creation of a new space and to a society's definition of itself: they trace a dividing line between 'us' and 'them'—a line that matters to saintly missionaries when they face heathen people.

---

[5] 'Guðlac shall rule this plain, you may not withhold this dwelling-place from him' (*Guthlac A* 702).

[6] Alvin A. Lee, *The Guest-Hall of Eden: Four Essays on the Design of Old English Poetry* (New Haven: Yale University Press, 1972), 113.

Various textual devices support territorial appropriation. For instance, the quality of the lands to which the saints journey changes; for the actions of holy men and holy women in remote regions transform the wilderness of pagan homelands into pleasant abodes, the possession of which is a source of joy. Also, the nature of the saints' travels deserves attention: their journeys are not random expeditions to the periphery, but they are in fact quests whose object is a particular piece of land. The discussion of *Beowulf* found in Chapter 2 has established that treading and stepping imagery commonly signals territorial appropriation; in vernacular hagiographic poetry, images of saints walking on the ground are pervasive. The very steps they take trace the contours of a new geography.

A brief comment on the corpus examined in this chapter is called for, for the following pages focus on *Andreas*, *Elene*, *Guthlac A*, and the *Fates of the Apostles*, with occasional glimpses at *Juliana*. The term 'saints' lives' is therefore taken here in its broadest sense, since the *Fates of the Apostles* for instance does not really narrate the life of a saintly individual or group of people. Yet, all these poems conform to one of the two broad categories according to which saints' lives can be classified: the *passio* and the *vita*. In the *passio*, the protagonist is martyred for his or her faith—like Andrew in Mermedonia and Christ's followers in the *Fates of the Apostles*. In the *vita*, the saint, through his or her unfailing service to God, accomplishes a real or a metaphorical martyrdom—like Helen in the land of the Jews or Guðlac in the wilderness, who both devote their lives to the greater glory of God.[7] The present chapter discusses exclusively Old English verse lives, although both vernacular prose hagiography and Latin saint's lives could without doubt illuminate many of the issues I am examining here.[8] The emergence of vernacular prose lives, which became more popular as the Old English period drew to a close, has been explained as a substitute for Latin texts that could no longer be understood, or that were understood only with difficulty.[9] Vernacular verse lives, which are very likely of an earlier date

---

[7] Michael Lapidge, 'The Saintly Life in Anglo-Saxon England', in Malcolm Godden and Michael Lapidge (eds.), *The Cambridge Companion to Old English Literature* (Cambridge: Cambridge University Press, 1991; repr. 1994), 243–63 (252–3).
[8] One needs only think of Ælfric's *Life of Saint Edmund*, for instance.
[9] E. G. Whatley, 'Late Old English Hagiography, ca. 950–1150', in Guy Philippart (ed.), *Histoire internationale de la littérature hagiographique latine et vernaculaire en occident des origines à 1550* 2 vols. (Turnhout: Brepols, 1994–), ii (1996), 429–99 (445 and 449–50).

of composition, were probably enjoyed alongside, rather than in place of their Latin originals. Old English poets could therefore more easily take liberties with their models and were free to elaborate on them.[10]

An analysis of Old English hagiographic poems evokes each of the three terms appearing in the title of this book. These verse lives of saints recall the creation narratives discussed in Chapter 2, in as much as they follow the progress of an advancing Christendom and thus trace the boundaries of a new space. Moving from a static to a dynamic vision of space, these texts introduce, with the importance they grant to the saints' travels, the migration stories which figure prominently in the last two chapters of the present study. The poems under consideration here, which tell of the influence holy men and holy women have on distant territories, help to shape the contours of the audience's mental map: the saints modify the world's spatial organization and redefine the distribution of familiar and alien regions. Hagiographic poems also narrate victorious battles waged in hostile lands and they chronicle the ensuing acquisition of new territories, thus announcing the narratives of conquest discussed in Chapter 7. It is indeed rewarding to think of saints' lives in terms of (re)conquest. Roaming the borderlands, their protagonists transform and claim them as part of the Christian world; land is being gained and occupied for Christianity. Jacques Le Goff has a happy expression to describe the territorial aspects of the saints' activities: he says that these holy people play 'un rôle d'intégrateurs d'espaces étrangers'.[11]

OFER MEARCPAÐU: OF PERIPHERIES AND BOUNDARIES

Andrew, Guðlac, Helen, the apostles, and even Juliana, all travel to distant lands. Their journeys draw the audience's attention to the periphery and their spatial relocation highlights the territorial aspects of their missions. More precisely, saints move toward the wilderness as they venture into a pagan world. As a result, the narratives of their lives foreground the position of boundaries and of territorial confines.

---

[10] On this point, see Whatley, 'Hagiography', 450.
[11] Jacques Le Goff, 'Discorso di chiusura', in *Popoli e paesi nella cultura altomedievale*, 2 vols., Settimane di studio del Centro italiano di studi sull'alto medioevo, 29 (Spoleto: Centro Italiano di Studi sull'Alto Medioevo, 1983), 805–83 (834).

Of course, the borders analysed here are 'imaginary' boundaries, which cannot be reduced to a line on a map. I do not wish to suggest that the actual frontiers of kingdoms and empires coincided with the mental limits discussed in this section—such as those separating Christians and pagans or culture and nature.[12]

A vital element of the Anglo-Saxon *imaginaire*, frontiers need to be constantly reasserted and secured for the world to endure, as a close reading of creation poems and of *Beowulf* has demonstrated. And yet, because of their spiritual and religious outlook, hagiographic poems are also influenced by Roman ideology, later adopted by Western Christianity, which grants both secular and spiritual Rome a universal destiny.[13] In the course of the early Middle Ages, therefore, a dialectic of unity and diversity emerges which combines an undivided imperial and later Christian Rome on the one hand, and an atomized, bounded world under external threats, on the other.[14] In the course of history, a totalizing political and religious ideology was being challenged by the triumph of division in reality and by the constitution of numerous realms and kingdoms following the disintegration of the Roman Empire.[15] Furthermore, a sense of local identity was promoted in Christian religious ideology by the development of the cult of relics; for, in the words of Peter Brown: 'this cult gloried in particularity. *Hic est locus*: "Here is the place" . . . The holy was available in one place, and in each such place it was accessible to one group in a manner in which it could not be accessible to anyone situated elsewhere.'[16] Such tensions run through Old English hagiographic verse, tensions between the universal aspiration of a Christian ideology and the constant necessity of protecting one's own territory.

In *Elene*, Cynewulf mentions a frontier that actually did exist: that separating the Roman Empire from its pagan neighbours. Famously, the Old English poem's opening scene is one of the few episodes where

---

[12] On the pre-eminence of the latter type of limits, see Walter Pohl, 'Conclusion: The Transformation of Frontiers', in Walter Pohl, Ian Wood, and Helmut Reimitz (eds.), *The Transformation of Frontiers from Late Antiquity to the Carolingians*, The Transformation of the Roman World, 10 (Leiden: Brill, 2001), 247–60 (260).

[13] Hanz-Werner Goetz, 'Concepts of Realm and Frontiers from Late Antiquity to the Early Middle Ages: Some Preliminary Remarks', in Walter Pohl, Ian Wood, and Helmut Reimitz (eds.), *The Transformation of Frontiers from Late Antiquity to the Carolingians*, The Transformation of the Roman World, 10 (Leiden: Brill, 2001), 73–82 (74–5).

[14] Le Goff, 'Discorso di chiusura', 806 and 837.   [15] Ibid., 807.

[16] Peter Brown, *The Cult of the Saints: Its Rise and Function in Latin Christianity* (Chicago: University of Chicago Press, 1981), 86.

Elene departs from its closest predecessor, the *Acta Cyriaci*.[17] Cynewulf significantly expands this episode and gives a detailed account of the barbarians' position on the shores of the Danube. Lines 36^b–39^a describe the barbarians' advance to war and read: 'on ælfylce | deareðlacende on Danubie, | stærcedfyrhðe, stæde wicedon | ymb þæs wæteres wylm'.[18] The enemy armies gather by the river. Cynewulf clearly says that they are planning to cross it, to invade Constantine's empire, and to plunder Rome. But the barbarians stop on the riverbank and their progression is halted by the Danube. The Latin account offers a different version of this episode: the enemies cross the border and occupy lands belonging to the Romans before the battle takes place. It says that Constantine 'invenit eos qui vindicaverant Romaniae partes, & erant secus Danubium'.[19] In the vernacular poem, the barbarian invasion remains a threat: although endangered, the boundaries of the Roman Empire are not violated. That Cynewulf modifies this very detail is significant. *Elene* recounts the rise and eventual triumph of Constantine's dominion; its borders are therefore expanding and the insular poet, by placing two enemy armies on each side of the Danube, graphically draws attention to the dividing line between the Emperor's dominion and the lands of his enemies.

When Helen initiates her quest to find the Cross on which Christ died, she steps over borders that are comparable to the ones the barbarians approach. Accompanied by a large crowd of retainers, the queen goes to the beach to sail to the land of the Jews. The poet specifies that the ships all stand ready 'ymb geofenes stæð', that they 'on stæðe stodon'.[20]

---

[17] *Cynewulf's 'Elene'*, ed. by P. O. E. Gradon (Exeter: University of Exeter Press, 1997; first publ. London: Methuen, 1958), 20; John P. Hermann, *Allegories of War: Language and Violence in Old English Poetry* (Ann Arbor: University of Michigan Press, 1989), 91; Earl R. Anderson, *Cynewulf: Structure, Style and Theme in his Poetry* (Rutherford, NJ: Fairleigh Dickinson University Press, 1983), 127, and Claes Schaar, *Critical Studies in the Cynewulf Group*, Lund Studies in English, 17 (Lund: Gleerup, 1949), 25. The *Acta Cyriaci* is the version of the invention of the Cross legend closest to the Old English poem. Numerous recensions in a variety of languages circulated in Europe during the Middle Ages. The Latin tradition is the most relevant for our purpose as *Elene* probably depended on a version of this type. On this point, see *Elene*, ed. Gradon, 17, Daniel G. Calder, *Cynewulf* (Boston: Twayne, 1981) 104–5, and Robert Dinapoli, 'Poesis and Authority: Traces of an Anglo-Saxon "agon" in Cynewulf's *Elene*', *Neophilologus*, 82 (1988), 619–30 (620).

[18] 'the warriors, resolute, encamped on the shore of the Danube, in a strange land, along the stream of water' (*Elene* 36^b–39^a).

[19] Constantine 'found that they had claimed parts of the Roman Empire and were living near the Danube' (*Acta Sanctorum*, ed. by Godfried Henschen and Daniel Papebroch, Maius, I (Antwerp, 1680), 445–8 (445)).

[20] 'along the shore of the ocean'; they 'stood on the shore' (*Elene* 227^a and 232^a).

The repetition of *stæð* a few lines apart invites an analysis of its other occurrences in the poem. The word is used twice during the account of Constantine's initial war. When they gather by the Danube, the hostile troops *stæðe wicedon* and the Roman Emperor sees them assembled 'ymb þæs wæteres stæð'.[21] Consequently, while the barbarians stop at the *stæð*, the shore of a stretch of water, Helen crosses it to launch her search for the Cross.

In the scene relating the queen's departure, the poet says that the troops accompanying the Emperor's mother press forward *ofer mearcpaðu*.[22] Although I translate *mearcpað* by 'path' in the note, the full meaning of the compound should be allowed to resonate, for it designates a path—*pæð*—that leads over a *mearc*, a mark, limit, or a border territory. When they go to the shore, the Roman soldiers and their queen therefore travel to the boundary of their realm. *Elene* draws attention to the Roman Empire's limits and to the very moment when the queen's journey takes her across them. The repetition of the word *stæð* and the use of the expression *mearcpað* indicate that Helen is able to cross a boundary that the empire's enemies could not transgress. It consequently suggests that when the queen travels to Jerusalem, she enters unfamiliar lands. Her sphere of action, like that of other saints, is situated in the periphery.

Although other hagiographic poems do not insist on the very moment when their protagonists cross the boundary and enter foreign areas, they nevertheless underscore the importance of the periphery. Words including a *mearc-* element, for instance, recur in all the poems under consideration here. In *Juliana* the holy virgin is not executed in the city of Nicodemia, but she is dragged to the *londmearce*, the boundary, before being martyred.[23] This specification is significant, for it indicates that Juliana's heroic fight for her faith occurs in the borderland. Like Andrew, Guðlac, or Helen, the holy virgin is active in the confines of her own world where she preaches and converts the people witnessing her martyrdom. Moreover, it is surely not a random detail that, following the saint's death, Heliseus leaves Nicodemia and drowns at the bottom of the sea. Juliana's wicked opponent does not—maybe he cannot—return to the city he used to rule and whose inhabitants are now Christians.[24] Once the holy woman has triumphed, her enemy is confined to the

---

[21] The troops 'encamped on the shore'; 'near the water's shore' (*Elene* 38[b] and 60[a]).
[22] 'over the paths' (*Elene* 233[a]).
[23] *Juliana* 635[b]. *The Exeter Book* (1936), 113–33.   [24] *Juliana* 692[b]–695[a].

periphery and dies while roaming the borders. Juliana's martyrdom therefore banishes Nicodemia's evil ruler from the city and gains a new territory for the Christian faith.

The *Guthlac A* poet introduces his hero in about seventy lines. He asserts the saint's excellence with a formula echoing the establishment of good rulers such as Scyld and Constantine. He says: 'God wæs Guðlac!',[25] at which point he specifies that an angel was always with the saint as he *mearclond gesæt*.[26] When establishing the distinction of Guðlac's virtue, the poet mentions the saint's dwelling-place: he links the holy man's fortitude to the residence the latter takes in the periphery. To settle in the wilderness is his claim to fame; for, like Juliana, Guðlac wins a new land for the Christian faith: he triumphs in the *beorg* and he takes control of a place to which the community of men previously had no access.

Andreas elaborates on this motif, for terms including a *mearc-* element resonate throughout the poem. Mermedonia is constantly associated with the periphery. It is called a *mearcland* at the very beginning of the poem when Matthew is first sent there.[27] Another *mearc-* compound is used in the scene reporting Andrew's subsequent travel to the city of the cannibals. Standing on the shore, eager to go, the saint asks sailors, who are in fact the Lord and his angels in disguise, for a passage to this distant land, to *þa leodmearce*.[28] This place is again associated with the margins when, after having freed the cannibals' captives and having led them out of the city, Andrew goes back to Mermedonia. The saint then awaits his fate *be mearcpaðe*.[29] In the poetic geography of the text, Andrew's sphere of action is this outlandish city confined to the borderlands.

Mearc- compounds also abound in another episode of the poem. On his way to Mermedonia, Andrew talks to the divine helmsman and gives him an account of his life with Christ. He relates one of the Saviour's miracles: he relates how Jesus called a statue to life and ordered it to travel to the land of the Canaanites to bring God's message 'on þa leodmearce'.[30] The stone figure obeys the divine command and journeys

---

[25] 'Guðlac was good!' (*Guthlac A* 170[a]). It echoes *Beowulf* 11[b], 863[b], 2390[b], and *Elene* 13[b].

[26] 'settled in the borderland' (*Guthlac A* 174[a]).

[27] 'a borderland' *Andreas* 19[a]. *The Vercelli Book*, ed. by George Philip Krapp, Anglo-Saxon Poetic Records, 2 (New York: Columbia University Press, 1932; repr. 1961), 3–51.

[28] 'that territory of a people' (*Andreas* 286[b]).

[29] 'by the path leading through the borderland' (*Andreas* 1061[b]).

[30] 'in that territory' (*Andreas* 777[b]).

ofer mearcpaðu to reach the tombs of Abraham, Isaac, and Jacob.[31] The miraculous envoy awakes the three patriarchs from death and sends them on an evangelizing mission. The poet says that 'geweotan ða ða witigan þry | modige mearcland tredan'.[32] Abraham, Isaac, and Jacob preach the word of God to distant people, to those living in the *mearcland*. Their mission takes them to the periphery, just as the miraculous statue was sent *ofer mearcpaðu*.

The recurrence of compounds including the element *mearc-* indicates that the question of the limits is a pervasive concern in *Andreas*: they are, in fact, the stage on which virtuous deeds are performed. The poem stresses the fact that Andrew and Matthew, as well as the statue and the three patriarchs, are active in remote regions. These holy envoys increase Christendom's domain and they draw attention to the frontiers separating Christian and heathen territories.

Lives of saints provide Christians with examples of good living and fortitude in the face of adversity. As such, they share many of their key features with heroic poetry because they Christianize a secular ideal of conduct. Heroes play a central role in establishing the area their tribe subsequently inhabits, and spatial issues are central to these ancient tales.[33] Paul Zumthor reminds his reader that 'le chant épique narre le combat contre l'Autre, l'étranger hostile, l'ennemi extérieur au groupe—que ce dernier soit une nation, une classe sociale ou une famille'.[34] It focuses hostility on a neighbouring or a distant people, thus justifying one's territorial ambitions. By confining their protagonists to the periphery, saint's lives adopt a similar agenda. As the hero secures and increases the space where his people live and prosper, the saint, in his or her missionary activities, expands Christianity's sphere of influence, gains new territories to his or her faith, and often puts an end to persecutions against Christians. Both the hero and the saint venture into the wilderness to confront hostile strangers; thanks to their triumphs, they delimit a territory which their community can enjoy. In this mental framework, the notion of the boundary is central: it is a line that protects and differentiates 'us' from outsiders on the one hand, and it is the place where heroic deeds, namely the appropriation of new territories, are performed on the other.

---

[31] 'over the paths leading through the borderland' (*Andreas* 788ᵃ).
[32] 'the three bold wise men then departed to tread the borderland' (*Andreas* 801ᵇ–802ᵃ).
[33] Paul Zumthor, *La Mesure du Monde* (Paris: Seuil, 1993), 383.
[34] Paul Zumthor, *Introduction à la poésie orale* (Paris: Seuil, 1983), 110.

WILDERNESS AND PLEASURABLE ABODES: THE QUESTION OF THE NATURE OF THE LAND

The missions the various saints undertake lead them to the periphery, to the confines of the Christian world. The preceding chapter, discussing localization and identity, has demonstrated that the articulation of proximity and distance is modelled on a pattern that understands what is close and familiar as pleasant, and that characterizes what is remote as untamed and dangerous. But it has also shown that the evaluation of distance and the nature of a place may vary according to the text's underlying ideological concerns. In the case of saints' lives, the periphery to which the protagonists travel is threatening, for it is populated by demons or wicked men. But as a close reading of these texts reveals, a distant region can also become pleasant and the possession of a particular tract of land can be a source of pleasure.

Guthlac A

The fiends Guðlac chases out constantly harass him; they hope that the holy man will leave the *beorg* and that they will eventually be able to reclaim the wilderness for themselves. They visit the hermit in his retreat to check 'hwæþre him þæs wonges wyn sweðrade'.[35] They wish he would stop enjoying the *beorg*, for they suppose that he would return to his homeland if his new abode was no longer pleasurable to him.

But if Guðlac eventually appreciates his shelter, his installation in the desert is no delight at first. The company of men and the security of the community are abandoned to earn salvation, and the *beorg* is not an inviting place. At the beginning of the text, the poet tells his audience that an angel helped the saint and that he 'lærde lenge hu geornor, | þæt him leofedan londes wynne, | bold on beorhge'.[36] There is happiness to be derived from the wilderness, but it does not come naturally and the saint has to be taught how to enjoy it. Moreover, the repugnant character of the original wilderness is not completely

---

[35] 'whether the pleasure of the land diminished for him' (*Guthlac A* 352).
[36] 'he taught him all the more eagerly so that the joys of the land, the house on the hill, were dear to him' (*Guthlac A* 138^b–140^a).

eradicated once Guðlac settles there, and horrors continue to lurk in the land. In the lines immediately following the mention of a good spirit helping the holy man to appreciate his *beorg*, the poet nuances this optimistic tableau. He says that 'oft þær broga cwom | egeslic ond uncuð, ealdfeonda nið'.[37]

The ambiguity surrounding the nature of the *beorg* (is it a pleasant or unpleasant dwelling?) continues throughout the poem. It is often described as a miserable place: a dark spot, a *mearclond* where Guðlac 'oferwon | frecnessa fela'.[38] The mound the saint inhabits is situated *on westenne*, in a *dygle stowe*, it is 'idel ond æmen'.[39] But at other times, the *beorg* seems to be an enjoyable location. The devils are, for instance, aggrieved that, because of Guðlac's coming, they have to leave *grene beorgas* and 'þone grenan wong'.[40] The land's positive and pleasurable aspects are emphasized as the poem unfolds. After the saint's first temptation, the demons bring him back to his retreat, 'to þam leofestan | earde on eorðan'.[41] The use of the adjective *leof* in the superlative degree indicates that the *beorg* is becoming a coveted corner of the earth. In the course of the poem, it changes into an increasingly agreeable place until its final transformation into a *sele niwe* and a *sigewong*.[42] The *beorg* is central to *Guthlac A* because of all the allegorical and symbolic meanings that have been read in it; but it also occupies a pre-eminent position because it spurs the saint and his enemies into action, because it whets their desire to possess this particular tract of ground.

The demons want to hold the *beorg* because, for them too, it is a source of joy, and Guðlac's arrival in the wilderness deprives them of it. This is how they react to the saint's settling on the land:

> To þon ealdfeondas   ondan noman,
> swa hi singales   sorge dreogað.

---

[37] 'the dreadful and unknown terror, the attack of the old foes, often came there' (*Guthlac A* 140ᵇ–141).

[38] a 'border-land' *Guthlac A* 174ᵃ; he 'overcame many perils' (*Guthlac A* 180ᵇ–181ᵃ).

[39] 'in the desert' (*Guthlac A* 208ᵇ), 'a hidden place' (*Guthlac A* 159ᵃ and 215ᵃ), 'desolate and deserted' (*Guthlac A* 216ᵃ).

[40] 'the green hills', 'the green plain' (*Guthlac A* 232ᵇ and 477ᵃ).

[41] 'to the most beloved place on earth' (*Guthlac A* 427ᵇ–428ᵃ).

[42] 'a new abode' (*Guthlac A* 742ᵇ); 'a plain of victory' (*Guthlac A* 742ᵃ). On this point, see also Daniel G. Calder, '*Guthlac A* and *Guthlac B*: Some Discriminations', in Lewis E. Nicholson and Dolores Warwick Frese (eds.), *Anglo-Saxon Poetry: Essays in Appreciation: For John G. McGaillard* (Notre Dame, IN: University of Notre Dame Press, 1975), 65–80 (74).

> Ne motun hi on eorþan   eardes brucan,
> ...
> ac hy hleolease   hama þoliað⁴³

Guðlac's presence divests the fiends of their home and the demons suffer because they have nowhere to go. The *beorg* is claimed as a home both by Guðlac and by the fiends, and it is critical for both of them to hold it. It is the cause of their enmity, and its changing nature reflects both its isolation and its desirable character. More importantly, it also illustrates the effects of the saint's settlement in the wilderness: the holy presence purifies the land.

Andreas

Although the reason why Andrew is sent to Mermedonia is to rescue Matthew, his mission to the cannibals has wider consequences, for it not only frees the captives, but it also changes the nature of this hostile land.

When the holy man liberates the prisoners, he deprives the cannibals of their sustenance. The latter are forced to find their food elsewhere, and they decide to eat one of their own people. A young boy is designated and Andrew, who cannot bear this miserable deed to happen, intercedes in his favour. In response to the apostle's prayer, God causes the weapons of the man-eaters to melt and the child is saved. The Mermedonians are dismayed by this miracle; they lament their fate and the poet very interestingly declares: 'næs him to eðle wynn'.⁴⁴ This is a curious observation. It occurs when the cannibals fear starvation; yet, as they eat human flesh, they do not rely on the land for their sustenance. What then are these joys that are no longer available to them in their homeland? The cause–effect relationship established between the saint's intervention and the enjoyment of the land recalls what happens between the saint and the fiends in *Guthlac A*. In *Andreas*, the apostle does not, or at least not immediately, dislodge the wicked inhabitants from their country. But his coming nevertheless induces a change in the relationships men entertain with the land on which they live. The joys the Mermedonians derive from their homeland dwindle and their native home eventually passes under Andrew's control.

---

⁴³ 'Thereupon the old foes felt horror, for they shall suffer perpetual sorrow. They may not enjoy their dwelling on earth ... but they, without a shelter, lack a home' (*Guthlac A* 218–22).

⁴⁴ 'there was no joy for them in their homeland' (*Andreas* 1162ᵇ).

Mermedonia is first described as a 'mearcland morðre bewunden'.[45] Yet at the end of the poem, it is a very different place. When Andrew steps out of prison, once the flood that had submerged the city has receded, the poem says that 'smeolt wæs se sigewang'.[46] Interestingly, the same half-line occurs at the end of *Guthlac A* where it refers to the transformed *beorg* after the hermit has withstood the demons' temptation at the doors of hell. Like the *beorg* therefore, Mermedonia is metamorphosed by the saint's presence and his virtuous living.

This change is effected progressively: Andrew's torture and the ensuing flood are landmarks in this process. The Mermedonians persecute the saint when he returns to the city after freeing the cannibals' captives. His enemies drag him for three days along the roads of their country and trees and flowers blossom where his blood has been shed.[47] Clearly, the nature of the land changes when Andrew's blood irrigates and fertilizes the ground. The flood later purges Mermedonia of its evil inhabitants. This passage immediately brings to mind the biblical episode, of course. In Genesis, the Flood punishes the sinful and marks the origin of a new race. Contrary to what happens with Noah and his descendants, it is not really a new race that takes possession of a now empty land in *Andreas*. The country of the cannibals becomes a place of resurrection; for, of the many people who perish in the waves, only a few are irremediably lost. Andrew raises the less guilty of the cannibals from death, he 'het þa onsunde ealle arisan, | geonge of greote, þa ær geofon cwealde'.[48] The bodies arise *of greote*, suggesting that the saint transforms Mermedonia into a fertile ground which produces a new population.[49] BT translates *greot* as 'sand, dust, earth, gravel': it clearly designates the materiality of the ground. From being a land of death where people are held captive in prison and are condemned to a certain death, Mermedonia becomes the place from which a regenerated population springs forth. The city of the cannibals is thus purged of its evil character.

---

[45] 'a distant land surrounded by murder' (*Andreas* 19).
[46] 'the plain of victory was smooth' (*Andreas* 1581ᵃ).   [47] *Andreas* 1448–9.
[48] He 'ordered all of them, the young people, to rise from the earth unharmed, those whom the sea had earlier killed' (*Andreas* 1623–4).
[49] The term *greot* is repeatedly linked with death and resurrection in *Andreas*: the three patriarchs whom the miraculous statue awakens from death rise *of greote* and the gaolers who guard the foreign captives destined to be eaten by the Mermedonians fall dead *on greote* when the saint enters the prison. See *Andreas* 794ᵃ and 1084ᵃ.

The idea that saints or heroes venture into foreign lands and cleanse them is widespread in Old English poetry. In the *Fates of the Apostles*, for instance, Cynewulf tells his audience that, thanks to Matthew's preaching in India, 'land wæs gefælsod'.[50] The saint's teachings transform not just the hearts of the people listening to him, but also the very land on which they live. The motif resurfaces in heroic poetry; in *Beowulf*, the hero announces that he intends to *Heorot fælsian*, that is, he will get rid of the monstrous presence haunting it.[51] The hero's actions, be he a pagan warrior fighting against monsters or a Christian saint converting heathen regions, modify the very nature of the land.

Both the *beorg* and Mermedonia are therefore metamorphosed by the actions of the saints. Guðlac and Andrew redeem hostile regions which become pleasant and enjoyable places, the possession of which gives rise to struggles and strife. The changing nature of these lands echoes my analysis, in the preceding chapter, of the descriptions of Britain. The importance of the context in which these depictions appear has been recognized: lands are hostile and frightening when they function as 'constituting others' or when they are the stage on which heroic deeds are performed; they are pleasant and attractive areas when they are inviting conquest or once they have been appropriated by the hero. The eventual transformation of the places to which the saints' missions take them signals that the holy man or the holy woman has taken control of a new territory. Furthermore, as the relocation of Britain on the map indicates the emergence of a new mental world, the changing nature of these outlandish regions marks the coming into being of a spatial *imaginaire* that conceives of pleasant homelands as places transformed by the beneficent action of a Christian champion.

THE JOURNEY AS A QUEST

Old English hagiographic poems tell how holy people leave the comfort and security of their homeland to spread God's word into distant lands. Unsurprisingly, therefore, the image of the journey plays a pivotal role in these texts. When they travel, Guðlac, Helen, Andrew, and the apostles

---

[50] 'the land was purified' (*Fates of the Apostles* 66^b). *The Vercelli Book*, 51–4.
[51] 'to purge Heorot' (*Beowulf* 432^b. See also 825^a, 1176^b, and 2352^b). *Beowulf and the Fight at Finnsburg*, ed. by F. Klaeber, 3rd edn. (Lexington, MA: Heath, 1922; repr. 1950).

do not roam the earth randomly, but their journeys are quests that aim for a particular land. Consequently, the descriptions of the saints' missions to the periphery can be interpreted as claims that the Christian envoys lay to the new territories they convert.

The *Fates of the Apostles*

Among Old English hagiographic poems, the text that most unambiguously revolves around the image of the journey is the *Fates of the Apostles*. It follows the apostles on their evangelical missions to far-away places after Christ's death. These journeys are quests to specific lands, as an analysis of three terms central to the poem shall demonstrate: the words *sið* and *secan*, and the possible emendations of the verb *woron* found in the manuscript.

The word *sið* is repeated throughout the poem and it is used when the poet characterizes the apostles. James, for instance, is not *siðes sæne*, and Simon and Thaddeus, who travel to the land of Persia, are *siðfrome*.[52] *Sið* also designates an otherworldly travel, that is, the journey that the soul undertakes after death. When recounting John's martyrdom in Ephesus, Cynewulf says that the holy man 'þanon lifes weg | siðe gesohte'.[53] In his edition of the poem, Kenneth Brooks offers a gloss on this occurrence *siðe* that renders the temporal meaning of the term: 'time, occasion',[54] a gloss which suggests that he understands the passage thus: 'at that time, John sought...' But as the meanings of *sið* are numerous and include 'journey, travel' as well as 'course of events' or 'time', the term has spatial undertones which it is possible to render here if one translates *siðe* as 'with a journey'. In this case, when John reaches the end of his earthly life, he seeks the kingdom of heaven 'with a journey', as he already pursued salvation with his missionary travels on earth. Both the physical journeys the apostles undertake on the surface of the globe and the spiritual ones that lead them to heaven are emphasized in this poem.

Daniel Calder has commented on the echoes uniting the apostles' missions to distant lands and Christ's Incarnation. He says that 'by seeking the lands to which lot directs them, they [the apostles] copy the

---

[52] 'reluctant to travel' (*Fates of the Apostles* 34ᵃ); 'eager to go' (*Fates of the Apostles* 77ᵃ).
[53] 'with a journey [he] sought from there the way to heaven' (*Fates of the Apostles* 31ᵇ–32ᵃ).
[54] *Andreas and the Fates of the Apostles*, ed. by Kenneth R. Brooks (Oxford: Clarendon Press, 1961), 163.

ultimate model of grace, Christ's Incarnation. A description of the birth of Christ within the section on John makes this identification explicit'.[55] Although Christ's Incarnation is not described as a *sið*, as a journey, a connexion exists between the birth of the Saviour and the mission of his followers; for, while mentioning the Incarnation, the poet says that 'engla ordfruma, eorðan sohte'.[56] The verb *secan* 'to seek (a person, a place, or immaterial things)' presents the Incarnation as a search for the earth, for a particular place.[57] Together with *gesecan* 'to seek, to go to',[58] it signals a change of location and it resonates throughout the *Fates of the Apostles*. As Jesus travels to the material world, his followers journey to the borderlands to announce God's word. Simon and Thaddeus, for instance, go to Asia; the two men 'land Persea | sohton siðfrome'.[59] The apostles hope, with their mission to the periphery, to earn salvation and to be taken, after their deaths, to the kingdom of heaven. As already mentioned, Cynewulf says that John goes to heaven when he dies—more precisely that the apostle *gesohte* the way there.[60] The verb *gesecan* is also used when Thomas's adventures in India are narrated. One reads that the holy man died by the sword and that 'þonon wuldres leoht | sawle gesohte'.[61] Similarly, after Philip has died crucified in Hiearpolis, his soul 'þanon ece lif | . . . ricene gesohte'.[62] All these occurrences of the verb *secan* or *gesecan* present the apostles' travels as a search for a special place, be it a distant land or a seat in heaven. In the *Fates of the Apostles*, the motif of travel is used to describe both 'horizontal' and 'vertical' motions. It denotes both journeys over the surface of the earth, peregrinations leading to distant and unfamiliar lands, and a progress away from this terrestrial life to an otherworldly realm.

The motif of travel is further foregrounded by the poem's narrative framework; for, the text stages a speaker who presents himself at the outset as *siðgeomor*. Critics disagree on how best to translate this term. Brooks affirms, without supporting his case, that 'the traditional interpretation "weary of travel" is very odd in the context'.[63] He recalls the possible translation of *sið* as 'experience' in order to translate the

---

[55] Calder, *Cynewulf*, 33.
[56] 'the Lord of the angels sought the earth' (*Fates of the Apostles* 28).
[57] BT, *secan* meaning 2.   [58] BT, *gesecan* meanings 2 and 4.
[59] 'eager to go, [they] looked for the land of the Persians' (*Fates of the Apostles* 76ª–77ᵇ).
[60] *Fates of the Apostles* 31ᵇ–32ª.
[61] 'his soul sought from there the light of glory' (*Fates of the Apostles* 61ᵇ–62ª).
[62] His soul 'at once sought eternal life from there' (*Fates of the Apostles* 38ᵇ–39).
[63] *Andreas and Fates*, ed. Brooks, 119.

word as 'weary of life'. Yet the pervasive image of the journey calls for the preservation of the meaning of *sið* as 'journey' in this compound.[64] BT translates *sið̄geomor* as 'sad and weary of travel'. From the very beginning, the *scop* and his poetic activities are equated with arduous journeys and, at the end of the poem, the speaker concludes that he is himself about to *sið asettan*.[65] At the moment of death, he says: 'ic sceal langne ham, | eardwic uncuð, ana gesecan'.[66]

In the context of the present discussion, it is illuminating to recall objections to the commonly accepted emendation of *woron* to *wæron* on line 4 of the *Fates of the Apostles*. The manuscript reads: 'Twelve woron | dædum domfæste'.[67] Christian Grein was the first to suggest emending *woron* to *foron*.[68] More recently, Howlett supports this change on palaeographic grounds: he bases his argumentation on the resemblance, in insular minuscule script, between the letters f and wyn.[69] The emendation to *foron* is also supported by the textual environment in which the word occurs, for it would link the apostles with the motif of travel from the very moment of their introduction in the poem.

In the *Fates of the Apostles*, the prominence of the word *sið* highlights the motif of travel and the numerous expressions built around the verb *secan* grant these peregrinations a direction: the holy travellers are indeed looking for a particular place.

Andreas

Like the *Fates of the Apostles*, and like its possible sources, *Andreas* opens with a scene depicting the apostles scattering over the face of the earth.[70] The Old English poem is, however, unique in specifying that it

---

[64] For a translation of *sið̄geomor* as 'weary of travel', see Nicholas Howe, *The Old English Catalogue Poems*, Anglisitica, 23 (Copenhagen: Rosenkilde and Bagger, 1985), 90; Calder, *Cynewulf*, 33, and Constance B. Hieatt, '*The Fates of the Apostles*: Imagery, Structure, and Meaning', in Robert E. Bjork (ed.), *Cynewulf: Basic Readings*, Basic Readings in Anglo-Saxon England, 4 (New York: Garland, 1996; first publ. in *Papers on Language and Literature*, 10 (1974)), 67–77 (70).

[65] 'set forth on a journey' (*Fates of the Apostles* 111ᵃ).

[66] 'I shall seek alone the grave, unknown habitations' (*Fates of the Apostles* 92ᵇ–93).

[67] *Fates of the Apostles* 4ᵇ–5ᵃ.

[68] *Bibliothek der Angelsächsischen Poesie*, ed. by Christian W. M. Grein, rev. by Richard Paul Wülker, 3 vols. (Kassel: Wigand, 1883–8), ii (1888), 7 n. 4.

[69] D. R. Howlett, '"Se Giddes Begang" of the *Fates of the Apostles*', *English Studies*, 56 (1975), 385–9 (387–8).

[70] Numerous possible predecessors of the poem can be identified, but none of them stands as its direct source. The Greek version of the Acts of Andrew among the

is God Himself who appoints the fate of his followers and who directs the lots.[71] It says that the holy men's courage did not fail 'syððan hie gedældon, swa him dryhten sylf, | heofona heahcyning, hlyt getæhte'.[72] In *Andreas*, the Lord personally intervenes in this process; as a result, Matthew, when going to Mermedonia, goes where God has directed him. However wild the city of the cannibals may be, it is the land to which the Lord wants his disciple to go. When he executes his mission therefore, the holy man arrives at a place selected for him by his Lord.

Andrew's journey to Mermedonia is even more clearly presented as a quest, for the holy man goes in search of Matthew, who is held prisoner there. Yet the land the apostle should reach is as important as the man he should rescue. The heavenly voice which first enjoins the saint to travel to Mermedonia tells him to 'siðe gesecan, þær sylfætan | eard weardigað'.[73] The use of the words *sið* and *secan þær* brings together the motif of the journey with that of the quest for a particular place. The focus then narrows from Mermedonia as a whole to the prison where Matthew is held; the voice says: 'Ðær ic seomian wat þinne sigebroðor | mid þam burgwarum bendum fæstne.'[74] The goal of the mission, that is, saving Matthew's life, comes last in these divinely imparted instructions.[75] The object of the quest is therefore as much the land of

---

Anthropophagi is the ultimate model for the Old English poem. On the sources of the poem, see *Andreas and Fates*, ed. Brooks, p. xv and *Bright's Old English Grammar and Reader*, ed. by Frederic G. Cassidy and Richard N. Ringler, 3rd edn. (New York: Holt, Rinehart and Winston, 1891; repr. 1971), 204–5. In addition to the Greek text, other possible sources for *Andreas* are the Latin version of the Andrew legend found in the Codex Casanatensis. It is preserved in a manuscript of a much later date than the Old English poem, but it is nevertheless the Latin version closest to it. There are also two Old English prose renderings, one preserved in CCCC 198 and one fragmentary version in the Blickling manuscript, Homily 19. With the exception of the Old English version found in CCCC 198, these texts are conveniently translated in *The Acts of Andrew in the Country of the Cannibals*, trans. by Robert Boenig, Garland Library of Medieval Literature, 70 (New York: Garland, 1991). *Bright's Old English Grammar and Reader* provides the Old English version of the text preserved in CCCC 198.

[71] On this point, see Brian Shaw, 'Translation and Transformation in *Andreas*', in M. J. Toswell (ed.), *Prosody and Poetics in the Early Middle Ages: Essays in Honour of C. B. Hieatt* (Toronto: University of Toronto Press, 1995), 164–79 (166).

[72] 'after they dispersed, as the Lord Himself, the High King of heaven, showed them their lot' (*Andreas* 5–6). In the other versions of the legend, the apostles cast lots to divide the regions of the earth among themselves.

[73] 'seek out with a journey where the cannibals keep a dwelling-place' (*Andreas* 175–176ª).

[74] 'There I know that your victorious brother lies fastened in bounds with these city dwellers' (*Andreas* 183–4).

[75] *Andreas* 185–8.

the cannibals as it is Matthew's release from prison—one should not forget that Andrew significantly returns to Mermedonia after having freed the cannibals' captives.

Andrew's crossing to Mermedonia is an important episode which literalizes the idea that the protagonist is guided there by the Lord. For, it is God in disguise, accompanied by two angels, who takes the holy man across the water to the place where he must fulfil his mission.[76] Once on dry land, God, appearing to Andrew as a child, again points his follower in the direction of Mermedonia. He says: 'Ðu in þa ceastre gong | under burglocan, þær þin broðor is.'[77] The importance of the place the apostle should reach at the end of his journey is again underscored.

Divine intervention plays a crucial role in initiating Matthew's and Andrew's journeys, and the lands these holy men seek are revealed by a miracle. The saints therefore travel with a clear goal in sight; they go to places that have been singled out for them by a miracle.

Guthlac A

Guðlac decides to settle in the wilderness because, as the poet tells his audience, God 'him giefe sealde | engelcunde, þæt he ana ongan | beorgseþel bugan'.[78] Like the apostles who scatter on missions of conversion, Guðlac obeys a holy intimation in retiring to the desert.

Guðlac does not choose the *beorg* randomly, but the Lord reveals it to him: 'wæs seo londes stow | bimiþen fore monnum, oþþæt meotud onwrah | beorg on bearwe'.[79] The *beorg* is disclosed especially for the saint: it had remained, up to that point, inaccessible to men, remote, and shrouded in mystery. Significantly, this passage is unique to the Old English poem.[80] *Guthlac A* implies that the *beorg* was uninhabited prior to the holy man's arrival. On the contrary, both Felix's *Vita* and

---

[76] *Andrew* 248–9.
[77] 'You shall go in that city, under the city walls where your brother is' (*Andreas* 939ᵇ–940).
[78] God 'granted him an angelic gift so that he began to stay alone in a mountainous abode' (*Guthlac A* 100ᵇ–102ᵃ).
[79] 'The location of that land was hidden from men until the Lord revealed the *beorg* in the grove' (*Guthlac A* 146b–148a).
[80] No single source lies behind *Guthlac A* as a whole, and whether Felix's Life of Saint Guðlac was used by the Old English poet remains open to debate. It seems, however, that the vernacular poem has little connexion with the Latin text. On the question of the sources of *Guthlac A*, see J. E. Cross, 'English Vernacular Saints' Lives before 1000 AD's, in Guy Philippart (ed.), *Hagiographies: Histoire internationale de la littérature hagiographique latine et vernaculaire en Occident des origines à 1550*, 2 vols. (Turnhout:

the Old English prose life of Guðlac explicitly say that vain attempts had previously been made to settle the *beorg*. In chapter 25 of the Latin text, Tatwine declares that he knows an island 'quam multi inhabitare temtantes propter incognita heremi monstra et diversarum formarum terrores reprobaverant'.[81] In this version, potential settlers have tried to dwell on the island, albeit unsuccessfully. The location of the *beorg* is therefore known to people; it is not, as in the Old English poem, a secret place whose existence is hidden until Guðlac's arrival. The land remains deserted until it receives the visit of its proper guardian, not because it is remote, but because God conceals it from men.[82] Foreignness and inaccessibility are not here a matter of distance but, as was already the case with the dragon's barrow in *Beowulf*, a particular place becomes accessible only when a suitable visitor approaches.

The *Guthlac A* poet further omits another important fact stipulated in Felix's *Vita*: that Tatwine actually ferries the saint to the *beorg* in a fisherman's boat.[83] In the Old English poem, there is no mention of Tatwine and it is God himself who discloses the location of the *beorg* to Guðlac. Such details, typical of the vernacular poem, make of the *beorg* a special site awaiting its original 'conqueror'. Guðlac inhabits a place chosen for him by the Lord, he travels there alone, and he is the first human being to occupy it.

Presenting the saints' journeys as quests for lands, vernacular poets tightly associate an individual with a tract of ground, since the holy traveller's destiny is to be fulfilled in this distant land. Analysing the

---

Brepols, 1994–), ii (1996), 413–27 (419); *The Guthlac Poems of the Exeter Book*, ed. by Jane Roberts (Oxford: Clarendon Press, 1979), 11; Rosemary Woolf, 'Saints' Lives', in Eric Gerald Stanley (ed.), *Continuations and Beginnings: Studies in Old English Literature* (London: Nelson, 1966), 37–66 (53); *Felix's Life of Saint Guthlac*, ed. and trans. by Bertram Colgrave (Cambridge: Cambridge University Press, 1956), 20, and Schaar, *Critical Studies*, 40–1.

[81] 'many had attempted to dwell there, but had rejected it on account of the unknown portents of the desert and its terrors of various shapes' (*Felix's Life of Saint Guthlac*, 88). For the translation, see this same volume, 89. The Old English prose version of the Guðlac legend is very close to the Latin text; Tatwine 'wiste sum ealand synderlice digle, þæt oft menige men eardian ongunnon, ac for menigfealdum brogum and egsum and for annysse þæs widgillan westenes þæt hit nænig man adreogan ne mihte, ac hit ælc forþan befluge' *Das angelsächsische Prosa-Leben des hl. Guthlac*, ed. by Paul Gonser, Anglistische Forschungen, 27 (Heidelberg: Carl Winter, 1909), 114.

[82] *Guthlac A* 215–17.

[83] 'Ipse enim imperiis viri annuens, arrepta piscatoria scafula, per invia lustra inter atrae paludis margines Christo viatore ad praedictum locum usque pervenit; Crugland dicitur' (*Felix's Life of Saint Guthlac*, 88). 'þa ferdon begen þurh þa rugan fennas, oþ þæt hi comon to þære stowe, þe man hateð Cruwland' (*Prosa-Leben*, ed. Gonser, 114).

expression *dygle stow* in *Guthlac A* as well as its resonance in other Old English poems, I would like to contend that the saints in fact take control of the territory they reach at the end of their voyages. Guðlac's *beorg* is a mysterious place: the saint takes up residence alone on a *dygle stowe*.[84] The same collocation of words occurs in the *Panther*. After having eaten, the wonderful animal rests for three nights in a 'dygle stowe under dunscrafum'.[85] As the panther is a figure of Christ, its three nights of sleep clearly refer to the Resurrection. The *dygle stow* in question thus designates the otherworld, possibly Hell, where Christ is said to have travelled before rising back to life. This association of the *dygle stow* with infernal regions lends additional significance to the description of the *beorg* in *Guðlac A*: it is not only a wild desert haunted by hostile fiends, it becomes a hellish place which the saint snatches away from Satan's control when he occupies it.

The Old English poetic corpus contains another well-known instance in which a *dygel lond*, a mysterious land, is being visited and appropriated. It occurs in *Beowulf*, more precisely in Hroðgar's description of the mere Grendel and his mother inhabit: the king says that they occupy a *dygel lond*.[86] The hero's expedition to the underwater cave and his defeat of its monstrous guardian purges the hostile domain.[87] Consequently, when Guðlac decides to settle on the *beorg*, to remain there until he has defeated the demons and until his shelter becomes a pleasant plain of victory, the saint performs a heroic deed similar to that of Beowulf. Both the saint and the hero venture into and cleanse hostile territories, ultimately taking control of them.

Elene

Like other hagiographic poems, *Elene* does not represent the journey of its protagonist as a mere spatial displacement. This text foregrounds the motif of the quest, for the queen looks for a desired object: the Cross on which Christ died. Margaret Bridges recognizes in the quest the poem's organizing principle: the lack of an object is revealed in an initial situation and, after several episodes, it is acquired by the hero

---

[84] 'a hidden place' (*Guthlac A* 159ª). See also *Guthlac A* 215ª.
[85] 'a hidden place in the hill-cave' (*The Panther* 37). *The Exeter Book*, 169–71.
[86] 'a hidden land' (*Beowulf* 1357ᵇ).
[87] The waters of the mere calm down. See *Beowulf* 1630ᵇ–1631.

for his or her community.[88] In the present case, Helen travels to the land of the Jews to find the Cross. Throughout the poem, one is never allowed to forget that the queen is seeking something; for instance, she says twice that she wants the Jews to answer her queries and to provide her with explanations about everything 'þe ic him to sece'.[89] Variations on this expression occur at other points in the text and all of them make use of the verb *secan*.[90]

In order to find the Cross, the queen first has to discover where it is hidden. Her journey is therefore also a quest for a precise site and she moves progressively towards it. After she has crossed the sea, she remembers Constantine and his command: 'þæt hio Iudeas | ofer herefeldas heape gecoste | lindwigendra land gesohte'.[91] In this quotation, the object of the verb *secan* is the *land* of the Jews. Once there, the focus of the search narrows further. The Emperor has indeed ordered his mother 'georne secan | . . . hwær se wuldres beam, | halig under hrusan, hyded wære'.[92] In the land of the Jews, the queen must therefore seek out a particular place, *hwær* Christ died.

The dialogue opposing the queen to Judas again foregrounds the site Helen is looking for. The queen knows that the crucifixion happened on Calvary and she asks Judas 'hwær seo stow sie | Caluarie'.[93] When Judas agrees to lead her there, the focus narrows again and this time, Helen wants to know 'hwær seo rod wunige'.[94] None of the characters, not even Judas, knows the exact spot.[95] Even though he is forced to collaborate with the queen, Judas cannot simply lead her to the Cross. Once on Calvary, he prays the Lord to reveal where the tools of martyrdom are buried, and it is a supernatural intervention which designates the place Helen is looking for. The entire poem unfolds as a quest for the Cross, a quest initiated in the Roman Empire, on the shores of the Danube, with Constantine's vision; it continues across the sea in the land of the Jews and brings all the protagonists to Calvary. There, a final miracle reveals where the holy rood is buried. Cynewulf doubles Helen's search

---

[88] Margaret Enid Bridges, *Generic Contrast in Old English Hagiographical Poetry*, Anglistica, 23 (Copenhagen: Rosenkilde and Bagger, 1984), 70–2.
[89] 'that I seek from them' (*Elene* 319^a and 410^b).
[90] *Elene* 325^b, 420^a, and 568^b.
[91] 'that she with an excellent crowd sought the land of the Jews, of the shield warriors, over the battlefield' (*Elene* 268^b–270).
[92] 'to seek eagerly . . . where the holy tree of glory was hidden under the earth' (*Elene* 216^b–218).
[93] 'where is that place, Calvary' (*Elene* 675^b–676^a).
[94] 'where the cross remains' (*Elene* 624^a).   [95] *Elene* 719^b–721.

for the cross with a quest for a piece of land, thus paying particular attention to spatial parameters and localization processes.

In her study of twelfth-century English historical writings, Monika Otter discusses *inventiones*, or narratives of the finding of a saint's relics. She uses the early fifth-century *Revelatio Sancti Stephani* as a model to trace the contours of the genre. The main plot elements are as follows: the relics are found by chance or by divine guidance through dreams and visions. An emphasis is put on the search for the right place and on the digging itself, and these texts stress that the relic is 'earned' by intense desire and hard work. An audience is always present when the remains are discovered and there is some confirmation proving that the relic is genuine. Finally, a *translatio* brings it to a more worthy shrine.[96]

The plot of the Old English *Elene* very easily fits into this pattern: a divine vision first reveals the cross to Constantine. The search for the right place forms the core of the poem, from the Emperor's first discovery of the site of the crucifixion in the Scriptures to the smoke that indicates the location of the Cross's grave on Calvary.[97] Judas is surrounded by a crowd when he finds the three crosses and a miracle confirms which of the three bore Christ.[98] The crucifix is finally enshrined in a jewelled reliquary which is described as its new dwelling-place where it 'siððan wunode | æðelum anbræce'.[99] The last step of the *inventio* consists in a *translatio* of the relic to a precious shrine, and the gems with which the Cross is inlaid can be understood as a transposition to a new receptacle.

The motif of the *translatio* deserves further attention, for it sheds new light on the spatial issues the poem foregrounds. Judas warns his fellow countrymen not to reveal the place where the Cross is hidden. He says: 'Ne bið lang ofer ðæt | þæt Israhela æðelu moten | ofer middangeard ma ricsian'.[100] Pondering over this declaration, Earl Anderson wonders which power the Jews stand to lose; for, the poem clearly establishes that both military might and political authority belong to Constantine. The critic contends that 'Judas's speeches make sense only when read in the context of the *translatio studii*'.[101] He

---

[96] Monika Otter, *Inventiones: Fiction and Referentiality in Twelfth-Century English Historical Writing* (Chapel Hill: University of North Carolina Press, 1996), 28–9.

[97] *Elene* 202^b–210^a and 802–803^a.   [98] *Elene* 883^b–889^a.

[99] 'it remained afterwards, inviolable in nobility' *Elene* 1027^b–1028^a. See also lines 1017–22^a.

[100] 'It will not be long after that that the lineage of Israel will be able to rule over the earth anymore' (*Elene* 432^b–434). See also lines 448–50^a.

[101] Anderson, *Cynewulf*, 124.

distinguishes three aspects of the *translatio*, the three pillars that sustain Christendom: the *imperium* (political authority), the *studium* (learning), and the *sacerdotium* (ecclesiastical authority).[102] The Jews still possess the *studium*, that is, their knowledge of Christ's Passion and of the site of the holy rood's burial. They have received this knowledge from their ancestors and they eventually transmit it to Helen. When Judas, confined to a dark pit, surrenders to the queen and agrees to inform her about holy mysteries, he is 'unearthed', prefiguring the subsequent discovery of the holy relics. The relics and his knowledge are both brought to light by Helen, they are retrieved from the earth, and they pass under Roman control. In this scene, Judas in fact abandons the *studium* to the queen.

Helen also appropriates the nails of the crucifixion. These objects are fixed on the bridle of Constantine's horse and the military power of the Emperor is increased as a result. The relics make him invincible and thus secure his victory over his enemies.[103] Thanks to the queen's successful mission to Jerusalem, ecclesiastical control falls into Constantine's hands: he is the agent of the discovery of the cross and of the nails, and he is consequently assigned an important role in Christian history. With his mother's expedition to Calvary, the Emperor acquires more than precious relics. Helen's quest results in an increase in his military power and in an affirmation of his role as a religious leader. In other words, the expedition grants the Roman Emperor control of the *studium* so far possessed by the Jews and it strengthens his control of the *sacerdotium* and of the *imperium*.

Gaining control of a piece of land can thus have wide-ranging consequences. In *Elene*, it allows both the coming into being of a solid Christian empire under Constantine and it secures the transfer of power, learning, and religion to the western parts of the oecumene. *Elene* tells of a quest for a holy site. Helen, Constantine, and Judas all look for a hallowed ground and the protagonists are led to this holy land by divine intervention. It is first Constantine receiving a sacred message through an angel in a dream and seeing the Cross in the sky. It is also Judas praying God to reveal the precise place of the rood's grave and the smoke that consequently rises from the ground.

---

[102] Helen's journeys follow an east–west axis and thus reinforce the idea that a *translatio* is taking place between the land of the Jews and Rome. See *Elene* 255^a, 995^a, and 1015^b.

[103] *Elene* 1181^b–1183^a.

Old English hagiographic poets, we see, carefully justify the necessity of their heroes' journeys. Because they are undertaken following a sacred command, they are all granted divine approval. The saints are directed to a particular place and the holy men and holy women travel with a precise goal in mind; neither the twelve apostles, Helen, Guðlac, Matthew, nor Andrew roam the land aimlessly. With their journeys, they literally or symbolically take over distant lands.

TERRITORIAL APPROPRIATION: THREE STRATEGIES

This concluding section examines three narrative strategies that support the territorial claims inherent in vernacular hagiographic poems. They include the accounts of the encounter between the saints and the indigenous inhabitants of the lands they convert, the emphasis granted to images of paths being traced on the new grounds the missionaries explore, and finally the pervasive motif of treading and stepping on the land.

Who Lives Here? The Question of Land Occupation

Among the many difficulties the saint has to face when settling in distant regions, one involves the hostility and the violent clashes with the area's previous inhabitants that the newcomer's arrival causes. The possible occupation of the land by natives before the coming of the holy man or the holy woman, and the status of these autochthonous people, are intriguing issues, for Helen, Guðlac, and Andrew do not venture into empty wastelands. The regions they reach are inhabited and their encounter with the population is brutal. Who therefore are these original inhabitants? How are they described by vernacular poets?

Mermedonia is clearly populated when Matthew and Andrew travel there, and the *Andreas* poet foregrounds the notion of the *eðel*, the native land which the cannibals enjoy in their city. The divine voice that orders Andrew to rescue the cannibals' pious captive directs him 'þær sylfætan | eard weardigað, eðel healdaþ'.[104] Mermedonia is unambiguously the domain of the anthropophagites. Moreover, one of the city's

---

[104] 'where the cannibals keep a dwelling-place, hold a home' (*Andreas* 175^b–176).

most striking characteristics is that it is a place 'þær ænig þa git | ellþeodigra eðles ne mihte | blædes brucan'.[105] Mermedonia belongs to the cannibals: only they possess the land and no outsider can dwell there.

The episode of the flood modifies this state of affairs: Mermedonia is purified, that is, it is emptied of its original population. This is not a mere side effect of the catastrophe: it is its very goal. When causing the flood, Andrew addresses a stone pillar and commands it to let waters flow forth. He says that God orders 'þæt ðu hrædlice | on þis fræte folc forð onsende | wæter widrynig to wera cwealme'.[106] The deluge happens specifically to eradicate the cannibals. They are replaced by a new generation of Mermedonians whom the apostle raises from the ground. The death and rebirth sequence the flood encapsulates is more than an image of conversion. The Mermedonians are not merely rebuked and transformed by the holy man's teachings: they are reborn. After the flood, a new population originates with Andrew. His actions therefore deprive the cannibals of their land: they are violently destroyed to make room for a new group of people. By depicting the city's inhabitants as wicked, the *Andreas* poet justifies the saint's conversion enterprise. By representing Mermedonia's new population as springing forth from the earth, the vernacular author stages the coming into being of a perfect autochthony, thus essentially and irremediably linking a rejuvenated population to a particular territory.

In *Guthlac A* the settling of the *beorg* by the saint is clearly a violent process, as exemplified by the ensuing fights opposing the holy man to the demons. The brutality of their encounters resurfaces at numerous points in the text, for instance on lines 206–9[b], where the demons 'cwædon þæt him Guðlac eac gode sylfum | earfeþa mæst ana gefremede, | siþþan he for wlence on westenne | beorgas bræce'.[107] The saint's arrival wounds and aggrieves the fiends. Interestingly, they accuse him of invading their mountainous abodes *for wlence*, because of pride. The expression most famously occurs in *Beowulf* when the

---

[105] 'where no foreigner could yet enjoy the prosperity of a home' (*Andreas* 15[b]–17[a]). See also line 280. On line 74b, Matthew calls himself *eðelleas* in Mermedonia.
[106] 'that you quickly send forth far-flowing waters on this obstinate people for the death of men' (*Andreas* 1505[b]–1507).
[107] 'They said that beside God Himself, Guðlac alone had inflicted them the greatest of troubles when he stormed the mountains in the desert because of pride' (*Guthlac A* 206–9[a]).

poet recounts Hygelac's ill-fated expedition among the Frisians.[108] It reappears at other points in the heroic poem, for instance when Unferð accuses the hero of having competed against Breca *for wlence*, or when the coastguard, greeting the Geats as they come ashore to fight Grendel, recognizes that they have undertaken this journey *for wlenco*, and not because they are exiles.[109] In *Beowulf*, the expression occurs in contexts of bold and heroic undertakings. Moreover, it always denotes a raid in a foreign country: the champion ventures into unknown territories where he confronts hostile creatures—the Frisians, Grendel and his mother, or sea-monsters. Because the demons accuse Guðlac of settling on the *beorg for wlence*, it indicates that the saint intends to defeat its previous inhabitants and to gain control of their land. Besides, he clearly informs the devils of his purpose: 'Mæg ic þis setl on eow | butan earfeðum ana geðringan.'[110] The saint's arrival on the *beorg* is thus a colonizing gesture signalling territorial conquest.

Yet, like the *Andreas* poet who, by presenting the Mermedonians as evil cannibals, justifies their territorial loss, the *Guthlac A* poet questions the status of the demons as the *beorg*'s first occupiers as well as their rights to this place. He says indeed that the mound is 'idel ond æmen', thus suggesting that the wilderness in which the saint sets up residence is empty.[111] Other passages in the poem however contradict this impression, for instance when the poet mentions that Guðlac was often attacked by devils who 'þær ær fela | setla gesæton'.[112] Was the *beorg* populated before Guðlac's arrival or not? This ambiguity invites us to reconsider the question of land occupation and to recognize here a textual strategy that, by negatively depicting a given population, undermines its claim to its own territory. This rhetorical device also appears in historico-geographical documents and will figure prominently in the descriptions of Britain and the narratives of migration discussed in Chapter 7.

Numerous critics have noted, somewhat uneasily, that Helen's actions toward Judas amount to persecution. Questioned by the queen and then confined to a dark pit, the latter suffers a reversed martyrdom in which

---

[108] *Beowulf* 1206^a.
[109] *Beowulf* 508^a and 338^a. Note also the occurrence of the adjective *wlonc* on lines 331^b and 341^a.
[110] 'I can gain this place alone from you without difficulty' (*Guthlac A* 244^b–245).
[111] 'desolate and deserted' (*Guthlac A* 216^a).
[112] 'had previously settled many residences there' (*Guthlac A* 143^b–144^a).

the oppressor is in fact the Christian queen.[113] While this interpretation of Helen's character cannot be denied, the violence of the heroine's deeds can also be read metaphorically. As we have seen above, the motif of the *translatio* calls for a figurative understanding of the scene recounting the burial and subsequent release of Judas. According to this interpretation, what is being unearthed is in fact a body of knowledge, the *studium*, which passes under Roman control.

Moreover, *Elene* presents the Jews as always already defeated. When Judas learns that Helen is inquiring about the cross, he tells his fellow countrymen that their might is about to vanish. This should happen at the moment when, as he was told, 'ðu gehyre ymb þæt halige treo | frode frignan'.[114] Jewish power shall decrease not when the cross is revealed, but already when inquires are made about it. From the very moment Helen arrives in Jerusalem and asks questions about the holy relic, the power of the Jews begins to dwindle. A close examination of the relationships between Helen and her opponents indicates that the latter are presented as powerless. As a result, the queen's actions are justified, for even though Judas resists Constantine's agent, Cynewulf has in fact already dispossessed the Jews from their land and knowledge.

Andrew, Guðlac, and Helen all clash with the original inhabitants of the lands to which their missions take them. Although the vernacular poets do not deny the violence of the encounter, they also carefully undermine the right of the saints' opponents to their own territory: they are wicked man-eaters, evil demons, or weaklings who cannot resist the coming of the holy man or the holy woman. The corollary of this is of course that the saints' moral claims to the land they reach and convert in the course of their missions are strengthened.

Treading the Ground and Territorial Control

The second strategy of territorial appropriation which elaborates on the image of characters stepping on the earth is not specific to vernacular hagiographic verse. It has already been discussed in Chapter 3, when considering *Beowulf* and *Judith*, and it will figure again in the next chapter devoted to scriptural poetry. Integrated into accounts of the saints' journeys of conversion to the periphery, this imagery conveys the

---

[113] See Dinapoli, 'Poesis and Authority', 623, Bridges, *Generic Contrast*, 78, and Calder, *Cynewulf*, 124.

[114] 'you hear wise people ask questions about the holy tree' (*Elene* 442–3ª).

idea that, with their travels, the holy envoys trace the contours of a new geography.

In *Andreas*, an episode relates how Christ calls a statue to life and sends it to Abraham, Isaac, and Jacob, an episode permeated with representations of characters stepping on the ground. When Christ orders the stone sculpture miraculously to descend from its wall and to go in search of the patriarchs, He commands 'þryðweorc faran, | stan on stræte of stedewange, | ond forð gan foldweg tredan, | grene grundas'.[115] *Stræt, stedewang, foldweg tredan*, and *grene grund*: all these words indicate that the statue walks on a solid surface. Only the Old English poem grants this motif such prominence: in the Greek text, Christ merely tells the statue to 'go into the country of Canaan and go into the double cave in the field of Mamre'.[116] In the Latin version, the statue remains where it is and Christ orders it back to the wall at the end of the miraculous episode, while the two Old English prose versions omit the passage altogether.[117]

When Abraham, Isaac, and Jacob are raised from death, the statue informs them that they should get ready for a journey. The three patriarchs are sent on a mission of conversion and they 'geweotan... mearcland tredan'.[118] With the expression *mearcland tredan*, the *Andreas* poet underscores the fact that the characters step on the land and that they progress on foot over the earth. Again, the vernacular poet is unique in stressing the motif of missionaries advancing on a tract of ground.[119]

More significantly still, after the flood, Andrew retrieves the land of Mermedonia from the fatal waters, and he does so by stepping on the ground. When the cannibals, terrified by the inundation, finally repent, the saint decides to still the waves; he 'stop ut hræðe' and leaves his prison.[120] The flood recedes at the apostle's command; more precisely,

---

[115] 'the mighty work, the stone, to travel from the floor onto the street, and to go forth and tread the earthway, the green plains' (*Andreas* 773ᵇ–776ᵃ).
[116] *The Acts of Andrew*, 10.
[117] See *The Acts of Andrew*, 39 and 60–1. See also *Bright's Old English Grammar and Reader*, 208–10.
[118] they 'departed... to tread the border-land' (*Andreas* 801ᵇ–802ᵃ).
[119] Nothing of the kind is reported in the Greek version of the legend of Andrew. In this case, the three patriarchs travel back to where Jesus is and they rebuke the High Priest for not believing what the Saviour says. After their intervention, Christ sends them back to where they come from: 'And Jesus said to them, "Go to your places." And they went.' See *The Acts of Andrew*, 10.
[120] 'he quickly stepped' (*Andreas* 1577ᵇ).

it ebbs before the holy man's feet: 'symble wæs dryge | folde fram flode, swa his fot gestop'.[121] At this point, a street miraculously appears before the saint who is again depicted as stepping on the ground. The *Andreas* poet resorts to treading imagery to suggest that the apostle's actions redefine the nature of this hostile land and that when he steps on it, he symbolically appropriates it.

Guthlac A sharply contrasts the fiends with the holy man: the former are described as *lyftlacende* while the latter is called *se bytla*.[122] It is legitimate therefore to conclude with Margaret Bridges that, unlike the saint, the demons, 'these nomads of the air have no solid grounds, no foundation for a home'.[123] Yet a close reading of the poem indicates that this clear dichotomy is called into question at other points in the text. For instance, once the saint has taken residence in the wilderness, he is harassed by demons who want to expel him from the *beorg*. They attempt to frighten him away and they warn him that they intend to gather a crowd of fiends and to destroy his dwelling. They say: 'We þas wic magun | fotum afyllan;... | Beoð þa gebolgne, þa þec breodwiað, | tredað þec ond tergað'.[124] The devils claim to be able to destroy the *beorg* by trampling it down with their feet; they menace Guðlac to crush him underfoot, to tread on him. They situate their power of action in their feet and their choice of words—*fotum afyllan*, *breodwian*, and *tergan*—suggests that it is by stepping on the land and its new occupant that they intend to reclaim their dwelling-place. In this case, treading a tract of ground is clearly a gesture of appropriation; were it ever to happen, it would deprive the saint of his abode.

Cynewulf depicts characters stepping on a particular tract of land at a crucial moment in *Elene*, namely when Judas agrees to lead the queen to Calvary. The poem reads: 'Stopon þa to þære stowe stiðhycgende | on þa dune up ðe dryhten ær | ahangen wæs, heofonrices weard'.[125] Calvary, and more precisely the place of the crucifixion, is the narrative's centre of attraction and the goal of Helen's trip. Just as the queen is

---

[121] 'always the land was dry from the flood as his foot tread [it]' (*Andreas* 1581ᵇ–1582).
[122] 'flying, sporting through the air' and 'the builder' (*Guthlac A* 146ᵃ and 148ᵇ).
[123] Bridges, *Generic Contrast*, 131. See also Robert E. Bjork, *The Old English Verse Saints' Lives: A Study in Direct Discourse and the Iconography of Style*, McMaster Old English Studies and Texts, 4 (Toronto: University of Toronto Press, 1985), 127.
[124] 'We can demolish this dwelling-place with our feet... There will be angry ones who will trample you down, tread on you, and torment [you]' (*Guthlac A* 284ᵇ–288ᵃ).
[125] 'The resolute ones stepped to that place, up on that hill where the Lord, the Guardian of the kingdom of heaven, had been crucified' (*Elene* 716–18).

the Emperor's surrogate in the land of the Jews, Judas—once he agrees to co-operate—acts on Helen's behalf when he steps on Calvary, for the queen is not present when the three crosses are discovered.[126] The use of the verb *stepan* at this point suggests that, through her deputy, Helen extends her control of the land and takes possession of the place of Christ's martyrdom. The site of the crucifixion has passed into Helen's control.

The recurrent scenes which represent the saints treading the land partake in the wider concern for spatial issues hagiographic verse betrays. In *Andreas*, characters stepping on the ground illustrate the progress of their conversion missions, be they the apostle himself or other divine messengers, such as the miraculously animated statue or the three patriarchs. In *Guthlac A*, to put one's feet on the ground clearly signals territorial possession. Finally, Helen's mission to the land of the Jews appropriates for Constantine the place of the crucifixion and the relics that are buried there. When the saints advance on the surface of the earth, therefore, their steps mark their recently acquired control over a new space.

Paths and Ways

In the article she devotes to the metaphor of the *lifes weg* in *Andreas*, Lisa Kiser notes that the image of the 'way' appears in all of the poem's major episodes and that with this metaphor, the vernacular author elaborates on a biblical notion, that of Christ presenting Himself as the Way.[127] This is a fundamental motif in *Andreas* and it 'appears again and again, not always as a metaphor, but often in the form of literalized "ways", that is, images of roads and streets'.[128] It is in this second sense, that is, ways as literalized roads, that the following pages examine the numerous mentions of paths and ways in *Andreas*.

When ordered by a voice from heaven to go to Mermedonia, Andrew objects that he is incapable of completing such a long journey in just three days (the time Matthew has left to live among the cannibals). To justify his reluctance to go, Andrew argues that he does not know

---

[126] People carry the relics to Helen and present them to the queen after their discovery. Helen herself is therefore not present on Calvary. See *Elene* 844^b–847.

[127] Lisa J. Kiser, '*Andreas* and the *lifes weg*: Convention and Innovation in Old English Metaphor', *Neuphilologische Mitteilungen*, 85 (1984), 65–75.

[128] Kiser, 'Convention and Innovation', 67.

the way. He suggests that God send one of his angels, for 'halig of heofenum con him holma begang, | sealte sæstreamas ond swanrade, |...| wegas ofer widland.'[129] Contrasting with other versions of the legend, *Andreas* stresses this point.[130] The saint clearly contrasts himself with a potential divine envoy and insists that the latter would easily master vast expanses. Andrew's mixed references to sea- and land-travel in the passage just quoted—'wegas ofer widland' being opposed to 'holma begang, | sealte sæstreamas'—have given rise to controversy among critics. Commenting on the expression 'wegas ofer widland', Claes Schaar argues that 'it is natural that the apostle, reluctant to make the perilous expedition himself, should recommend the powerful angel with his knowledge of all ways on sea and land'.[131] This interpretation, which distinguishes clearly between travel at sea and travel over land, is opposed by Karin Olsen. She observes that to view the sea as a tract of land is a common feature of Old English poetry.[132] She argues in favour of a metaphorical understanding of 'wegas ofer widland', but she nevertheless concludes that both interpretations—the literal meaning of path over dry land as well as a signification including the nuances pertaining to a maritime context—are possible.

Any reading of these lines should keep both meanings in play; for, an interpretation that sees Andrew's travel to Mermedonia as a sea-journey emphasizes the remoteness of the land of the cannibals and underlines its foreign character.[133] Moreover, an understanding of this passage that combines evocations of land and sea is in keeping with the path imagery pervasive in the poem. The concluding lines of Andrew's answer to

---

[129] 'the holy one from heaven knows the expanse of the water, the salty waters of the ocean, and the sea, ... the roads over the extensive country' (*Andreas* 195–8ª).

[130] In the Greek text, Andrew does not mention the fact that he does not know the way to Mermedonia; he simply says that he cannot travel there quickly enough to save Matthew. In the Latin and the two Old English texts, Andrew points to his ignorance of the way, but he does not insist that the angel God should send would know it, that he would be familiar with the paths leading to the city of the cannibals. See *The Acts of Andrew* 3, 30, and 59, and *Bright's Old English Grammar and Reader*, 207–8.

[131] Schaar, *Critical Studies*, 50–1.

[132] Karin Olsen, 'The Dichotomy of Land and Sea in the Old English *Andreas*', *English Studies*, 79 (1998), 385–94 (385).

[133] The depiction of Mermedonia as an island seems to be another point on which the Old English poem departs from other versions of the legend where no such detail is mentioned. On this point, see *Andreas and the Fates*, ed. Brooks, 62, where Brooks quotes Klaeber on *Beowulf* 2334 and George Philip Krapp in his 'Notes on the *Andreas*', *Modern Philology*, 2 (1904–5), 403–10 (403–4). See also Olivier J. H. Grosz, 'The Island of Exiles: A Note on *Andreas* 15', *English Language Notes*, 7 (1970), 241–2.

the divine voice sending him to Mermedonia once more resort to this metaphorical model; the apostle says: 'ne me herestræta | ofer cald wæter cuðe sindon'.[134] The compound *herestræta* suggests that the sea-travel is conceived as a journey over land along a *stræt*.[135] Even when talking about the sea, the *Andreas* poet continues to use an imagery that alludes to paths and roads. In so doing, he foregrounds the progress of the travelling saint's journeys, journeys which follow a precise path.

During the crossing to Mermedonia, Andrew talks with the divine steersman and he recalls the time he spent with Christ. He remembers how Jesus sent his apostles to convert the nations. He told them: 'Faraþ nu geond ealle eorðan sceatas | ... | oððe stedewangas stræte gelicgaþ'.[136] Jesus' companions are to walk the earth until the end of the roads. Paths are again present in Andrew's account of Christ's interview with the High Priest. The apostle says that the latter knows 'þæt we soðfæstes swaðe folgodon'.[137] Here, the metaphor of Christ as the Way resonates with its full potential, for the road the disciples follow is also a spiritual way that leads to salvation. Yet a few lines below, the literal meaning of this expression resurfaces. The High Priest's words are quoted in direct speech and he tells the disciples that they *wadað widlastas*,[138] that they venture on miserable journeys for the love of their divine master. Within a short passage therefore, the *Andreas* poet puts the image of the road to two different uses and he adapts it both to spiritual and to literal contexts. The road on which the apostles advance is both a road to salvation and a track on which they step, following Christ.

The most striking example of this complex path imagery probably occurs when the water recedes after the flood: as already mentioned, a street miraculously appears before Andrew. The poet says: 'him wæs gearu sona | þurh streamræcce stræt gerymed'.[139] Kiser interprets this passage as a return to the metaphorical realm: 'the street that opens up before Andreas during the flood recalls...Moses crossing the Red Sea. More important, perhaps, than Andreas' own "gerymed stræt" is the

---

[134] 'the military roads over the cold water are not known to me' (*Andreas* 200^b–201).

[135] A similar association bringing together the image of a street with the crossing of a stretch of water is found when the divine steersman says that Andrew and his followers have no sustenance to get them through their journey *on faroðstræte*. (*Andreas* 311^b).

[136] 'Go now to all the corners of the earth...as far as the roads lie upon the plains' (*Andreas* 332–4).

[137] 'that we [the apostles] followed the tracks of the righteous One' (*Andreas* 673).

[138] They 'travel over long roads' (*Andreas* 677^a).

[139] 'immediately a street was prepared, was cleared for him through the water-course' (*Andreas* 1579^b–1580).

via that he creates for the people in Mermedonia'.[140] The episode of the flood in *Andreas* echoes the Hebrews' journey out of Egypt recounted in Exodus. It also conjures up the image of baptism—the beginning of a new life in Christ. Yet this passage should be also read as part of a wider poetic imagery: the land of Mermedonia emerging from the flood is a new territory. When Andrew walks through this regenerated expanse, he takes possession of it for his faith.

The journeys and actions recounted in saints' lives are structured around an expanding movement, an attraction that leads the protagonists to the periphery. In her study of the symbolic construction of geographical space, Mary Helms examines the politics of distance.[141] Reflecting on how foreigners and unfamiliar lands are perceived, she presents her reader with numerous anthropological examples, most of which are taken from the colonial enterprise. She mentions an opinion often expressed in the colonial world, an opinion that associates the essence of the foreigners and the nature of their environment. She mentions in particular the Spanish friars active in the Philippines and she indicates that they drew a parallel 'between the deplorable social character of the Ilongots and the alleged wild, untended, and "uncontrolled" nature of their habitat prior to its being "reworked" and "civilized" by an orderly layout of roads and schools'.[142] Although the temporal displacement existing between a colonial context and Old English literature limits the use of such concepts, nevertheless the idea that a habitat can be reworked, and especially that it can be done using roads, is relevant here. In *Andreas*, roads do not of course form an 'orderly layout'. Yet, the emphasis on the paths Andrew treads is significant. It is an expression of the apostle's 'colonizing' enterprise, of the fact that when evangelizing, he tames an alien space by imposing, with his journeys through the periphery, a network of roads that transforms and maps the wilderness. *Andreas* is thus a text in which path imagery is complexified and which allows for various interpretations: it makes use of the metaphor of Christ as the way, but it also illustrates how the saint domesticates and appropriates the border-lands to which he is sent.

---

[140] Kiser, 'Convention and Innovation', 73.
[141] Mary W. Helms, *Ulysses' Sail: An Ethnographic Odyssey of Power, Knowledge, and Geographical Distance* (Princeton: Princeton University Press, 1988).
[142] Helms, *Ulysses' Sail*, 50.

CONCLUSION

Old English hagiographic poems tell of ventures into unknown and distant lands, of the combat of holy men or holy women against hostile forces. These texts also tell of beginnings and origins, namely of the genesis of one's own religious community. What is at stake in the encounters between the saints and their opponents is thus to gain control of a new territory, and when these poems narrate how a particular land is won for Christianity, they conjure a new mental space: the border-lands now integrated into the familiar world.

Andrew, Helen, Guðlac, and the apostles: all the saints whose acts are related in these texts travel to the periphery, the stage where they carry out their missions. Consequently, the motif of the journey, especially of the journey understood as a quest for land, figures prominently in these poems. With their actions, the holy men or the holy women modify the nature of the place they reach at the end of their travels, as is most clearly exemplified by what happens to Mermedonia or to Guðlac's *beorg*.

The territorial aspects of Old English hagiographic verse are at the heart of two contrasting ideological pulls. On the one hand, they serve the totalizing dream which characterizes Christian thinking, with its idea of a universal mission that should bring Christ's faith to the remotest corners of the earth. Vernacular poets legitimize this expansionist thrust when they suggest that the regions to which the saints travel have been divinely appointed, or when they question the status of a given area's original inhabitants and of their right to their land. On the other hand, as Peter Brown observes, Christianity shifted the balance between places and non-places in the ancient man's map of civilization.[143] The cult of relics, which allowed for the delocalization of the holy away from a few privileged areas, modifies the map of Christian sites.[144] Thus hagiographic poems also reflect this scattering of communities and the relationships that unite distant places to privileged areas, such as the Holy Land. They redefine centrality and periphery (for instance, when *Elene* makes of Jerusalem the first of Constantine's religious 'foundations') and they transform the border-lands—non-places—into religious centres.[145]

[143] Brown, *Cult of the Saints*, 8.   [144] Ibid., 90.
[145] See *Andreas* 1675–97 and *Guthlac A* 744[b]–751.

6
Searching for Land: Scriptural Poetry and Migration

THE remaining two chapters of this book adopt a new perspective on the motif of travel that has figured so prominently in Chapter 5: they envisage it more particularly as a migration. They recognize in it a key feature of the Anglo-Saxons' spatial *imaginaire*. Yet, with the concept of migration, the stakes are no longer to map, to tame, and eventually to control the wild and unknown periphery. It is rather to reach, at the end of the migration journey, a homeland to which one is rightfully entitled and destined. This scenario, analysed here in the context of vernacular scriptural poetry, is also developed by the historiographic narratives recounting the Anglo-Saxons' journey to and conquest of England.

Chapter 2 has studied vernacular verse based on the Book of Genesis (the beginning of *Genesis A*, *Genesis B*, *Christ and Satan*, and Cædmon's *Hymn*); whereas Chapter 2 dealt with creation narratives, what follows focuses on the question of migration and it is devoted to a close reading of *Genesis A* and *Exodus*, with allusions to *Daniel* when relevant. Precisely because these poems are translations, because they are rewritten by vernacular authors, they are good witnesses to what John P. Hermann calls the 'culturally specific deployment of tradition'.[1] They invite an investigation into what is typically Old English in them.[2] More precisely, the tradition against which *Genesis A*, *Exodus*, and *Daniel* will be read is that of the biblical topos which understands the Israelites as a people migrating in search of land. Old English poets, while adapting and reworking their sources, played with this theme and juxtaposed it to the Anglo-Saxons' memory of their own ancestral migration from the

---

[1] John P. Hermann, *Allegories of War: Language and Violence in Old English Poetry* (Ann Arbor: University of Michigan Press, 1989), 82.
[2] On for instance Old English poets' contributions to landscape description and to an appreciation of nature, see George K. Anderson, *The Literature of the Anglo-Saxons* (New York: Russel and Russel, 1962), 117–19.

Continent. This convergence of the biblical and the native migrations is pervasive in Old English literature, as convincingly demonstrated by Nicholas Howe in his now classic *Migration and Mythmaking in Anglo-Saxon England*.[3] *Exodus* and *Genesis A* are no exceptions: because of the content of the biblical text on which it is based, it is not surprising that the former should centre on the migration itself. The vernacular poet furthermore limits his treatment of the biblical text to Chapters 13 and 14 of the Book of Exodus, that is, to the account of the Israelites' journey out of Egypt and to the pursuit and destruction of Pharaoh's army.[4] The Old English author concentrates on the Israelites' change of location, namely on their progress through the desert and their crossing of the Red Sea. More surprisingly, however, the notion of migration is also central to *Genesis A*: it is especially prominent in the episodes dealing with the Flood and with the construction of the Tower of Babel.[5] In this poem, the Hebrews are indeed constantly searching for *rumre land*, a broader land, the Promised Land toward which they initiated their journey under Abraham's leadership.[6]

The very idea of migration implies the passage from one space to another and it draws attention to the territory to be reached at the end of the journey, an area waiting to be occupied. Because they involve a change of location, migration narratives allowed Anglo-Saxon poets to articulate concerns having to do with spatial organization, with the importance of land ownership, and with the question of territorial appropriation. After reflecting on the relevance of the migration motif for the study of the Anglo-Saxons' spatial *imaginaire*, the present discussion turns to the recurrent depiction of the protagonists of these poems as people in search of a specific place. These descriptions foreground the importance granted to land possession since rest and safety are reserved for those who control a tract of ground and since punishment often takes a territorial form. To migrate also ranks among the heroic deeds one can perform, for it entails the crossing and the mastering of

---

[3] Nicholas Howe, *Migration and Mythmaking in Anglo-Saxon England* (New Haven: Yale University Press, 1989).

[4] Paul Remley, *Old English Biblical Verse*, Cambridge Studies in Anglo-Saxon England, 16 (Cambridge: Cambridge University Press, 1996), 9; Hermann, *Allegories of War* 57; and Howe, *Migration and Mythmaking*, 51–2.

[5] On this point, see *Genesis A: A New Edition*, ed. by A. N. Doane (Madison: University of Wisconsin Press, 1978), 81–2.

[6] *Genesis A* 1651[b]. *The Junius Manuscript*, ed. by George Philip Krapp, Anglo-Saxon Poetic Records, 1 (New York: Columbia University Press, 1931; repr. 1964), 3–87. See also *Genesis A* 1895[b], 1910[b], and 1913[a].

strange, unfamiliar, and sometimes dangerous areas; as such, it becomes an instance of heroic action. Finally, as the itinerant protagonists eventually have to establish their authority on the land promised to them at the end of their journey, vernacular poets developed various narrative strategies to express control over an area, in particular in scenes which represent characters treading the ground or following paths and ways marked out for them. In short, this chapter revolves around the following two questions: how did Anglo-Saxon poets articulate their interest in spatial and territorial issues with the concept of migration? How can the latter be used to redefine spatial organization?

MIGRATION MYTH AND THE PRODUCTION OF TERRITORY

The *OED* offers the following definition of the word *migration*: 'the action of moving from one country, locality, etc. to settle in another; also, simply, removal from one place of residence to another'. This definition hinges on two central notions which provide the structural principle of this chapter and of the next: the passage from one place to another and the establishment of a residence in the new country. The last step of the migration process, that is, a settlement in the area that has just been reached, might not be actually realized, but it is firmly established as the migrating people's horizon of desire.

In *Migration and Mythmaking in Anglo-Saxon England*, Howe demonstrates the existence of a myth of migration and he analyses its influence on Old English literature. This myth permeates Anglo-Saxon England's literary production, from Gildas's *De Excidio Britonum*, which sows its first seeds, to Wulfstan's *Sermo Lupi ad Anglos*, which stands as its last flowering. According to Howe, the Anglo-Saxons juxtaposed biblical and Germanic migration narratives and used this association to shape their collective memory of their own past. The Anglo-Saxons, he argues, viewed their ancestral migration from the continent as 'a reenactment of the biblical exodus'.[7] The *adventus Saxonum* was moreover crucial to the Anglo-Saxons' perception of themselves as a people.[8] The myth helped the Germanic tribes that crossed the Channel to create a common identity and it grounds their awareness of themselves as a people. 'In the absence of the political cohesiveness offered by nationhood,'

---

[7] Howe, *Migration and Mythmaking*, 2.   [8] Ibid., p. ix.

says Howe, 'a myth of origin provides a people with some means for determining its organic status as a group.'[9] And migration narratives did indeed function as a myth of origin for the Anglo-Saxons, for these accounts deal with their past history and with the imagined genesis of their community. Their impact affects many areas of Anglo-Saxon cultural and literary tradition. To quote Howe once more: 'To study the Anglo-Saxon myth, then, is to examine both a culture's reordering of its past and also some of the finest expressions of its imagination.'[10] Chapter 7 will focus on the *adventus*'s influence on the Anglo-Saxons' conception of their own past; in the present chapter, the migration myth will guide my reading of the Old English renderings of scriptural poetry. Both chapters resort to the migration myth to introduce issues more specifically linked to this book's starting ambition, namely an investigation into the Anglo-Saxons' spatial *imaginaire*. Both argue that with the motif of the *adventus* Old English authors articulate concerns having to do with spatial organization, land appropriation, and territorial ownership. Although deeply indebted to *Migration and Mythmaking*, Chapters 6 and 7 move beyond it to reflect on how vernacular poets, drawing on and elaborating a specific spatial imagery, eventually 'produce a territory' for their people.

Spatially speaking, migration narratives foreground the existence of an *ailleurs* from which the group first emerged. By leaving behind its former dwelling-place, it comes into being precisely thanks to its first migration. Yet, even though such narratives usually tell of events that happened in a distant past, they always retain currency and relevance for the interpretation of present and future circumstances: they offer patterns for understanding the present and for anticipating what is to come.[11] The appearance of new spaces is a crucial ingredient of any myth of origin, including a migration myth; for such tales chronicle how a people found its home after an original journey. In migration narratives, the expanses that will eventually form a people's territory are reached only after a change of location; they are a land to be conquered and occupied. These accounts look to the past to define a desired spatial organization and to justify its implementation by the society in which they originate.

Old English poets tend to view migrations in positive terms. These journeys do not only benefit from the aura surrounding the Israelites'

---

[9] Howe, *Migration and Mythmaking*, 179.   [10] Ibid., 6.
[11] See Howe, *Migration and Mythmaking*, 4 and Mary W. Helms, *Ulysses' Sail: An Ethnographic Odyssey of Power, Knowledge, and Geographical Distance* (Princeton: Princeton University Press, 1988), 42.

biblical exodus; adopting a secular point of view, Paul Battles points out that 'migration, like sea voyages and battle, constitutes heroic action, and as such is generally depicted in approving terms'.[12] Heroic action is tightly linked to the establishment of new territories; the present study has shown how both epic and hagiographic poems equate their protagonists' pursuits with the delimitation of an original space where a group can exist and prosper. Commemorating the founding exploits of a people's champion, heroic verse chronicles the emergence of a territory, that is, the creation of the space of the community. Hagiographic verse similarly registers the expansion of Christendom's sphere of influence through the various saints' missionary journeys, thus ideally allowing religious communities peacefully to dwell in territories newly gained from pagan people. Just as these two groups of texts address territorial issues, scriptural poems, inspired by migration narratives, also relate the emergence of a new homeland resulting from a founding and heroic migration.

Hagiographic and heroic poems celebrate the achievements of outstanding individuals. *Beowulf* traces the career of an extraordinary warrior and king, and even though his fate and his unfortunate death do affect his people, the poem's focal point clearly remains Beowulf himself. Hagiographic verse recalls the adventures of single men or women who travel and undertake their missions of conversion alone. Guðlac, for instance, struggles against the fiends of the wilderness on his own; the apostles separate at the beginning of the *Fates of the Apostles* and each follows his own road. If Helen and Andreas travel with a retinue, yet attention constantly remains focused on the two protagonists, and the group never figures prominently in these poems.

In the scriptural poems discussed here, the hero is no longer a single individual, but it is a whole community who venture into distant lands. Critics have noticed the pre-eminence these texts grant to the *folc*, the people, against the individual.[13] Paul Battles, for instance, notes that the *Genesis A* poet amplifies the tribal movement which precedes the Babel episode, a magnification encapsulated in the description of the Israelites as a *folc ferende*.[14] Geoffrey Shepherd for his part contends that Abraham is the most prominent figure of the second half of *Genesis A*, but he also recognizes that the patriarch is depicted as a national leader,

---

[12] Paul Battles, '*Genesis A* and the Anglo-Saxon "migration myth"', *Anglo-Saxon England*, 29 (2000), 43–66 (59). See also Howe, *Migration and Mythmaking*, 81.
[13] See e.g. Howe, *Migration and Mythmaking*, 76–8.
[14] 'a travelling people' (*Genesis A* 1653ª).

thus conjuring up the notion of the people.[15] A similar focus on the *folc* characterizes the Old English *Exodus*. This poem reports only the Israelites' crossing of the Red Sea and it describes this episode in heroic terms: as a result, it elevates the Hebrews as a whole to the rank of protagonists and heroes of the narrative.[16] In *Genesis A* and in *Exodus*, therefore, it is a group, not an individual, who accomplish the migratory journey. Agency is granted to a people who, contrary to what happens in *Beowulf* for instance, no longer need an extraordinary, heroic being acting on its behalf. The group's efforts aim at finding and appropriating a territory for itself: it is striving to define and secure a space, a tract of land where it can exist.

Daniel opens with a lavish praise of the Hebrew people; mindful of their covenant with God, they live happily in Jerusalem, and the poet says: 'Þæt wæs modig cyn!'[17] The presence of this common formula, which combines the construction *þæt wæs* with a laudatory adjective to praise champions such as Scyld, Hroðgar, or Beowulf, casts the Hebrews in the role of the hero and confirms the central part they play in *Daniel*.[18] Their fall from grace, their defeat at the hands of the Chaldeans, and their subsequent captivity are all recorded without the poet mentioning a single Hebrew name. Individualization occurs only when the three children appear in the narrative. Moreover, the song Azarias utters in the blazing furnace can be read, as Robert Bjork suggests, as a prayer for national deliverance.[19] If Azarias first asks God to help him and his two companions in the fire, he quickly starts speaking on behalf of his whole people. He laments: 'siendon we towrecene geond widne grund, | heapum tohworfene'.[20] Because of their ancestors' crimes, all the Hebrews suffer and are scattered over the face of the earth. Thus, when Azarias prays the Lord, he implores divine mercy on his entire people, not just on his companions and himself.

In granting the *folc* collective agency in the gaining and retaining of its territory, these three scriptural poems highlight the sense of collective identity that is derived from territorial possession. Contrary to heroic

---

[15] Geoffrey Shepherd, 'Scriptural Poetry', in Eric G. Stanley (ed.), *Continuations and Beginnings: Studies in Old English Literature* (London: Nelson, 1966), 1–36 (29).
[16] See Howe, *Migration and Mythmaking*, 80. Lucas contends that the true 'hero' of the poem is God. *Exodus*, ed. Peter J. Lucas (London: Methuen, 1977), 63–4.
[17] 'That was a brave people!' (*Daniel* 7b). *The Junius Manuscript*, 111–32.
[18] *Beowulf* 1812b. See also *Beowulf* 11b, 863b, and 2390b.
[19] Robert E. Bjork, 'Oppressed Hebrews and the Song of Azarias in the Old English *Daniel*', *Studies in Philology*, 77 (1980), 213–26 (223).
[20] 'we are scattered throughout the wide earth, dispersed in bands' *Daniel* (300–1a).

verse that establishes a 'legendary' sense of self and hagiography that bases identification on religious premises, the texts under consideration here, together with the narratives discussed in the following chapter, develop a more political perception of the group.[21] They link self-perception and spatial parameters, and they underscore how much a group's sense of its own identity is based on geographical circumstances.

PEOPLE IN SEARCH OF LAND

Central to the notion of migration is the image of a people journeying in search of its territory, an image which permeates both *Genesis A* and *Exodus*. In *Genesis A*, the narrative pattern according to which characters undertake a journey at the end of which they will reach a promised place of residence occurs many times. It is first mentioned very early in the poem, just after Adam and Eve eat the forbidden fruit. God, angry at his creatures for their sinful behaviour, begins his speech to the first man thus: 'Þu scealt oðerne eðel secean, | wynleasran wic, and on wræc hweorfan | nacod niedwædla'.[22] Although the idea of banishment is implicitly present in the Bible at this point, Genesis 3: 17–19, which reports the Lord's words to Adam, does not specify that Adam will have to look for a new abode. In the Vulgate, God chastises the first human beings, gives them some clothes, and only then does the text say that Adam has to go and cultivate the land from which he was first taken.[23] The Old English poem stresses that the first man's penance is territorial by opening the Lord's speech to his creature with the announcement that Adam now has to look for a place to live and that his punishment includes searching for a new dwelling-place, a *wynleasran wic*. The sinner is deprived of his residence and exile

---

[21] Of course, these three aspects are closely linked and cannot be unambiguously distinguished. But I suggest that there is a difference of emphasis between these three groups of texts.

[22] 'you shall seek another abode, a less joyful dwelling-place, and depart in exile, a naked, poor wretch' (*Genesis A* 927–9ᵃ).

[23] 'emisit eum Dominus Deus de paradiso voluptatis ut operaretur terram de qua sumptus est' Genesis 3: 23. *Biblia Sacra iuxta Vulgatam Versionem*, ed. by Bonifatius Fischer and others, rev. by Robert Weber, 3rd edn. (Stuttgart: Deutsche Bibelgesellschaft, 1969; repr. 1983). Please note that since the Old English prose version of the Book of Genesis follows the biblical text so faithfully, I have decided not to comment upon it. See *The Old English Version of the Heptateuch: Ælfric's Treatise on the Old and New Testament and his Preface to Genesis*, ed. by S. J Crawford, EETS os. 160 (London: Oxford University Press, 1922).

is part of the divine sentence passed on him. From this archetypal moment when the first man sets off in search of a new abode, the motif runs through the Old English rendition of the Book of Genesis and resurfaces, for instance, with the narrative of the Flood, the Babel episode, and Abraham's journeys.

In his account of the episode of the Flood, the vernacular poem insists that Noah's companions are eager to disembark on dry land. When the waters recede, the patriarch sends a raven first, and then a dove, to check whether a tract of ground is available. The poet explains that the people in the ark are impatient to get out and they await the moment: 'hwonne hie of nearwe ofer nægledbord | ofer streamstaðe stæppan mosten | and of enge ut æhta lædan.'[24] The Hebrews wish to leave the ark and to enjoy land once more; they especially resent their confinement in a tight space. The Book of Genesis does not mention this eagerness of Noah's fellow travellers to leave the ark.[25] This motivation behind the biblical leader's attempt to find dry land for his people is a notion added by the Old English author. Thus, in the vernacular poem, people in the ark are searching for a wider territory on which to dwell.

It is worth noting that all the occupants of the ark, and not only human beings, are keen to leave their shelter; for the dove sent off to scout around is described as being *rumgal*.[26] According to BT, this term is a *hapax legomenon* meaning 'rejoicing in ample space'. The vernacular poet, with his choice of this peculiar adjective for which there is no equivalent in the Vulgate, draws his audience's attention to the pleasure derived from roaming the earth and from enjoying its spacious expanses.

The episode of the Flood and the mention of the desire for land animating the ark's occupiers prefigure the Hebrews' depiction as they travel on the plain of Shinar before Babel; for, they decide to build the tower as a commemorating token before they scatter over the face of the earth *on landsocne*.[27] This last expression is repeated when, after the confusion of tongues, men disband throughout the world.[28] Once more, the two corresponding passages in the Vulgate mention the fact that the Israelites are about to disperse, but not

---

[24] 'when they could step out of the ship, out their place of confinement, onto the shore and carry their possessions out of the narrow place' (*Genesis A* 1433–5).
[25] Genesis 8: 5–6.   [26] *Genesis A* 1466ª.
[27] 'in search of land' (*Genesis A* 1665ᵇ).   [28] *Genesis A* 1699ª.

that they need to find a tract of land on which to live.[29] Moreover, the *Genesis A* poet says that when they travel from the east and settle on the plain of Shinar, 'rofe rincas sohton rumre land'.[30] The Old English poet adds this idea to his text and the Hebrews' tribal movement thus becomes 'motivated by the need for a more spacious domain'.[31] In *Genesis A*, the Hebrews are striving to possess an ample stretch of ground. And yet, as Battles shrewdly points out, 'population pressure or insufficient territory can scarcely be the reason why Noah's descendants journey to Shinar, since the flood has just destroyed all but Noah's lineage'.[32] If everything on earth has just been wiped out by the Deluge, why should the Israelites need to find *rumre land*?

The poet does not make explicit the comparison implied by the form *rumre* but he uses the notion of a (more) spacious domain at other points in his text. For instance, when the Lord leads Abraham out of Haran, He tells him that He will show him *brade foldan*.[33] When the patriarch arrives at Sichem and looks at the Promised Land, God again speaks to him and He announces that He will 'on geweald don, | rume rice'.[34] The land which God promises to Abraham is described as broad and extensive. *Genesis A* repeatedly mentions the necessity for a people to enjoy a vast territory. Not only does a group need to acquire a land where it can reside, but this dwelling-place should also be vast.

Expectation of a wider domain also permeates the account of Abraham and Lot's parting. Uncle and nephew are forced to go separate ways because the land on which they dwell can no longer sustain them both. Whereas Genesis 13: 6 simply says that the ground cannot provide enough subsistence for the two of them, *Genesis A* specifies that 'sceoldon arfæste, | þa rincas þy rumor secan | ellor eðelseld'.[35]

---

[29] Genesis 11: 4: 'et celebremus nomen nostrum antequam dividamur in universas terras' and Genesis 11: 9: 'et inde dispersit eos Dominus super faciem cunctarum regionum'

[30] 'the brave warriors sought a wider land' (*Genesis A* 1651). Genesis 11: 2: 'invenerunt campum in terra Sennaar'.

[31] Battles, '*Genesis A*', 46.   [32] Ibid., 46–7.

[33] 'a broad land' (*Genesis A* 1752^a).

[34] 'give the broad kingdom into your power' (*Genesis A* 1789^b–1790^a). In both these instances, the Old English poet elaborates on the simple term *terra* found in the Vulgate (Genesis 1: 2 and 1: 6).

[35] 'because of that, the honourable warriors had to look more widely for a settlement elsewhere' (*Genesis A* 1894^b–1896^a). On *Genesis A*, lines 1890–927, see Battles, '*Genesis A*', 51–4. The Vulgate has: 'nec poterat eos capere terra ut habitarent simul' (Genesis 13: 6).

The vernacular poet clearly indicates that another dwelling-place has to be found further away and Abraham finally gives Lot the following advice '[we should] unc staðolwangas | rumor secan'.[36] The repetition of the expression *rumor secan* a few lines apart, and especially of the comparative form of the adverb *rume*, emphasizes the spatial aspect at the heart of the scene which chronicles the separation of Lot and Abraham.

Abraham is a central figure in *Genesis A*, and he also figures prominently in *Exodus*: in the latter poem, he is the Israelite named most frequently after Moses.[37] This is surprising because Abraham does not take part in the Exodus (he dies in chapter 25 of the Book of Genesis) and because he is not mentioned in the biblical passages on which the vernacular poem is based. William Helder explains this oddity by contending that the Old English poet, with his numerous allusions to this character, refers to a 'homeland motif', namely that he reminds his audience that the Hebrews are entitled to Canaan because Abraham is their ancestor and because this land has been promised to him. The various allusions to the covenant existing between God and Abraham scattered throughout the poem, and more precisely the attention paid to its spatial components, support this argument.

Exodus opens with the figure of Moses who is presented first as a lawgiver and then as the leader who guides the Hebrews out of Egypt. Among the divine gifts granted to the patriarch, the poet mentions not only victory over his enemies, but also the life of his people and 'onwist eðles, Abrahames sunum'.[38] The very first lines of the poem therefore recall God's promise that he will bestow a land on the Hebrews. Moses and his people are heirs to a pledge first made to their ancestor, Abraham. Later in the poem, as the Israelites are crossing the Red Sea, the poet again alludes to Abraham: the Hebrews are united because they all descend from the patriarch who *landriht geþah*.[39] In this passage, what matters is the Hebrews' expectation that they will reach the Promised Land, a place to which they are entitled and that has been divinely selected for them. This territorial hope, and not their common ancestry in Abraham or their migration out of Egypt, secures their existence as a group.

---

[36] We should 'seek more widely homelands for ourselves' (*Genesis A* 1912^b–1913^a).

[37] Moses is named ten times and Abraham seven. William Helder, 'Abraham and the Old English *Exodus*', in Henk Aertsen and Rolph H. Bremmer (eds.), *Companion to Old English Poetry* (Amsterdam: Vu University Press, 1994), 189–200 (194).

[38] 'the dwelling of the homeland to the sons of Abraham' (*Exodus* 18). *The Junius Manuscript*, 91–107.

[39] 'received the right to the land' (*Exodus* 354^b).

But references to the 'homeland motif' also occur independently of Abraham. For instance, when camping on the shores of the Red Sea, the Hebrews realize that the Egyptian army is pursuing them, and they are frightened.[40] *Exodus* follows the Vulgate which says that the Israelites *timuerunt valde* when they see Pharaoh approaching.[41] Yet, the Old English poet elaborates on their state of mind at this precise moment and he adds that they 'wæron orwenan eðelrihtes'.[42] The Hebrews do not only fear for their lives; in the vernacular text, they also lose hope ever to possess their own territory. This allusion to the Promised Land occurs when the Hebrews 'nahton maran hwyrft',[43] that is, when land availability becomes a problem. Squeezed between the sea and the Egyptians, the Israelites risk being eradicated because they have nowhere else to go. They are on the verge of despair and reach the lowest point in their fortunes when no further stretch of ground lies open to them. To have a homeland or a land on which to reside becomes here a matter of life or death.

After the Hebrews have successfully crossed the Red Sea, Moses delivers a speech which includes two interesting territorial allusions. First, the leader reminds his people that God, who led the journey through the waters, has granted them 'burh and beagas, brade rice'.[44] Secondly, the patriarch recalls God's pledge to the virtuous that they 'gesittað sigerice be sæm tweonum'.[45] In both cases, the reward reserved to those who remain faithful to God is territorial. Although the Old English *Exodus* focuses on the crossing of the Red Sea, the poet nevertheless insists that the migration does not come to an end when the Hebrews successfully escape from Pharaoh's army: they are still searching for their territory.

The *Exodus* poet constantly emphasizes the territorial aspects inherent in the Hebrews' escape from Egypt. To do so, he resorts to the figure of Abraham and to the notion of the Promised Land. He also pays close attention to the space which the Israelites have at their disposal. The climax of the poem is reached when the Chosen People is caught on the

---

[40] *Exodus* (135–7ª and 200–2).   [41] Exodus 14: 10.

[42] 'they were despairing of their right to a country' (*Exodus* 211).

[43] 'did not have a further course' (*Exodus* 210ᵇ). Lucas recognizes that the notion that the Israelites were caught between Pharaoh and the Red Sea was probably not original with the poet. But the emphasis on land and on its availability is striking. On this point, see *Exodus*, ed. Lucas, 107.

[44] 'a fortified city and rings, a wide kingdom' (*Exodus* 557).

[45] They 'shall occupy the victorious kingdom between two seas' (*Exodus* 563). On the expression 'be sæm tweonum' and its biblical antecedents, see *Exodus*, ed. Lucas, 131 n. 443. For a different view, see Howe, *Migration and Mythmaking*, 90–2.

shores of the Red Sea with nowhere else to go. As in *Genesis A*, the motif of a land to settle and to enjoy is central to the spatial arrangements the text sets up. The heroic actions performed by the protagonists of these two poems consist in a search for their own land.

LAND POSSESSION AND TERRITORIAL BENEFITS

Exodus, and to a certain extent *Genesis A*, chronicle a change of location leading to a new homeland, and the travel itself is spurred by the expectation that one will enjoy land at the end of the journey. But once the destination is reached, what is at stake in controlling the space newly occupied? To answer this question, I will reflect on the value and benefits attached to territorial ownership.

On the third night of their exodus out of Egypt, the Hebrews encamp at Etham. They perceive, the poet says, 'þæt þær drihten cwom | weroda drihten, wicsteal metan'.[46] The place where they stop has been selected by the Lord himself; it is divinely set aside for them. God delineates the contours of the camp only in the Old English poem—in the Vulgate Exodus, it is nowhere specified that He marks out the boundaries of the Israelites' camp.[47] In the vernacular poem, God determines who dwells where, and in that, he echoes the representations of the Lord found in the creation narratives discussed in Chapter 2, which equated divine power with control over the occupation and the settlement of space. In *Exodus*, therefore, the Chosen People's obedience to the Lord is spatial: they travel and encamp where God directs them. About Etham, the poet also says: 'Þa wæs þridda wic | folce to frofre.'[48] The expression 'folce to frofre' belongs to a common stock of poetic phrases recurring throughout the Old English corpus.[49] It suggests that the Hebrews derive comfort and benefit from their place of residence as others do from a good and powerful leader: in *Beowulf*, for instance, God sends a descendant to Scyld 'folce to frofre'.[50] The place marked

---

[46] 'that the Lord, the Lord of the armies, came there to mark out a camping place' (*Exodus* 91^b–92).

[47] Exodus 13: 21.

[48] 'The third camp was a comfort to the people' (*Exodus* 87^b–88^a).

[49] See *Andreas* 606^a, *Beowulf* 14^a, *Christ* 1421^a, *Elene* 502^a and 1142^a, and *Menologium* 228^a. J. B. Bessinger, Jr., *A Concordance to the Anglo-Saxon Poetic Records* (Ithaca, NY: Cornell University Press, 1978).

[50] *Beowulf* 14^a. *Beowulf and the Fight at Finnsburg*, ed. by F. Klaeber, 3rd edn. (Lexington, MA: Heath, 1922; repr. 1950).

out for the Israelites in the wilderness is a solace to them, and to have a dwelling-place is as essential to a people's social organization as to be ruled by a competent leader.

In *Genesis A*, the land emerging from the deadly waters of the Flood also appears as a comfort to the people in the ark. For instance, when the streams recede and Noah sees the dove he sent out come back with a twig of olive tree, the Vulgate says: 'intellexit ergo Noe quod cessassent aquae super terram'.[51] The patriarch understands the branch the bird brings back as a sign that the waters are ebbing. The Old English poet elaborates on this point; for, the olive twig announces that help has come to the people in the ark since: 'þa ongeat hraðe | flotmonna frea þæt wæs frofor cumen'.[52]

The Old English poet again fleshes out his source a few lines below when he adds a first sentence to God's speech to Noah. In Genesis 8: 16 the Lord orders him to leave the ark. But in the vernacular poem, before this command, we read: 'Þe is eðelstol eft gerymed, | lisse on lande, lagosiða rest | fæger on foldan.'[53] Doane demonstrates that this passage plays on the meaning of the name 'Noah': 'rest for the sea-journey'.[54] But it also foregrounds the idea that a new dwelling-place is ready for the patriarch and his companions after the Flood. It has been prepared for them and the Lord guides them to it. While still in the ark, Noah perceives that land possession brings comfort, and the words the poet attributes to God—*lisse, fæger rest*—stress the delights inherent in possessing a home.

In the Babel episode, the vernacular poet emphasizes once more the pleasant nature of the ground when the Hebrews reach the plain of Shinar and look for a residence there. The earth has just been cleared by the Flood and the survivors of the Deluge finally reach a place 'þær hie fæstlice | æðelinga bearn, eard genamon'.[55] At this point, the *Genesis A*

---

[51] 'So Noah knew that the waters were abated from the earth' Genesis 8: 11. The English version of the Bible is from: *The Holy Bible: Containing the Old and New Testaments: Translated out of the Original Tongues: and with the Former Translations Diligently Compared and Revised by His Majesty's Special Command* (New York: Nelson, [n.d.]).

[52] 'then the ruler of the sailors realized that help had come' (*Genesis A* 1474ᵇ–1475).

[53] 'a native land is provided for you, joy on the land, a beautiful place to rest from your journeys on earth' (*Genesis A* 1485–7ᵃ).

[54] *Genesis A*, ed. Doane, 272. See also Fred C. Robinson, 'Names in Old English Literature', *Anglia*, 86 (1962), 14–58 (33).

[55] 'where they, the children of noble men, firmly took up a dwelling-place' (*Genesis A* 1653ᵃ–1654).

poet details the pleasant nature of the land and he adds to the Vulgate where the account of this scene is more concise and simply states that when the Israelites reach Shinar, *habitaverunt in eo*.[56] The land on which the Hebrews settle is carefully described in the vernacular text, and its green and fertile plains are a continual blessing to the people: to them, they are 'wilna gehwilces weaxende sped'.[57] By emphasizing the bounteous aspects of the soil and the benefits the Israelites derive from it, the Old English poet establishes a link between land and people, between the availability of the former and the welfare of the latter.

Land is again considered a valuable possession toward the end of the poem, in the dialogue between Abimelech and Abraham. The Philistine king realizes that the patriarch is a man of God and begs him to be benevolent toward his people and himself. In his plea, he reminds Abraham of the favours he bestowed on him in the past. The Vulgate account of this conversation is succinct; the king merely says: 'sed iuxta misericordiam quam feci tibi facies mihi et terrae in qua versatus es advena'.[58] Once again, the vernacular poet seizes this opportunity to highlight the motif of land possession and he renders this biblical verse thus: 'Gyld me mid hyldo, þæt ic þe hneaw ne wæs | landes and lissa'.[59] Since the Old English author does not clearly state what joys Abimelech granted Abraham, one is induced to believe that the two words—*land* and *liss*—are virtually synonymous. To have the former (land) unavoidably brings the latter (joy). In *Genesis A*, Abimelech's kindness toward Abraham is territorial.

Lines 1759 and following narrate the blessing of Abraham. The Old English author alters his source again and Doane, in his edition of the poem, comments on this change. The critic observes that the vernacular poet brings together the two main components of the blessing: on the one hand, the fact that through Abraham all the nations of the earth shall be blessed and, on the other, the promise to make Abraham a great nation.[60] He mentions that commentators, Augustine for instance, have usually granted a higher value to the first part of the blessing and that

---

[56] They 'dwelt there' (Genesis 11: 2).

[57] 'a growing prosperity in their every wish' (*Genesis A* 1660).

[58] 'but according to the kindness that I have done unto thee, thou shalt do unto me, and to the land wherein thou hast sojourned' (Genesis 21: 23).

[59] 'Repay me with kindness, because I was not stingy with land and joy towards you' (*Genesis A* 2824–5ª).

[60] *Genesis A*, ed. Doane, 287.

the Old English poet does the same. Moreover, Doane assumes that the lesser blessing, the increase of Abraham's family, 'is of little immediate worth to an audience of Anglo-Saxon Christians, in a word, seems no real blessing at all'.[61] According to the critic therefore, this explains why the Old English poet modified the wording of this passage. For Genesis 12: 2: 'faciamque te in gentem magnam',[62] he renders

>   Wriðende sceal
> mægðe þinre monrim wesan
> ...
> oðþæt fromcyme   folde weorðeð,
> þeodlond monig   þine gefylled.[63]

And Doane concludes that the Old English text thus 'accords with the needs and expectations of the Christian audience'.[64] He does not however specify what these needs and expectations are. Inscribing this passage in the wider context of my argument, I would like to offer another possible explanation for the change outlined above; for, it suggests that to be a great nation is to rule over and to occupy many lands. The lines just quoted assure Abraham that his family will fill the earth and settle numerous regions on earth: this is the promise made to the patriarch according to the vernacular poet and what is appealing in it is certainly that Abraham's descendants will enjoy the entire earth as their home.

To conclude with *Genesis A*, let us return to Adam and Eve at the beginning of the poem. The first human beings are banished from Paradise, the 'liðsa and wynna | hihtfulne ham' because they have eaten the forbidden fruit.[65] In the Vulgate, the punishment God reserves to Adam for his transgression is precisely directed at the soil: it will no longer be fertile and the first man will have to struggle to get his subsistence from it.[66] The biblical account does not mention any mitigating circumstances to the first man's afflictions, but the vernacular text does. The poet elaborates on his source and adds that God was

---

[61] *Genesis A*, ed. Doane, 287.   [62] 'And I will make of thee a great nation'.
[63] 'The total number of people of your tribe shall be growing... until the earth, many inhabited lands, shall be filled with your race' (*Genesis A* 1762^b–1766).
[64] *Genesis A*, ed. Doane, 288.
[65] 'the pleasant home of joys and delights' (*Genesis A* 945^b–946^a).
[66] 'ad Adam vero dixit quia audisti vocem uxoris tuae et comedisti de ligno, ex quo praeceperam tibi ne comederes maledicta terra in opere tuo in laboribus comedes eam cunctis diebus vitae tuae' (Genesis 3: 17).

reluctant to withdraw all favours from his creatures.[67] Although Adam and Eve have sinned, the Lord still wishes them to enjoy the bounty of a fertile earth. Consequently, he orders the sea and the earth to bring forth sustenance for the first couple. He also allows them to reside under a starry sky and He 'him grundwelan ginne sealde'.[68] Adam and Eve's terrible loss when expelled from Paradise is alleviated by the enjoyment of a fruitful earth. This precise point is completely independent from the biblical version. It suggests that in keeping with the Old English poet's outlook, land is so precious that to hold sway over it necessarily entails some benefits.

Although *Daniel* is structured around the image of the city—Jerusalem and Babylon—issues comparable to those addressed in relation to *Genesis A* and *Exodus* permeate the poem. In *Daniel*, 'the happiest state of man is an urban one'.[69] Robert Finnegan observes that the *burh* reflects the moral state of its citizens and that on this spiritual condition depend not merely the happiness of the *burhsittend* but also their right to hold the city.[70] *Daniel* opens indeed with a description of the faithful Israelites who can 'in Hierusalem, goldhord dælan, | cyningdom habban'.[71] This state of affairs lasts as long as the Hebrews keep their covenant with God; faithfulness and good living are thus rewarded in territorial terms: with control over a stretch of land and enjoyment of a home. Land possession is also crucial for the Hebrews' enemies; for, once Nebuchadnezzar has captured Jerusalem and led its population in captivity, the Babylonian king still wishes to control the city of the defeated. After his military victory, Nebuchadnezzar 'onsende þa sinra þegna | worn þæs werudes west toferan, | þæt him þara leoda land geheolde, | eðne eðel, æfter Ebreum.'[72] Lines 1 to 79 in *Daniel* have no direct source in the Book of Daniel, although an account of the destruction of Jerusalem can be found in 2 Kings 24: 10–18. In the biblical text, Nebuchadnezzar names his uncle as his successor to rule over Jerusalem. And yet, the biblical passage does not foreground territorial aspects in the same way as the Old English poem does. In the

---

[67] *Genesis A* 952–64.
[68] He 'granted them ample earthly riches' (*Genesis A* 957).
[69] Robert Emmett Finnegan, 'The Old English *Daniel*: The King and his City', *Neuphilologische Mitteilungen*, 85 (1984), 194–211 (204).
[70] Finnegan, '*Daniel*', 204.
[71] 'distribute treasure in Jerusalem, hold the kingdom' (*Daniel* 2–3ª).
[72] 'He sent his followers, a crowd from that army, west so that they held the land of that people for him, the desolate native land, after the Hebrews' (*Daniel* 75–8).

passage just quoted, the Babylonian king is anxious to keep control of the land of the Jews, of their *eðel*. Nebuchadnezzar wants to rule over the city even though it is now *eðe*, desolate, waste. In this, he echoes the figures of Grendel who rules over Heorot when the hall has ceased to function properly and of the fiends who oppose Guðlac and fight to retain control of the wilderness. In all these examples, the lands in question are barren, that is, they are not put to any proper use. And yet, it is still important to possess them. This apparent paradox may be resolved when one realizes that to own the enemies' land seals victory over one's opponents.

When Daniel interprets Nebuchadnezzar's second dream, the Old English poem links the notion of happiness to urban surroundings. The king ignores Daniel's explanation of his vision and his warnings that his own impending downfall and exile in the wilderness are being foreshadowed. After the holy man's speech, Nebuchadnezzar contemplates Babylon, his city, and he just cannot imagine that he might one day no longer enjoy it. He addresses Babylon directly and says: 'þu eart seo micle and min seo mære burh | þe ic geworhte to wurðmyndum, | rume rice. Ic reste on þe, | eard and eðel, agan wille.'[73] Nebuchadnezzar claims ownership of the city. Interestingly, he equates possession of a dwelling-place, *eard*, of a home, *eðel* with rest, *rest*. Territorial control is thus associated with the enjoyment of peacefulness.[74]

It is crucial for a people to possess land because by granting it a territory where it can live, it ensures its survival. It is given to those who are faithful and obey God's commands, as the Hebrews in *Daniel* and in *Exodus*. The enjoyment of a tract of ground is also a source of delight and sustenance for those who dwell on it. The land that emerges from the Flood waters is a comfort to the people in the ark, and Nebuchadnezzar, unable to imagine that he could lose control of Babylon, is certain that he will always find rest and quiet in his city. *Daniel*, *Exodus*, and *Genesis A* all link well-being and land possession.

---

[73] 'You are mine, a great and famous city which I constructed in my honour, a spacious domain. In you, I will have rest, a dwelling-place, and a home' (*Daniel* 608–11). Unlike Farrell who takes *reste* here as a form of the verb *restan* 'to remain', I understand the word as the accusative feminine singular form of *rest*. For similar translations of the lines, see also *The Cædmon Poems*, trans. by Charles W. Kennedy (London: Routledge, 1916) and Finnegan, '*Daniel*', 206.

[74] A similar association of rest and territorial location appears in *Exodus* 134[a], where the fourth camp of the migrating Israelites is called *randwigena ræst*, the 'resting-place of the warriors'.

LOSS OF LAND AND TERRITORIAL PUNISHMENT

Commenting on Nebuchadnezzar's words quoted above, in which the king says that he will find rest in Babylon, J. R. Hall notes that the Old English poet is original in introducing the idea of rest at this point, for it cannot be traced to the Book of Daniel.[75] Thinking further about these lines, I would like to contrast them with the mention, in Daniel's interpretation of the king's dream, that 'ne rest witod' for the Babylonian ruler in his exile.[76] These two passages unambiguously connect prosperity and dwelling-place. For Nebuchadnezzar, rest can only be had in Babylon, that is, in a space he controls. To be deprived of this original home is, for the king, a terrible loss, and it is equivalent to becoming one of the wild beasts which roam the wilderness, as we will see below. One remembers here that when Guðlac deprives the fiends of the *beorg*, he also denies them their shelter: the *beorg* was the place where they could, like Nebuchadnezzar in Babylon, 'restan ryneþragum, rowe gefegon'.[77] In both cases, territorial dispossession is a terrible injury.

In *Daniel*'s account of Nebuchadnezzar's downfall, the central difference between the Old English poem and the Vulgate lies, according to Claire Fanger, in the nature of the king's error and the reason for God's retaliation.[78] The vernacular poem underscores the king's pride before he contemplates Babylon and rejoices at the sight; the Old English author says 'wearð ða anhydig ofer ealle men, | swiðmod in sefan'.[79] Nebuchadnezzar forgets that he holds the city by the grace of God and not of his own power. He thus repeats Satan's mistake, the rebellious angel who fell when he refused to acknowledge that the Lord had ultimate control over creation. Both Nebuchadnezzar and Satan question God's spatial authority and presume that they can create their own space and rule over it independently. As a result, they are humbled and are denied the piece of land they consider theirs: heaven or Babylon.

---

[75] J. R. Hall, '*Daniel*, Line 610b', *The Explicator*, 45/2 (1987), 3–4 (3).

[76] 'no resting place [shall be] appointed' (*Daniel* 575ᵃ).

[77] 'rest for a while, enjoy quietness' (*Guthlac A* 213). *The Exeter Book*, ed. by George Philip Krapp and Elliott van Kirk Dobbie, Anglo-Saxon Poetic Records, 3 (New York: Columbia University Press, 1936; repr. 1966), 49–88.

[78] Claire Fanger, 'Miracle as Prophetic Gospel: Knowledge, Power and the Design of the Narrative in *Daniel*', *English Studies*, 72 (1991), 123–35 (131).

[79] 'he was proud beyond all men, arrogant in his heart' (*Daniel* 604–5ᵃ). The Vulgate does not mention Nebuchadnezzar's pride. See the Book of Daniel 4: 25–7.

Because he refuses to heed the warnings contained in his dream, the king is condemned to roam the wilderness for seven years: 'seofon winter samod susl þrowode, | wildeora westen, winburge cyning'.[80] Alliteration underlines the contrast between the *winburg*, the chief city which Nebuchadnezzar rules, the *westen*, the desert to which he is banished, and the *wildeor*, the wild beasts which populate it. The city and the wilderness are two contrasting locations, the first an ideal dwelling-place and the second a place of punishment and suffering. Fittingly, therefore, for Nebuchadnezzar, whose sin is to contest divine control of space, the sentence is territorial.

The Israelites also lose their city because of their sinful behaviour. When they turn away from God and disregard his laws, the Lord allows the Chaldeans to go 'to ceastre forð, | þær Israela æhta wæron'.[81] The focus of the retaliation is the city, the *ceastre*, in which the Israelites keep their treasures. Jerusalem shelters material riches which Nebuchadnezzar plunders. His warriors: 'gestrudan gestreona under stanhliðum, | ... | oðþæt hie burga gehwone abrocen hæfdon, | þara þe þam folce to friðe stodon.'[82] More importantly, however, the poet says that the heathen king deprives the Israelites of the city which was their protection.[83] In this passage, the precious objects robbed by the enemy army and the quietness afforded by a fortified and secure settlement are almost synonymous. It is crucial to possess Jerusalem because it is the place where the Hebrews can exist as a people. When they lose their capital city to the Chaldeans, they are led into captivity.

The connexion between loss of land and punishment is also made by the *Genesis A* poet, from the expulsion of the first humans from Paradise to the destruction of Sodom and Gomorrah. Genesis 19: 25 reports the two cities' annihilation thus: 'et subvertit civitates has et omnem circa regionem universos habitatores urbium et cuncta terrae virentia'.[84] In the Old English poem, this passage is expanded and provides a more detailed account of the ravages wrought by the fire: 'lig eall fornam | þæt he

---

[80] 'for seven years together the king of the capital city suffered torment, the wilderness of wild beasts' (*Daniel* 620–1).

[81] 'forth to that city where the possessions of the Israelites were' (*Daniel* 42ᵇ–43).

[82] 'They plundered treasures under the stone walls ... until they had destroyed every stronghold which stood as a protection to the people' (*Daniel* 61–4).

[83] The possible biblical source for this passage, 2 Kings 24: 10–17, mentions the fact that Nebuchadnezzar loots Jerusalem's temple, but it does not comment on the destruction of the city itself and on its consequences.

[84] 'and he overthrew those cities, and all the plain, and all the inhabitants of the cities, and that which grew upon the ground'.

grenes fond goldburgum in' and 'bearwas wurdon | to axan and to yslan, eorðan wæstma'.⁸⁵ The devastation of the land is vividly depicted, with trees being burned down to ashes and all vegetation disappearing. Not only Sodom and Gomorrah's lofty buildings are destroyed, but the very ground on which they are built is also charred. God's retaliation for the sinful living of the population is terrible and the territorial destruction that befalls the two cities graphically conveys this impression. As God's blessing to Abraham is modified to refer more directly to the lands over which the patriarch's descendants will rule, similarly the destruction of Sodom and Gomorrah includes territorial allusions with details that depict a land completely laid waste. Both God's anger and his blessing are metaphorically expressed in territorial terms.

Similar stress is laid on the importance of land possession earlier in the poem, in the account of the institution of the circumcision. As a token of the covenant established between God and men through Abraham, the Lord tells the patriarch that every male child should be circumcised, lest he shall be 'of eorðan | þurh feondscipe feor adæled, | adrifen from duguðum'.[86] This translates Genesis 17: 14 which simply says that the uncircumcised child shall be cut off from his people.[87] The Old English poet once again adds a reference to a tract of ground and its possession: it will be denied to the one who does not follow God's orders. The man who is not circumcised will not only be separated from his family, but also from the earth. Punishment is not merely relational, as is the case in the Vulgate where social ties are threatened, but it becomes territorial.

In *Exodus*, land possession is a matter of life or death for the Egyptians. When they perceive the impending disaster about to befall them, Pharaoh and his army wish to turn tail and go back home. In this, they adopt the coward's typical attitude when caught in the middle of battle. But as the deadly waters engulf the entire army, the Egyptians have nowhere to go. The poet specifies that their retreat has been cut off: 'behindan beleac | wyrd mid wæge'.[88] In an image that recalls the Israelites' predicament on the shore of the Red Sea before the waters

---

[85] 'the flame destroyed all that it found green in the cities rich in gold' (*Genesis A* 2550ᵇ–2551) and 'forests, the fruits of the earth, became cinders and ashes' (*Genesis A* 2554ᵇ–2555).

[86] 'through hostility separated far from the earth, driven away from salvation' (*Genesis A* 2323ᵇ–2325ᵃ).

[87] 'masculus cuius praeputii caro circumcisa non fuerit delebitur anima illa de populo suo quia pactum meum irritum fecit' (Genesis 17: 14).

[88] 'with waves, fate closed in behind [them]' (*Exodus* 457ᵇ–458ᵃ).

open, the Egyptians are trapped in the waves: 'mægen wæs on cwealme | fæste gefeterod, forðganges nep'.[89] *Forðganges nep* is a notorious crux, as Peter Lucas warns in his notes. George Krapp resolves it in emending *nep* to *weg*.[90] In the context of the present discussion, it is worthwhile pondering on the manuscript reading *nep*. The etymology of this term is obscure but the word is found in the compound *nepflod*, 'neap tide', that is, a tide of minimum height. Lucas deduces that 'the basic sense of the word is probably "lacking power", "enfeebled", and the general sense of the verse is thus that the Egyptians were unable to move in any direction'.[91] The interpretation is appealing, for it suggests that the Egyptians die because, contrary to what happens to the Israelites, they are not saved by a road miraculously appearing and allowing them to continue their voyage. No escape is offered to Pharaoh's army when the walls of water crush on them. They perish because they have nowhere to go.

Land is a source of security and sustenance for human beings; therefore, to be denied its possession and enjoyment is a punishment. The Israelites lose control of their strongholds when they displease God; Nebuchadnezzar is exiled from Babylon when pride takes hold of him; in his anger, God takes a dreadful revenge on Sodom and Gomorrah and devastates the very ground on which they stand; and finally, the man who is not circumcised will be estranged from the land. This cluster of images echoes the wider interest in spatial distribution and territorial ownership that the three scriptural poems under examination here betray. More precisely, in these migration narratives, the original desertion, the first loss of land, the ensuing journey, and the expectation of a new dwelling-place are instrumental in shaping a people's sense of itself.

SPATIAL TRIALS AND THE PERIPHERY

The three scriptural poems analysed here stage, at one point or another, protagonists who undertake a journey. In *Exodus* and *Genesis A* especially, this displacement is modelled on the motif of migration. The

---

[89] 'the army was firmly fettered in death, without power of advance' (*Exodus* 469ᵇ–470).

[90] *Exodus*, ed. Lucas, 134; *Junius Manuscript*, ed. Krapp, 213. See also Stephen F. Kruger, 'Oppositions and their Opposition in the Old English *Exodus*', *Neophilologus*, 78 (1994), 165–70 (165).

[91] *Exodus*, ed. Lucas, 134.

travels the characters undertake often lead them through frightening and unpleasant regions. Their odyssey is a trial or an ordeal during which they display courage and fortitude. Equivalent to the saints' missions of conversion and to Beowulf's or Judith's expeditions against monstrous or cruel enemies, the migrating journeys examined below amount to heroic deeds, the reward of which is enjoyment of a new space.

When fleeing Egypt in *Exodus*, the Israelites follow a route leading them through alien spaces. The bottom of the Red Sea, on which they walk between two high walls of water, obviously constitutes a strange environment. When Moses opens up the sea, he bids his followers to witness the miracle. He says that the waters have receded, that the ways are dry, the 'ealde staðolas, þa ic ær ne gefrægn | ofer middangeard men geferan'.[92] Moses and his people are about to enter a new sphere where no human being has ever ventured. By engaging on this extraordinary crossing and by following the tracks that miraculously appear before them, the Hebrews prove their faith in God and their obedience to his commands. Peter Clemoes identifies the passage through the Red Sea as 'the phase when the Israelites' resolve had been tested and not found wanting in a narrow, artificially produced space between two towering walls of water'.[93]

This episode echoes the end of *Genesis B* where Adam, lamenting his past actions, tells Eve of his desire to repent and to make amends for their original sin.[94] He declares that if only he knew it were God's will, he would not hesitate to go into the sea and to walk on the bottom of the ocean regardless of how deep it is.[95] Adam and the Israelites are both ready to step on alien grounds where no one has ever set foot before. These mysterious regions are situated in the depths of the sea in both cases. The obedience of the first man and of the Chosen People manifests itself by venturing into strange spaces.

The spectacular aspect of the Red Sea episode should not overshadow the fact that, from the very moment they leave Egypt, the Israelites in fact enter unfamiliar surroundings. When they escape from Pharaoh's country, they follow 'uncuð gelad, | oðþæt hie on Guðmyrce gearwe

---

[92] 'the old foundations which I have never heard before that men traversed over the earth' (*Exodus* 285–6).
[93] Peter Clemoes, *Interactions of Thought and Language in Old English Poetry*, Cambridge Studies in Anglo-Saxon England, 12 (Cambridge: Cambridge University Press, 1995), 294.
[94] *Genesis B* 828–35ª.
[95] See Ch. 2 for a discussion of this passage.

bæron'.⁹⁶ The paths on which they advance are unknown to them. The word *guðmyrce* is difficult to translate. Older critics tended to understand it as a proper name, most often designating Ethiopians, occasionally Nubians.⁹⁷ Consensus has now emerged and the term is usually translated as 'warlike border-dwellers'. This interpretation is based on the presence in the compound of the element *-myrce*, a form of *mearc*, 'border, boundary'.⁹⁸ Allusions to border-lands abound in the opening lines of *Exodus* as a result of the Old English poet's intensive use of *-mearc* compounds.⁹⁹ The Israelites reach *mearchofu* (l. 61ª), 'border dwellings', they encamp on *mearclandum* (l. 67ᵇ), in 'the border-lands', they tread the *mearc* (l. 160ᵇ), the 'border-land', and the Hebrew army is called a *mearcþreate* (l. 173ᵇ), a 'border-army'. The whole of the exodus therefore symbolically takes the Chosen People through alien spaces, to the dangerous periphery of their world, an observation that recalls hagiographic poems and the saints' heroic deeds set in the periphery.

As Hall remarks, while in the desert Moses and his followers are surrounded by a threatening wilderness.¹⁰⁰ The pillar of fire protects them 'þy læs him westengryre, | har hæðbroga, holmegum wederum | on ferclamme ferhð getwæfde'.¹⁰¹ The Hebrews risk their lives on land when journeying through the regions surrounding Egypt. They do so again at the bottom of the sea when they cross the Red Sea, as the poet specifies on lines 570–572ª, a passage for which no biblical parallel has been found.¹⁰² The wilderness around Egypt and the paths appearing at the bottom of the Red Sea are analogous environments. A linguistic analysis supports this parallel: both the roads crossing the desert and those lying at the bottom of the sea are unknown, and the

---

⁹⁶ 'unknown paths until they bore arms to warlike border-dwellers' (*Exodus* 58ᵇ–59).
⁹⁷ For a discussion of this question, see *Junius Manuscript*, ed. Krapp, 200.
⁹⁸ See Tolkien's notes in *The Old English Exodus: Text, Translation and Commentary by J. R. R. Tolkien*, ed. by Joan Turville-Petre (Oxford: Clarendon Press, 1981), 40; *Exodus*, ed. Lucas, 84; *Andreas and the Fates of the Apostles*, ed. by Kenneth R. Brooks (Oxford: Clarendon Press, 1961), 76–7; and *The Old English Exodus*, ed. by Edward Burroughs Irving, Jr., Yale Studies in English, 122 (New Haven: Yale University Press, 1953), 71.
⁹⁹ On this emphasis on border-land in *Exodus*, see Howe, *Migration and Mythmaking*, 89, and *Exodus*, ed. Lucas, 83–4.
¹⁰⁰ J. R. Hall, 'Old English *Exodus* and the Sea of Contradiction', *Mediaevalia*, 9 (1986 for 1983), 25–44 (28).
¹⁰¹ 'unless the terror of the desert, the grey heath-danger should, in a sudden clutch, put an end to their lives with storms from the sea' (*Exodus* 117b–119).
¹⁰² 'Life gefegon þa hie oðlæded hæfdon | feorh of feonda dome, þeah ðe hie hit frecne geneðdon, | weras under wætera hrofas' (*Exodus* 570–2ª). Hall, 'Old English *Exodus*', 5. See Exodus 14: 22–31.

expression *uncuð gelad* is repeated twice.¹⁰³ The Israelites enter an alien, extraordinary space as soon as they venture out of Egypt, and although in so doing they escape slavery, their entire journey is a trial which tests their mettle.

Since *Exodus* narrates the Hebrews' flight out of Egypt, it is hardly surprising that the protagonists should advance through unfamiliar areas. Yet this same motif also appears in *Daniel*, even though this text does not explicitly recount a communal journey. The episode of the three children thrown into the furnace can metaphorically be read as a spatial trial and as a prefiguration of the journey toward freedom of the whole Hebrew people. In the furnace, the youths are plunged into a hostile environment, to say the least. And when they are thrown in the flames, an angel comes to their rescue. He joins them in the middle of the fire, at which point danger recedes: 'wearð se hata lig | todrifen and todwæsced þær þa dædhwatan | geond þone ofen eodon, and se engel mid'.¹⁰⁴ The flames abate before the advancing steps of the youths and their guardian angel; the Book of Daniel says that the divine envoy pushes the flames away.¹⁰⁵ There is thus a difference of emphasis between the biblical and the Old English versions, and the vernacular text conceives of the trial in the furnace as a journey through menacing surroundings: the fire is extinguished where—*þær*—the children and the angel walk. The three children, like the Israelites in the desert or at the bottom of the Red Sea, cross a hostile space with fortitude.

In *Genesis A* the episode of the Flood with its depiction of the ark floating on the waves is the epitome of the dangerous voyage taking a chosen people through many perils. Contrary to the Vulgate account, the Old English poem clearly conceives of Noah's and his companions' sojourn in the holy vessel as a journey. When, following God's orders, the patriarch has finished building the ark, the Lord tells him: 'Ic þe þæs mine, monna leofost, | wære gesylle, þæt þu weg nimest | and feora fæsl þe þu ferian scealt | geond deop wæter'.¹⁰⁶ The expressions *weg niman* and 'ferian geond deop wæter' indicate that Noah will be steering the ark

---

¹⁰³ 'unknown paths' (*Exodus* 58ᵇ and 313ᵇ).
¹⁰⁴ 'The hot flame was scattered and extinguished where the ones bold in deeds, and the angel with them, went through the furnace' (*Daniel* 351ᵇ–353).
¹⁰⁵ Daniel 3: 49: 'angelus autem descendit cum Azaria et sociis eius in fornacem et excussit flammam ignis de fornace'.
¹⁰⁶ 'Accordingly I give you my promise, dearest of men, that you shall get under way and take the offspring of living beings which you shall ferry across the deep water' (*Genesis A* 1328–1331ᵃ). No allusion to the sojourn in the ark as a sea-journey is found in the Vulgate. See Genesis 6: 17–7: 24.

and travelling over the waters during the Deluge. And indeed, once the waves cover the earth, the vessel floats on the waves and: 'siððan wide rad wolcnum under | ofer holmes hrincg hof seleste, | for mid fearme.'[107] The use of the verbs *ridan* and *faran* further suggests that, in the ark, Noah and his companions sail over the waves. In the Old English poem, therefore, the episode of the Flood also narrates a heroic journey.

The voyage of the people in the ark takes them through a deadly Flood: everything outside the vessel is doomed to perish.[108] Its destructive character is further conveyed by the poet's use of compounds such as *wællregn* and *wægþreate* to designate the waters of the Deluge.[109] These words are *hapax legomena* which underline the exceptionally hostile nature of the streams. Like the Israelites who flee Egypt and cross the Red Sea in *Exodus*, Noah and his companions are tested with a perilous expedition across hostile surroundings. But in neither case does the courage of the Chosen People fail, and their readiness to carry out God's command never slackens.

The heroes of our poems therefore all undergo spatial trials: they cross unfamiliar or dangerous spaces and emerge victorious. They have to leave the familiarity of their own world and pass through marginal areas. The periphery becomes a ground testing the protagonists before they are deemed worthy of the land awaiting them at the end of their migration. Contrary to what happens in hagiographic poetry, these people do not seize marginal spaces; their territorial gain lies beyond the periphery, in the domains they will eventually reach. Yet, in successfully crossing the border-lands, the Hebrews, Noah, and the three children in the furnace nevertheless redefine the contours of their world. Thanks to their successful passage through the margins, they create a new space for themselves and their people, as heroes and saints do for their community.

STRATEGIES OF APPROPRIATION

To migrate is to move, to leave one's place of residence to embark on a difficult journey. But a migration also entails—or at least promises—the settlement in another country, the establishment of a new home at the

---

[107] 'Afterwards the best of houses moved over the circle of the ocean under the clouds, it sailed with its cargo' (*Genesis A* 1392–4ª).

[108] See *Genesis A* 1353–4.

[109] 'destroying rain' (*Genesis A* 1350ª) and 'wave-army' (*Genesis A* 1352ᵇ).

end of the journey. For the prospect of enjoying its own territory incites the migrating group to get under way. The travellers are moved by the hope of finding a place where they can live, where they can develop their own territory, and where they enjoy the fertility of the earth. Migration narratives are thus also tales which chronicle a territorial gain: that of the land promised at the end of the journey. The rest of the present chapter examines how *Genesis A*, *Exodus*, and *Daniel* deal with questions of territorial appropriation. More precisely, it focuses on two narratives strategies—which should by now have become familiar—that Old English poets elaborate to convey the idea that a migrating group rightly seizes and occupies a piece of land: the image of characters stepping on the ground, and allusions to and descriptions of paths and roads.

Treading the Land

In the narrative of the Fall, God punishes both the first human beings for having sinned and the serpent for the role he played in this episode, that is, for having successfully tempted Eve. In the Vulgate, the Lord's first words to the serpent lay a curse on him. He says: 'quia fecisti hoc maledictus es inter omnia animantia et bestias terrae'.[110] The Old English poet omits this section of the biblical verse and, in *Genesis A*, the Lord's speech opens directly with the condemnation for the tempter to move on its belly: 'Þu scealt wideferhð werig þinum | breostum bearm tredan bradre eorðan'.[111] The obligation to move over the earth on one's breast is the central and essential element of God's retribution against the serpent. In the vernacular version, it is enough of a plight without the biblical curse being added. Even though the idea that the serpent will from now on have to crawl on the earth clearly derives from the Vulgate account of the Fall,[112] the fact that God's speech starts with it and that the Old English poet silences any mention of a curse on the tempter draws the audience's attention to the motif of treading the land, of walking on the earth.

---

[110] 'because thou hast done this, thou art cursed above all cattle, and above every beast of the field' Genesis 3: 14.

[111] 'You, weary, shall forever tread on your breast the bosom of the broad earth' (*Genesis A* 906–7). For alternative translations and emendations of this passage, see *Genesis A*, ed. Doane, 243–4 and *DOE* microfiches *bearm*.

[112] 'super pectus tuum gradieris, et terram comedes cunctis diebus vitae tuae' (Genesis 3: 14).

The episode of the Flood is another moment when such issues are foregrounded, especially when Noah and his companions step out of the ark. Earlier in this chapter, I have shown that the *Genesis A* poet is original in suggesting that those who survive the Deluge are eager to leave their shelter and to find dry land once the rain stops. They wish to know when they 'ofer streamstaðe stæppan mosten'.[113] What they are looking for is specifically to feel the land under their feet, to tread on it.

Before leaving the ark, Noah checks whether the waters have receded enough and dry ground is available. To this end, he first sends a raven, and then a dove, over the streams. In the Vulgate, the first bird does not come back to the vessel but flies to and fro over the waters until land appears.[114] The Old English poet's account of how the raven fares is much more detailed. Noah expects it to fly back to the ark if it does not find a tract of ground on which to land. But the patriarch is mistaken: 'eft him seo wen geleah, | ac se feonde gespearn fleotende hreaw; | salwigfeðera secan nolde.'[115] In his edition of the poem, Doane analyses the vernacular poet's elaboration on these lines, and especially the fact that the bird does not keep flying over the waters but actually lands on dead bodies.[116] The critic contends that this feature does not relate to the conventional Germanic 'beasts of battle' scene, but that it springs from a similar Talmudic tradition that passed into Christian exegetical thinking. This image may not originate with the Old English poet, but the vernacular author nonetheless innovates at this point, integrating the image of stepping and treading into a wider pattern that structures his account of the Flood. After the raven, Noah sends a dove out of the ark. The bird comes back because 'nohweðere reste fand, | þæt heo for flode fotum ne meahte | land gespornan ne on leaf treowes | steppan for streamum'.[117] The vernacular poem follows the biblical account fairly closely and it borrows from it the mention of the bird's foot and the

---

[113] They 'may step on the seashore' (*Genesis A* 1434).
[114] 'dismisit corvum qui egrediebatur et revertebatur donec siccarentur aquae super terram' (Genesis 8: 6–7).
[115] 'Afterwards his hope deceived him, but the enemy perched on floating corpses; the raven did not return' (*Genesis A* 1446[b]–1448).
[116] *Genesis A*, ed. Doane, 271.
[117] 'Nowhere did it find rest, so that it could not, because of the flood, step on the land with its feet nor perch on the leaf of a tree because of the waters' (*Genesis A* 1456[b]–1459[a]). This passage renders Genesis 8: 9 'quae cum non invenisset ubi requiesceret pes eius reversa est ad eum in arcam' (Vetus Latina: 'non inveniens columba requiem pedibus suis reversa est ad eum in arcam'. This reading is from *Genesis A*, ed. Doane, 148).

notion of rest. Yet it is worth noting that the *Genesis A* poet structures this entire episode around the two following elements—stepping on the ground and finding a resting place on land.

A few lines below, the same cluster of details reappears with the dove's second journey out of the ark.[118] This time, the bird does not come back: 'seo wide fleah | oðþæt heo rumgal restestowe | fægere funde and þa fotum stop | on beam hyre'.[119] The Vulgate does not report what happens to the dove on its second excursion out of the ark. It simply says that, in the evening, it comes back to Noah with an olive twig in its beak.[120] But the Old English poet follows the bird's fortunes and resorts to familiar images: the dove on her journey *fotum stop* on a tree and thus found a *restestowe*. The tree is a place of rest for the dove and, as such, it announces the land, the resting place of men that will soon be freed from the waters. To appropriate a tract of ground, one, be it the dove or Noah's companions on the seashore, steps on it with one's foot.

Noah sends the dove out of the ark one last time. The bird does not return from its journey, for 'heo land begeat, | grene bearwas'.[121] The Old English poet volunteers the information that the dove has found land and pleasant groves and that, consequently, it does not return to the ark. Once again, the biblical account of the Flood is not so specific at this point.[122]

Treading the ground signals land appropriation and in *Exodus*, the account of the Egyptians' destruction in the Red Sea conjures up this same motif. The poet says of Pharaoh: 'He onfon hraðe, | siððan grund gestah godes andsaca, | þæt wæs mihtigra mereflodes weard'.[123] It is significant that Pharaoh should perceive the extent of God's power precisely when he reaches the bottom of the Red Sea. Punishment strikes at a meaningful moment for, according to my analysis, the Egyptians are chastised when they step on the foundations of the sea, that is, when they are bold enough to venture their lives in this alien space. Their

---

[118] For an exegetical interpretation of the journeys of the raven and of the dove, see Doane (ed.), 271–2.
[119] 'It flew far and wide until, rejoicing in ample space, it found a beautiful resting place and the gentle one stepped with its feet on a tree' *Genesis A* 1465^b–8^a.
[120] 'at illa venit ad eum ad vesperam portans ramum olivae virentibus foliis in ore suo' Genesis 8. 11.
[121] 'it found land, green forests' *Genesis A* 1479^b–80^a.
[122] 'et emisit columbam quae non est reversa ultra ad eum' (Genesis 8: 12).
[123] 'he quickly realized, God's enemy, after he reached the bottom of the sea, that the Guardian of the sea was the mightier' (*Exodus* 502^b–504).

change of location is an act of defiance, and their spatial transgression, like that of Lucifer, is immediately punished.

Genesis A's account of Noah's and his companions' coming out of the ark and of the first steps taken on land, either by human beings or by birds, exemplifies the importance of the stepping imagery. Treading the land with one's feet is the sign of a gradual repossession of land in the episode of the Flood, or of a failure to recognize exactly the limits of one's power in *Exodus*'s account of the Egyptians' death.

Paths and Ways

The second narrative strategy analysed here consists in paying particular attention to the paths over which the characters travel: given the subject-matter of the poem, this imagery unsurprisingly occupies a prominent place in *Exodus*, When they leave Egypt, the Hebrews are eager to go and the poet describes them as 'fus on forðweg'.[124] The word *forðweg* recurs four times in the poem. Its first occurrence is in the opening presentation of Moses: he is Pharaoh's enemy and God strengthens him *on forðwegas*.[125] Lucas, in the notes to his edition of the poem, refers this half-line to the patriarch's exile in Midian. While there is nothing in the poem which contradicts this interpretation, there is also no element supporting it. Tolkien's translation is thus also acceptable: *on forðwegas* becomes 'on the march from Egypt'.[126] Besides, with this second rendering, this instance of *forðweg* is made part of the exodus out of Pharaoh's country. When they are trapped between the Red Sea and the advancing Egyptian army, the Israelites are again described as *fus forðwegas*.[127] This is the moment when they need new roads to follow in order to escape their enemies. These *forðwegas* are finally found at the bottom of the sea: the one who guided the Hebrews—who, according to the poem's syntax, can be either God or Moses—became famous along them.[128] *Forðweg*, with the presence of the prefix *forð*–, 'thence, hence, forwards, onwards', emphasizes the idea of a movement forward, of a progress that follows a particular path.

There is, in addition to *forðweg*, another *weg*- compound that deserves attention: *lifweg*. It describes the Israelites' route across the desert when

---

[124] 'eager for the onward journey' (*Exodus* 129ᵃ). See also *Exodus* 248ᵃ.
[125] *Exodus* 32ᵇ.
[126] *Old English Exodus* (Tolkien, ed. Turville-Petre), 20.
[127] *Exodus* 248ᵃ.   [128] *Exodus* 350ᵃ.

the travelling people see 'lifes latþeow lifweg metan'.[129] The repetition of the word *lif* in this line underscores the vital character of the voyage the Hebrews are about to undertake. In the desert, the Chosen People progress along the 'life-way'. God guides them and, before them, they see the road they will follow up to the sea: 'gesawon randwigan rihte stræte'.[130] Lucas glosses *riht* as 'straight', but the word also means 'proper, just, correct'. Both meanings surely come into play here and if the road to the Red Sea is a direct one, it is also the one appointed by God. The *Exodus* poet is thus particularly careful in his depiction of the paths along which the Hebrews progress through the desert.

The vernacular author again insists on the roads the Hebrews follow when they cross the Red Sea. As the waters recede, Moses tells his followers: 'wegas syndon dryge, | haswe herestræta, holm gerymed'.[131] Paths appear, on which the Chosen People will tread. It is striking that roads should immediately be visible when the sea opens and that they should appear on a ground on which no one has ever travelled, therefore in a space that has not yet been mapped. This passage echoes *Andreas*; for, when the saint steps out of prison after the flood, a *stræt gerymed* appears before the saint's feet.[132] Both in the hagiographic and in the scriptural poems, the roads found on untrodden expanses invite the protagonists to move, to advance on the land: in short, it invites them to take possession of new spaces.

When the characters' journeys are not sanctioned by God and challenge divine control over the world's spatial organization, paths simply disappear. For instance, the waters close down on the Egyptians just as they reach the bottom of the Red Sea. The roads on which they were advancing vanish: 'þær ær wegas lagon, | mere modgode'.[133] They lose their ground against the tide, and, with literally no way out of it, they are doomed to perish.

Ways symbolically figure the spiritual guidance offered by the Lord to his creatures. They also conjure up a poetic space in which the characters move. In this, they justify the motions of the travelling group; for, the protagonists progress along roads divinely marked out for them. Path imagery is thus used to initiate the migration—it follows inviting ways. *Genesis A* and *Daniel* do not foreground this motif as clearly as *Exodus*

[129] 'the guide of life [God or Moses] marking out the life-way' (*Exodus* 104).
[130] 'the warriors saw the straight/correct road' (*Exodus* 126).
[131] 'the ways are dry, the main roads grey, the sea lays open' (*Exodus* 283ª–284).
[132] 'a cleared street' *Andreas* 1580ᵇ.
[133] 'where ways had previously laid, the sea raged' (*Exodus* 458ᵇ–459ª).

does, but they nevertheless deserve attention because they associate the road with military action. Four compounds—*herpað* (military road) and *milpað* (track) in *Exodus*, *rancstræt* (warrior-street) in *Genesis A* and *herestræt* (army road) in *Daniel*—shed light on the link between path imagery and fighting.

In *Exodus*, the Egyptians 'ne mihton forhabban helpendra pað' when the Red Sea closes down on them.[134] Several editors have suggested emending *pað* to *pæð* or *wað*. In an article in which he argues for the retention of the manuscript reading -*pað*, Hall refers to a similar passage in *Judith*.[135] When the Bethulians attack their enemies, they 'herpað worhton | þurh laðra gemong'.[136] Hall uses this other occurrence of *herpað* to argue for a 'specialized poetic sense of the morpheme [*pað*], "passage made through an enemy's rank"'.[137] The compound *milpæð* appears when the Israelites are trapped between the shores of the Red Sea and the pursuing Egyptians.[138] Military confrontation is expected, the beasts of battle are howling, hoping for carrion, and the Hebrews 'mæton milpaðas meara bogum'.[139] *Milpæð* is a crux which BT translate as 'a road along which miles are reckoned'. Against this translation, Andrew Breeze conjectures that in this instance, the component *mil-* might be a loan element from the Welsh *mil*, 'army'.[140] He thus suggests rendering *milpæð* as 'road used by an army, highway'. In this case, *milpæð* would partake in the pervasive military imagery characterizing *Exodus*. Anyway, the gesture of the Jewish riders whose horses pace the road is a reaffirmation of territorial control, a claim that the tract of ground on which the army stands will be defended against advancing enemies. The context, characteristic of *Exodus*, is clearly military, although the actual battle never occurs.[141]

---

[134] The Egyptians 'could not restrain the track of the helpers' *Exodus* 488.

[135] J. R. Hall, '*Exodus* 448b, *helpendra pað*', *American Notes and Queries*, NS 5 (1992), 3–7 (4). For views supporting emendation, see Tolkien's notes in Turville-Petre (ed.), *The Old English Exodus*, 73 and Edward B. Irving, 'New Notes on the Old English *Exodus*', *Anglia*, 90 (1972), 289–324 (319). On this point, see also *Exodus*, ed. Lucas, 197.

[136] They 'cut an army-passage through the enemies' troop' (*Judith* 302b–303a). *Beowulf and Judith*, ed. by Elliott van Kirk Dobbie, Anglo-Saxon Poetic Records, 4 (London: Routledge and Kegan Paul, 1953), 101–9.

[137] Hall, '*Exodus* 448b, *helpendra pað*', 4. [138] *Exodus* 171a.

[139] 'measured [traversed] the army roads on horseback' (*Exodus* 171).

[140] Andrew Breeze, '*Exodus*, *Elene* and the *Rune Poem*: *milpæþ*, "Army Road, Highway"', *Notes and Queries*, NS 38 (1991), 436–8 (436).

[141] Breeze also discusses the other two instances of *milpæð* in Old English: *Elene* 1262[a] and the *Rune Poem* 15[b].

The third term of the present discussion, *rancstræt*, is used in the episode of Abimelech's blessing of Abraham.[142] The high priest tells the patriarch that he is blessed and that God helped him in battle. Abimelech says: 'and þe wæpnum læt | rancstræte forð rume wyrcan'.[143] The image of the road opened up by the swords and weapons of the battling armies is peculiar to the vernacular poem.[144] Doane acknowledges two possible translations for *rancstræt*: 'a path for warriors to pass through', and this is the meaning of *herpað* in *Judith* 302, or 'the act of cutting down the enemies causing the path to appear'.[145] The critic himself opts for 'a path of bold ones, warrior-street', but the two interpretations are possible and both associate paths imagery with military action.

Let me now discuss a final passage from *Daniel*. On line 38ª, the poet uses the compound *herestræt*. The context in which the word appears is relevant: lines 35–42 recount how, in days of yore, the Chosen People, still dear to the Lord, was shown the way to Jerusalem:

> Wisde him æt frymðe,   ða ðe on fruman ær ðon
> wæron mancynnes   metode dyrust,
> dugoða dyrust,   drihtne leofost;
> *herepað tæhte   to þære hean byrig,*
> *eorlum elðeodigum,*   on eðelland
> þær Salem stod   searwum afæstnod,
> weallum geweorðod.   To þæs witgan foron,
> Caldea cyn,   to ceastre forð[146]

This passage chronicles how the Hebrews were granted enjoyment of Jerusalem because of their virtue and faithfulness.[147] I would like to

---

[142] *Genesis A* 2112ª.

[143] 'and [God] allowed you to clear with your weapons a wide road of the bold ones' (*Genesis A* 2111ᵇ–2112).

[144] At this point, the Vulgate has: 'et benedictus Deus excelsus quo protegente hostes in manibus tuis sunt' (Genesis 14: 20).

[145] *Genesis A*, ed. Doane, 301.

[146] *Daniel* 35–42. See translation below. Emphases are mine.

[147] Kennedy translates 'To them, *a wandering folk*, who once were dearest of mankind to God, dearest of all peoples and best loved of the Lord, *He had showed a highway to their lofty city* and their native land, where Salem stood, walled around about and girt with battlements. Thither the wise men, the Chaldean people, came up against the city' (*Cædmon Poems*, trans. Kennedy, 122). Bradley offers: 'He at the start had guided them who, before that, had in the beginning been dearest to God among the human race, dearest of communities, most loved by the Lord; he had shown these men, being strangers, the military road to the lofty city, into the land of their inheritance where Salem stood, fortified by defensive works and dignified by ramparts—until the Chaldean tribe, those sorcerers, advanced against the city'. *Anglo-Saxon Poetry*, trans. by S. A. J. Bradley (London: Dent, 1982), 68. Emphases are mine.

argue that we can discern in these lines a slipping from the Hebrews to the Chaldeans: the Lord would show the latter the *herepað*, the 'highway' (as Kennedy translates it) or, more accurately, 'a road for an army, military road, road large enough to march soldiers upon'.[148] In this case, it is the Chaldeans who march against Jerusalem under divine guidance, so that they conquer it from the sinful Israelites. Their characterization as agents of God's wrath would be reinforced and *eorlum elðeodigum* would no longer designate the Hebrews, but their enemies. Lines 35–42 could then be translated as follows:

> He had directed them [the Hebrews] first, those who in the beginning were the dearest of mankind, the dearest of nations to the Creator, the Lord's most beloved; *He showed the foreign noblemen* [the Chaldeans] *the army-road to the lofty city* into the country where Jerusalem stood, skilfully made fast, adorned with walls. The wise men, the Chaldeans, went forth to that city

The ambiguity at the heart of this passage allows for the two readings of this scene: it can describe how the Israelites, led by the Lord, reached Jerusalem, but it can also depict how an enemy army conquers its opponents and their fortress. The Chaldeans carry out divine punishment against the Hebrews when the Lord allows them to follow the *herepað* successfully, the 'army road' that leads to the city.

Exodus, *Daniel*, and *Genesis A*: all link paths and military advance. The recurrent association between roads and fighting supports my contention that to follow a path, to step upon it, is equated with taking possession of a new space. A *milpað* is trodden just when battle is expected in *Exodus*. In *Genesis A* and *Daniel*, a *herepað* and a *rancstræt* are violently cut through the ranks of the opponents; the space of the enemy army is invaded and the warriors opening the military road take control of it. Violence is inherent in stepping on the ground, an activity which marks control of enemy territory and which brings about the destruction of one's foes. Any change of location, including migration, involves violent clashes with the people encountered in the course of the journey.

CONCLUSION

To focus on the migration motif omnipresent in the three scriptural poems under consideration here casts an interesting light on these narratives. Episodes relating a people's change of location echo each other

---

[148] See BT.

and draw attention to representations of journeys which lead a tribe to a new land. A migration is not an exile; for expectation of future abodes motivates the voyage itself. The migrating group sets out in search of a land hoping eventually to enjoy it. The migration motif also lends itself to traditional heroic colouring and the journey becomes an extraordinary achievement against overwhelming odds. In establishing a link between migration and heroic action, these poems therefore foreground spatial issues, especially those dealing with the institution of a territory. A careful reading of the depictions of roads and paths, and of the characters who step on them, shows how claims to land possession are poetically expressed.

The hoped-for enjoyment of a territory, a fount of joy and abundance promised at the end of the migration, is instrumental in creating a people's sense of itself; for, as Paul Zumthor phrases it: 'l'aboutissement de l'itinéraire...signifie une redéfinition de soi'.[149] The preceding reflections on *Genesis A*, *Exodus*, and *Daniel* were mostly focused on the representation of the migrating travel and on the goal of the journey, the expectation of land that incited a given people to move. But Nicholas Howe reminds us that a migration is always 'remembered as a transit between two places, between a home that has been left behind and the one that has been found or, more likely, seized on arrival.'[150] The concept of migration thus develops around a tension between two poles: between a place of departure and a place of arrival. Chapter 7, the book's last, clearly acknowledges this dynamic aspect of migration and investigates how a dialectics between 'here' and 'there' helps to construct identity. For the Anglo-Saxons never forgot that they only reached England after a group journey from the Continent. The memory of themselves as those who came from elsewhere never completely disappeared and undoubtedly bore upon the emergence and the character of their collective identity. It portrayed them as those who had deservedly established themselves over England; but, more problematically, it also defined them as brutal invaders. Chapter 7 addresses the difficulties which, for the Anglo-Saxons, inevitably lie at the heart of their memory of the migration and, in examining narratives of the *adventus Saxonum*, sees how Old English authors worked around this paradox.

---

[149] Paul Zumthor, *La Mesure du Monde* (Paris: Seuil, 1993), 311.
[150] Nicholas Howe, 'Looking for Home in Anglo-Saxon England', in Nicholas Howe (ed.), *Home and Homelessness in the Medieval and Renaissance World* (Notre Dame IN: University of Notre Dame Press, 2004), 143–63 (157).

PART III

CONQUEST

7

The *descriptiones Britanniae* and the *adventus Saxonum*: Narrative Strategies for the Conquest of Britain

IN the opening pages of the *Old English Orosius*, which Chapter 4 analysed at some length, there is a curious allusion which deserves further attention. Ohthere tells of his journey from *Sciringesheal* (a place identified with modern Kaupang in south-east Norway) to *Hæþum* (Hedeby, in the south-east of the Jutland peninsula). He incidentally mentions that he passed on his starboard 'Gotland 7 Sillende 7 iglanda fela—on þæm landum eardodon Engle, ær hi hider on land coman'.[1] In her notes, Janet Bately comments on the term *Engle*, but she does not explain this unexpected reference to the Germanic tribes' migration.[2] Yet this passage is striking in a work that proves so reluctant to talk about the history and the geography of its country of origin, that is, Anglo-Saxon England.[3] There are two possible sources for this allusion: it might initially have been part of the traveller's narrative and may thus be Ohthere's own comment or it might be a later scribal interpolation. If this observation was from the outset part of the Scandinavian explorer's report, it suggests that the Germanic tribes' migration was so much part of Anglo-Saxon England's history that even a Norwegian would know about it and refer to it more than four hundred years later to situate the land he is talking about. If it is a scribal interpolation, it implies that this event was so central to Anglo-Saxon history that a copyist perceived a gap in Ohthere's report and added this piece of information to the original narrative. In any case, it indicates that the *adventus Saxonum* was still considered, in the ninth century, to be a significant event. The

---

[1] 'Jutland and Sinlendi, and many islands—the Angles dwelt on that land before they came hither' *The Old English Orosius*, ed. by Janet Bately, EETS ss. 6 (Oxford: Oxford University Press, 1980), 16.
[2] *The Old English Orosius*, 196.   [3] See Ch. 4.

knowledge of this founding migration was still alive, so much so that it was irremediably conjured up by the mention of the Anglo-Saxons' continental home.

Following on from the preceding chapter which addressed the question of migration in a specifically scriptural context, the present chapter discusses this same motif as it appears in texts of a more historical nature. In addition to returning to Bede's *Ecclesiastical History of the English People*, I will also examine the two following texts: Gildas's *De Excidio Britonum* and the Anglo-Saxon Chronicle to which I will add, when relevant, Asser's *Life of King Alfred* and Æthelweard's *Chronicle*. As was already the case with the material analysed in Chapter 4, these texts claim to be historical records. They thus invite the audience to trust in the coincidence of their poetic geography with an actual, external topographical reality. Once again, my focus is not on the nature and reliability of this coincidence. Although these accounts draw on and transmit a body of spatial knowledge, that is, a culture of space dealing specifically with the nature and the topography of Britain, they cannot free themselves from the pervasive influence of the *imaginaire*. Ideological considerations about geography and identity thus bear on the picture of the island these texts elaborate. The documents under scrutiny here will be studied precisely insofar as they are situated at the intersection of the two main concepts of space considered in this book: a culture of space and space as a mental construct.

Identifying and analysing various strategies of land appropriation and territorial dispossession, the present chapter falls into two parts. The first one embarks on a close reading of the descriptions of Britain with which the *Ecclesiastical History* and the *De Excidio Britonum* open, focusing on what insular authors say about the nature of their homeland. The second part turns to episodes which chronicle the migration of the Germanic tribes from the Continent to Britain and their subsequent conquest of the island. This last chapter brings together migration and conquest, a conquest leading to the emergence of a new territory, thus joining the three threads that form the framework of this book; for the motif of creation is not absent from what follows. Descriptions of Britain and migration narratives can both be considered to be, in the broad sense of the term, creation stories. When Old English authors portray their island's topography and its outstanding characteristics, they imagine an ideal place, a land as it was before the start of history. In so doing, they suggest that they are representing an original order as it existed, uncorrupted and untouched, in some primordial past. At the same time, they also create an imaginary place which their audience will adopt and integrate in its mental map: this is how the homeland was like 'in the beginning'. Accounts of migration also foreground the question of origin. They narrate the passage from an earlier settlement to a land promised at the end of the journey, a land which the migrants eventually occupy and control. Furthermore, these tales often pay attention to their various protagonists' ancestry and comment on their genealogy. Migration narratives are indeed creation stories in as much as they generate new poetic spaces in which to inscribe a people's idealized past—in the present case, the Germanic tribes' *adventus*. And in so doing, they shape the Anglo-Saxons' imaginary geography.

In Anglo-Saxon England the vividly remembered migration of the Germanic tribes helped to generate a sense of community among their descendants. But at the same time this foundation myth also commemorated the fact that the Anglo-Saxons were not Britain's first inhabitants: they arrived in a land which was already settled and which they had to conquer militarily. How could they therefore atone for and justify the violence inherent in the establishment of their rule over England? The disturbing link that, during the major part of their history, could be drawn between themselves and the Vikings as heathen invaders dispossessing Christians from their homeland undermined any supposedly moral superiority Old English authors could have invoked to base their claim to the land. The Viking raids which afflicted Anglo-Saxon England started at the end of the eighth century and culminated at the close of the period with the accession of the Danish king Canute to the English throne in 1016. These northern invaders threatened the survival of Anglo-Saxon rule in Britain and the descendants of the Germanic tribes did not miss the similarities existing between their own migration from the Continent during the fifth century and the arrival of the Scandinavians; Wulfstan clearly articulates the correspondences between these two invasions at the end of his *Sermo Lupi ad Anglos*.[4] Nicholas Howe sums up this delicate situation when he points out that the Anglo-Saxons' 'story of place had always to deal with the intertwined acts of possession and dispossession, both as historical fact and as future possibility'.[5]

---

[4] *Sermo Lupi ad Anglos*, ed. by Dorothy Whitelock (London: Methuen, 1963), 65–6, lines 184–99.

[5] Nicholas Howe, 'The Landscape of Anglo-Saxon England: Inherited, Invented, Imagined', in John Howe and Michael Wolfe (eds.), *Inventing Medieval Landscapes:*

The present chapter's concluding sections examine how Bede and the compiler of the Chronicle reacted to this dilemma and what poetic devices they developed to resolve it. Two narrative strategies will be singled out: the recourse to biblical rhetoric, focusing especially on allusions to the Promised Land or on the identification of the Anglo-Saxons as the Chosen People on the one hand, and the use of heroic diction with particular attention to the glorification of the military and violent conquest of the island on the other. Both textual devices also redefine the main protagonists involved in the *adventus Saxonum*: the Anglo-Saxons and the Britons, of course, but also the Romans, the Picts, and the Irish.

DESCRIPTIONS OF BRITAIN

To use geographical descriptions as preludes to the text that follows is a common literary device in medieval literature. In a specifically English context, Margaret Bridges observes that 'depuis le haut Moyen Age anglais, il était d'usage, dans les textes à caractère historique, de faire précéder le récit chronologique des événements constitutifs de l'histoire en question par une description topographique délimitant un espace encore vierge des événements qui vont s'y déployer.'[6] These descriptions are part of a tradition that Monika Otter traces back to Orosius: 'In imitation of Orosius's geographical introduction, many early British historians like to begin their work with a "descriptio Britanniae", a brief topographical description and panegyric of Britain.'[7] The critic names several landmarks in this tradition: Gildas and Bede of course, but also Geoffrey of Monmouth and Henry of Huntingdon in the twelfth century. These narratives as it were set up an empty stage where subsequent events will take place. They depict the land before it was inhabited, before the arrival of any immigrant, before the start of history. After this static description, these topographical theatres come to life

---

Senses of Place in Western Europe (Gainesville: University of Florida Press, 2002), 91–112 (93).

[6] Margaret Bridges, 'Discours du réel, discours de l'imaginaire: cours et étendues d'eau dans la *Descriptio Britanniae* médiévale', in *Sources et fontaines du moyen âge à l'âge baroque*, Colloques, Congrès et Conférences sur la Renaissance, 12 (Paris: Champion, 1998), 16.

[7] Monika Otter, *Inventiones: Fiction and Referentiality in Twelfth-Century English Historical Writing* (Chapel Hill: University of North Carolina Press, 1996), 71.

and history unfolds in an originally empty space. Implicitly claiming merely to mirror what was there 'in the beginning', these depictions seem to portray Britain factually—what its climate is like, whether the land is fertile or not, and so on. And yet, a close look at these narratives will show that their apparent neutral character is deceptive.

The two *descriptiones Britanniae* on which the following pages focus are those of Gildas and Bede, both natives of the British Isles. The rhetoric to which they resort calls for a careful study: both historians build their texts around biblical images, in particular the idea of the Promised Land and of the Chosen People. They insist on the opposition between an elected community and its sinful enemies, and they draw on the traditional motif which transforms pagan invaders into the wicked agents of a just punishment.[8] Gildas's and Bede's topographical descriptions adopt different perspectives on the events they relate. While Gildas enhances the Britons' guilt as the cause of the Germanic tribes' coming, Bede highlights the outstanding religious role granted to the Anglo-Saxons. Just as insular geographers revisit their sources when situating their island on the map of the world, these two authors distance themselves from classical accounts of Britain and its inhabitants, and they strategically redefine the nature of their homeland and of their fellow countrymen.

Gildas, De Excidio Britonum

During the sixth century Gildas, a Welshman, wrote the *De Excidio Britonum*, a treatise in which he justifies the invasion of his country by pagan Anglo-Saxons.[9] According to him, these enemies' coming is part of a divine plan devised to punish the Britons for their sins. The historian opens his pamphlet with a description of Britain, providing the following information: it is an isolated land; it has a length of eight hundred and a width of two hundred miles; it is surrounded by stormy seas; twenty-eight cities and a number of castles were built on the island, which is fertile and blessed with clear springs. This description probably derives from a traditional source, although no precise origin has been

---

[8] On this traditional motif, see Malcolm Godden, 'Apocalypse and Invasion in Late Anglo-Saxon England', in Malcolm Godden, Douglas Gray, and Terry Hoad (eds.), *From Anglo-Saxon England to Early Middle English* (Oxford: Clarendon Press, 1994), 130–62 (135 and 155).

[9] Gildas, *The Ruin of Britain and Other Works*, ed. and trans. by Michael Winterbottom (London: Phillimore, 1978). The translations are from this edition.

identified for this passage. Gildas may have found information about the isolation and dimensions of Britain in Pliny and Solinus. In the textual notes to the *Ruin of Britain*, John Morris suggests that the Welsh author drew on a late Roman geographer, a source that Orosius may have used too.[10] The critic also traces the allusion to Britain's twenty-eight cities to Ptolemy.[11]

Three elements in this description are worth commenting upon here: the twenty-eight cities, the absence of any reference to the Britons, and the fertility of the land that leads Gildas to compare it to a bride. When the historian comments on the cities which were built on the island, he says that they are no longer populated as they once were: 'sed ne nunc quidem, ut antea, civitates patriae inhabitantur; sed desertae dirutaeque hactenus squalent'.[12] This affirmation conjures up a picture of urban areas once buzzing with people: it contrasts a lost age of prosperity with present-day decay. Gildas also mentions delightful rivers and springs that lull to sleep people dwelling nearby. Interestingly, his account of Britain pictures a land without its population but with traces of human occupation. Some people must indeed have dwelt there to build beautiful cities and to hear the murmurs of its rivers, but the historian does not mention them in his *descriptio*.

In fact, Gildas does not introduce the Britons, who must already have been living on the island, until he turns his attention to Roman Britain. Nowhere does he account for their arrival on the island: he does not provide a narrative of their migration, an omission which implies that Britain was inhabited from the very beginnings of its history.[13] Gildas thus suggests that the Britons are the island's rightful inhabitants since they have always been there. By silencing their migration story, the Welsh scholar also contrasts the Britons with all the subsequent invaders who reach Britain, such as the Romans and the Anglo-Saxons.[14] He

---

[10] Gildas, *The Ruin of Britain*, 148. On the links between Orosius and Gildas, see Neil Wright, 'Did Gildas read Orosius?', *Cambridge Medieval Celtic Studies*, 9 (1985), 31–42.

[11] Ptolemy named thirty-eight cities south of Hadrian's wall. Morris explains the change from the original xxxviii to the xxviii found in Gildas as a possible scribal error. See Gildas, *The Ruin of Britain* 148.

[12] 'but the cities of our land are not populated even now as they once were; right to the present they are deserted, in ruins and unkempt' (Gildas, *The Ruin of Britain* 26. 2, p. 98). For the translation, see p. 28.

[13] Gildas simply says 'ex quo inhabitata est [Britain]' (Gildas, *The Ruin of Britain* 4. 1, p. 90).

[14] The coming of the Romans and of the Anglo-Saxons is narrated in chs. 5 and 22 respectively.

further explains that the latter's coming is a punishment,[15] and that the Britons' territorial loss is due to their own wickedness. In so doing, he grounds land possession on moral criteria.

Even if Britain's golden past is gone, Gildas offers a favourable description of the island: it is *decorata* with cities and *ornata* with fertile plains and hills. The historian highlights the land's attractiveness by comparing it to a bride: 'electa veluti sponsa monilibus diversis ornata'.[16] Britain is personified and the comparison indicates that the island—like a bride—is ready to be possessed and enjoyed. This image conjures up an idea of virginity that, when applied to the land, denotes both purity and fertility. At the same time, Gildas's bride is adorned: it has beautified itself and appears to be waiting for its possessor. In fact, if the ideas of purity and that of adornment seem contradictory at first, they serve the same end, that is, they work as incentives for a future invader, a future owner. The coding of 'nature', of a space over which man has no control, as feminine is a topos of Western intellectual tradition; it partakes in a sexualization of the land according to which it is readily available and it awaits fertilization.[17] Consequently, the land becomes a horizon of desire for the invaders. By drawing this comparison, Gildas presents Britain as a land open to settlement, ready to welcome its rightful inhabitants, who are, in his case, the Britons.

The preceding remarks call to mind Otter's comments on twelfth-century historians and especially on Geoffrey of Monmouth. She says: 'there is no such thing, it seems, as an unoccupied territory. In fact, the literary imagination of the historians seems unable to conceive of untouched land; it is always imagined as already cultivated, or at least so "apta" to cultivation that it has no true existence apart from the cultivators and their desires.'[18] These observations are also valid for Gildas's *descriptio Britanniae*; for, in the account of the Welsh author too, the island cannot be evoked independently of its possessors: it is always an object of desire and of possible exploitation. In the poetic geography of the *De Excidio*, Britain is only conceived of in relation to its occupiers.

---

[15] 'ultionis iustae praecedentium scelerum causa' (Gildas, *The Ruin of Britain* 24. 1, p. 97).
[16] 'Like a chosen bride arrayed in a variety of jewellery' (Gildas, *The Ruin of Britain* 3. 4, p. 90). For the translation, see pp. 16–17.
[17] Derek Gregory, *Geographical Imaginations* (Cambridge, MA: Blackwell, 1994), 129. See also Bridges, 'Discours du réel', 19–20.
[18] Otter, *Inventiones*, 83.

When reporting Britain's conversion to Christianity, Gildas provides a very different picture of the island: the new faith is offered to 'glaciali frigore rigenti insulae'.[19] Britain is no longer fertile and grassy, but cold and chilled, and only the light of Christ, who is compared to the sun, warms it up. The difference between these two descriptions is due to the different narrative environments in which they appear. Both are inscribed in a religious framework, but they draw on different images. The first one conjures up the motifs of the Golden Age and the Promised Land: the island is a pleasant area inviting settlement. The second plays on the opposition between the worlds of Christians and of pagans: Britain belongs to the latter. It cannot therefore be presented as an idyllic place. Interestingly, Gildas does not recoil from providing two strikingly different portrayals of Britain only a few chapters apart, demonstrating thereby that geographical situation, distance, and the nature of the land vary according to the narrative context.

Gildas's *descriptio* is grounded on tradition (Pliny, Solinus, probably Orosius) but it is nevertheless an original narrative; for the author manages at the same time to praise the land and to condemn its original inhabitants. Britain is depicted as an attractive land and the Britons, who should hold the island by right, are not worthy of it. The opening lines of the *De Excidio Britonum* chronicle and justify this process of territorial dispossession. The Welsh historian's narrative paves the way for Bede and the opening of the *Ecclesiastical History*, which adopts a different perspective on Britain and its inhabitants. It praises both the land and its later conquerors, the Anglo-Saxons. Yet, following Gildas, Bede also assumes the existence of an essential link between land and people and he exploits it to validate the Germanic invaders' right to Britain.

Bede, *The Ecclesiastical History*

Bede, in the first chapter of the *Ecclesiastical History*, offers a description of Britain based on Pliny, Solinus, Orosius, and Gildas.[20] From Gildas,

---

[19] 'an island numbed with chill ice' (Gildas, *The Ruin of Britain* 8. 1, p. 91). For the translation, see p. 18.

[20] *Bede's Ecclesiastical History of the English People*, ed. and trans. by Bertram Colgrave and R. A. B. Mynors (Oxford: Clarendon Press, 1969; repr. 1991), i. 1, p. 14 n. 1.

the Old English author retains the idea that Britain is an attractive place. His description provides the following information: the island's situation in relation to the rest of Europe, its dimensions, its crossing points from the Continent, and the presence of the Orkney Islands toward the north. Commenting further on the nature of the land, the Anglo-Saxon historian adds that it produces vines, that it is bountiful in plants and animals, that it has wonderful hot springs and metal veins in its subsoil, and that it counts twenty-eight cities that were once famous. He discusses the length of the summer days before turning his attention to the languages spoken on the island and to the migration history of each people settled in Britain. He concludes this first chapter with a portrayal of Ireland. Several aspects of Bede's description are discussed below: the evaluation of the distance separating the island from the Continent, the fertility of the land, the twenty-eight cities and their evocation of a lost golden age, the identification of this *descriptio* as a creation scene, and finally the link these lines establish between the Anglo-Saxons and the land of Britain.

Bede writes a laudatory narrative of his own island and his own people. Logically, therefore, he presents Britain as an alluring land clearly worth conquering. Even though the historian does not repeat Gildas's metaphor of Britain as a bride, his presentation of the island as a pleasant place, rich in trees, crops, cattle, and fish, makes it a desirable target for potential invaders. In the Christian framework of the *Ecclesiastical History*, Bede further elaborates on the concept of the land of plenty. Contrasting with Gildas's homeland which generates tyrants, the Anglo-Saxon historian's Britain becomes fertile ground for the Church.[21] After Augustine starts his work of conversion among the descendants of the Germanic tribes, he writes to Pope Gregory, and Bede says that he 'suggesserat ei multam quidem sibi esse messem sed operarios paucos', quoting the Gospels of Matthew and Luke.[22] The *Ecclesiastical History* is a panegyric of the Anglo-Saxon Church; it is not

---

[21] In his condemnation of the Britons' sins, Gildas quotes Porphyry who says: 'Britannia . . . fertilis provincia tyrannorum' (Gildas, *The Ruin of Britain* 4. 3, p. 90). In the notes, Morris points out that the quotation is in fact from Jerome Ep. 133, 9; see 148. It is fitting that Gildas's Britain should produce tyrants, as they are the epitome of the Britons' misbehaviour.

[22] he 'had advised him that the harvest was great and the workers were few' (Bede, *Ecclesiastical History*, i. 29, p. 104). Another example can be found in Bede's account of Alban's martyrdom, where Bede quotes Venantius Fortunatus: 'Albanum egregium fecunda Britania profert' (Bede, *Ecclesiastical History*, i. 7, p. 28). For the biblical source, see Matthew 9: 37 and Luke 10: 2.

surprising, therefore, that the land where it flourishes should bring forth numerous saints.

Given Bede's favourable bias toward his homeland, one might wonder why he retains some of the traditional *topoi* of the descriptions of Britain, in particular those stressing its remoteness. This question becomes all the more relevant when one remembers that, as Chapter 4 has shown, Bede develops a different geography in his scientific writings, a geography that does not insist on Britain's isolation. In the *Ecclesiastical History*, however, the insular scholar chooses not to downplay his homeland's remoteness, but he revisits some of the traditional elements found in classical accounts of Britain, transforming distance into a positive attribute. This outlying island is adorned with beautiful cities and its fertility is remarkable. The Anglo-Saxon author models this image of his fatherland on the Promised Land. As such, he transforms it into a special place reserved for elected settlers, in this case the Anglo-Saxons.

But distance is not always auspicious and a contrasting picture emerges at other points in the text. For instance, in the account of the Roman missionaries' first journey to Britain, the Pope's envoys turn back before reaching Britain's shores. They are paralysed with terror at the idea of facing the island's inhabitants, whom the historian describes as 'barbaram feram incredulamque gentem'.[23] In the *Ecclesiastical History*, the evaluation of distance is closely linked to its author's Christian perspective. The island's remoteness has positive connotations when it inscribes the election of place and people within a wider religious scheme. But isolation becomes an ominous characteristic when linked to paganism. Distance does not always conform to scientific measurements but, subject to affective variations, it often reflects a particular author's agenda.

Bede's *descriptio* fails to picture the island empty of its population. Following his Welsh predecessor, Bede mentions cities and hot baths beneficial for men and women of all ages. The twenty-eight urban areas are beautiful and Britain was once *insignita*, famous, because of them.[24] They testify to the ability of Britain's inhabitants to build spectacular edifices that embellish the island. The reader is not told who erected these buildings or for whom they made Britain famous. If we assume that Bede and Gildas refer to twenty-eight existing cities, then they were probably constructed by the Romans. But this link is never explicitly drawn and in these two narratives the cities appear

---

[23] 'a barbarous, fierce, and unbelieving nation' (Bede, *Ecclesiastical History*, i. 23, p. 68).

[24] Bede, *Ecclesiastical History*, i. 1, p. 16.

before the country's earliest inhabitants are first mentioned. Thus, the reader is left with the impression that the twenty-eight towns predate the coming of the Romans and that, at one point in its history, Britain was blessed with a golden age, now forever gone. Chapter 1 has shown how narratives conjuring up a lost ideal almost inevitably also put forth an aspiration for the future. Articulating these two temporal poles, Margaret Bridges observes that in Bede's description, Britain's richness is both that of a lost Eden and that of the Promised Land.[25] These comments are in fact pertinent to both Bede's and Gildas's descriptions: the picture they present is not merely an evocation of the past, but it should be read as a promise of a brighter future for the island. This happy tomorrow is linked to the (re)establishment of a territorial rule, that of the Britons' for Gildas and that of the Anglo-Saxons' for Bede.

The allusion to the golden age detected in the mention of Britain's twenty-eight beautiful cities should be linked to the idea, put forward by several critics, that Bede's opening chapter gestures toward the beginning of the Book of Genesis, to Paradise and the Fall.[26] The notion that this portrayal of Britain amounts to a creation scene is of crucial importance for the present discussion.[27] For it suggests that Bede's *descriptio Britanniae* chronicles the coming into being of an imaginary place, that of Britain before it was inhabited. It draws attention to the question of settlement, which the narrative foregrounds, for the island will successively become the home of the Britons, the Romans, and the Anglo-Saxons. The issue of the occupation of space also figures prominently in creation narratives and, as demonstrated in Chapter 2, there is no such thing as an empty space: any tract of ground needs to be settled. The *Ecclesiastical History*'s opening chapter documents the coming into being of a land—Britain—and its population—the Anglo-Saxons. It shapes a poetic, almost Edenic space: Britain as it should 'originally' have been and, as such, it can be read as a creation scene.

---

[25] Bridges, 'Discours du réel', 21.
[26] See e.g. Calvin B. Kendall, 'Imitation and the Venerable Bede's *Historia Ecclesiastica*', in Margot H. King and Wesley M. Stevens (eds.), *Saints, Scholars and Heroes: Studies in Medieval Culture in Honour of Charles W. Jones* 2 vols. (Collegeville, MN: Hill Monastic Manuscript Library, St John's Abbey and University, 1979), i. 161–90 (188 n. 63).
[27] J. M. Wallace-Hadrill calls it a creation scene by *imitatio*. J. M. Wallace-Hadrill, *Bede's* Ecclesiastical History of the English People: *A Historical Commentary* (Oxford: Clarendon Press, 1988), 6.

Bede's *descriptio Britanniae* supports the Anglo-Saxons' claim to Britain and partakes in a strategy that justifies land seizure. To support this territorial appropriation, the medieval historian links the extraordinary character of both the land and its inhabitants. This association becomes manifest when one reads the *Ecclesiastical History*'s first chapter together with the anecdote of the Anglo-Saxon slave boys. In the opening lines of the text, the island's twenty-eight beautiful cities and the fertility of the soil imply that Britain is a place of delight even before it is settled by the Britons. Contrasting with traditional depictions of the periphery, it is not presented as a wild and hostile place, populated by monsters and pagans. In the episode of the insular youths in Rome, the boys, although coming from a distant land, are at their best: they are God's Chosen People and they are proleptic Christians destined to promote orthodoxy in Britain. Compared with the initial *descriptio*, this scene shifts the focus of the praise away from the land on to its inhabitants. But these two passages are indissociable; for, just as the land is 'civilized' even before any form of human occupation takes hold of it, its inhabitants' election is anterior to their conversion to Christianity. Each reflects positively on the other and Bede implicitly ties the people to the land. They deserve each other because they are both extraordinary.

Gildas and Bede offer a new image of Britain. Insisting on its fertility, they present it as a land worth conquering, as a desirable place to occupy. The question of who does and who should control Britain is central to both texts. Gildas resorts to moral criteria to justify land ownership and he explains the coming of the pagan Germanic invaders as a divine punishment. Yet he does not present the Anglo-Saxons as Britain's rightful inhabitants nor does he deem the land to be irremediably lost. In the picture he puts forward, the Britons, because they are natives to the island, contrast with all the other tribes dwelling in Britain. Their right is that autochthony: they do not have a distant homeland which they left behind before migrating to a new land. Bede builds the Anglo-Saxons' claim to Britain on different bases—among which their migration from the Continent. Turning to biblical rhetoric, he inscribes the invaders' conquest of Britain in a Christian scheme of history. Consequently, the *adventus Saxonum* becomes an event willed by God and it is the 'elected' character of both land and inhabitants that legitimizes territorial appropriation.

MIGRATION NARRATIVES

Some key elements of the migration motif so pervasive in Old English literature have already been highlighted in the preceding chapter and they are still relevant here. They include the importance of the territory left behind and/or of the place to be reached, the various processes of land seizure that operate once the journey is over, and the temporal ambiguity characterizing narratives that commemorate past events, that justify a present order, and that gesture toward a desirable future. This section concentrates on two accounts of the migration of the Anglo-Saxons' ancestors: the ones found in the *Ecclesiastical History* and in the Anglo-Saxon Chronicle. These narratives present a very different picture of the Germanic tribes' journey and of their settlement in Britain. Bede mitigates the violence of the conquest, while the compiler of the Anglo-Saxon Chronicle does not. The former resorts to biblical rhetoric and provides a historical-looking account of origin; the latter values heroic ethos and offers a legendary view of Anglo-Saxon England's beginnings.

Commenting on the notion of 'cultural myth'—in the present case, the memory of the Anglo-Saxons' original migration—Nicholas Howe observes that 'by its very nature, a cultural myth looks back to depict the outcome of history as inevitable.'[28] He adds that, when a myth is deeply inscribed in a culture, it becomes difficult to interpret the present except as it accords with the pattern of the past.[29] Old English authors exploit the inevitability inherent in their cultural myth to justify the Germanic tribes' appropriation of Britain. They revisit British history and reinterpret it as announcing their arrival. In what follows, I analyse several narrative strategies that legitimize the Anglo-Saxons' journey to and conquest of Britain. For instance, the inflexions given to the account of the island's Roman past ensure continuity between the Mediterranean and the Germanic invaders. At the same time, the Anglo-Saxons construct their identity against the island's former inhabitants and they recast themselves as Britain's rightful occupiers. Repeating a practice already at work in the *descriptiones Britanniae*, they establish privileged links between their own people and the land of Britain.

---

[28] Nicholas Howe, *Migration and Mythmaking in Anglo-Saxon England* (New Haven: Yale University Press, 1989), 4.
[29] Howe, *Migration and Mythmaking*, 4–5.

Bede, *The Ecclesiastical History*

In the course of the *Ecclesiastical History*, Bede successively narrates the migration story of each invading people: the Britons, the Picts, the Irish, the Romans, and the Anglo-Saxons. The Britons come first, leaving Armorica behind. Then the Picts, who according to the Northumbrian historian come from Scythia, reach Ireland. As there is no land available there, they sail to Britain. Also from the west comes the portion of the Irish who live in Britain. Next, the Romans arrive from the south and, lastly, the Germanic tribes cross from the Continent. Each people has its own migration story and no group is really native to Britain. Contrary to what is found in Gildas, the Britons are no longer the island's autochthonous inhabitants; for the Anglo-Saxon historian clearly says that they are those 'qui de tractu Armoricano, ut fertur, Brittaniam aduecti australes sibi partes illius uindicarunt'.[30] The Britons are simply the island's earliest settlers; they are the first in a long series of invaders. They are consequently denied the special status they were granted in the *De Excidio Britonum*, where they were not associated with any other land except Britain. A close reading of the migration stories of each of the tribes who contributed to the island's population will help to identify the various textual devices which operate in the *Ecclesiastical History* and which aim at supporting the Anglo-Saxons' claim to Britain.

The Britons

Bede presents a very unfavourable picture of the Britons: they are weak and they are cowards who do not know how to fight. Consequently, they are unable to defend themselves and cannot resist the attacks of the Irish and the Picts: 'Brittania . . . praedae tantum patuit, utpote omnis bellici usus prorsus ignara'.[31] The Britons therefore need to be helped by the Romans or to be spurred on by famine to repel their northern enemies.[32] On their own, they have no military power, no means to ensure their existence as a group.

The Britons however do win a couple of military victories, such as their success at Mount Badon (discussed below) or their defeat of an

---

[30] The Britons who 'sailed to Britain, so it is said, from the land of Armorica, and appropriated to themselves the southern part of it' (Bede, *Ecclesiastical History*, i. 1, p. 16).

[31] 'Britain . . . lay wholly exposed to plunderers and the more so because the people were utterly ignorant of the practice of warfare' (Bede, *Ecclesiastical History*, i. 12, p. 40).

[32] Bede, *Ecclesiastical History*, i. 12–13, pp. 40–6, and i. 14, pp. 46–8.

alliance of Saxons and Picts at the time when Lupus and Germanus, two bishops from Gaul, fight against the Pelagian heresy in Britain. But success on the battlefield owes nothing to the Britons' own prowess. For, they fight under the two bishops' leadership, and the historian observes that: 'itaque apostolicis ducibus Christus militabat in castris.'[33] When they take up arms, Germanus offers to be their leader, and victory is won when the army shouts 'Alleluia' and thus scares away the Picts and the Saxons who fear that heaven is going to fall down on their heads.[34] It is clearly Lupus's and Germanus's guidance and faith which secure victory over the enemies — Bede unambiguously says so: 'ultionem suam innocens exercitus intuetur, et uictoriae concessae otiosus spectator efficitur.'[35] The Anglo-Saxon historian deprives the Britons of any agency in this military success.

It is worth noticing that when the Britons ask the Romans for military support, they define themselves as a Roman province. They send to Rome envoys who beg for assistance 'ne penitus misera patria deleretur, ne nomen Romanae prouinciae . . . exterarum gentium inprobitate obrutum uilesceret'.[36] The Britons do not display any sense of themselves as an independent and sovereign people. Bede further consolidates his negative portrayal of this people in not depicting independent Britain, this period between the departure of the Romans and the coming of the Anglo-Saxons during which the Britons would have had their own social organization. According to the historian, when the Romans finally abandon the Britons to their fate, the latter are unable to set up a lasting kingdom and an efficient army; instead, they give themselves to civil war, which is indeed the very negation of a group's collective identity.[37]

In the *Ecclesiastical History* therefore, the Britons are unfit for independence and self-determination: they need to be ruled by foreign princes, be they Roman or Anglo-Saxon. To gauge the impact of such a depiction, one should recall Paul Zumthor's comments on the notion of *territoire*. The critic says that 'l'union de l'homme et de l'espace fonde le "territoire", espace civilisé de qui, par son travail, se l'est approprié et y a

---

[33] 'Indeed, with such apostolic leaders, it was Christ Himself who fought in their camp' (Bede, *Ecclesiastical History*, i. 20, p. 62).

[34] Bede, *Ecclesiastical History*, i. 20, p. 62.

[35] 'The army, without striking a blow, saw themselves avenged and became inactive spectators of the victory freely offered to them' (Bede, *Ecclesiastical History*, i. 20, p. 64).

[36] 'so that their wretched country might not be utterly destroyed, and the name of a Roman province . . . might not be obliterated and disgraced by the barbarity of foreigners' (Bede, *Ecclesiastical History*, i. 12, p. 42).

[37] See Bede, *Ecclesiastical History*, i. 12, p. 44.

créé un droit.'[38] This quotation combines three important notions: the settlement in a given area, the transformation of a space by a civilizing human presence, and the establishment a right over a tract of land. In Bede's account, the Britons are unable to institute a stable political rule. In Zumthor's terms, therefore, they do not assert their ownership of Britain, for one element of the equation—political right—is missing. They thus fail to establish their own territory. By implication, therefore, their claim to the land of Britain is undermined.

Bede also resorts to a specifically religious perspective to blame the Britons and to justify the Anglo-Saxon tribes' conquest of their island. Their disastrous idea to call the Germanic tribes to their aid from across the sea is part of God's plan to chastise the Britons: 'quod Domini nutu dispositum esse constat, ut ueniret contra inprobos malum, sicut euidentius rerum exitus probauit.'[39] The Anglo-Saxons' coming thus conforms to divine providence and their victory over the Britons is justified. Bede's negative view of the Britons is not limited to the early chapters of the *Ecclesiastical History* but continues throughout the text, as the historian chronicles orthodox Christianity's progressive triumph in the British Isles. He insists that, when in contact with the pagan Anglo-Saxons, the Britons refuse to share their faith with the newcomers, and this is the main argument in his condemnation.[40] Their religious stubbornness has heavy consequences, some of which are of course territorial. Bede concludes his *History* with a contemporary picture of Britain.[41] He comments on the general situation of the various tribes who dwell there: the Anglo-Saxons, the Picts, the Irish, and the Britons. He mentions one more time the latter's opposition to the Anglo-Saxons and to the Catholic Church, and he says that it is because of this opposition that they cannot obtain all of what they want and are partly under Anglo-Saxon rule.[42] They are refused the possession of a piece of land where they would dwell independently and which they could call their own. Bede's religious perspective legitimates the Britons' territorial dispossession.

---

[38] Paul Zumthor, *La Mesure du Monde* (Paris : Seuil, 1993), 78.
[39] 'As events plainly showed, this was ordained by the will of God so that evil might fall upon those miscreants' (Bede, *Ecclesiastical History*, i. 14, p. 48).
[40] Bede adds to Gildas's account of their crimes; the worst of all is that 'numquam genti Saxonum siue Anglorum, secum Brittaniam incolenti, uerbum fidei praedicando committerent' (Bede, *Ecclesiastical History*, i. 22, p. 68).
[41] Bede, *Ecclesiastical History*, v. 23, pp. 558–60.
[42] 'nonnulla tamen ex parte Anglorum sunt seruitio mancipati' (Bede, *Ecclesiastical History*, v. 23, p. 560).

The *Ecclesiastical History* repeatedly undermines the Britons' claim to the land: adopting a military point of view, it implies that they are not strong enough to control a tract of ground. It also stresses their inability to establish a solid political rule, an inability that explains their territorial loss. And finally, the text resorts to theological arguments to justify the Anglo-Saxons' subjection of the Britons.

The Romans

Even though no large immigration is mentioned in connexion with the Romans, they nevertheless figure prominently in Bede's account of Britain's early history. Clearly superior to the Britons militarily, they exercise martial control over Britain and they administer it as a province. When Claudius invades Britain, he hardly encounters any resistance: Bede says that the Britons surrender without fighting. The Roman leader crosses to Britain: 'ibique sine ullo proelio ac sanguine intra paucissimos dies plurimam insulae partem in deditionem recepit'.[43] The Britons do not resist foreign invasion and they cannot put up a serious military opposition to their enemies.

But what about Mount Badon? The episode is instructive, for if the Britons win this fight against the invaders, they are led by Ambrosius Aurelianus, a Roman general. The foreign origin of the Britons' providential leader is all the more remarkable since Bede presents him as the only Roman left in Britain. The historian says that he is a modest man 'qui solus forte Romanae gentis praefatae tempestati superfuerat'.[44] The fact that he becomes the Britons' general suggests that the latter are unable to protect their own interests alone and that this British victory is due to a Roman general.

Rome constitutes a powerful pole of attraction throughout the *History*, and the eternal city's inhabitants play a crucial role in the development of Christianity in the British Isles. The papal city's importance is underscored at various points in Bede's text and I will only mention two significant instances here: the Augustinian mission and the anecdote of the Anglo-Saxon slave boys. Although the Britons do not preach the Christian faith to their Germanic invaders, it does not mean that God has forsaken the Anglo-Saxons. Quite on the contrary, this is

---

[43] 'and without any fighting or bloodshed he received the surrender of the greater part of the island within a very few days' (Bede, *Ecclesiastical History*, i. 3, p. 22).
[44] 'who was, as it happened, the sole member of the Roman race who had survived this storm [the Germanic tribes' attacks of their former British allies]' (Bede, *Ecclesiastical History*, i. 16, p. 54).

part of a divine scheme devised for a special people; the historian says: 'Sed non tamen diuina pietas plebem suam, quam praesciuit, deseruit; quin multo digniores genti memoratae praecones ueritatis, per quos crederet, destinauit.'⁴⁵ By *digniores praecones*, Bede means the Augustinian mission, and the Anglo-Saxons are thus privileged to receive their faith directly from Rome. In the insular historian's account of the spread of Christianity in Britain, no intermediary comes between the descendants of the Germanic tribes and the heart of Christendom. These continental missionaries moreover continue a line of Roman travellers to Britain. At first, there were emperors waging military campaigns; later, there are missionaries preaching the Christian faith: the Augustinian mission signals the restoration of Roman influence in Britain.

The anecdote of the insular youths put up for sale in a Roman market is a central episode in the development of the relationships between the Romans and the Anglo-Saxons, for it clearly is the founding event of insular Christianity. Yet it does not take place in Anglo-Saxon England: it occurs away from the homeland, in Rome, and it involves Gregory, the future Pope. The Anglo-Saxons' religious destiny thus starts at the very centre of the Christian world under the auspices of the Church's highest official. As a consequence, a privileged, direct link is established between the papal city and Anglo-Saxon England. This scene in fact announces the creation of a new spiritual centre in England; for it is indeed the English who eventually convert the Picts, who bring the Scots to accept Roman religious observances, and who launch conversion missions to the Continent.⁴⁶

This focus on Rome is part of Bede's polemical and religious agenda, an agenda which aims at supporting orthodox observances in the Christian Church. It is also meant to associate Rome and Anglo-Saxon England. The Romans prefigure the role the Anglo-Saxons will play in Britain when they hold sway over the island both in questions of military rule and of religious leadership. But there is more to the prominence granted to Rome; for there was, to borrow Mayke De Jong's expression, a 'Rome in the mind' above the Alps to which northern rulers turned to ground their political rule and their religious orthodoxy.⁴⁷ The former

---

⁴⁵ 'Nevertheless God in His goodness did not reject the people whom He foreknew, but He had appointed much worthier heralds of the truth to bring this people to the faith' (Bede, *Ecclesiastical History*, i. 22, p. 68).

⁴⁶ For the conversion missions to the Continent, see Bede, *Ecclesiastical History*, v. 9–11, pp. 474–86.

⁴⁷ Mayke De Jong and Frans Theuws, 'Topographies of Power: Some Conclusions', in Mayke De Jong and Frans Theuws, with Carine van Rhijn (eds.), *Topographies of*

centre of the Empire and the heart of Christendom, both located in Rome, were two significant elements constitutive of sacred and secular medieval thinking. This ideology, based on the theory of the primacy of the city of Rome, adopts a spiritual as well as a temporal outlook. Political and religious power is thus located in Rome, and the association Bede establishes between the papal city and his own people implicitly supports the latter's territorial claims. According to this mental framework, the Anglo-Saxons are heirs to the Romans and their control of Britain is justified not only from a military, but also from a religious point of view.

The Picts and the Irish

The relationships the Picts and the Irish entertain with the Anglo-Saxons in the religious sphere throughout the *Ecclesiastical History* is especially interesting. For Bede's account of the contacts between these three peoples does not so much serve to support territorial claims as to recentre the descendants of the Germanic tribes in a new religious geography.

The Picts, first introduced as fierce warriors plaguing their neighbours, are eventually redeemed toward the end of Bede's text when they opt for religious conformity with Rome. When the Pictish king Nechtan decides to follow the Roman observances, he asks the Anglo-Saxons for help in easing the change to orthodoxy and in implementing it with *maiore auctoritate*.[48] Significantly, therefore, the Anglo-Saxons become the missionaries who introduce the Picts to correct rituals, thus clearly holding a position of religious authority.

Pre-eminence is similarly conferred on the Anglo-Saxon Church in its dealings with the Irish; for Iona, the Irish monastery founded by Columba, is eventually won to Roman Christianity by Egbert, an Englishman.[49] This episode, recounted at the very end of the *Ecclesiastical History*, is seen as the summit of the text.[50] Henry Mayr-Harting says: 'that was the crowning moment of Bede's book, that was the end of those labours which had begun in the year of the Synod of Whitby'.[51] Egbert's mission to Iona is recounted just after Nechtan's

---

Power in the Early Middle Ages, The Transformation of the Roman World, 6 (Leiden: Brill, 2001), 533–45 (538).

[48] 'greater authority' (Bede, *Ecclesiastical History*, v. 21, p. 532).
[49] Bede says that he is 'de natione Anglorum' (Bede, *Ecclesiastical History*, iii. 4, p. 224).
[50] See Wallace-Hadrill, *Historical Commentary*, 198.
[51] Henry Mayr-Harting, *The Coming of Christianity to Anglo-Saxon England* (London: Batsford, 1972), 113.

adoption of the Roman observances. Consequently, the *Ecclesiastical History* closes on an image of Anglo-Saxon England constituting a new religious centre: it becomes the point from which orthodox rituals radiate over the island, from which missions are sent to the Picts and to the Irish.

The Synod of Whitby marks the turning point in the relationships between the Anglo-Saxons and the Irish. It is the moment when their religious differences are officially discussed and when Oswiu, King of Northumbria, decides against the Irish. The account of the Synod is an interesting passage of the *Ecclesiastical History* for, in this episode, Bede plays on the notion of distance and refers to it both to condemn and to excuse diverging religious practices. Let me examine first the dialogue taking place between Wilfrid, who defends the Roman observances, and the Irish bishop Colman. The former, trying to convince his opponent of his error, opposes Roman rites to what the Irish, the Picts, and the Britons practise. He says that these people fight against the whole world 'de duabus ultimis Oceani insulis'.[52] A few lines below, he further asks Colman whether he really thinks that the rites of a few isolated people are to be preferred to those of the universal Church. In Wilfrid's words, this rebel minority dwells in 'uno de angulo extremae insulae'.[53] Twice, the speaker insists on the distance separating the British Isles from Rome, and his choice of words stresses his religious opponents' geographical isolation. Remoteness is here an argument used against the Irish.

But once more, Bede grants distance different connotations when he recounts Columba's founding of Iona: he uses it to excuse Iona's doubtful calculation of the date of Easter. The Anglo-Saxon historian says that because the Irish dwell so far away from Rome, there is no one to bring them the acts of the synods, and thus to rectify their Easter observances. They are wrong 'utpote quibus longe ultra orbem positis nemo synodalia paschalis obseruantiae decreta porrexerat'.[54] Geography here atones for unorthodox faith. In his account of the Irish, Bede adopts different points of view toward the question of distance, as he did both in his description of Britain early in the *Ecclesiastical History* and in his scientific writings examined in Chapter 4.

---

[52] 'in the two remotest islands of the Ocean' (Bede, *Ecclesiastical History*, iii. 25, p. 300).
[53] 'in one corner of the remotest of islands' (Bede, *Ecclesiastical History*, iii. 25, p. 306).
[54] 'since they were so far away at the ends of the earth that there was none to bring them the decrees of the synods concerning the observance of Easter' (Bede, *Ecclesiastical History*, iii. 4, p. 224).

Bede's comments on the isolation of the Irish, the Picts, and the Britons indirectly reflect on the Anglo-Saxons. In the dichotomy between centrality and marginality that structures the question of religious observances in the *Ecclesiastical History*, the Anglo-Saxons are no longer confined to the periphery, and marginality becomes the special preserve of those who do not follow the Catholic rituals. By implication, Bede's insistence on the distance separating the Irish from Rome and his account of the role the Anglo-Saxons play in the diffusion of orthodoxy in the British Isles serve to recentre his own people in a larger Christian geography.

The Anglo-Saxons

The Anglo-Saxons are the main protagonists of the *Ecclesiastical History* and their migration story figures prominently in the text. In the first book, Chapter 16, of the *History*, Bede relates how the Germanic tribes reach Britain and fight the Picts and the Irish at first, but then betray their British allies and turn against them. When the war is over, the Anglo-Saxon historian specifies that 'hostilis exercitus...domum reuersus est'.[55] This is an intriguing comment and its interpretation is difficult. In their edition of the text, Colgrave and Mynors declare that this 'can hardly mean more than that the invaders returned to their headquarters on some island or islands near the coast, perhaps Thanet'.[56] Wallace-Hadrill is more categorical; he says: 'We cannot tell what "home" the "exercitus" returned to...The word is in Gildas: Bede repeats it and makes no guess. Neither writer can have supposed that the "exercitus" went back to the continent.'[57] This assumption sheds a very reasonable light on Bede's passing comment. And yet, earlier in the account of the Anglo-Saxons' coming, *domus* (home) is used to designate their dwelling-place on the Continent. Discovering a fertile and pleasant land in Britain, the invaders announce their finding to their own people back home. Bede says that when this report 'domi nuntiatum est', more people come from the Continent.[58] Here, *domus* is without doubt a region on the Continent. When Bede says that the invading tribes return 'home', he does not specify where that is. What is

---

[55] 'the army of the enemy...returned home' (Bede, *Ecclesiastical History*, i. 16, p. 52).
[56] Bede, *Ecclesiastical History*, i. 16, p. 52 n. 2.
[57] Wallace-Hadrill, *Historical Commentary*, 25.
[58] 'reached their homes' (Bede, *Ecclesiastical History*, i. 15, p. 50).

certain is that the Germanic tribes leave the area where they have fought the Britons and that their 'home' is still situated elsewhere.

The narrative of the settlement proper deserves closer scrutiny, for if Bede foregrounds the Anglo-Saxons' migration story, he later eludes the very process of land seizure. Immediately following the account of the Anglo-Saxons' first coming (and going), the historian offers a detailed report of Germanus's and Lupus's mission to Britain to fight the Pelagian heresy. Returning to the question of the relationships between Britain's inhabitants and the newcomers, he narrates the victory the Britons win under the two bishops' leadership. A peaceful interval follows, during which the Britons return to their criminal and sinful ways. A new generation arises and Bede specifies that they do not preach the Christian faith to the 'genti Saxonum siue Anglorum, secum Brittaniam incolenti'.[59] The Anglo-Saxons seem already to dwell among the Britons at this point. This impression is confirmed by the following chapter of the *History* which deals with the beginnings of the Augustinian mission of conversion; for the mission takes place once the Anglo-Saxons are securely settled in Britain. Consequently, Bede never depicts the invasion itself; he jumps from a British victory to the time when the invaders inhabit Britain. The Germanic tribes' settlement, that is, their appropriation of a land that formerly belonged to the Britons, remains a blank in the *Ecclesiastical History*.

Moreover, Bede describes the Britons as a people unfit for independence and self-determination and such a characterization of the island's first inhabitants strongly suggests that the Anglo-Saxon invaders arrive in a social vacuum. If the Britons are unable to create their own territory, that is, if they are unable to secure a right over a given tract of ground, then implicitly the land of Britain is there for the taking. The Germanic tribes cannot therefore be accused of destroying an existing social organization and depriving a people of its homeland. Such narrative devices downplay the fact that the Anglo-Saxons take over the living space of the Britons and it grounds the invaders' claim to the land on political and military bases.

Bede inscribes, at other points in the *Ecclesiastical History*, the Germanic tribes' invasion of Britain in a religious framework. With the seminal episode of the Anglo-Saxon slave boys, the historian promises a grand role to his people in the history of the Church. And in Bede's

---

[59] 'the Saxons or Angles who inhabited Britain with them' (Bede, *Ecclesiastical History*, i. 22, p. 68).

narrative, the Anglo-Saxons fulfil it: they establish a new religious centre in England and their homeland becomes the place from which missions of conversion are sent to their neighbours. The Anglo-Saxons' religious destiny is highlighted and their conquest of the island is equivalent to a step in the development of Christianity and orthodoxy in Britain. The *adventus* was appointed by divine providence and the violence inherent in the conquest of Britain is denied: Bede's Christian rhetoric legitimizes the coming of the Anglo-Saxons.

The opening chapters of the first book of the *Ecclesiastical History* offer a neat picture of the migration of the Angles, the Jutes, and the Saxons. Three tribes leave their homeland on the Continent, and three tribes settle in Britain, each in a different part of the country. Bede alludes to this founding event again toward the end of his text, in a passage that starkly contrasts with his earlier report. In book V, Chapter 9, the historian mentions the migration in the context of the missions of conversion which insular preachers launch on the Continent. Bede reminds his reader that the ancestors of many Anglo-Saxons now living in Britain descend from tribes dwelling in Germany. He names several of them: the Frisians, the Rugians, the Danes, the Huns, the Old Saxons, and the Bructeri.[60] These lines have been taken to be an expansion, or even a correction of the earlier narration of the *adventus Saxonum*. Discussing the discrepancies between these two accounts, John Hines considers it more than plausible that Bede derived information for this list from his knowledge of recent and projected missionary expeditions to the Continent.[61] However that may be, it is surprising to find, in the *Ecclesiastical History*, two irreconcilable accounts of an episode so central to its narrative project.

Along the same lines, Nicholas Howe observes that Bede makes little of the fact that there were Germanic people dwelling in Britain for at least a century before the *adventus*.[62] Bede seems to have disregarded a complex reality in order to promote a simplified account of the migration. The opening chapter of the *History* makes of the *adventus Saxonum* a single event, and not a process extending over several decades and happening more or less at random. The Anglo-Saxon historian understands the migration as an occurrence willed by God and

---

[60] Bede, *Ecclesiastical History*, v. 9, p. 476.
[61] John Hines, 'The Becoming of the English Identity: Material Culture and Language in Early Anglo-Saxon England', *Anglo-Saxon Studies in Archaeology and History*, 7 (1994), 49–59 (50). On this point, see also Wallace-Hadrill, *Historical Commentary*, 181.
[62] Howe, *Migration and Mythmaking*, 60 n. 3.

inscribed in a providential view of history. Consequently, it happened once, in conformity with divine providence, and its validity cannot be questioned. Moreover, Bede associates each of the three migrating tribes with one region on the Continent and one in Britain.[63] In so doing, he associates one given people to one territory, first the homeland left behind and then the land reached at the end of the journey. This is yet another strategy aiming at supporting the Anglo-Saxons' right to the land of Britain, for it stresses the link that unites them to the area they reach at the end of their migration.

The *Ecclesiastical History* memorializes the migration story of the many tribes that reached Britain's shores in the course of the island's history. Bede's account is biased toward the Anglo-Saxons: it aims at justifying their conquest and at supporting their claim to the land. As a result, the historian presents a negative picture of the Britons, the island's first inhabitants, implicitly undermining the rights they might have had to their homeland. He further recasts the Picts and the Irish as the beneficiaries of the Anglo-Saxons' religious missions, at the same time creating a new Christian centre in Anglo-Saxon England. Bede finally insists on the links uniting his own people to Rome. To sum up, Bede revisits Britain's history: according to him, it foreshadows and legitimates the Anglo-Saxons' conquest and occupation of Britain. The new geographical distribution violently generated by the *adventus* becomes the inevitable outcome of history.

The *Anglo-Saxon Chronicle*

During the reign of King Alfred, England produced another major account of Britain's early history, namely the Anglo-Saxon Chronicle. When narrating the migration to and the conquest of the island, this text substitutes a detailed account of the battles opposing the invaders to the Britons for Bede's moderate picture of the *adventus*. For instance, the entry for the year 491 clearly indicates that the Anglo-Saxons have to fight for Britain and that victims fall on the battlefield: 'Her Ælle 7 Cissa ymbsæton Andredescester 7 ofslogon alle þa þe þærinne eardedon; ne wearþ þær forþon an Bret to lafe.'[64] The mention here of the complete

---

[63] Howe, *Migration and Mythmaking*, 60.
[64] 'In this year Ælle and Cissa besieged *Andredesceaster*, and killed all those who were inside, and there was not even a single Briton left alive' (*The Anglo-Saxon Chronicle: A Collaborative Edition: III MS A*, ed. by Janet Bately (Cambridge: Brewer, 1986), 491, p. 19). I quote the Parker Chronicle from this edition.

annihilation of the Britons engaged in this battle testifies to the violence of the encounter, a violence that the compiler does not attempt to mitigate.

The Chronicle adopts an original perspective on the events it relates: it depicts the conquest of Britain as a brutal process and it does not address the moral issue raised by the fact that the Anglo-Saxons invade a peaceful land. Although it eschews the biblical rhetoric Bede uses, the Anglo-Saxon Chronicle has recourse to some of the textual devices to which the Northumbrian historian resorted. For example, it forges an essential link uniting the land of Britain and the Germanic tribes, and it also establishes a special connexion between the invaders and Rome. But in addition to these narrative strategies, the vernacular text also develops new devices to account for the conquest. It exploits, for instance, the question of the provenance of the invaders' leaders: although it grants them a pan-Germanic genealogy, it obscures their precise place of origin. The compiler also highlights the role played by names and name-giving, an action which he construes as signalling territorial appropriation. In so doing, he creates a topography of commemoration that immortalizes the early history of Britain's conquerors. Finally, the Anglo-Saxon Chronicle provides only scant information about the island's British past but still defines Britain's first inhabitants as the Anglo-Saxons' enemies. The lines that follow focus on four important aspects of the Chronicle's early annals: the genealogical material it provides, the origins of the Germanic tribes, the migration stories of the Romans and the Anglo-Saxons, and finally the question of toponymy.

The Anglo-Saxon Chronicle has a complicated manuscript history. Seven recensions of the text survive, and when we refer to the Anglo-Saxon Chronicle, we refer to an organic work for which we do not have a definitive manuscript version.[65] I base my comments on the Parker *Chronicle*: it is the oldest surviving version of the seven variants, even though it is at least two removes from an original text.[66] Æthelweard's *Chronicle* and Asser's *Life of King Alfred*, which are both Latin translations of parts of the Chronicle, will be brought into the

---

[65] Alfred P. Smyth, *King Alfred the Great* (Oxford: Oxford University Press, 1995), 461.

[66] On the manuscript history of the Chronicle, see Smyth, *Alfred* 455–64; *The Anglo-Saxon Chronicle*, pp. xiii–xx, and *The Parker Chronicle (832–900)*, ed. by A. H. Smith (London: Methuen, 1935; repr. 1954), 2–9. On Alfredian manuscripts, see James Campbell, Eric John, and Patrick Wormald, *The Anglo-Saxons* (London: Penguin, 1991; first publ. London: Phaidon, 1982), 158–9.

discussion when relevant.[67] To conclude these prefatory comments, the bias toward Wessex which characterizes the Chronicle should be mentioned. The earlier sections of these vernacular annals—dealing with Roman Britain and with *adventus Saxonum*—can be seen as an introduction to the history of the West-Saxons and to King Alfred's conflict with the Danes; for this is, to quote Alfred Smyth, 'the very essence of the Chronicle'.[68]

Prefaces and Genealogies

Rehearsing King Alfred's genealogy, the preface to the Parker *Chronicle* gives an account of his ancestry and it crucially links the West-Saxon king with the Germanic chieftains Cerdic and Cynric. Cerdic and Cynric are the very first names mentioned by the compiler, for the preface opens thus: 'Þy geare þe wæs agan fram Cristes acennesse cccc wintra 7 xciiii uuintra, þa Cerdic 7 Cynric his sunu cuom up æt Cerdicesoran mid v scipum'.[69] In the following lines, their lineage is traced back through a legendary past to Woden. The preface then enumerates the kings who have held the kingdom of Wessex, from Cerdic, the first sovereign, to Æthelwulf, Alfred's father. Having reached this point, the narrative recapitulates the same material ascending through the genealogy of the West-Saxon kings from Æthelwulf back to Cerdic. And only then does the text introduce Alfred as one of Æthelwulf's sons. A direct line of descent is thus firmly established between Alfred and the two Germanic leaders.

The very wording of the preface to the Parker *Chronicle* further elaborates on the association of King Alfred with Cerdic and Cynric. The compiler says that the two Germanic leaders 'uuærun þa ærestan cyningas þe Westseaxna lond on Wealum geeodon'.[70] Toward the end of the preface, the chronicler echoes this passage when he says that after the rule of Æthelbald, Ethelbert, and Ethelred, 'þa feng Ælfred hiera broþur to rice ... ccc 7 xcvi wintra þæs þe his cyn ærest Westseaxna lond

---

[67] *The Chronicle of Æthelweard*, ed. and trans. A. Campbell (London: Nelson, 1962) and Asser, *Life of King Alfred*, ed. W. H. Stevenson (Oxford: Clarendon Press, 1904; repr. 1959).

[68] Smyth, *Alfred*, 478.

[69] 'In the year when 494 years had passed from Christ's incarnation, Cerdic and his son Cynric came to *Cerdicesora* with five ships' (*The Anglo-Saxon Chronicle*, Preface to MS A, p. 1).

[70] Cerdic and Cynric 'were the first kings who conquered the land of the West-Saxons from the Welsh' (*The Anglo-Saxon Chronicle*, Preface to MS A, p. 1).

on Wealum geeodon'.⁷¹ The repetition of the verb *gegan* and of the expression *on Wealum* in these two quotations strengthens the parallel between Alfred and Cerdic and Cynric. Moreover, it draws attention to the violence inherent in the conquest of Britain. The mention that there were Britons (the *Wealas*) dwelling in the island is also striking, for the compiler does not entertain the illusion of an empty land waiting to be occupied. Britain belonged to someone before the coming of the Anglo-Saxons and their migration to and settlement in the island amounts to a military conquest.⁷²

Asser's *Life of King Alfred* also lingers on the king's lineage. The royal biography opens with Alfred's birth and with a genealogy which goes back to the king's Germanic ancestors, and then beyond them, to Adam. More interestingly, the second chapter turns to the king's maternal descent and the biographer presents Alfred's mother thus: 'mater . . . quae erat filia Oslac . . . Qui Oslac Gothus erat natione; ortus enim erat de Gothis et Iutis'.⁷³ With this allusion, Asser anchors the king's origins in the continental tribes of the ninth century. In so doing, he includes in Alfred's background the continental homeland of the Germanic tribes.⁷⁴ A traditional legendary account of origin and an innovative genealogy that conjures up people dwelling on the Continent are thus juxtaposed in Asser's narrative. With these two genealogies, the biographer articulates Alfred's role as a Christian leader with the aura conferred by his legendary Germanic background and with his inscription in a larger northern European political context.

A close reading of the Anglo-Saxon Chronicle and of Asser's *Life of King Alfred* demonstrates the central role played by issues of origin and of space in the legitimation of power. In the vernacular annals, the initial land seizure is reported in detail and a military rhetoric is

---

⁷¹ 'Then their brother Alfred succeeded to power . . . 396 years after his people first conquered the land of the West-Saxons from the Welsh' (*The Anglo-Saxon Chronicle*, Preface to MS A, p. 2).

⁷² MS E has a different preface, also found in D and F, which is based on the first chapter of Bede's *Ecclesiastical History*.

⁷³ 'His mother . . . was the daughter of Oslac . . . Oslac was a Goth by race; for he was descended from the Goths and the Jutes' Asser, *Life of King Alfred*, § 3, 4. On the description of Oslac as a Goth, and on Asser's possible attempt to convey the idea that Oslac was of Danish extraction, see *Alfred the Great: Asser's Life of Alfred and Other Contemporary Sources*, ed. and trans. by Simon Keynes and Michael Lapidge (London: Penguin, 1983), 229–30.

⁷⁴ On this point, see Janet L. Nelson, 'Reconstructing a Royal Family: Reflections on Alfred, from Asser, chapter 2', in Ian Wood and Niels Lund (eds.), *People and Places in Northern Europe, 500–1600* (Woodbridge: Boydell, 1991), 47–66 (52).

used to support Alfred's rule. Something similar to the observations developed in Chapter 4, which demonstrated that an association of the Alfredian court with foreigners and with distant lands reflects positively on the King, may be discerned in Asser's biography. Its opening chapters associate Alfred with a wider Germanic world. Mary Helms reminds us of the importance for all political-religious elites to mediate somehow between the homeland and the world beyond their own realms.[75] Asser's genealogies grant visibility to the West-Saxon king's long-distance associations. Their scope is both temporal and historical: on the one hand, they include the whole of Christian chronology, since Alfred is linked to Adam, the first man, and on the other, they encompass an extensive geographical extent. The King's connexions with distant lands in fact ground his kingship.

The Invaders' Origins

In addition to this view of origins drawing on the notion of genealogy, the Anglo-Saxon Chronicle also addresses the problem of the invaders' territorial provenance, thus foregrounding geographical issues. Interestingly, the Parker *Chronicle*, occulting Cerdic and Cynric's place of origin, does not specify where these two heroes' homeland is located. It could be argued that the compiler did not mention this particular element because it was common knowledge for an Anglo-Saxon audience. But a closer examination of this question invalidates this hypothesis. The Parker *Chronicle* silences the origins not only of Cerdic and Cynric, but also of Hengest and Horsa. The entry relating their landing in Britain says: 'On hiera dagum Hengest 7 Horsa from Wyrtgeorne geleaþade Bretta kyninge gesohton Bretene on þam staþe þe is genemned Ypwinesfleot, ærest Brettum to fultume, ac hie eft on hie fuhton.'[76] This gap has subsequently been filled by hand 8, a post-Conquest hand which adds, at this point in the annals, an account of the Germanic tribes' continental home based on Bede.[77] The interpolation indicates that a later scribe felt it necessary to specify the Anglo-Saxons' origins. Other versions of the Chronicle also compensate for this absence: the preface to the northern recensions incorporates Bede's material on the origins

---

[75] Mary W. Helms, *Ulysses' Sail: An Ethnographic Odyssey of Power, Knowledge, and Geographical Distance* (Princeton: Princeton University Press, 1988), 166–71.

[76] 'In this year Hengest and Horsa, invited by Vortigern, king of the Britons, reached Britain in that place that is called Ebbsfleet, first to help the Britons, but they afterwards fought against them' (*The Anglo-Saxon Chronicle*, 449, p. 17).

[77] *The Anglo-Saxon Chronicle*, pp. 17 and xl–xli.

of Britain's inhabitants, and Æthelweard clearly mentions a home for the invaders. He gives a detailed account of the *adventus Saxonum* in the first book of his chronicle and says that Vortigern and his noblemen decided to ask for help from Germany.[78]

By not specifying the provenance of the Germanic leaders, the Parker *Chronicle* plays on a traditional motif, that of the mysterious ruler coming from afar and whose origins are unknown. It is a figure which resurfaces at several points in the Old English corpus, for instance with the characters of Scyld in *Beowulf* and of Sceaf in Æthelweard's *Chronicle*. In the epic poem's opening lines, Scyld appears from beyond the sea and reaches Denmark in a boat.[79] Æthelweard refers to Sceaf in Æthelwulf's genealogy and he says that he came as a young boy from overseas.[80] Discussing the character of Scyld Scefing in *Beowulf*, Clive Tolley postulates the existence of a legend about a foundling infant sent by God as a gift from the unknown.[81] Echoes of such a figure possibly resonate in Æthelweard's allusion to Sceaf and in the *Beowulf* poet's account of Scyld, and it might also have influenced the compiler of the Parker *Chronicle* in his decision not to mention the invaders' place of origin.[82] The silencing of Cerdic's and Cynric's provenance and its exploitation of the mysterious ruler's motif in the Parker *Chronicle* furthermore create a solid link between the newcomers and the island they have just reached. Since the two Germanic leaders have no place of origin, the only land to which they are attached is that in which they settle at the end of their journey: they are bound to their destination and not their point of departure. Associated exclusively with the land of Britain, the Germanic tribes have no other place they can call their own.

---

[78] 'et hoc maluerunt ut de Germania eis adduxissent suffragium' (*The Chronicle of Æthelweard*, 7).
[79] See *Beowulf* 4–11. *Beowulf and the Fight at Finnsburg*, ed. by F. Klaeber, 3rd edn. (Lexington, MA.: Heath, 1922; repr. 1950). Because Heremod precedes Scyld in Anglo-Saxon genealogies, Scyld may be understood as Heremod's descendant, restoring his kingdom in Denmark (see the *Anglo-Saxon Chronicle*, 855 MS A, D, E; 856 MS C and F; Asser, *Life of King Alfred*, 67; Æthelweard omits all the names between Scyld and Sceaf, including therefore Heremod, see *The Chronicle of Æthelweard*, 33). But this connexion is not explicitly drawn by the *Beowulf* poet himself. On this point, see also Ch. 2.
[80] 'Ipse Scef cum uno dromone aductus est in insula oceani que dicitur Scani, armis circundatus, eratque ualde recens puer, et ab incolis illius terræ ignotus' (*The Chronicle of Æthelweard*, 33).
[81] Clive Tolley, 'A Comparative Study of Some Germanic and Finnic Myths', D.Phil. thesis, Oxford, 1993, 106.
[82] *English Historical Documents: c.500–1042*, ed. by Dorothy Whitelock (London: Eyre and Spottiswoode, 1955), 175.

British Past and Roman History

The preface to the Parker *Chronicle* unambiguously foregrounds one migration story: that of the Anglo-Saxons. Contrasting with the *Ecclesiastical History*'s opening chapter, nothing is said of the coming of the other tribes dwelling in Britain. The annals predating the advent of the Germanic tribes in the year 449 convey mostly information about the Roman presence on the island. The Chronicle does not dwell on the land's British past and does not narrate for instance the wars opposing the Britons to their hostile northern neighbours. The Britons are mentioned at the very beginning of the Chronicle, when Caesar's failed conquest of the island is reported. They reappear with the account of Claudius's conquest of Britain in the year 46 and when their King Lucius asks to be baptized in 167.[83] The entries for 381 and 409, recounting respectively the birth of the Emperor Maximus in Britain and the Gothic invasion of Rome, concern in fact not British, but Roman history. The Britons are therefore only shadowy figures whose history is played down in the Parker *Chronicle*'s early annals. This narrative arrangement has two consequences. First, the Britons are deprived of their history and, as a result, of an independent identity. They exist only as the enemies of the Romans or, later, of the Anglo-Saxons. Secondly, the dearth of information about British history suggests that, for the compiler, its only highlights are the comings of the Romans and of the Anglo-Saxons respectively. The text therefore links these two arrivals: in the Parker *Chronicle*, only two waves of invaders reach Britain's shores and the Germanic tribes are implicitly cast as the Romans' successors.[84]

Annal 418 further reinforces the association between these two people. It relates how the Romans, when they return home, take gold with them before leaving Britain. The compiler specifies that they bury what they cannot carry with them: 'Her Romane gesomnodon al þa goldhord þe on Bretene wæron 7 sume on eorþan ahyddon þæt hie nænig mon siþþan findan ne meahte'.[85] This is a curious observation, for why would

---

[83] Note that the mention of the year 189, which says that Severus built a wall across Britain, does not mention any of the island's inhabitants. In the Parker Chronicle, the audience is therefore left to guess why such a wall was needed. *The Anglo-Saxon Chronicle*, 189, p. 9.

[84] In Mss D, E, F, the inclusion of Bede's material on the immigration of all of Britain's inhabitants blurs the parallel.

[85] 'In this year, the Romans collected all the treasures that were in Britain, and hid some in the ground, so that no one could find them afterward' (*The Anglo-Saxon Chronicle*, 418, p. 16).

the Romans bury treasure if they do not come back to get it? And more intriguingly, why should the compiler record this detail when narrating the Romans' departure? This comment has a metaphorical import which gestures toward the worth of Britain. The treasure signals something precious to which the Britons do not have access: the Romans hide it so that no one can find it once they have left. It is striking that the gold should be buried, that is, that the earth should hold it. Although buried treasures are a widespread motif which occurs in a variety of contexts, it is worth noting that in this entry of the Chronicle, attention is drawn to the soil, to the materiality of the land of Britain. Pushing the argument further, I contend that the Anglo-Saxon Chronicle suggests that the Romans symbolically bequeath the gold, or the land's worth, to the Germanic tribes who will succeed them in Britain. The gold, intact in the earth, is preserved for later users. As such, it signals continuity over time and temporal distance is replaced by spatial proximity. The mention of the gold buried in the ground thus partakes in the wider pattern that strives both to associate the Anglo-Saxons with their prestigious Roman predecessors and to link them to the land of Britain.

Names and Naming

Complex links exist between name giving and the proper names of heroes, conquerors, and founders. Naming is an activity which evidently signals appropriation, and, in Zumthor's words: 'Nommer un lieu, c'est en prendre possession.'[86] In his *Chronicle*, Æthelweard provides an explicit illustration of this fact when he declares that the conquest of the island by the Germanic tribes has modified its name. He says: 'Ideoque Brittannia nunc Anglia appellatur, assumens nomen uictorum.'[87] The victorious newcomers give their name to the land they now control and the toponymic modification signals a change of political rule.

In the *Anglo-Saxon Chronicle*, the name of an invader is often made to coincide in a complex way with a place-name. Let us consider the year 501 as an example; it reads: 'Her cuom Port on Bretene 7 his ii suna Bieda 7 Mægla mid ii scipum on þære stowe þe is gecueden Portesmuþa'.[88] Portsmouth seems at first sight to have been called thus

---

[86] Zumthor, *Mesure du Monde*, 54. On this point, see also Tzvetan Todorov, *La Conquête de l'Amérique: la question de l'autre* (Paris: Seuil, 1982), 39–40.

[87] 'And so Britain is now called England, taking the name of the victors' (*The Chronicle of Æthelweard*, 9).

[88] 'In this year, Port, with his two sons Bieda and Mægla, came to Britain with two ships at the place that is called Portsmouth' (*The Anglo-Saxon Chronicle*, 501, p. 20).

because of Port. But quite evidently in the present case, this process is likely to have gone the other way, and the personal name to have been abstracted from the toponym. More generally, this suggests that the Anglo-Saxons may have deduced the existence of some at least of their legendary rulers from place-names.[89] And if conquerors sometimes give their names to the areas they take over, in legendary accounts of origin, the land also 'generates', in a reversed eponymic process, its own indigenous ancestors and founders.

Whichever comes first—the toponym or the leader—the coincidence of the two names connects the land with the individual. When legendary heroes are abstracted from a place-name, the invaders reinvent their ancestors so that they fit in the land which they appropriate. In so doing, they create a ' "storied" landscape', to borrow Otter's wording, a 'spatial deployment of collective memory'.[90] This inscription of history on the ground becomes an important factor in the constitution of a community. Howe observes that what holds a group together, at least in part, is 'the territory with its shared stories, the topography that commemorates the names and events that must be honoured'.[91] A common history and identity are thus associated with a tract of land. By stamping its own past on the ground, a community makes this space its own and imposes on it a new horizon of intelligibility. Analysing European colonialism, Derek Gregory discusses this operation which makes the landscape 'at once familiar to its colonizers and alien to its native inhabitants'.[92] Because it forces a new topography of commemoration on a piece of ground, naming is a process of dispossession: it erases and denies the relationship previous inhabitants entertained with the land.[93] In the Anglo-Saxon Chronicle, the Britons are deprived of their history: almost absent from the account of the years predating the *adventus*, they exist only as the Germanic tribes' enemies. An analysis of the Chronicle's toponyms further deprives them of their geography and,

---

[89] See Plummer's and Earle's notes on this entry. *Two of the Saxon Chronicles Parallel*, ed. by Charles Plummer and John Earle, reissued by Dorothy Whitelock, 2 vols. (Oxford: Oxford University Press, 1892–9; repr. 1980), ii. 13. See also note to the year 495, p. 12 and to the year 544, p. 14.

[90] Otter, *Inventiones*, 70.

[91] Nicholas Howe in his preface to the paperback edition. Howe, *Migration and Mythmaking*, p. xv.

[92] Gregory, *Geographical Imaginations*, 172.

[93] On the process that describes appropriation through a series of linguistic acts, see Stephen Greenblatt, *Marvelous Possessions: The Wonder of the New World* (Oxford: Clarendon Press, 1991), 57–8.

to quote Gregory once more, they 'become not only "people without history"... but also "people without geography" '.[94] As a result, their land is symbolically taken away from them.

The establishment of the Anglo-Saxon rule over Britain continues the Chronicle's exploitation of the symbolic potential inherent in names and naming. When, in the year 519, Cerdic and Cynric succeed to power, the entry reads: 'Her Cerdic 7 Cynric Westsexena rice onfengun 7 þy ilcan geare hie fuhton wiþ Brettas þær mon nu nemneþ Cerdicesford.'[95] The two appellations Cerdic and *Cerdicesford* furnish yet another example of the process according to which place generates leader.[96] But it is the name Cynric which interests me here; for Plummer and Earle note that 'it is possible that the name Cynric is an abstraction from this establishment of the "cynerice" '.[97] If this is the case, that is, if there never was an actual Germanic leader called Cynric, then this entry actually offers a legendary account of how the Anglo-Saxons came to have authority over Britain. Here, the existence of a Germanic chieftain is derived from a political concept, kingship. This passage thus associates the Anglo-Saxons with the establishment of *cynerice*, with the emergence of a new political organization. Proper names and place-names in the early annals of the Chronicle thus bring together not only the people and the land, but also political authority. The three terms of this equation create a territory, that is, the union of a land (Britain), of a people (the Anglo-Saxons), and of territorial control (the *cynerice*).

The Anglo-Saxon Chronicle presents an original account of the Germanic tribes' coming to Britain and of their subsequent conquest of the island. It does not attempt to mitigate the violence of the invasion and it clearly bases on military power and on fighting the right a people might have to possess a given tract of land. In addition to this martial argument, the Chronicle implements other strategies to justify the Anglo-Saxons' appropriation of Britain. A judicious recourse to genealogy enhances the wide-ranging connections, and the aura and prestige, of the Germanic rulers. The right the Anglo-Saxons have to the land of Britain is diversely underscored: the silence surrounding the invaders' precise continental origins, the parallel drawn between the Romans and the Anglo-Saxons, as well as the belittling of British history,

---

[94] Gregory, *Geographical Imaginations*, 130–1.
[95] 'In this year, Cerdic and Cynric succeeded to power and that same year they fought against the Britons at a place now called *Cerdicesford*' (*The Anglo-Saxon Chronicle*, 519, p. 20).
[96] *Saxon Chronicles*, ed. Plummer and Earle, ii. 12.   [97] Ibid, ii. 13.

all concord to rob Britain's former inhabitants of their past, and, as the analysis of names and naming has shown, of their geography.

CONCLUSION

The *adventus Saxonum* is a major landmark in the Anglo-Saxons' remembered history. The texts which allude to this event in the Old English corpus are numerous: Wulfstan mentions it at the end of the *Sermo Lupi ad Anglos*, the *Battle of Brunnanburh* celebrates the Anglo-Saxons' victory as a slaughter never seen since this people first came to Britain, Alcuin gauges the terror of the Viking attacks on Lindisfarne against the 350 years that the descendants of the Germanic tribes have spent in England.[98] This founding migration also influences the Anglo-Saxons' perception of spatiality, both of their immediate environment and of lands lying further away; for the memory of this event not only reminds them that they originally came from afar and that they are linked to a wider Germanic world,[99] but it also constantly allows them to rehearse their claim to the land of Britain.

Descriptions of Britain and narratives of migration are the two poles around which this chapter has revolved and I hope that, by reading the two together, I might have shed new light on the Anglo-Saxons' imaginary and imagined homeland(s). The *descriptiones Britanniae* present a space that is socially constructed and culturally encoded. Waiting to be possessed and enjoyed, Britain is imagined as a space which invites the migrations that are reported subsequently. It is true, as Howe observes, that in Bede's *Ecclesiastical History* and in the Anglo-Saxon Chronicle, the Germanic tribes 'did not find an empty island, as did those who

---

[98] See *The Anglo-Saxon Chronicle*, preface to MS A, p. 2; *Sermo Lupi ad Anglos*, ll. 184–99; the *Battle of Brunanburh* 65^b–73, in *The Anglo-Saxon Minor Poems*, ed. by Elliott van Kirk Dobbie, Anglo-Saxon Poetic Records, 6 (London: Routledge, 1942; repr. 1968), 16–20; 'Letter of Alcuin to Ethelred, king of Northumbria', in *English Historical Documents: c.500–1042*, 776. See also Bede, *Ecclesiastical History*, iv. 2, p. 334 and the *Chronicle of Æthelweard*, 1.

[99] For a testimony of the Anglo-Saxons' enduring memory of their continental roots, see Boniface's famous letter to the English people. In it, he encourages the English to convert the pagan continental Saxons who say 'de uno sanguine et de uno osse sumus'. Michael Tangl, ed., *Die Briefe des Heiligen Bonifatius und Lullus*, Monumenta Germaniae Historica, Epistolae Selectae, 1 (Munich: Monumenta Germaniae Historica, 1989; first pub. Berlin: Weidmann, 1916), 75. For a translation of the letter, see 'Letter of Boniface to the whole English Race', in *English Historical Documents*, 748.

settled Iceland, or a virgin land, as those who imagined America.'[100] But Howe also claims that 'having come to Britain as pagan mercenaries and then as conquerors of the native Celts in the fifth century A. D., the Anglo-Saxons could hardly indulge in edenic fantasies about the island as an unspoiled paradise'.[101] It cannot be gainsaid that in the fifth century the Germanic tribes did not disembark on an empty island when they reached Britain's shores. But it did not really prevent them from dreaming this place as having been a paradise waiting for their arrival, and Bede builds his text's early chapters around the images of the lost Eden and of the Promised Land. The paradox with which Anglo-Saxon authors had to work when imagining their settlement in Britain thus incited them to engage in a constant (re)definition of themselves and of their homeland. And the Germanic tribes, who for Gildas were a punishment sent by God, become for Bede a chosen people destined for great achievements in the Christian Church.

The Anglo-Saxon Chronicle does not inscribe the migration in a divine scheme of retribution. The Anglo-Saxons have to fight for Britain; their violent appropriation of British territory indicates that their right to the land is based on military conquest. Although with its records of battles and slaughters the Chronicle gives special weight to acts of dispossession, it counterbalances this violent bias with strategies aiming at securing the Anglo-Saxons' legitimate claims to Britain, using the invaders' genealogies and origins, the island's Roman past, and the symbolic value attached to names and naming. Descriptions of Britain and accounts of migration both open up new mental spaces for their audience. The former create a new spatial entity, a static space waiting to be conquered, while the latter contribute to a dynamic vision of space, raising questions of territorial distribution and land occupation. Although Bede's and Gildas's *descriptiones Britanniae* are heirs to a classical culture of space, and although the Anglo-Saxon Chronicle's recording of events is rooted in history, all are shaped by the *imaginaire* and are clearly indebted, in the way they map out and represent their environment, their homeland, as well as Britain's geographical situation in northern Europe, to space as a mental construct: they are profoundly informed by the complex and manifold symbolic values attributed to space and localization.

[100] Howe, 'Landscape', 92.   [101] Ibid., 92.

Conclusion

THE Greek historian Dionysius of Halicarnassus (fl. c.20 BC) reports, in his *Roman Antiquities*, the most elaborated version of a well-known Roman myth: the Capitol head.[1] It tells how, under the reign of Tarquinius Superbus, a temple dedicated to Jupiter was built on the Capitoline Hill in Rome. As the new sanctuary's foundations are being dug up, a human head is found buried in the ground. Roman soothsayers prove unable to make sense of this wonderful prodigy, but they admit that Etruscan seers have the necessary skills to interpret the sign. Consequently, the king sends an official delegation to the most famous of all Etruscan soothsayers. Before they meet him, the Roman envoys talk to his son, who informs them that his father will not lie—for this is not permitted to a soothsayer—but that he will try to lead them into error. This is how he will proceed: he will hear what the Romans have to say, and then, alleging that he did not fully understand what they meant, he will

> circumscribe with his staff some piece of ground or other; then he will say to you [them, the Romans]: 'This is the Tarpeian Hill, and this is the part of it that faces the east, this the part that faces the west, this point is north and the opposite is south.' These parts he will point out to you with his staff and then ask you in which of these parts the head was found. What answer, therefore, do I advise you to make? Do not admit that the prodigy was found in any of these places he shall inquire about when he points them out with his staff, but say that it appeared among you at Rome on the Tarpeian Hill. If you stick to these

---

[1] Dionysius of Halicarnassus 2. 4. 59. 2–61. 2, pp. 457–63. See also Livy 1. 55, pp. 88–9; Pliny the Elder 28. 4. 14–16, pp. 280–1; and Varro 5. 41, p. 26. *The Roman Antiquities of Dionysius of Halicarnassus*, ed. and trans. by Earnest Cary, 7 vols. (London: Heinemann, 1937–50; repr. 1961–71), ii (1961); *C. Plini Secundi: Naturalis Historiae: Libri* XXXVII, ed. by Charles Mayhoff, 5 vols. (Leipzig: Teubner, 1892–1909; repr. 1967–70), IV (1967); Tite-Live, *Histoire Romaine: Tome I: Livre I*, ed. by Jean Bayet, trans. by Gaston Baillet, rev. by Richard Adam, 15th edn. (Paris: Belles Lettres, 1997); and Varro, *De Lingua Latina: Livre V*, ed. and trans. by Jean Collart (Paris: Belles Lettres, 1954).

answers and do not allow yourselves to be misled by him, he, well knowing that fate cannot be changed, will interpret to you without concealment what the prodigy means.[2]

The Romans, duly warned, avoid the Etruscan's trick and the soothsayer eventually interprets the prodigy as announcing that the place where the head was found shall be the head of all Italy.

A thorough analysis of this complex and rich narrative is obviously beyond the scope of this Conclusion.[3] And yet, this episode distant in time and place from Anglo-Saxon England is worth pondering over, for it echoes many of the issues discussed in this book. In addition to underscoring the intimate relationship between language and acts of foundation—the mythical anecdote justifies Roman imperialist ambitions and the city's bright future is articulated by the seer who 'reads' the meaning of the severed head—the narrative also emphasizes the institution and the localization of power. Foretelling Rome's dominion over its neighbours, it symbolically anchors the city's expansionist impulses in a precise time (Tarquinius's reign, at the time when Jupiter's temple was being built) and place (the Capitol or, more precisely, the foundations of the sanctuary dedicated to the greatest of all Roman gods). But crucially here the prodigy of the head is not enough to ensure Rome's greatness. To become irrevocable, the oracular sign needs the soothsayer's mediation and interpretation.

But why an Etruscan diviner? Historically speaking, the Romans did indeed largely borrow their art of divination from the Etruscans. But beside this traditional explanation, the relocation of the source of knowledge away from Rome also lends itself to political and ideological interpretations. This mythical narrative presents a wise outsider acknowledging, and thus at the same time accepting, Rome's pre-eminence. Furthermore, it is his very son who helps the Roman envoys avoid the trap they might fall into when consulting his father. In so doing, he anticipates the latter's elucidation of the omen, namely the seer's avowal that the eternal city has been granted an exceptional political and military fortune. More generally, the soothsayer and his son figure the awareness of those who will eventually be dominated that they 'need' to be ruled by foreigners, that they cannot by themselves achieve self-determination. In this, the son's co-operation with the Roman delegation recalls the

---

[2] Dionysius of Halicarnassus, *The Roman Antiquities* 2. 4. 60. 3–4, p. 461.
[3] On this episode, and especially on its narrative context, see Philippe Borgeaud, *Exercices de mythologie* (Geneva: Labor et Fides, 2004), 157–77.

negative portrayals of the Britons analysed in Chapter 7, portrayals that characterize them as unable to defend their best interests, as deprived of any agency in the forging of an independent destiny.

The trick the Etruscan seer threatens to play on his Roman visitors betrays the arbitrariness inherent in the location of power and in the establishment of sovereignty. Before interpreting the meaning of the bloody head found on the Capitol, the oracle attempts to move the fount of power and to appropriate it for his people. When he points to his rudimentary map and asks if this is where the head has been found, the soothsayer is 'literalizing' representation and he is playing on the ambiguity surrounding the precise place he is designating: is it a site figured on the map, that is, the Capitoline Hill, or is it the Etruscan soil on which he has drawn the chart? Does his deictic point at the map or at the ground? The diviner hopes that representation—his rough map—might work as a smokescreen allowing him to displace the head, that is, the source of authority. Then sovereignty would escape Rome: it would be usurped and the eternal city be deprived of its destiny. While seemingly confirming, on the map, the place where the omen was found, the oracle plans to relocate it. In so doing, he exposes the complex interplay that unites symbolic representation and an actual location rooted in the ground. The myth of the Capitol head reminds us that an imaginary territory needs to be attached somehow to an external reality, while at the same time revealing that an actual site—the Etruscan ground at which his staff points—is also a symbolic point in space, that place is always already inscribed in an *imaginaire*.

The myth of the Capitol head works to anchor Rome in Rome, and its collective identity hinges on the fidelity to a particular site. Rome's early history is not told in terms of autochthony, that is, it does not resort to a myth which sees a population emerging from the ground on which the city is subsequently built. Romulus, after killing his twin brother Remus, increases the population of his embryonic settlement by offering asylum to exiles and fugitives. The link between people and land may thus seem arbitrary, and even disputable: Rome's future inhabitants come from elsewhere and the city's foundation is associated with an act of violence—Remus's death. The myth of the Capitol head, one among many such myths, counters this arbitrariness: it is a rite of fixation fostering the sense of a common destiny.[4]

---

[4] See Borgeaud, *Exercices*, 164.

There are, as Marcel Detienne reminds us, different ways to lay claim to a place and to produce a 'territory'.[5] Migration, as articulated over and over again by Old English authors, is one of them. The Anglo-Saxons remembered that they were not native to Britain and they cultivated the memory of their distant origins. Their imagined history and their sense of place were infused by the thought that they came from elsewhere. Despite Nicholas Howe's optimistic belief that stories of migration might provide a possible corrective against the sense of triumphalism that comes when a population believes that it has always lived in a place and that it is self-righteously convinced of its right to land possession, the Anglo-Saxons' versions of their myth of migration do not really betray an awareness that things might have been different.[6] For a careful study of their spatial *imaginaire* inevitably draws attention to the many and various 'fixation rites' which they elaborated to secure their claim and their control over England.

This study began with uncertainty on how to understand the spatial representations and the geographical descriptions found in the Old English literary corpus; for some intriguing inconsistencies can be detected in the elaboration of a poetic space. In *Beowulf* or in *Guthlac A*, the poet depicts the same location once as an unknown place hidden from men, and once as an outstanding feature in the countryside. If these variations may be ascribed to the literary effects of poetic geography, similar phenomena occur in works with a stronger claim faithfully to mirror the external world. Bede, for instance, presents two different geographies in his scientific writings and in the *Ecclesiastical History*'s opening lines. In the former, Britain is part of the known world, it is just one in a series of lands extending toward the north; in the latter, the historian describes his own island as clearly isolated from continental Europe. Also intriguing is the Anglo-Saxon Chronicle's silencing of the continental origins of the first Anglo-Saxon invaders. These ambiguities incited me to consider in more detail both the Anglo-Saxons' sense of space and their imaginary geography, examining how they organized and represented space in their works of literature. A series of questions structured and stimulated

---

[5] Marcel Detienne, *Comment être autochtone: du pur Athénien au Français raciné* (Paris: Seuil, 2003), esp. 14–15.
[6] See Howe's preface to the paperback edition. Nicholas Howe, *Migration and Mythmaking in Anglo-Saxon England* (Notre Dame: University of Notre Dame Press, 2001; first publ. New Haven: Yale University Press, 1989), p. xv. See also Nicholas Howe, 'Introduction', in Nicholas Howe (ed.), *Home and Homelessness in the Medieval and Renaissance World* (Notre Dame, IN: University of Notre Dame Press, 2004), 8.

my reflections. First, most obvious: how did the Anglo-Saxons organize and represent space? But also: are there points of contact uniting the imaginary spaces emerging from the Old English poetic and historiographic corpuses? How should one understand the spatial features and geographical descriptions set up in Old English texts? What can it tell us of the Anglo-Saxons' perception of what is at stake in geographical positioning? What are the modalities according to which one relates to a place? How are homeland and territory imagined and appropriated?

This last question in particular brought to light the many fixation rites scattered throughout the Anglo-Saxons' works of literature. In addition to the motif of migration which replays their original journey away from a continental homeland toward the British Isles as the Hebrews' wanderings through the desert in search of the Promised Land, the Anglo-Saxons' claim to the land is obsessively asserted. To possess and to rule over space is a constant concern in the texts examined in the preceding pages, as is the desire to explore and to map distant regions. Symbolic gestures, for instance when characters step on the ground or when they trace new paths in an indefinite landscape, signal spatial domination. Enclosures, boundaries, and a need to control who dwells where, delimit a territory and its extension. Finally, the emergence of a new centrality around one's homeland and the various recentring attempts operating in the Old English literary corpus foreground the intimate links between localization, identity, and collective destiny. All these strategies, which inform the Anglo-Saxons' spatial *imaginaire*, also aim to anchor the descendants of the Germanic tribes in the land they reached at the end of their migration, and they contribute to the emergence of a territory, which is, according to Zumthor, the union of human beings and space.[7]

This book, I hope, has gone beyond inquiring how a population symbolically relates to its environment. For to study a spatial *imaginaire* raises wide-reaching issues; articulating a collective sense of self in geographical terms, it reveals who we are but also, reorganizing collective memory, who we wish we had been and, containing human history, who we think we will be.

[7] Paul Zumthor, *La Mesure du Monde* (Paris: Seuil, 1993), 78.

Select Bibliography

PRIMARY TEXTS

Acta Sanctorum, ed. by Godfried Henschen and Daniel Papebroch, Maius, 1 (Antwerp, 1680).

[ÆLFRIC], *The Old English Version of the Heptateuch: Ælfric's Treatise on the Old and New Testament and his Preface to Genesis*, ed. by S. J. Crawford, EETS os. 160 (London: Oxford University Press, 1922).

—— *De Temporibus Anni*, ed. by Heinrich Henel, EETS os. 213 (London: Oxford University Press, 1942).

—— *Ælfric's Catholic Homilies. The First Series Text*, ed. by Peter Clemoes, EETS ss. 17 (Oxford: Oxford University Press, 1997).

[ÆTHELWEARD], *The Chronicle of Æthelweard*, ed. by A. Campbell (London: Nelson, 1962).

Andreas and the Fates of the Apostles, ed. by Kenneth R. Brooks (Oxford: Clarendon Press, 1961).

[Andreas] *The Acts of Andrew in the Country of the Cannibals*, trans. by Robert Boenig, Garland Library of Medieval Literature, 70 (New York: Garland, 1991).

Anglo-Saxon and Old English Vocabularies, ed. by Thomas Wright, 2nd edn., ed. by Richard Paul Wülcker, 2 vols. (London: Trübner, 1884).

[Anglo-Saxon Chronicle] *The Parker Chronicle (832–900)*, ed. by A. H. Smith (London: Methuen, 1935; repr. 1954).

The Anglo-Saxon Chronicle, trans. by Dorothy Whitelock (London: Eyre and Spottiswoode, 1961; repr. 1965).

The Anglo-Saxon Chronicle, trans. by G. N. Garmonsway (London: Dent, 1953; repr. 1972).

[Anglo-Saxon Chronicle] *Two of the Saxon Chronicles Parallel*, ed. by Charles Plummer and John Earle, reissued by Dorothy Whitelock, 2 vols. (Oxford: Clarendon Press, 1892–9; repr. 1980).

[Anglo-Saxon Chronicle] *The Anglo-Saxon Chronicle: A Collaborative Edition: III MS A.*, ed. by Janet Bately (Cambridge: Brewer, 1986).

The Anglo-Saxon Minor Poems, ed. by Elliott van Kirk Dobbie, Anglo-Saxon Poetic Records, 6 (London: Routledge, 1942; repr. 1968).

Anglo-Saxon Poetry, trans. by S. A. J. Bradley (London: Dent, 1982).

Anonymi Leidensis De Situ Orbis Libri Duo, ed. by Riccardo Quadri (Padua: Antemore, 1954).

ASSER, *Life of King Alfred*, ed. by W. H. Stevenson (Oxford: Clarendon Press, 1904; repr. 1959).

[ASSER] *Alfred the Great: Asser's* Life of Alfred *and Other Contemporary Sources*, ed. and trans. by Simon Keynes and Michael Lapidge (London: Penguin, 1983).

[BEDE] *Bedae Venerabilis: Opera: Pars* II: *Opera Exegetica 2*, ed. by D. Hurst, Corpus Christianorum Series Latina, 119 (Turnhout: Brepols, 1962).

Bede's Ecclesiastical History of the English People, ed. and trans. by Bertram Colgrave and R. A. B. Mynors (Oxford: Clarendon Press, 1969; repr. 1991).

[BEDE], *Bedae Venerabilis: Opera: Pars* VI: *Opera Didascalica*, ed. by C. W. Jones, Corpus Christianorum Series Latina, 123 B (Turnhout: Brepols, 1975).

[———] *The Old English Version of Bede's Ecclesiastical History of the English People*, ed. and trans. by Thomas Miller, EETS os. 95 and 96, 2 vols. (London: Oxford University Press, 1890–1; repr. 1997).

[*Beowulf*] *The Deeds of Beowulf*, trans. by John Earle (Oxford: Clarendon Press, 1892).

Beowulf and the Fight at Finnsburg, ed. by F. Klaeber, 3rd edn. (Lexington, MA: Heath, 1922; repr. 1950).

Beowulf and Judith, ed. by Elliott van Kirk Dobbie, Anglo-Saxon Poetic Records, 4 (London: Routledge and Kegan Paul, 1953).

Beowulf, trans. by E. T. Donaldson, in *The Norton Anthology of English Literature*, ed. by M. H. Abrams and others, 6th edn., 2 vols. (New York: Norton, 1962; repr. 1993), 27–68.

Beowulf: A Student Edition, ed. by George Jack (Oxford: Clarendon Press, 1994).

Beowulf: An Edition with Relevant Shorter Texts, ed. by Bruce Mitchell and Fred C. Robinson (Oxford: Blackwell, 1998).

Beowulf, trans. by Kevin Crossley-Holland (Oxford: Oxford University Press, 1999).

Beowulf, trans. by Seamus Heaney (London: Faber and Faber, 1999).

[Bible] *The Holy Bible: Containing the Old and New Testaments: Translated out of the Original Tongues: and with the Former Translations Diligently Compared and Revised by His Majesty's Special Command* (New York: Nelson, [n.d.])

Biblia Sacra iuxta Vulgatam Versionem, ed. by Bonifatius Fischer and others, rev. by Robert Weber, 3rd edn. (Stuttgart: Deutsche Bibelgesellschaft, 1969; repr. 1983).

Bibliothek der Angelsächsischen Poesie, ed. by Christian W. M. Grein, rev. by Richard Paul Wülker, 3 vols. (Kassel: Wigand, 1883–98).

[BONIFACE], *Die Briefe des Heiligen Bonifatius und Lullus*, ed. by Michael Tangl, Monumenta Germaniae Historica, Epistolae Selectae, 1 (Munich: Monumenta Germaniae Historica, 1989; first publ. Berlin: Weidmann, 1916).

The Book of Settlements: Landnámabók, trans. by Herman Pálsson and Paul Edwards, Icelandic Studies, 1 (Winnipeg: University of Manitoba, 1972).

Bright's Old English Grammar and Reader, ed. by Frederic G. Cassidy and Richard N. Ringler, 3rd edn. (New York: Holt, Rinehart and Winston, 1891; repr. 1971).

The Cædmon Poems, trans. by Charles Kennedy (London: Routledge, 1916).

[CAESAR] César, *Guerre des Gaules*, ed. and trans. by L.-A. Constans, rev. by A. Balland, 2 vols. (Paris: Belles Lettres, 1995–6).

[*Christ*] *The Advent Lyrics of the Exeter Book*, ed. by Jackson J. Campbell, (Princeton: Princeton University Press, 1959).

Christ and Satan: A Critical Edition, ed. by Robert Emmett Finnegan (Waterloo, Ontario: Laurier University Press, 1977).

Daniel and Azarias, ed. by R. T. Farrell (London: Methuen, 1974).

Dicuili Liber de Mensura Orbis Terrae, ed. and trans. by J. J. Tierney, Scriptores Latini Hiberniae, 6 (Dublin: Dublin Institute for Advanced Studies, 1967).

[DIONYSIUS OF HALICARNASSUS], *The Roman Antiquities of Dionysius of Halicarnassus*, ed. and trans. by Earnest Cary, 7 vols. (London: Heinemann, 1937–50; repr. 1961–71).

[EINHARD] Eginhard, *Vie de Charlemagne*, ed. and trans. by Louis Halphen, 4th edn. (Paris: Belles Lettres, 1938, repr. 1967).

[*Elene*] *Cynewulf's 'Elene'*, ed. by P. O. E. Gradon (Exeter: University of Exeter, 1977; first publ. London: Methuen, 1958).

An Eleventh-Century Anglo-Saxon Illustrated Miscellany, ed. by P. McGurk and others, Early English Manuscripts in Facsimile, 21 (Copenhagen: Rosenkilde and Bagger, 1983), 79–87.

English Historical Documents: c. 500–1042, ed. by Dorothy Whitelock (London: Eyre and Spottiswoode, 1955).

The Exeter Book, ed. by George Philip Krapp and Elliott van Kirk Dobbie, Anglo-Saxon Poetic Records, 3 (New York: Columbia University Press, 1936; repr. 1966).

[*Exodus*] *The Old English Exodus*, ed. by Edward Burroughs Irving, Jr., Yale Studies in English, 122 (New Haven: Yale University Press, 1953).

Exodus, ed. by Peter J. Lucas (London: Methuen, 1977).

[*Exodus*] *The Old English Exodus: Text, Translation and Commentary by J. R. R. Tolkien*, ed. by Joan Turville-Petre (Oxford: Clarendon Press, 1981).

Felix's Life of Saint Guthlac, ed. and trans. by Bertram Colgrave (Cambridge: Cambridge University Press, 1956).

Genesis A: A New Edition, ed. by A. N. Doane (Madison: University of Wisconsin Press, 1978).

[*Genesis B*] *The Saxon Genesis*, ed. by A. N. Doane (Madison: University of Wisconsin Press, 1991).

GILDAS, *The Ruin of Britain and Other Works*, ed. and trans. by Michael Winterbottom (London: Phillimore, 1978).

The Gospel according to Saint Luke and according to Saint John, ed. by Walter W. Skeat (Cambridge: Cambridge University Press, 1874; repr. Darmstadt: Wissenschaftliche Buchgesellschaft, 1970).

[Gregory] *S. Gregorii Magni: Registrum Epistularum Libri VIII–XIV, Appendix*, ed. by Dag Norberg, Corpus Christianorum Series Latina, 140A (Turnhout: Brepols, 1982).

[*Guthlac*], *Das angelsächsische Prosa-Leben des hl. Guthlac*, ed. by Paul Gonser, Anglistische Forschungen, 27 (Heidelberg: Carl Winter, 1909).

The Guthlac Poems of the Exeter Book, ed. by Jane Roberts (Oxford: Clarendon Press, 1979).

A Hand-Book to the Land Charters and other Saxonic Documents, ed. by John Earle (Oxford: Clarendon Press, 1888).

Isidori Hispalensis Episcopi: Etymologiarum Sive Originum: Libri xx, ed. by W. M. Lindsay, 2 vols. (Oxford: Clarendon Press, 1911; repr. 1985).

Íslendingabók: Landnámabók, ed. by Jakob Benediktsson, Íslenzk Fornrit, 1 (Reykjavík: Hið Íslenzka Fornritfélag, 1968).

Judith, ed. by B. J. Timmer (London: Methuen, 1952).

Judith, ed. by Mark Griffith (Exeter: University of Exeter Press, 1997).

The Junius Manuscript, ed. by George Philip Krapp, Anglo-Saxon Poetic Records, 1 (New York: Columbia University Press, 1931; repr. 1964).

The Laws of the Earliest English Kings, ed. and trans. by F. L. Attenborough (New York: Russel and Russel, 1922; repr. 1963).

[Livy] Tite-Live, *Histoire Romaine: Tome I: Livre I*, ed. by Jean Bayet, trans. by Gaston Baillet, rev. by Richard Adam, 15th edn. (Paris: Belles Lettres, 1997).

Old English Minor Poems, ed. by Joyce Hill, Durham and St Andrews Medieval Texts, 4 (Durham: Durham and St Andrews Medieval Texts, 1983).

The Oldest English Texts, ed. by Henri Sweet, EETS os. 83 (London: Oxford University Press, 1885; repr. 1966).

[Orosius], *The Old English Orosius*, ed. by Janet Bately, EETS ss. 6 (Oxford: Oxford University Press, 1980).

—— *Histoires (Contre les Païens)*, ed. and trans. by Marie-Pierre Arnaud-Lindet, 3 vols. (Paris: Belles Lettres, 1990–1).

[Pliny], *C. Plini Secundi: Naturalis Historiae: Libri* xxxvii, ed. by Charles Mayhoff, 5 vols. (Leipzig: Teubner, 1892–1909; repr. 1967–70).

[Pytheas] Roseman, Christina Horst, *Pytheas of Massalia: On the Ocean: Text, Translation and Commentary* (Chicago: Ares, 1994).

[Solinus], *C. Iulii Solini: Collectanea Rerum Memorabilium*, ed. by T. Mommsen (Berlin: Weidmann, 1895; repr. 1958).

[Strabo], *The Geography of Strabo*, ed. and trans. by H. L. Jones, 8 vols. (London: Heinemann, 1917–32; repr. 1966–70).

Sweet's Anglo-Saxon Reader, rev. D. Whitelock, 15th edn. (Oxford: Clarendon Press, 1967; repr. 1988).

[Tacitus] Tacite, *Vie d'Agricola*, ed. and trans. by E. de Saint-Denis (Paris: Belles Lettres, 1942; repr. 1967).

THIETMAR VON MERSEBURG, *Chronik*, ed. by Werner Trillmich, Ausgewählte Quellen zur Deutschen Geschichte des Mittelalters, 9 (Darmstadt: Wissenschaftliche Buchgesellschaft, 1957; repr. 1970).
[VARRO] Varron, *De Lingua Latina: Livre V*, ed. and trans. by Jean Collart (Paris: Belles Lettres, 1954).
The Vercelli Book, ed. by George Philip Krapp, Anglo-Saxon Poetic Records, 2 (New York: Columbia University Press, 1932; repr. 1961).
[VIRGIL] Virgile, *Enéide: Livres I–IV*, ed. and trans. by Jacques Perret, rev. by R. Lesueur, 2nd edn. (Paris: Belles Lettres, 1999).
[WIDUKIND], *Quellen zur Geschichte der Sächsischen Kaiserzeit: Widukinds Sachsengeschichte, Adalberts Fortsetzung der Chronik Reginos, Liudprands Werke*, ed. by Albert Bauer and Reinhold Rau with the transl. of Paul Hirsch, Max Büdinger, and Wilhelm Wattenbach, Ausgewählte Quellen zur Deutschen Geschichte des Mittelalters, 8 (Darmstadt: Wissenschaftliche Buchgesellschaft, 1971).
[WULFSTAN], *Sermo Lupi ad Anglos*, ed. by Dorothy Whitelock (London: Methuen, 1963).

SECONDARY TEXTS

ABRAHAM, LEONORE, 'Cædmon's *Hymn* and the 'geþwærnysse' (Fitness) of Things', *American Benedictine Review*, 43 (1992), 331–44.
ABULAFIA, DAVID, and NORA BEREND (eds.), *Medieval Frontiers: Concepts and Practices* (Aldershot: Ashgate, 2002).
ALAMICHEL, MARIE-FRANÇOISE, 'Voyage dans les paysages du *Beowulf*', in Marie-Françoise Alamichel (ed.), *Beowulf: Symbolismes et interprétations* (Paris: Éditions du Temps, 1998), 87–106.
ANDERSON, BENEDICT, *Imagined Communities: Reflections on the Origin and Spread of Nationalism* (London: Verso, 1983; repr. 1989).
ANDERSON, EARL R., *Cynewulf: Structure, Style and Theme in his Poetry* (Rutherford, NJ: Fairleigh Dickinson University Press, 1983).
ANDERSON, GEORGE K., *The Literature of the Anglo-Saxons* (New York: Russel and Russel, 1962).
An Anglo-Saxon Dictionary, ed. by J. Bosworth and T. N. Toller (Oxford: Oxford University Press, 1882–98), with a *Supplement* by N. T. Toller (Oxford: Oxford University Press, 1921).
ARNAUD, PASCAL, 'L'Affaire Mettius Pompusianus ou le crime de cartographie', *Mélanges de l'École Française de Rome. Antiquité*, 95 (1983), 677–99.
AUGÉ, MARC, 'Eroi', in *Enciclopedia Einaudi*, ed. by Giulio Einaudi, 16 vols. (Turin: Einaudi, 1977–82), v. 636–56.
BAKHTIN, MIKHAIL, *The Dialogic Imagination: Four Essays by M. M. Bakhtin*, trans. by Caryl Emerson and Michael Holquist (Austin: University of Texas Press, 1981).

BARNEY, STEPHEN A., *Word-Hoard: An Introduction to Old English Vocabulary* (New Haven: Yale University Press, 1977).
BATELY, JANET M., 'The Relationship between Geographical Information in the *Old English Orosius* and Latin Texts other than Orosius', *Anglo-Saxon England*, 1 (1972), 45–62.
—— 'Old English Prose before and during the Reign of Alfred', *Anglo-Saxon England*, 17 (1988), 93–138.
BATTLES, PAUL, '*Genesis A* and the Anglo-Saxon "migration myth" ', *Anglo-Saxon England*, 29 (2000), 43–66.
BAUDET, HENRY, *Paradise on Earth: Some Thoughts on European Images of Non-European Man*, trans. by Elisabeth Wentholt (New Haven: Yale University Press, 1965).
BERESFORD, MAURICE, *The Lost Villages of England*, rev. edn. (London: Lutterworth, 1954; repr. Phoenix Mill: Sutton Publishing, 1983).
—— *History on the Ground*, rev. edn. (London: Lutterworth, 1957; repr. Phoenix Mill: Sutton Publishing, 1998).
BESSINGER, J. B. Jr., 'Homage to Cædmon and Others: A Beowulfian Praise Song', in Robert B. Burlin and Edward B. Irving, Jr. (eds.), *Old English Studies in Honour of John C. Pope* (Toronto: University of Toronto Press, 1974), 91–106.
—— *A Concordance to the Anglo-Saxon Poetic Records* (Ithaca, NY: Cornell University Press, 1978).
BJORK, ROBERT E., 'Oppressed Hebrews and the Song of Azarias in the Old English *Daniel*', *Studies in Philology*, 77 (1980), 213–26.
—— *The Old English Verse Saints' Lives: A Study in Direct Discourse and the Iconography of Style*, McMaster Old English Studies and Texts, 4 (Toronto: University of Toronto Press, 1985).
—— 'Speech as Gift in Beowulf', *Speculum*, 69 (1994), 993–1022.
BOLTON, D. K., 'The Study of the Consolation of Philosophy in Anglo-Saxon England', *Archives d'Histoire Doctrinale et Littéraire du Moyen Age*, 44 (1977), 33–78.
BORGEAUD, PHILIPPE, *Exercices de mythologie* (Geneva: Labor et Fides, 2004).
BREEZE, ANDREW, '*Exodus*, *Elene* and the *Rune Poem*: *milpæþ*, "Army Road, Highway" ', *Notes and Queries*, NS 38 (1991), 436–8.
BRIDGES, MARGARET ENID, *Generic Contrast in Old English Hagiographical Poetry*, Anglistica, 23 (Copenhagen: Rosenkilde and Bagger, 1984).
—— 'Of Myths and Maps: the Anglo-Saxon Cosmographer's Europe', *SPELL*, 6 (1992), 69–84.
—— 'Discours du réel, discours de l'imaginaire: cours et étendues d'eau dans la *Descriptio Britanniae* médiévale', in *Sources et fontaines du moyen âge à l'âge baroque*, Colloques, Congrès et Conférences sur la Renaissance, 12 (Paris: Champion, 1998), 13–30.

BROWN, PETER, *The Cult of the Saints: Its Rise and Function in Latin Christianity* (Chicago: University of Chicago Press, 1981).
BUISSERET, DAVID, *The Mapmaker's Quest: Depicting New Worlds in Renaissance Europe* (Oxford: Oxford University Press, 2003).
CALDER, DANIEL G., 'Setting and Ethos: The Pattern of Measure and Limit in *Beowulf*', *Studies in Philology*, 69 (1972), 21–37.
—— '*Guthlac A* and *Guthlac B*: Some Discriminations', in Lewis E. Nicholson and Dolores Warwick Frese (eds.), *Anglo-Saxon Poetry: Essays in Appreciation: For John G. McGaillard* (Notre Dame, IN: University of Notre Dame Press, 1975), 65–80.
—— *Cynewulf* (Boston: Twayne, 1981).
CAMPBELL, JAMES, ERIC JOHN, and PATRICK WORMALD, *The Anglo-Saxons* (London: Penguin, 1991; first publ. London: Phaidon, 1982).
CARR, CHARLES T., *Nominal Compounds in Germanic*, St Andrews University Publications, 41 (London: Oxford University Press, 1939).
CASEY, EDWARD S., *Representing Place: Landscape Painting and Maps* (Minneapolis: University of Minnesota Press, 2002).
Catalogue général des manuscrits des bibliothèques publiques des départements, i (Paris: Imprimerie Nationale, 1849).
ČERMÁK, JAN, '*Hie dygel lond warigeað*: Spatial Imagery in Five Beowulf Compounds', *Linguistica Pragensia*, 1 (1996), 24–34.
CLEMOES, PETER, *Interactions of Thought and Language in Old English Poetry*, Cambridge Studies in Anglo-Saxon England, 12 (Cambridge: Cambridge University Press, 1995).
COHEN, JEFFREY JEROME, 'Old English Literature and the Work of Giants', *Comitatus*, 24 (1993), 1–32.
CONWAY, CHARLES ABBOTT, 'Structure and Idea in "Cædmon's Hymn"', *Neuphilologische Mitteilungen*, 96 (1995), 39–50.
CRONAN, DENNIS, 'The Origin of Ancient Strife in *Beowulf*', *Germanic Studies in Honour of Anatoly Liberman: North-Western European Language Evolution (NOWELE)*, 31–2 (1997), 57–68.
CROSS, J. E., 'English Vernacular Saints' Lives before 1000 AD', in Guy Philippart (ed.), *Hagiographies: Histoire internationale de la littérature hagiographique latine et vernaculaire en Occident des origines à 1550*, 2 vols. (Turnhout: Brepols, 1994–), ii (1996), 413–27.
DAVIS, KATHLEEN, 'National Writing in the Ninth Century: A Reminder for Postcolonial Thinking about the Nation', *Journal of Medieval and Early Modern Studies*, 28 (1998), 611–37.
DAY, DAVID D., 'Hands across the Hall: The Legalities of Beowulf's Fight with Grendel', *Journal of English and Germanic Philology*, 98 (1999), 313–24.
DE JONG, MAYKE, and FRANS THEUWS, 'Topographies of Power: Some Conclusions', in Mayke De Jong and Frans Theuws, with Carine van Rhijn (eds.),

Topographies of Power in the Early Middle Ages, The Transformation of the Roman World, 6 (Leiden: Brill, 2001), 533–45.
DEROLEZ, RENÉ, '*Genesis*: Old Saxon and Old English', *English Studies*, 76 (1995), 402–23.
DESTOMBES, MARCEL, *Mappemondes: AD 1200–1500* (Amsterdam: Israel, 1964).
DETIENNE, MARCEL, *Comment être autochtone: du pur Athénien au Français raciné* (Paris: Seuil, 2003).
Dictionary of Old English, ed. by A. diP. Healy and others (Toronto: Pontifical Institute of Medieval Studies, 1986–).
Dictionnaire de Théologie Catholique, ed. by A. Vacant and others, 21 vols. (Paris: Letouzey et Ané, 1903–72).
Dictionnaire Encyclopédique de la Bible, ed. by Centre: Informatique et Bible, Abbaye de Maredsous, resp. scient. Pierre-Maurice Bogaert and others ([Turnout]: Brepols, 1987).
DINAPOLI, ROBERT, 'Poesis and Authority: Traces of an Anglo-Saxon "agon" in Cynewulf's *Elene*', *Neophilologus*, 82 (1988), 619–30.
DRAGLAND, S. L., 'Monster-Man in *Beowulf*', *Neophilologus*, 61 (1977), 606–18.
EARL, JAMES W., *Thinking about Beowulf* (Stanford, CA: Stanford University Press, 1994).
EDSON, EVELYN, *Mapping Time and Space* (London: British Library, 1997).
ÉLIADE, MIRCEA, *Patterns in Comparative Religions*, trans. by Rosemary Sheed (London: Sheed and Ward, 1958).
The New Encyclopaedia Britannica, ed. by Jacob Safra and others, 15th edn., 32 vols. (Chicago: Encyclopaedia Britannica, 2003).
FANGER, CLAIRE, 'Miracle as Prophetic Gospel: Knowledge, Power and the Design of the Narrative in *Daniel*', *English Studies*, 72 (1991), 123–35.
FINNEGAN, ROBERT EMMETT, 'The Old English *Daniel*: The King and his City', *Neuphilologische Mitteilungen*, 85 (1984), 194–211.
FONTAINE, JACQUES, 'De l'universalisme antique aux particularismes médiévaux: la conscience du temps et de l'espace dans l'antiquité tardive', in *Popoli e paesi nella cultura altomedievale*, 2 vols., Settimane di studio del Centro italiano di studi sull'alto medioevo, 29 (Spoleto: Centro Italiano di Studi sull'Alto Medioevo, 1983), 15–45.
FOOT, SARAH, 'The Making of *Angelcynn*: English Identity before the Norman Conquest', *Transactions of the Royal Historical Society*, 6th ser., 6 (1996), 25–49.
FOUCAULT, MICHEL, 'Of Other Spaces', *Diacritics*, 16 (1986), 22–7.
FRENK, JOACHIM (ed.), *Spatial Change in English Literature* (Trier: Wissenschaftlicher Verlag, 2000).
FRY, DONALD K., 'The Heroine on the Beach in *Judith*', *Neuphilologische Mitteilungen*, 68 (1967), 168–84.

FRYE, NORTHROP, *Anatomy of Criticism: Four Essays* (Princeton: Princeton University Press, 1957).
GAUTIER DALCHÉ, PATRICK, 'Tradition et renouvellement dans la représentation de l'espace géographique au XIe siècle', in *Géographie et culture: La représentation de l'espace du VIe au XIIe siècle* (Aldershot: Ashgate, 1997; first publ. in *Studi Medievali*, 24 (1983)), iv. 121–65.
—— *La 'Descriptio Mappae Mundi' de Hugues de Saint-Victor* (Paris: Études Augustiniennes, 1988).
—— 'De la glose à la contemplation. Place et fonction de la carte dans les manuscrits du haut Moyen Age', in *Géographie et culture: La représentation de l'espace du VIe au XIIe siècle* (Aldershot: Ashgate, 1997; first publ. in *Testo e immagine nell'alto medioevo*, Settimane di studio del Centro italiano di studi sull'alto medioevo, 41 (Spoleto: Centro Italiano di Studi sull'Alto Medioevo, 1994)), viii. 693–771.
—— 'Notes sur la "carte de Théodose II" et sur la "mappemonde de Théodulf d'Orléans" ', in *Géographie et Culture: La représentation de l'espace du VIe au XIIe siècle* (Aldershot: Ashgate, 1997; first publ. in *Geographica Antiqua*, 3–4 (1994–5)), ix. 91–107.
—— *Conférence d'Ouverture de M. Patrick Gautier Dalché: 8 janvier 2001*, École Pratique des Hautes Études: Sections des Sciences Historiques et Philologiques (Paris: La Sorbonne, 2002), 35–60.
—— 'Principes et modes de la représentation de l'espace géographique durant le haut moyen âge', in *Uomo e spazio nell'alto medioevo*, 2 vols., Settimane di studio del Centro italiano di studi sull'alto medioevo, 50 (Spoleto: Centro Italiano di Studi sull'Alto Medioevo, 2003), 117–50.
GELLING, MARGARET, 'The Landscape of *Beowulf*', *Anglo-Saxon England*, 31 (2002), 7–11.
GLORIE, F. (ed.), *Itineraria et alia geographica*, Corpus Christianorum Series Latina, 175 (Turnhout: Brepols, 1965).
GNEUSS, HELMUT, 'Bücher und Leser in England im zehnten Jahrhundert', in *Books and Libraries in Early England* (Aldershot: Variorum, 1996; first publ. in H. L. C. Tristram (ed.), *Medialität und mittelalterliche insulare Literatur*, Scriptoralia, 43 (Tübingen: Günter Narr, 1992)), iv. 104–31.
GODDEN, MALCOLM, 'Apocalypse and Invasion in Late Anglo-Saxon England', in Malcolm Godden, Douglas Gray, and Terry Hoad (eds.), *From Anglo-Saxon England to Early Middle English* (Oxford: Clarendon Press, 1994), 130–62.
—— and MICHAEL LAPIDGE (eds.), *The Cambridge Companion to Old English Literature* (Cambridge: Cambridge University Press, 1991; repr. 1994).
GOETZ, HANS-WERNER, 'Concepts of Realm and Frontiers from Late Antiquity to the Early Middle Ages: Some Preliminary Remarks', in Walter Pohl, Ian Wood, and Helmut Reimitz (eds.), *The Transformation of Frontiers from*

Late Antiquity to the Carolingians, The Transformation of the Roman World, 10 (Leiden: Brill, 2001), 73–82.

GORRICHON, M., 'La Bretagne dans la "Vie d'Agricola" de Tacite', in R. Chevallier (ed.), *Littérature Gréco-Romaine et Géographie Historique: Mélanges offerts à Roger Dion*, Caesarodunum, 9bis (Paris: Picard, 1974), 191–205.

GREENBLATT, STEPHEN, *Marvelous Possessions: The Wonder of the New World* (Oxford: Clarendon Press, 1991).

GREENFIELD, STANLEY B., *Hero and Exile: The Art of Old English Poetry* (London: Hambledon, 1989).

GREGORY, DEREK, *Geographical Imaginations* (Cambridge, MA: Blackwell, 1994).

GRIMM, JACOB, *Deutsche Mythologie*, 4th edn. by Elard Hugo Meyer, 3 vols. (Berlin: Dümmlers, 1875–8).

GROSZ, OLIVIER J. H., 'The Island of Exiles: A Note on *Andreas* 15', *English Language Notes*, 7 (1970), 241–2.

GRUNDY, G. B., 'The Development of the Meanings of Certain Anglo-Saxon Terms', *Archaeological Journal*, 99 (1943), 67–98.

HAINES, DOROTHY, 'Vacancies in Heaven: The Doctrine of Replacement and *Genesis A*', *Notes and Queries*, 44 (1997), 150–4.

HALL, J. R., 'Old English *Exodus* and the Sea of Contradiction', *Mediaevalia*, 9 (1986 for 1983), 25–44.

—— '*Daniel*, Line 610b', *The Explicator*, 45/2 (1987), 3–4.

—— '*Exodus* 448b, *helpendra pað*', *American Notes and Queries*, NS 5 (1992), 3–7.

HALVERSON, JOHN, 'The World of *Beowulf*', *Journal of English Literary History*, 36 (1969), 593–608.

HÄNGER, CHRISTIAN, *Die Welt im Kopf: Raumbilder und Strategie im Römischen Kaiserreich*, Hypomnemata, 136 (Göttingen: Vandenhoeck and Ruprecht, 2001).

HARLEY, J. B., and DAVID WOODWARD (eds.), *The History of Cartography*, 6 vols. (Chicago: University of Chicago Press, 1987–   ).

HARRISON, DICK, 'Invisible Boundaries and Places of Power: Notions of Liminality and Centrality in the Early Middle Ages', in Walter Pohl, Ian Wood, and Helmut Reimitz (eds.), *The Transformation of Frontiers From Late Antiquity to the Carolingians*, The Transformation of the Roman World, 10 (Leiden: Brill, 2001), 83–93.

HARSH, CONSTANCE, '*Christ and Satan*: The Measured Power of Christ', *Neuphilologische Mitteilungen*, 90 (1989), 243–53.

HARVEY, P. D. A., *Medieval Maps* (Toronto: University of Toronto Press, 1991).

—— *Mappa Mundi. The Hereford World Map* (London: British Library, 1996).

HELDER, WILLIAM, 'Abraham and the Old English *Exodus*', in Henk Aertsen and Rolph H. Bremmer, Jr. (eds.), *Companion to Old English Poetry* (Amsterdam: Vu University Press, 1994), 189–200.

HELMS, MARY W., *Ulysses' Sail: An Ethnographic Odyssey of Power, Knowledge, and Geographical Distance* (Princeton: Princeton University Press, 1988).

HERMANN, JOHN P., *Allegories of War: Language and Violence in Old English Poetry* (Ann Arbor: University of Michigan Press, 1989).

HIEATT, CONSTANCE B., 'The *Fates of the Apostles*: Imagery, Structure, and Meaning', in Robert E. Bjork (ed.), *Cynewulf: Basic Readings*, Basic Readings in Anglo-Saxon England, 4 (New York: Garland, 1996; first publ. in *Papers on Language and Literature*, 10 (1974)), 67–77.

—— 'Cædmon in Context: Transforming the Formula', *Journal of English and Germanic Philology*, 84 (1985), 485–97.

HILL, DAVID, *An Atlas of Anglo-Saxon England* (Oxford: Blackwell, 1981).

HILL, JOYCE, '*Widsið* and the Tenth Century', *Neuphilologische Mitteilungen*, 85 (1984), 305–15.

HILL, THOMAS D., 'Apocryphal Cosmography and the "stream uton sæ": A Note on *Christ and Satan*, lines 4–12', *Philological Quarterly*, 48 (1969), 550–4.

—— 'Hwyrftum scriþað: *Beowulf*, line 163', *Medieval Studies*, 33 (1971), 379–81.

—— 'Sapiential Structure and Figural Narrative in the Old English *Elene*', in R. E. Bjork (ed.), *Cynewulf: Basic Readings in Anglo-Saxon England*, 4 (New York: Garland (rev. version), 1996, 207–28 (first publ. in *Traditio*, 27 (1971) 159–77)).

HINES, JOHN, 'The Becoming of the English Identity: Material Culture and Language in Early Anglo-Saxon England', *Anglo-Saxon Studies in Archaeology and History*, 7 (1994), 49–59.

HODGKIN, R. H., *A History of the Anglo-Saxons*, 3rd edn., 2 vols. (Oxford: Clarendon Press, 1935; repr. 1952).

HOSKINS, W. G., *English Landscapes* (London: British Broadcasting Corporation, 1973).

HOWE, NICHOLAS, *The Old English Catalogue Poems*, Anglistica, 23 (Copenhagen: Rosenkilde and Bagger, 1985).

—— *Migration and Mythmaking in Anglo-Saxon England* (Notre Dame, IN: University of Notre Dame Press, 2001; first publ. New Haven: Yale University Press, 1989).

—— 'An Angle on this Earth: Sense of Place in Anglo-Saxon England', *Bulletin of the John Rylands University Library of Manchester*, 82 (2000), 3–27.

—— 'The Landscape of Anglo-Saxon England: Inherited, Invented, Imagined', in John Howe and Michael Wolfe (eds.), *Inventing Medieval Landscapes: Senses of Place in Western Europe* (Gainesville: University of Florida Press, 2002), 91–112.

Howe, Nicholas (ed.), *Home and Homelessness in the Medieval and Renaissance World* (Notre Dame, IN: University of Notre Dame Press, 2004).

—— and Michael Wolfe (eds.), *Inventing Medieval Landscapes: Senses of Place in Western Europe* (Gainesville: University of Florida Press, 2002).

Howlett, D. R., '"Se Giddes Begang" of the *Fates of the Apostles*', *English Studies*, 56 (1975), 385–9.

Hume, Kathryn, 'The Concept of the Hall in Old English Poetry', *Anglo-Saxon England*, 3 (1974), 63–74.

Huppé, Bernard F., *The Web of Words: Structural Analysis of the Old English Poems* Vainglory, The Wonders of Creation, The Dream of the Rood *and* Judith (Albany: State University of New York Press, 1970).

Irving, Edward B. Jr., *A Reading of* Beowulf (New Haven: Yale University Press, 1968).

—— 'New Notes on the Old English *Exodus*', *Anglia*, 90 (1972), 289–324.

—— *Rereading Beowulf* (Philadelphia: University of Pennsylvania Press, 1989).

Jacob, Christian, *L'Empire des cartes: approche théorique de la cartographie à travers l'histoire* (Paris: Albin Michel, 1992).

Jacquart, Danielle, 'Conférence de Mme Danielle Jacquart, Directeur d'études', in *Conférence d'Ouverture de M. Patrick Gautier Dalché: 8 janvier 2001*, École Pratique des Hautes Études: Sections des Sciences Historiques et Philologiques (Paris: La Sorbonne, 2002), 25–33.

Johnson, David F., 'The Fall of Lucifer in *Genesis A* and Two Anglo-Latin Royal Charters', *Journal of English and Germanic Philology*, 97 (1998), 500–21.

Kendall, Calvin B., 'Imitation and the Venerable Bede's *Historia Ecclesiastica*', in Margot H. King and Wesley M. Stevens (eds.), *Saints, Scholars and Heroes: Studies in Medieval Culture in Honour of Charles W. Jones*, 2 vols. (Collegeville, MN: Hill Monastic Manuscript Library, St John's Abbey and University, 1979), i. 161–90.

Kiser, Lisa J., '*Andreas* and the *lifes weg*: Convention and Innovation in Old English Metaphor', *Neuphilologische Mitteilungen*, 85 (1984), 65–75.

Klein, Bernhard, 'Constructing the Space of the Nation: Geography, Maps, and the Discovery of Britain in the Early Modern Period', *Journal for the Study of British Cultures*, 4 (1997), 11–29.

Kline, Naomi Reed, *Maps of Medieval Thought: The Hereford Paradigm* (Woodbridge: Boydell and Brewer, 2001).

Krapp, George Philip, 'Notes on the *Andreas*', *Modern Philology*, 2 (1904–5), 403–10.

Kruger, Stephen F., 'Oppositions and their Opposition in the Old English *Exodus*', *Neophilologus*, 78 (1994), 165–70.

Lapidge, Michael, and others (eds.), *The Blackwell Encyclopaedia of Anglo-Saxon England* (Oxford: Blackwell, 1999).

LARRINGTON, CAROLYNE, *A Store of Common Sense: Gnomic Theme and Style in Old Icelandic and Old English Wisdom Poetry* (Oxford: Clarendon Press, 1993).
LAVEZZO, KATHY, 'Another Country: Ælfric and the Production of English Identity', *New Medieval Literatures*, 3 (1999), 67–93.
LE DOEUFF, MICHÈLE, *Recherches sur l'imaginaire philosophique* (Paris: Payot, 1980).
LEE, ALVIN A., *The Guest-Hall of Eden: Four Essays on the Design of Old English Poetry* (New Haven: Yale University Press, 1972).
LEFEBVRE, HENRI, *La Production de l'espace* (Paris: Anthropos, 1974).
LE GOFF, JACQUES, 'Discorso di chiusura', in *Popoli e paesi nella cultura altomedievale*, 2 vols., Settimane di studio del Centro italiano di studi sull'alto medioevo, 29 (Spoleto: Centro Italiano di Studi sull'Alto Medioevo, 1983), 805–38.
—— *L'Imaginaire médiéval* (Paris: Gallimard, 1985).
—— 'Qu'est-ce que l'histoire de l'imaginaire', in *Sens et place des connaissances dans la société*, 3 vols. (Paris: Centre National de la Recherche Scientifique, 1986–7), i (1986), 217–50.
Lexikon des Mittelalters, ed. by Robert Auty and others, 10 vols. (Munich: Artemis, Winckler, and Lexma; Stuttgart: Metzler, 1980–99).
LIONARONS, JOYCE TALLY, 'Bodies, Buildings and Boundaries: Metaphors of Liminality in Old English and Old Norse', *Essays in Medieval Studies*, 11 (1994), 43–50.
—— 'Beowulf: Myth and Monsters', *English Studies*, 77 (1996), 1–14.
LOCHRIE, KARMA, 'Gender, Sexual Violence, and the Politics of War in the Old English *Judith*', in Britton J. Harwood and Gillian R. Overing (eds.), *Class and Gender in Early English Literature: Intersections* (Bloomington: Indiana University Press, 1994), 1–20.
LOHSE, B., 'Zu Augustins Engellehre', *Zeitschrift für Kirchengeschichte*, 70 (1959), 278–91.
LÖNNROTH, LARS, 'Iörð fannz æva né upphiminn: A Formula Analysis', in Ursula Dronke and others (eds.), *Speculum Norœnum: Norse Studies in Memory of Gabriel Turville-Petre* (Odense: Odense University Press, 1981), 310–27.
LÖW, MARTINA, *Raumsoziologie*, Suhrkamp Taschenbuch Wissenschaft, 1506 (Frankfurt: Suhrkamp, 2001).
LUCAS, PETER J., 'Loyalty and Obedience in the Old English *Genesis* and the Interpolation of *Genesis B* into *Genesis A*', *Neophilologus*, 76 (1992), 121–35.
MAGENNIS, HUGH, *Images of Community in Old English Poetry*, Cambridge Studies in Anglo-Saxon England, 18 (Cambridge: Cambridge University Press, 1996).
MALONE, KEMP, 'King Alfred's North: a Study in Medieval Geography', *Speculum*, 5 (1930), 139–67.

MANES, CHRISTOPHER, 'The Substance of Earth in *Beowulf*'s Song of Creation', *English Language Notes*, 31/4 (1994), 1–5.

MAYR-HARTING, HENRY, *The Coming of Christianity to Anglo-Saxon England* (London: Batsford, 1972).

MILLER, KONRAD, *Mappae Mundi: die ältesten Weltkarten*, 6 vols. (Stuttgart: Roth'sche, 1895–8).

MOLINARI, MARIA VITTORIA, 'La caduta degli angeli ribelli: considerazioni sulla *Genesis B*', *Annali, Istituto Orientale di Napoli (AION)*, Filologia Germanica, 18–19 (1985–6), 417–40.

MORLAND, LAURA, 'Cædmon and the Germanic Tradition', in J. M. Foley (ed.), *De Gustibus: Essays for Alain Renoir* (New York: Garland, 1992), 324–58.

NELSON, JANET L., 'Reconstructing a Royal Family: Reflections on Alfred, from Asser, chapter 2', in Ian Wood and Niels Lund (eds.), *People and Places in Northern Europe, 500–1600* (Woodbridge: Boydell, 1991), 47–66.

NEVILLE, JENNIFER, *Representations of the Natural World in Old English Poetry*, Cambridge Studies in Anglo-Saxon England, 27 (Cambridge: Cambridge University Press, 1999).

OGILVY, J. D. A., *Books Known to the English, 587–1066* (Cambridge, MA: Medieval Academy of America, 1967).

—— 'Books Known to the English, AD 597–1066: *Addenda et Corrigenda*', *Mediaevalia*, 7 (1981), 281–325.

OLSEN, KARIN E., 'The Dual Function of the Repetitious in Exodus 447–515', in L. A. J. R. Houwen and A. A. MacDonald (eds.), *Loyal Letters: Studies on Medieval Alliterative Poetry and Prose* (Groningen: Egbert Forsten, 1994), 55–70.

—— 'The Dichotomy of Land and Sea in the Old English *Andreas*', *English Studies*, 79 (1998), 385–94.

ORCHARD, ANDY, *Pride and Prodigies: Studies in the Monsters of the* Beowulf-Manuscript (Cambridge: Brewer, 1995).

OTTER, MONIKA, *Inventiones: Fiction and Referentiality in Twelfth-Century English Historical Writing* (Chapel Hill: University of North Carolina Press, 1996).

OVERING, GILLIAN R., 'The Women of *Beowulf* : A Context for Interpretation', in P. S. Baker (ed.), *Beowulf: Basic Readings*, Basic Readings in Anglo-Saxon England, 1 (New York: Garland, 1995), 219–60.

The Oxford English Dictionary, ed. by J. A. Simpson and E. S. C. Weiner, 2nd edn., 20 vols. (Oxford: Clarendon Press, 1989).

PÀROLI, TERESA, 'La soglia come cronotopo narrativo ed esistenziale nel medioevo germanico', in Paola Cabibbo (ed.), *Sulla soglia: questioni di liminalità in letteratura* (Rome: Il Calamo, 1993), 37–65.

POHL, WALTER, 'Conclusion: The Transformation of Frontiers', in Walter Pohl, Ian Wood, and Helmut Reimitz (eds.), *The Transformation of Frontiers from*

Late Antiquity to the Carolingians, The Transformation of the Roman World, 10 (Leiden: Brill, 2001), 247–60.

RACKHAM, OLIVER, *The Illustrated History of the Countryside* (London: Weidenfeld and Nicolson, 1994; repr. London: Phoenix Illustrated, 1997).

REMLEY, PAUL, *Old English Biblical Verse*, Cambridge Studies in Anglo-Saxon England, 16 (Cambridge: Cambridge University Press, 1996).

RENOIR, ALAIN, ' "Romigan ures rices": A Reconsideration', *Modern Language Notes*, 72 (1957), 1–4.

RICHARDS, MARY P., 'Anglo-Saxonism in the Old English Laws', in Allen J. Frantzen and John D. Niles (eds.), *Anglo-Saxonism and the Construction of Social Identity* (Gainseville: University Press of Florida, 1997), 40–59.

RICOEUR, PAUL, 'Mythe: l'Interprétation Philosophique', *Encyclopaedia Universalis*, xv (1989), 1041–8.

ROBINSON, FRED C., 'Names in Old English Literature', *Anglia*, 86 (1962), 14–58.

ROY, GOPA, 'The Anglo-Saxons and the Shape of the World', in Jane Roberts and Janet Nelson (eds.), *Essays on Anglo-Saxon and Related Themes in Memory of Lynne Grundy* (London: King's College London, 2000), 455–81.

RUSSELL, JEFFREY BURTON, *Inventing the Flat Earth* (New York: Praeger, 1991).

SAID, EDWARD W., *Orientalism: Western Conceptions of the Orient* (London: Penguin, 1978; repr. 1995).

—— *Culture and Imperialism* (London: Vintage, 1994).

SCHAAR, CLAES, *Critical Studies in the Cynewulf Group*, Lund Studies in English, 17 (Lund: Gleerup, 1949).

SCHNEIDER, UTE, *Die Macht der Karten: Eine Geschichte der Kartographie vom Mittelalter bis heute* (Darmstadt: Primus Verlag, 2004).

SCHREB, VICTOR, 'Setting and Cultural Memory in Part II of *Beowulf*', *English Studies*, 79 (1998), 109–19.

SCHWAB, UTE, 'The Miracles of Cædmon', *English Studies*, 64 (1983), 1–17.

—— *Einige Beziehungen zwischen altsächsischer und ängelsächsischer Dichtung*, Centro italiano di studi sull'alto medioevo, 8 (Spoleto: Centro Italiano di Studi sull'Alto Medioevo, 1988).

SHAW, BRIAN, 'Translation and Transformation in *Andreas*', in M. J. Toswell (ed.), *Prosody and Poetics in the Early Middle Ages: Essays in Honour of C. B. Hieatt* (Toronto: University of Toronto Press, 1995), 164–79.

SHEPHERD, GEOFFREY, 'Scriptural Poetry', in Eric G. Stanley (ed.), *Continuations and Beginnings: Studies in Old English Literature* (London: Nelson, 1966).

SIMPSON, JACQUELINE, *Everyday Life in the Viking Age* (London: Batsford, 1967).

SLEETH, CHARLES R., *Studies in 'Christ and Satan'* (Toronto: University of Toronto Press, 1982).

SMITH, ANTHONY D., *The Ethnic Origins of Nations* (Oxford: Blackwell, 1986).

SMITH, JONATHAN Z., and RICHARD G. A. BUXTON, 'Myth and Mythology', in *The New Encyclopaedia Britannica*, xxiv (2003), 715–32.
SMYTH, ALFRED P., *King Alfred the Great* (Oxford: Oxford University Press, 1995).
SØRENSEN, PREBEN MEULENGRACHT, 'Thor's Fishing Expedition', in Gro Steinsland (ed.), *Words and Objects: Towards a Dialogue between Archaeology and History of Religion*, Institute for Comparative Research in Human Culture. Serie B; Skrifter, 71 (Oslo: Norwegian University Press, 1986), 257–78.
STANLEY, ERIC G., *In the Foreground:* Beowulf (Cambridge: Brewer, 1994).
SZARMACH, PAUL E., M. TERESA TAVORMINA, and JOEL T. ROSENTHAL (eds.), *Medieval England: An Encyclopedia* (New York: Garland, 1998).
TAYLOR, PAUL BEEKMAN, 'Heorot, Earth and Asgard: Christian Poetry and Pagan Myth', *Tennessee Studies in Literature*, 11 (1966), 119–30.
THER, PHILIPP, 'Niemand will im Osten sein: Barbarisch, rückständig und despotisch: Die Erfindung Osteuropas von der Aufklärung bis heute', *Süddeutsche Zeitung am Wochenende*, 2–3 December 2000, p. I.
TODOROV, TZVETAN, *La Conquête de l'Amérique: la question de l'autre* (Paris: Seuil, 1982).
TOLKIEN, J. R. R., 'Beowulf: The Monsters and the Critics', in R. D. Fulk (ed.), *Interpretations of Beowulf: A Critical Anthology* (Bloomington: Indiana University Press, 1991; first publ. in *Proceedings of the British Academy*, 22 (1936), 245–95), 14–44.
—— *Finn and Hengest: The Fragment and the Episode* (London: Allen and Unwin, 1982).
TOLLEY, CLIVE, 'A Comparative Study of Some Germanic and Finnic Myths', D.Phil. thesis, Oxford, 1993.
TURVILLE-PETRE, THORLAC, *England the Nation: Language, Literature and National Identity, 1290–1340* (Oxford: Clarendon Press, 1996).
Uomo e spazio nell'alto medioevo, 2 vols., Settimane di studio del Centro italiano di studi sull'alto medioevo, 50 (Spoleto: Centro Italiano di Studi sull'Alto Medioevo, 2003).
VERGER, JACQUES, 'Conférence de M. Jacques Verger, Correspondant de l'Institut', in *Conférence d'Ouverture de M. Patrick Gautier Dalché: 8 janvier 2001*. École Pratique des Hautes Études: Sections des Sciences Historiques et Philologiques (Paris: La Sorbonne, 2002), 11–24.
VICKREY, JOHN F., 'The Vision of Eve in *Genesis B*', *Speculum*, 44 (1969), 86–102.
VIDIER, A., 'La Mappemonde de Théodulfe et la mappemonde de Ripoll', *Bulletin de géographie historique et descriptive*, 26 (1911), 285–318.
WALLACE-HADRILL, J. M., *Bede's* Ecclesiastical History of the English People: *A Historical Commentary* (Oxford: Clarendon Press, 1988).
WEHLAU, RUTH, 'Rumination and Re-Creation: Poetic Instruction in the *Order of the World*', *Florilegium*, 13 (1994), 65–77.

—— 'The Riddle of Creation': Metaphor Structures in Old English Poetry, Studies in the Humanities: Literature–Politics–Society, 24 (New York: Lang, 1997).

—— 'The Power of Knowledge and the Location of the Reader in *Christ and Satan*', *Journal of English and Germanic Philology*, 97 (1998), 1–12.

WESTREM, SCOTT D., *The Hereford Map: A Transcription and Translation of the Legends with Commentary*, Terrarum Orbis, 1 (Turnhout: Brepols, 2001).

WHATLEY, E. G., 'Late Old English Hagiography, ca. 950–1150', in Guy Philippart (ed.), *Histoire internationale de la littérature hagiographique latine et vernaculaire en occident des origines à 1550*, 2 vols. (Turnhout: Brepols, 1994–), ii (1996), 429–99.

WOOLF, R. E., 'The Devil in Old English Poetry', *Review of English Studies*, NS 4 (1953), 1–12.

—— 'Saints' Lives', in Eric G. Stanley (ed.), *Continuations and Beginnings: Studies in Old English Literature* (London: Nelson, 1966), 37–66.

WORMALD, PATRICK, 'Bede, the *Bretwaldas* and the Origins of the *Gens Anglorum*', in P. Wormald, D. Bullough, and R. Collins (eds.), *Ideal and Reality in Frankish and Anglo-Saxon Society* (Oxford: Blackwell, 1983), 99–129.

WRIGHT, NEIL, 'Did Gildas read Orosius?', *Cambridge Medieval Celtic Studies*, 9 (1985), 31–42.

ZUMTHOR, PAUL, *Introduction à la poésie orale* (Paris: Seuil, 1983).

—— *La Mesure du Monde* (Paris: Seuil, 1993).

Index

Adam and Eve 26, 39, 43, 46, 55, 62–3, 69–73, 204–5, 212–13, 219, 223, 261–2
Ælfric 20, 61, 131, 135
Æthelweard, *Chronicle* 158, 236, 259, 263, 265
Alamichel, Marie-Françoise 80, 89
Albi map; *see* maps, mapping
Alcuin 268
Alfred, king 23, 26, 27, 134, 137, 138, 139, 157–60, 258, 259, 262
Anderson, Benedict 2, 11, 12
Andreas 25, 37, 164, 165, 170–1, 174–6, 179–81, 187–8, 191–2, 193–6, 202, 227
Anglo-Saxon Chronicle 32, 134, 157–8, 236, 238, 258–68, 269, 273
   ancestral migrations 247, 260–9
      Cerdic and Cynric 260–1, 262, 263, 267
      Hengest and Horsa 262
   genealogies 259–62
architectural metaphors 24–5, 44, 52–5, 73
Asser, *Life of King Alfred* 236, 259–62
Augustine, bishop of Hippo 61, 211
Augustinian mission 243, 251–2, 256
Augustus, emperor 143–5

Bakhtin, Mikhail 29
Bately, Janet 132–5, 136, 139, 235
Battle of Brunnanburh viii, 268
Battle of Maldon 20
Battles, Paul 202, 206
Beatus of Liebana, *Commentary on the Apocalypse of St John*, *see* maps, mapping; Saint-Sever map
Bede, *Ecclesiastical History of the English People* 28, 32, 37, 39–45, 117, 127–30, 157, 160, 236, 238, 239, 242–6; *see also* Cædmon, *Hymn*
   conversion of the English 21–2, 42, 116–17, 129–30, 160, 243, 244, 246, 250, 251–3, 256

geography 21–2, 127–30, 135, 157, 242–6, 273
   ancestral migrations 28, 157, 247–8, 250–1, 255–8
   missions to the continent 257, 258
De Temporum Ratione 128
In Regum xxx Quaestiones 128–9
Old English translation 134
Whitby, synod of 253–4
Beowulf 20, 24, 25, 26, 28, 30, 32, 37, 74–114, 165, 167, 176, 188–9, 190, 202, 203, 219, 273
   Breca 108, 111
   centres 25, 134, 138
   creation motif vii, 47–52
   Finn episode 90, 99–101
   geography in
      Beowulf's barrow 25, 76–9, 80, 81, 82, 86–9, 94, 97, 105, 109
      Beowulf's hall 25, 76–9, 82, 86–9, 94, 97
      dragon's lair 21, 25, 76, 79–82, 86–9, 90, 93–4, 95, 97, 104–5, 108, 111
      Heorot 22, 24–5, 37, 47–8, 50, 52, 54–5, 76–9, 80, 82–6, 88–9, 90, 92–3, 94, 95, 96, 97, 102–3, 107, 109–10, 176, 214
      Grendel's mere 20, 21, 76, 79–86, 88–9, 94, 95, 96, 97, 107, 110–11, 183
   Heathobard episode 101, 105
   history, vision of 84, 103–4
   Scyld 37, 48–52, 90, 170, 203, 209, 263
Bible 14, 15, 16, 64
   Daniel 158, 213, 215, 221
   Exodus 196, 198–9, 208, 209
   Genesis 14, 15, 46, 52, 71, 175, 198–9, 204–5, 206, 210–11, 212–13, 216, 217, 221, 223, 224, 225 245
   Gospel 19–20, 53, 54, 68
   Isaiah 15, 56, 64

Bjork, Robert E. 203
boundaries 2, 9–10, 17, 21–5,
    30, 56–8, 63–4, 72–3, 75,
    106–9, 112, 114, 135–6,
    137, 164, 166–9, 171,
    274
Breeze, Andrew 228
Bridges, Margaret 127, 183–4, 192,
    238, 245
Britain, location of 115–60, 239, 242,
    243, 244
Britons 28, 115–17, 120–1, 122–3,
    237, 239, 240–1, 242, 245,
    246, 248–51, 255, 256,
    258–9, 261, 264–5, 266–8,
    272
Brooks, Kenneth R. 177, 178–9
Brown, Peter 167, 197
Buisseret, David x

Cædmon, *Hymn* 33, 37, 39–45, 54,
    56, 198; *see also* Bede,
    *Ecclesiastical History of the
    English People*
Caesar, *Gallic Wars* 117, 119, 120–1,
    124, 137, 143
Calder, Daniel G. 177–8
Capella, Martianus, *Marriage of
    Philology and Mercury* 15
Casey, Edward S. x
celestial spheres 13, 15
centre, centrality 6, 9, 10, 13, 17, 21,
    25, 54, 75, 82–3, 84, 91–7,
    100–2, 106, 107, 113–14,
    117–18, 120, 126–7, 130,
    134, 138, 139, 141–2, 146,
    157, 160, 197, 254–5, 257,
    258, 274; *see also* periphery
Chaplin, *Great Dictator* 11
Charlemagne 27
Chosen People, the Anglo-Saxons
    as 238, 239, 246, 269
Christ I 53, 56
Christ II 59
Christ and Satan 24, 33, 55–9, 62–3,
    64, 67–9, 70 71, 198
Clemoes, Peter 74, 219
Colgrave Bertram and R. A. B.
    Mynors 255
colonizing,colonialism 11, 189, 196,
    266–7
conversion: *see also* Bede; Gregory the
    Great

of the English 21–2, 116–17,
    129–30, 160, 243–4, 246,
    251–3, 256–7
missions of conversion 17, 18, 28,
    34, 53, 163–97, 202, 219,
    244, 252, 253–4, 256–7,
    258
cosmos, cosmography vii, viii, 4, 6,
    8–9, 12–17, 19, 24, 28, 30–1,
    37–73, 143
Cotton map; *see* maps, mapping

Danes, Danelaw; *see* Vikings
Daniel 34, 198, 203, 213–16, 221,
    223, 227–8, 229–30, 231
Davis, Kathleen 11, 12, 160
Day, David D. 93
De Jong, Mayke 252
De Situ Orbis 27, 126–7
Detienne, Marcel 273
Dicuil, *Liber de Mensura Orbis
    Terrae* 27, 34, 117, 127, 135,
    139–42, 145, 157, 160
distance, evaluation of 1–2, 9–10,
    21–2, 28–9, 30, 59–60, 72,
    80–1, 115–60, 172, 182, 196,
    242, 243, 244, 254–5, 262,
    265, 268–9
Dionysius of Halicarnassus 270–2
Doane, A. N. 63, 64, 65, 66, 71, 210,
    211–12, 224, 229

Earl, James W. 76
East, the 6–7, 16, 29, 156, 158–9
Eden, edenic 14, 17, 27, 29, 62, 73,
    245, 269; *see also* paradise
Elene 34, 37, 50–2, 53–4, 67, 164,
    165, 167–9, 183–7, 189–90,
    192–3, 197, 202
Eliade, Mircea 38, 40
Europe viii, 2, 7, 16, 137–9, 159–60,
    243, 261, 269, 273
    boundaries of 32, 117, 119, 122,
    126–9, 131, 132–41,
    147–57
Eve; *see* Adam and Eve
Exodus vii, viii, 32, 34, 198–9, 203,
    204, 207–9, 213, 214, 217–21,
    222, 223, 225–7, 228, 230,
    231
exile 26, 50, 65, 73, 87, 99, 157–8,
    189, 204–5, 214, 215–16,
    218, 226, 231, 272

Fanger, Claire 215
Fates of the Apostles 34, 37, 164, 165, 176, 177–9, 202
Felix, *Life of Saint Guthlac* 181–2
Finnegan, Robert Emmett 213
folc, see nation, nationalism
Foucault, Michel 5
frontiers; *see* boundaries
Frye, Northop 40

Gautier-Dalché, Patrick x, xi, 118
gaze 58, 60, 70–1, 102–6
genealogies 18, 50, 237, 259–62, 263, 267, 269; *see also* origins
Genesis A 24, 34, 37, 43, 46–9, 52, 54, 59, 60–2, 64–5, 67, 198–9, 202–3, 204–7, 209, 210–13, 214, 216–17, 218–19, 221–2, 223–5, 226, 227–8, 229, 230, 231
Genesis B 24, 62, 64–6, 69, 70, 72, 73, 85–6, 198, 219
Geoffrey of Monmouth 238, 241
geography 4, 13–18, 19, 141–3, 236
  knowledge of 13–18, 142–3, 156–7
Gildas, *De Excidio Britonum* 34, 127, 200, 236, 238, 239–42, 243, 244, 245, 246, 248, 255, 269
Goetz, Hans-Werner 22–3
Gradon, P. O. E. 51
Gregory the Great, pope 21–2, 116–17, 129–30, 243, 252
Gregory, Derek x, 266–7
Griffith, Mark 112
Guthlac A 21, 34, 37, 47–8, 53, 163–4, 165, 170, 172–4, 175, 176, 181–3, 188–9, 192–3, 202, 214, 215, 273

Haines, Dorothy 61
Hall, J. R. 215, 220, 228
Hänger, Christian x
Harley, J. B. and David Woodward x
Helder, William 207
Helms, Mary 10, 196, 262
Henry of Huntingdon 238
Hereford map; *see* maps, mapping
Hermann, John P. 198
Hill, Joyce 40
Hines, John 257
home, homeland ix, 2, 26, 44, 47, 48, 56, 62–3, 65, 69–70, 74–5, 98–9, 116–17, 129–30, 157, 158–60, 163, 165, 172, 174, 176, 187–8, 192, 198, 201, 202, 207–8, 209, 210, 212–14, 215, 222–3, 231, 235–7, 239, 244–5, 246, 252, 255–6, 257–8, 261–3, 268–9, 274
Hoskins, W. G. 23
Howe, Nicholas 21, 29, 98, 231, 237, 247, 257, 266, 268–9, 273
  Migration and Mythmaking xi, 199, 200–1
Howlett, D. R. 179
Hume, Kathryn 78, 84–5
Huppé, Bernard F. 57–8

Iceland 141, 156, 269
identity ix, 2–3, 5, 6–7, 11–12, 21, 25–6, 28, 30–1, 32, 33, 34, 62, 73, 79, 117–18, 130, 160, 164, 167, 172, 200, 203–4, 231, 236, 247, 249, 264, 266, 272–4
imaginaire viii, ix, xi, 2, 3, 4–5, 8–9, 21, 32, 74, 76, 102, 118, 160, 176, 198, 199, 201, 236, 269, 272, 273–4
Ireland 15, 115, 121, 125, 135, 139, 141, 151, 156, 243, 248
  Irish, the 139–41, 157–8, 238, 248, 250, 252, 253–5, 258
  Irish hermits 140, 141
Irving, Edward B. Jr. 85, 105
Isidore of Seville, *Etymologies* 15, 119, 126, 140

Jack, George 100
Jerusalem, *see also* centre, centrality 17, 53–4, 158–9, 168–9, 184–7, 190, 197, 203, 213–16, 229–30
Judith 34, 75, 82, 89–90, 105–6, 111–13, 190, 219, 228, 229
Juliana 37, 164, 165, 166, 169–70

Kiser, Lisa 193, 195–6
Klaeber, F. 100, 101
Klein, Bernhard 12
Kline, Naomi Reed x
Krapp, George Philip 218

Lambert of Saint Omer, *Liber Floridus* 144
landscape 7–8, 21, 23, 80, 90–1, 266

language 11, 21–2, 26–7, 38–42, 44, 54–5, 65, 72, 116–17, 122–3, 125, 130, 203, 207, 210, 220, 243, 259, 260, 265–8, 269, 270–2
Larrington, Carolyn 40
Lee, Alvin 164
Lefebvre, Henri xi, 1, 3, 4–5, 78–9
Le Goff, Jacques xi, 3, 8, 18, 25–6, 31–2, 166
Lionarons, Joyce Tally 49, 107–8
Löw, Martina x
Lucas, Peter J. 218, 226, 227
Lucifer; *see* Satan

Macrobius, *Commentary on the Dream of Scipio* 15
Magennis, Hugh 90–1
Malone, Kemp 133
Manes, Christopher 42–3
mappae mundi 9, 16–17, 132, 142–57
maps, mapping viii, ix, x, 2, 3, 6, 7, 8–9, 10–11, 13–15, 21, 22, 25, 27, 30, 32, 34, 60, 115–60, 164, 166, 176, 196, 197, 198, 227, 237, 239, 269, 270–2, 274
    Albi map 142, 146–9, 151, 152, 157
    Cotton map 32, 42, 154–7, 159
    Hereford map 142, 145–6
    Ripoll map 147–2, 157
    Saint-Sever map 151–4, 157
Mayr-Harting, Henry 253
Maxims 26–7, 56
McGurk, Patrick 156

nation, nationalism 1–2, 11–12, 28, 74, 159–60, 171, 200–1, 202–3, 211–12
Neville, Jennifer x–xi, 23–4, 29, 38, 46, 102, 107
Norsemen; *see* Vikings
north, the 17, 64, 115–17, 119–60, 243, 261, 269, 273; *see also* periphery

Olsen, Karin E. 194
Order of the World 37, 57–8
origins 2, 11, 26, 28–30, 37–42, 45, 51, 52–5, 71, 72, 73, 74–6, 84, 95–6, 116–17, 175, 182, 187–8, 197, 201–2, 215, 235–7, 247, 251–2, 259, 261–3, 266–9, 273–4; *see also* genealogies
Orosius, *Historiarum adversum Paganos Libri septem* 16, 127, 132–3, 134, 135–6, 138, 238, 240, 242
[Orosius] Old English *Orosius* 26, 27, 32, 33, 34, 117, 127, 132–9, 141, 157, 158–9, 235–6
    Ohthere 26, 27, 129, 132, 134, 135, 136–9, 142, 160, 235
other, otherness ix, 7, 10, 11, 21, 27–8, 30–1, 51–2, 55, 119, 160, 176, 188–90, 197
Otter, Monika 117–18, 185, 238, 241, 266

Panther 183
paradise 14, 39, 43, 6, 73, 151, 212–3, 216, 245, 269; *see also* Eden, edenic
periphery ix, 2, 6, 10, 11, 21, 25, 26, 28, 31, 34, 75, 76, 92, 94, 103, 106–9, 114, 115–60, 164, 165, 166–71, 172, 175, 177–8, 196, 197, 198, 218–22, 246, 254–5, 261–2; *see also* centre; centrality
Picts, the 238, 248, 249, 250, 252, 253–5, 258
place, notions of ix, 2, 6–7, 19–20, 25, 26, 43–4, 60–3, 73, 75, 76–91, 113–14, 116–17, 134, 157, 160, 167, 172, 184, 197, 199–200, 231, 270–3
Pliny the Elder, *Natural History* 15, 16, 119, 125, 127, 128, 140, 145, 240, 242
Plummer, Charles and John Earle 158, 267
Pomponius Mela, *Chorography* 16
Ptolemy 240
    Almagest 14
Pytheas of Massalia, *On the Ocean* 124–5, 126, 128

Renoir, Alain 66
Richard of Holdingham 145
Ripoll map; *see* maps, mapping
Riddle 40 33, 37, 56, 58
Riddle 66 33, 37, 60
Rome; the Romans 3, 17–18, 22–3, 28, 50–1, 115–17, 120,

122–3, 124, 129–30, 134, 138, 143–5, 167–9, 185–6, 190, 238, 240, 248–9, 258
and Anglo-Saxon England 21–2, 28, 116–17, 129–30, 157–9, 243–4, 246, 247, 252–5, 256–7, 259, 264–5, 267, 269

Said, Edward 10
Saint-Sever map; *see* maps, mapping
Satan 24, 26, 38, 39, 46, 47, 58–9, 60–3, 64–73, 85–6, 183, 215, 225–6
Sceaf 263
Schaar, Claes 194
Schneider, Ute x
Shepherd, Geoffrey 202–3
Sleeth, Charles R. 67
Smith, Anthony D. 2
Smyth, Alfred P. 260
Solinus, *Collectanea Rerum Memorabilium* 16, 119, 127, 128, 140, 240, 242
space:
   culture of 3–5, 7–8, 12–18, 30–1, 118, 160, 236, 269
   as a mental structure 4–8, 17, 18, 21, 30–1, 118, 136, 169
   terminology 19–21
Strabo, *Geography* 115–17, 119, 121, 125, 137

Tacitus, *Agricola* 117, 119, 120, 121–3, 124, 126
territory ix, 2, 10, 11, 19, 22, 26–7, 29, 30, 39, 43, 50, 74–5, 97, 171, 189, 199–200, 201–4, 208–9, 223, 231, 236, 241, 249–50, 256, 266–7, 273–4
Theodosius, emperor 27, 143–5
Ther, Philip 6–7
Thule 124–6, 127, 128–9, 131, 140–2
Tolkien, J. R. R. 100, 101, 226
Tolley, Clive 263
translatio imperii / translatio studii 17, 158–9, 185–6, 190
Turville-Petre, Thorlac 12

Virgil, *Aeneid* 17
Vikings, the 23, 27, 31, 126–7, 133–4, 138, 140, 237, 260, 268
Vickrey, John F. 71

Wallace-Hadrill, J. M. 255
Wehlau, Ruth 32, 41–2, 45, 52
Westrem, Scott D. x
Widsiþ 33, 37, 39, 40–4, 54
Wormald, Patrick 12
Wulfstan 61
   Sermo Lupi ad Anglos 200, 237, 268

Zumthor, Paul xi, 5–6, 11, 13, 24, 25, 30, 33, 43, 52, 53, 60, 74, 75, 76, 171, 231, 249–50, 265, 274